XML in IE5
Programmer's Reference

Alex Homer

Wrox Press Ltd. ®

XML in IE5 Programmer's Reference

© 1999 Wrox Press

Published by Wrox Press Ltd,
Arden House, 1102 Warwick Road, Acocks Green, Birmingham B27 6BH, UK.
Printed in Canada
3 4 5 6 7 8 9 TRI 00 99
ISBN 1-861001-57-6

Trademark Acknowledgements

Wrox has endeavored to provide trademark information about all the companies and products mentioned in this book by the appropriate use of capitals. However, Wrox cannot guarantee the accuracy of this information.

Credits

Author
Alex Homer

Development Editor
Anthea Elston

Editors
Julian Skinner
Jon Hill

Technical Reviewers
Michael Corning
Richard Harrison
Michael Kay
Mark Oswald

Cover
Andrew Guillaume
Image by Rita Ruban

Design/Layout
Noel Donnelly

Index
Martin Brooks

About the Author

Alex Homer lives and works in the idyllic rural surroundings of Derbyshire, UK. His software company specializes in office integration and Internet-related development, and produces a range of vertical application software. He has worked with Wrox Press on several projects.

Table of Contents

Table of Contents

Table of Contents

Table of Contents

Table of Contents

Appendix F: XML Behaviors Reference   429
Default Behaviors Reference   429

Custom Behaviors Reference   444

Introduction

A year ago, it may have seemed like it was all just typical software industry hype. Now it's here and it's going to be big. Six months ago, it looked like it was all done with smoke and mirrors. Now there are solid, working applications that actually use it. We're talking about the **Extensible Markup Language**, or **XML**.

In the early days, a lot of people made a lot of predictions about where XML would go. Some said it would replace HTML as the web page language of choice. Others said it was the only way to achieve true platform independence, and (as a useful side effect) reduce Microsoft's domination of the desktop. Still others said it was all about transferring data in standard formats, or adding styles to web page elements in a structured way.

As ever in our industry, some of these predictions are coming true and some of them aren't. The prospect of XML pushing Microsoft off course has faded, because it has in fact embraced (some would say embraced and extended) the still-evolving standards. Their latest browser, Internet Explorer 5 (IE5), includes a whole raft of features designed to make working with XML and its associated technologies much easier.

Of course, other browsers and applications also provide XML support in a range of ways, and I'm not suggesting for a moment that IE5 has the field to itself. Netscape's upcoming Navigator 5 software should include similar XML support to IE5. Based on past experience, however, this doesn't mean that the implementations in Navigator 5 and IE5 will be fully compatible, and if they're not then another expectation of XML — full cross-browser compatibility — may fall by the wayside.

What Is This Book About?

The availability and standard of XML support in other browsers and applications is not directly relevant to this book. *This* book is about the support available in Microsoft Internet Explorer 5 for XML and its associated technologies, such as the **Extensible Stylesheet Language** (XSL) and the **Document Object Model** (DOM) that provides access to XML documents.

Microsoft has undertaken to provide full support for XML and other associated standards in IE5. These standards are set by the **World Wide Web Consortium** (W3C), and cover a whole range of different technologies. Reassuringly, IE5 also conforms to most other browser technology standards set by other organizations. For example, the built-in scripting language **JScript** is documented as being fully compatible with the **ECMAScript** scripting language definition — a standard based around JavaScript, and controlled by the European Computer Manufacturer's Association.

This early commitment to full standards-level support in IE5 may be the key that will give XML the chance to succeed in the compatibility stakes where HTML failed. Provided that other browser manufacturers follow the published standards, we can look forward to a time when a page will behave identically in all browsers. However, Microsoft is also adding support for proposals that it has put forward to the W3C, and which are not yet ratified. This book covers these extensions to the standards too.

> To help you, I've stated clearly in the text when I'm talking about a feature that is part of Microsoft's proposed extensions, rather than a ratified standard. Bear in mind, though, that the development and ratification of standards is a continuing process, whereas (at some point) Microsoft has to freeze the feature set of its product. This means that the extensions I've flagged as being outside current standards may have been accepted by the time that you read this, or may have even have been rejected in favor of a different proposal.

Who Is This Book For?

XML is creeping into both the vocabulary and the arsenal of every web page author and web application programmer. Even if you haven't actually noticed it yet, it's there and growing in influence. For example, the "Channels" feature of IE4 was implemented using XML to create the Channel Definition Format (CDF) language that specifies the way that the channels behave.

Some corporations have already built web-based applications that transfer data between client and server in XML format rather than as HTML within a page, or as traditional recordsets through Remote Data Services. IE4 supported XML through a series of ActiveX controls and Java applets that could be embedded into a web page, and which could parse and display data contained within an XML-format file.

This book, then, is for anyone involved in creating web pages or web-based applications. XML still looks to be the best (and only) way for web page definition and construction to move forward. HTML will not die, but as the level of compatible browser support (hopefully) grows, XML (together with XSL and other related technologies) will begin to take over. More and more of the tasks of defining the transport of data within web pages, of defining the styles and appearance of elements, and of controlling the way that data is displayed, will be handed over to XML.

What Do I Need To Use This Book?

This book focuses closely on a set of features within Internet Explorer 5 — specifically, the ways that it supports and uses XML and XML-related technologies. We won't be discussing the way the browser is used, or other programming techniques such as HTML and Dynamic HTML, except when this is directly relevant to the topic at hand.

This means that you will need to be reasonably familiar with the basics of creating web pages and (of course) using the Internet Explorer browser. This includes the structure of HTML, the Dynamic HTML object model, and the way it can be manipulated using script code. We'll also be using a few client-side components to extend the way the browser works, and so you should be familiar with the outline principles of using ActiveX controls and Java applets.

To create the example web pages you'll see in this book, you can use any page-design tool you wish. To get you started, Microsoft provides a cut-down version of FrontPage with IE5, but there is a range of other tools available. However, bear in mind that many of these are *HTML* design tools, and not *XML* design tools. Of course, all the pages and XML documents in this book can be also created with that old favorite, the Windows Notepad.

Resources and Samples for This Book

You can download and install Internet Explorer 5 from the Microsoft web site at http://www.microsoft.com/ie/. You'll also find a series of links to other pages where you can download tools and add-ins for IE5.

The Microsoft XML web site is at http://www.microsoft.com/xml/, and this contains a series of articles, reference materials and white papers that describe Microsoft's vision of the future for XML.

For examples, reference tools, and other information about all the IE5 programming topics, including XML, visit the Microsoft SiteBuilder Workshop pages at http://www.microsoft.com/workshop/default.asp.

The officially ratified standards for XML, XSL and the DOM, together with links to other sources of XML information, can be found at the W3C web site at http://www.w3.org/.

The Wrox Web-Developer site also contains useful information and examples of XML at work, at http://webdev.wrox.co.uk/xml/.

You'll find the examples that are described in this book available for download, or ready to run directly, at the main support page for this book: http://webdev.wrox.co.uk/books/1576/.

Conventions

We have used a number of different styles of text and layout in the book to help differentiate between the different kinds of information. Here are examples of the styles we use, and an explanation of what they mean:

Advice, hints, and background information comes in this type of font.

> **Important pieces of information come in boxes like this.**

Important Words are in a bold type font.

Words that appear on the screen in menus, like <u>F</u>ile or <u>W</u>indow, are in a similar font to the one that you see on screen

Keys that you press on the keyboard, like *Ctrl* and *Enter*, are in italics.

Code comes in a number of different styles. If it's something we're talking about in the text — when we're discussing a `For...Next` loop, for example — it's in a fixed-width font. If it's a block of code from a program, then it's also in a gray box:

```
<SCRIPT>
   ' Some VBScript...
</SCRIPT>
```

Sometimes you'll see code in a mixture of styles, like this:

```
<HTML>
<HEAD>
<TITLE>Cascading Style Sheet Example</TITLE>
<STYLE>
   style1 {color: red; font-size: 25}
</STYLE>
</HEAD>
```

The code with a white background is something that we've already looked at and don't wish to examine further.

These formats are designed to make sure that you know exactly what you're looking at. We hope they make life easier.

Tell Us What You Think

We've worked hard on this book to make it enjoyable and useful. Our best reward would be to hear from you that you liked it and that it was worth the money you paid for it. We've done our best to try to understand and match your expectations.

Please let us know what you think about it. Tell us what you liked best and what we could have done better. If you think this is just a marketing gimmick, then test us out — drop us a line! We'll answer, and we'll take whatever you say on board for future editions. The easiest way is to use e-mail:

feedback@wrox.com

You can also find more details about Wrox Press on our web site. There you'll find the code from our latest books, sneak previews of forthcoming titles, and information about the authors and the editors. You can order Wrox titles directly from the site, or find out where your nearest local bookstore with Wrox titles is located. The address of our site is:

http://www.wrox.com

Customer Support

If you find a mistake in the book, your first port of call should be the errata page on our web site. Appendix G outlines how can you can submit an erratum in much greater detail.

If you can't find an answer there, send e-mail to support@wrox.com telling us about the problem. We'll do everything we can to answer promptly. Please remember to let us know the book your query relates to, and if possible the page number as well. This will help us to get a reply to you more quickly.

What is XML?

The future for all data manipulation and transmission, they tell us, is XML. In fact, if you listen to all the hype that surrounds it, you would think that it really is (to borrow a phrase from Douglas Adams' *Hitchhiker's Guide to the Galaxy*) the answer to the ultimate question of life, the universe and everything. Microsoft mentions XML support in all its new product announcements, with a fervor that makes most other innovations look distinctly unimportant.

But is it really all hype? The answer is a resounding, "No," because XML finally offers us the prospect of creating a globally accepted and cross-platform way of managing and communicating data and information. The World Wide Web Consortium (W3C) has already ratified the first version specification, and groups within the consortium are working on associated standards that are bound up with it. Along with other vendors such as Sun and IBM, the two major browser vendors (Microsoft and Netscape) have both announced that they intend to provide full support for these standards, and Internet Explorer 5 has XML parsing abilities built into the browser.

XML is the **Extensible Markup Language**, a subset of the Standard Generalized Markup Language (SGML) and a companion to the HTML that we all know and love. On top of XML are related technologies such as the **Extensible Stylesheet Language** (XSL), **XML Query Language** (XQL), and various other three-letter acronyms that we'll be meeting later in the book. For the meantime, in this chapter, I'll aim to explain where XML came from, what it can do, and why we would use it. The plan, then, is to:

- ❑ Describe the foundations, development, and future of XML
- ❑ Examine the differences between HTML and XML
- ❑ Take an overview of the ways XML is supported in Internet Explorer 5
- ❑ See some simple but practical uses of XML-based behaviors in IE5
- ❑ Look at how web-based applications might be constructed to use XML

Internet Explorer 5 uses XML techniques to program several parts of the browser, including new built-in and custom 'behavior' objects. We'll briefly see what these can do in this chapter, as we attempt to overview all the different ways that IE5 can use XML. We'll start, however, with a brief summary of what XML and XSL actually *are*.

Where Did XML Come From?

At first inspection, XML looks quite similar to the HTML we use to build traditional web pages. It uses elements that are defined by being enclosed in angled brackets, just like HTML elements. It also uses attributes in much the same way as most HTML elements do.

SGML and DTDs

This similarity between XML and HTML arises because they are both related, albeit in different ways, to a parent language definition standard called **Standard Generalized Markup Language**, or SGML. (XML is a *subset* of SGML, while HTML is an *application* of SGML.) It's important to note that despite its name, SGML is *not* a language in itself, but a way of defining languages that are developed along its general principles.

SGML defines the way that a markup language is built by specifying the syntax and definitions for the elements and attributes that compose it. However, SGML doesn't itself define the structure of any particular application; this is the job of a **Document Type Definition**, or **DTD**. The DTD uses the syntax specified by SGML to define the structure of elements and their associated attributes that will make up a valid document — that is, SGML is used to define a particular markup language using a DTD. As a subset of SGML, XML is *also* a generalized language in the sense that it too is used to define specific markup languages with a DTD.

HTML is a particular application of SGML; the definition of the language has been fixed in an SGML DTD. As a result, the <TABLE> element (for example) has the same logical role in all programs using HTML. Although the results of displaying HTML may in reality differ between browsers, the intrinsic meaning of HTML documents is fixed. The defined standard (the SGML DTD) dictates what the structure of an HTML document should be, and the logical roles that the elements within the document should play.

> *To be more specific, the content type and internal structure composed of sub-elements for the <TABLE> element is fixed by the DTD. Strictly speaking, though, the interpretation of these structures is up to the programmer of the application that uses them.*

In XML (as in SGML), documents and the elements that they contain can have whatever structure and meaning their creator wants them to have, because these definitions are up to the user. In effect, users can define their own standard for the structure of a type of document. While this might seem to be a recipe for total anarchy, the situation is actually redeemed by the DTD. This defines the grammar for the XML application and describes the structure that the elements must adhere to in order for the document to be a valid instance of that application. The great thing is that DTDs can be shared, and so if a DTD is available for a certain type of data, all valid XML files using that DTD can be understood by everyone.

*Internet Explorer 5 also supports an alternative document definition method called **XML-Data schemas**. This is presently under consideration by W3C, but is supported to a considerable degree by IE5. We'll be looking at this together with some other technologies still in development in Chapter 3.*

The Definition of HTML

Almost since its inception, HTML has been defined by W3C using a Document Type Definition. However, HTML is fairly relaxed as far as syntax is concerned. Element and attribute names are not case sensitive, and attribute values don't usually need to be enclosed in double quotes (unless they contain spaces or certain other characters). As well as this, many of the elements carry optional closing tags, such as <TR>, <TH> and <TD> in tables, <LI> and <DT> in lists, and the mundane <P> element.

Because of this, many browsers automatically compensate for 'lazy' programming techniques, or for pages that contain minor errors or omissions. The problem is that different browsers compensate in different ways, and with differing levels of success. Omitting a closing </TD> or </TR> tag in Netscape Navigator, for example, can cause the final table cell to disappear or to be merged with the previous cell.

As a result, W3C publishes two DTDs for each of the recent versions of HTML. A **strict** definition describes the language with all the rules consistently and fully applied, while a **loose** definition attempts to describe the minimum level of conformance that is acceptable. Provided that page authors stick as closely as possible to the strict definition, their pages should work on all browsers that support the particular version of the HTML standard.

Strict Conformance Rules in XML

All this loose and strict definition confusion, along with the increasing divergence of feature sets between browsers, makes future development of the HTML standard difficult. It also makes it a lot harder for browser or HTML-parsing application manufacturers to build their rendering engines. There are so many different ways for the syntax to vary but still be valid that a large amount of development effort — and processing time — tends to be wasted.

As a result, in an attempt to avoid such wastage, one of the main aims of the XML development workgroup at the W3C was to standardize the syntax of XML using a strict set of rules. XML is far less relaxed about incorrect syntax than is HTML. It's vital that every element and attribute used in XML, along with the other instructions that are required to build a valid XML document, follows the syntax rules precisely. In most situations, this even extends to case sensitivity. We'll look at the exact syntax requirements in more detail in Chapter 2, but as a taster the following section describes some of the fundamental differences.

HTML Syntax vs. XML Syntax

To give you a better idea of how HTML and XML differ in syntax, a few simple examples follow. Broadly speaking, the differences fall into six areas. Before we begin, note the terminology for the different parts of the element that I use in this section, both for XML and HTML:

Item	Description
Tag	The individual character string that defines the opening or closing part of an element.
Attribute	A name and value pair enclosed within the element's opening tag.
Element	The complete string of characters making up the element, including the opening tag, any attribute names and their values, the content of the element, and any closing tag.

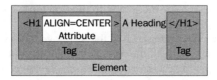

The Role of the Document Type Definition

The **Document Type Definition** is fixed in HTML. It dictates, for example, that a <TABLE> element always defines a fixed table structure in HTML. <TABLE> elements can contain <TR> elements, and these in turn contain <TD> elements:

```
<TABLE>
    <TR>
        <TD>Cell One</TD>
        <TD>Cell Two</TD>
    </TR>
</TABLE>
```

In XML, <TABLE> could mean absolutely anything, and have any internal structure that you want. For a furniture manufacturer, it might be used to define an item in their catalogue:

```
<TABLE>
    <SHAPE>Round</SHAPE>
    <SIZE>36</SIZE>
    <LEGCOUNT>4</LEGCOUNT>
    <MATERIAL>African Teak</MATERIAL>
</TABLE>
```

Element Nesting

Most browsers' interpretations of HTML are reasonably relaxed about the way elements are nested, and they give predicable results in most cases:

```
This text has <B>bold, <I>bold italic</B> and italic</I> words.
```

This is not **well formed**, and is certainly not legal in XML. Instead, each element must nest completely or not at all, so the proper equivalent XML syntax would be:

```
This text has <B>bold, <I>bold italic</I></B><I> and italic</I> words.
```

Optional Closing Tags

HTML is also relaxed (at least in the loose DTD) about closing tags being omitted from certain elements. For example, the following definition of a list is valid in almost every browser:

```
<UL>
   <LI>List Item One
   <LI>List Item Two
   <LI>List Item Three
</UL>
```

In XML, however, this is not allowed. If the DTD defines a list element <MYLIST> that contains nested items of type <LISTITEM>, the code *must* use closing element tags:

```
<MYLIST>
   <LISTITEM>List Item One</LISTITEM>
   <LISTITEM>List Item Two</LISTITEM>
   <LISTITEM>List Item Three</LISTITEM>
</MYLIST>
```

Single Tag Elements

Some elements in HTML do not enclose content, and hence do not have a closing tag. An example is the <HR> element, which always exists alone or with optional attributes within the single element tag:

```
<HR>
<HR SIZE="5">
```

In XML, there is no such concept as a 'single tag' element. All elements must be properly closed. If they have no content, however, there is a shorthand way of doing this: by adding a backslash character within the single element tag. For example the equivalent syntax for an imaginary XML <MYRULE> element would be:

```
<MYRULE />
<MYRULE SIZE="5" />
```

Double-quote Value Delimiters

HTML allows attribute values to be used with or without double-quotes, as long as they don't contain spaces:

```
<HR SIZE=5>
<H1 ALIGN=CENTER>This is a Heading</H1>
<TABLE WIDTH=75%> ..some table content.. </TABLE>
```

In strict HTML, and certainly in XML, single or double-quotes must *always* be present (double quotes are the more commonly used in HTML, but either are perfectly legal). Remember that *all* attribute values, including things like size and width, are in fact text strings and not numbers. The browser interprets them as numbers where appropriate when it parses the document:

```
<HR SIZE="5">
<H1 ALIGN="CENTER">This is a Heading</H1>
<TABLE WIDTH='75%'> ..some table content.. </TABLE>
```

Case Sensitivity

Finally, unlike HTML, XML is case sensitive. As HTML has evolved, there have been various recommendations for the case of element names, attributes names and values. In HTML 4.0, the recommendation is to use all lower case, as this gives better compression when sent across the Net because the words and character strings are more likely to appear in the document text as well.

However, many authors prefer upper case element and attribute names, as this makes it easier to read the HTML code afterwards, assimilate each element, and follow the document structure. Others still prefer a mixture; but the point is that in HTML, all the following are valid and identical:

```
<H1 ALIGN="CENTER">This is a Heading</H1>
<h1 ALIGN="center">This is a Heading</h1>
<h1 align="CENTER">This is a Heading</H1>
<H1 align="center">This is a Heading</H1>
```

When we come to use XML, we have to match the cases of names in the document type definition to those of the elements and attributes in the document. Case sensitivity is particularly important in the **processing instructions** that define a document's type and version, and the way it is linked to other documents. We'll be discussing these aspects in more detail in Chapter 2.

Why Use XML?

As we grow towards a global, information-sharing society, XML provides an application-independent format in which data can be shared. At present, one way to achieve this is for disparate groups to agree to build and/or use a defined DTD for their applications. Groups employing the same DTD then know that they can use data from applications created by any of the other groups. Already forums like http://www.xmlx.com and sites like http://www.schema.net are appearing, where groups can define standard DTDs for use in commerce or other areas of data exchange over the Web.

More importantly, though, *anyone* can access that same DTD; it will be made open to anyone who needs to determine the validity of the structure of the data they are receiving from some third party. Because of this, there is the potential for the exchange of data between parties without significant prior agreement — a DTD sent with the XML data can provide the recipient of the data with all the information they need to interpret and use it.

Secondly, when you build client/server or web-based applications that use XML to format and structure the data, you enable interoperability across disparate computing platforms. This is because the nature of XML data is not dependent on specific features of the platform on which it is used. This may not seem important at first, as both ends of the process (the client and the server) can be designed to accept data in any agreed format. However, as you adapt, upgrade, and extend a system or application — and add new clients or servers to it — it becomes easier to work with the data if it is in a format that different operating systems, browsers and applications can recognize. This means that they can interpret it without requiring additions to the system foundations (like emulators). XML provides such an opportunity.

Thirdly, if you make data or information publicly or widely accessible to others, you should consider XML as the format for that data. An example might be exposing information about products on your web site. If the data is available in a self-describing format like XML, visitors can use it in a way most suited to their specific requirements, enhancing accessibility and promoting data reusability. In other words, instead of just looking at a list of your products as an HTML page, clients can access the XML file as a *source of data* for their own applications and web pages.

As an example, consider the information received by a buying department from various vendors' catalogues. If the information from separate vendors could be readily integrated into one spreadsheet, for example, it would save buyers a lot of time and effort. And because XML allows the styling of the document content to be completely separated from the informational content through the use of stylesheets (as we'll see in Chapter 7), it is ideal for this task. An application could search for products of a particular type on several web sites and then display the resulting integrated dataset within any user interface (on any platform), styled to the user's preference.

> *At Wrox, we expose a range of information about our books in XML on our*
> **Web-Developer** *site. You can view this page at*
> *http://webdev.wrox.co.uk/xml/:*

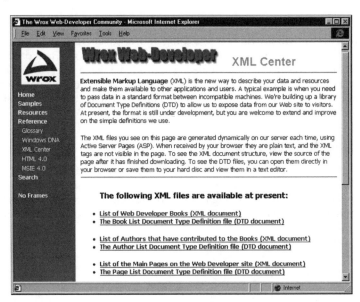

Of course, you may have other reasons for exposing your data as XML. It might be done to suit another company's custom, client-side application, or as an ongoing project to interface with other web sites and applications, or even just because (like a mountain) it's there, and you can do it...

What About XSL and XQL?

As you'll see in this and later chapters, XML support in Internet Explorer 5 allows styling to be applied using Cascading Style Sheet (CSS) rules, or **selectors**, to affect particular XML elements exposed within a document. This provides a simple way to control the appearance of the contents of the XML data or document, in exactly the same way as we would for normal HTML elements.

Often, however, this isn't enough. When we come to look at how to represent *repeating* data in XML (that is, data rows or 'records' that effectively mirror the structure and content of a traditional database table or recordset), we need to be able to exert more control over the way it is displayed. CSS, with a few minor exceptions, is all about positional layout, element size, and text formatting. It simply applies a set of visible effects to the elements that appear in the page.

Extensible Stylesheet Language (XSL), together with the associated technology **XML Query Language** (XQL) can do a lot more than this. The XSL standard defines a set of rules (in XML syntax) that can be used to transform and style the contents of an XML document. This includes sorting the 'records' (or repeating rows) of data into a different order, filtering the data so that only certain rows are placed in the page, and formatting the individual items of the data based on their value. It can also insert new elements into the page, and even transform the page into a different XML or XSL file, rather than outputting it as HTML for display in a traditional format by the browser. XSL effectively allows you to transform the data to conform to the structure of a different DTD or other text file format. All these features allow for effects that just aren't possible with CSS.

The support for XQL that Microsoft has included in IE5 is an extension to the capabilities of XSL that will provide for searching into, and data retrieval from, XML documents. At the time of writing, it is unclear exactly what form the final proposals for XQL will take. However, the general feeling seems to be that a `source` attribute could be added to certain elements within an XSL stylesheet to specify data that could be queried and linked into the originating document. We will look in more detail at the syntax that the query/linking statements use in Chapter 7.

Where is XML Going?

One of the limitations of HTML is that every element has a pre-defined meaning, specified by the HTML standard and interpreted in a reasonably similar way by all the browser manufacturers. There's nothing to stop you adding your own elements to a page by inventing your own tag names, but the browser won't know anything about them.

The chances are that it will ignore the tags (unless they coincidentally match the name of an HTML element tag) and just render the content — that is, the text or HTML between the opening and closing tags of the element.

Fundamentally, this is what XML is all about, and it's why the world is getting excited about it. Rather than having pre-defined meanings for the elements, each one can mean whatever the XML document author wants it to mean. Perhaps Lewis Carroll could see into the future when he wrote *Alice in Wonderland*?

The 'Meaning' Of XML Elements

A world where words can mean whatever the speaker (or author) wants them to mean doesn't bode well for standardized methods of data interchange. In fact, though, this is exactly where the strength of XML comes from. The Document Type Definition for XML documents is not fixed, as it is in HTML, and every document can have its own DTD. The DTD defines the structure of that particular document, constraining (to some degree) the meaning of the elements within it.

In other words, XML is a way of describing your data using a standardized syntax (the DTD) *and* of specifying the data itself. In some circles, this is referred to as a **self-describing document**, and it's responsible at least in part for the technology's cross-platform compatibility — the data carries a description of its format with it. Also, because it is just text, the data can be sent from one place to another easily, using a variety of transport methods. Amongst the most potentially useful, of course, is HTTP. XML documents can be referenced and downloaded across a network or the Internet in exactly the same way as an HTML page or a text file.

The Future Of XML

So, despite all the hype, XML is really just a new format for data stored in text files. However, its simplicity, combined with its platform and application independence, means that it is being used in an increasing number of areas where the exchange of data is required — especially between disparate systems.

New uses for XML are being found all the time, as new tools are being released that can create and parse XML data and make it easier to work with. However, in this book we'll be mainly concentrating on the ways that XML (and associated technologies such as XSL, XQL and XML-Data schemas) can be used in Internet Explorer 5.

XML Support in Internet Explorer 5

This book is about XML, XSL and related technologies. However, it's also a book that is based on Internet Explorer 5. All new technologies go through a period when they are developing and being standardized. During this period, applications appear that support particular subsets of the standards or proposed standards. Each application may also attempt to extend the standards by adding new proprietary features of its own. The result of this 'feature creep' is that it's often difficult to pin down precisely which features are supported where, and which standards a particular product covers. It also means that if you advertise that your product is compatible with "all the current standards", you risk becoming out-of-date very quickly as they change.

Fixing the Feature Set

This can be a particular problem for software application manufacturers, who can find their products outdated almost as soon as they're released in markets where standards and features change rapidly (and these days, there aren't many places where this isn't the case). The result is that each manufacturer must make a decision as to when and where they fix the feature set for their product. This is sometimes referred to colloquially as "putting a stake in the ground".

At this point, the plan is complete, the decisions are made, and the customer gets what is in the package. If the standards change or are extended, the product is obsolete.

Driving Standards

Of course, Microsoft tends to be less easily influenced by market pressures than smaller software companies would be. Their share of the browser market is large enough for their product — in some respects — to set its own standards. In the recent history of the Web, Netscape and Microsoft have both exercised their marketing muscle and tried to drive standards by building new features into their applications. And, in many cases, this was successful: the current HTML 4.0 specification contains a range of features that were built into browsers long before acceptance by the W3C.

What all this is coming to is that at some point, each manufacturer must put its proverbial "stake in the ground" and ship a product. In the case of Microsoft's browser range, this is Internet Explorer 5. In its collaboration with the W3C, Microsoft has tried to ensure that the technologies it supports are the same as those specified in W3C standards, and thus its "stake in the ground" suits as many users as possible. In the case of some of the XML-based features within IE5, the technologies as implemented by Microsoft represent advances upon the W3C standards. To some extent, then, they represent Microsoft taking a risk as to how it sees the market evolving.

It may be that Microsoft is wrong about the future, and that the forthcoming standards will evolve along a different route. However, it's at least equally possible — as has happened in the past with both major browser manufacturers — that a large installed user base will influence the way that the standards evolve.

What's Supported, and What's Not

Although we are working with the most recent version of Internet Explorer available at the time of writing, you'll appreciate from the previous discussion that this means we may not be working to the latest ratified W3C standards for all the XML, XSL and other technologies that we'll cover. The standards will grow and change after this book is released, and over the life of the browser. Furthermore, the browser itself will change over time (particularly through the Windows Update feature that can update it and add new components), and so its XML/XSL support will be fine-tuned.

All this means that we are looking at two flexible and converging environments. I'll attempt to point out where the standards differ at present from the support available in Internet Explorer 5, and which IE5 features are non-standard or likely to change. I'll also try and provide you with enough information that you can check out the latest changes, and find out exactly what position the browser or standards are at.

Our "stake in the ground" suddenly looks a lot less permanent that we might have assumed, but don't worry too much on this count. The things you learn here will always be useful, and they'll make it far easier for you to assimilate the emerging new technologies, as well as any changes to existing ones.

Core XML Support

The thing that most differentiates IE5 from the cosmetically very similar IE4 is the new built-in XML support. The core 'engine' of IE4 (and of other browsers such as Navigator) knew basically nothing about XML.

It could, however, be made to *look* intelligent when presented with an XML document by means of a custom plug-in, applet, or ActiveX control that parsed the XML document and made it available to script in the page.

> IE4 does, *however, support the* **Channel Definition Format** *(CDF) used to create Active Channels, and the* **Open Software Description** *(OSD) software download file format that can be used to install and update files over the Net. Both of these are* applications *of XML.*

The following is a simple XML file named `booklist.xml`, which contains details of three books. Don't worry about what the elements mean for the time being — we'll see more about them in Chapter 2:

```
<?xml version="1.0"?>
<BOOKLIST>
    <BOOK>
        <CODE>16-041</CODE>
        <CATEGORY>HTML</CATEGORY>
        <RELEASE_DATE>1998-03-07</RELEASE_DATE>
        <SALES>127853</SALES>
        <TITLE>Instant HTML</TITLE>
    </BOOK>
    <BOOK>
        <CODE>16-048</CODE>
        <CATEGORY>Scripting</CATEGORY>
        <RELEASE_DATE>1998-04-21</RELEASE_DATE>
        <SALES>375298</SALES>
        <TITLE>Instant JavaScript</TITLE>
    </BOOK>
    <BOOK>
        <CODE>16-105</CODE>
        <CATEGORY>ASP</CATEGORY>
        <RELEASE_DATE>1998-05-10</RELEASE_DATE>
        <SALES>297311</SALES>
        <TITLE>Instant Active Server Pages</TITLE>
    </BOOK>
</BOOKLIST>
```

If you open this file in Internet Explorer 4, the browser displays it as plain text. It knows nothing about XML or the meaning of the elements in our document, so it ignores the tags and just displays the content. However, notice how it thinks that the <CODE> element is an HTML formatting instruction, and displays it in a fixed-width font:

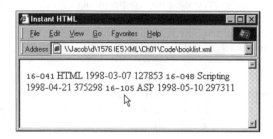

In Navigator 4, we don't even get this far. It simply doesn't recognize an
XML file as a valid HTML document (and who can blame it?), so it doesn't
display anything at all. However, if you view the page's source code, you can
see the XML document.

In contrast, IE5 has XML support built right into the rendering engine. Given an XML
file, it will display it with the elements formatted, color-coded, and as a collapsing tree.
OK, so it just looks like the original XML document. Perhaps this is why fancy
formatting is provided — to convince us that it really does know about XML:

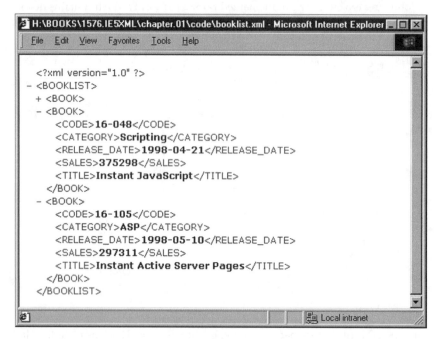

However, if you feed it an XML document that contains *no* obvious formatting or line
breaks, you'll see that really *does* know about XML. If we load the following file
instead, we get exactly the same result displayed:

```
<?xml version="1.0"?><BOOKLIST><BOOK><CODE>16-
041</CODE><CATEGORY>HTML</CATEGORY><RELEASE_DATE>1998-03-
07</RELEASE_DATE><SALES>127853</SALES><TITLE>Instant
```

```
HTML</TITLE></BOOK><BOOK><CODE>16-
048</CODE><CATEGORY>Scripting</CATEGORY><RELEASE_DATE>1998-04-
21</RELEASE_DATE><SALES>375298</SALES><TITLE>Instant
JavaScript</TITLE></BOOK>
<BOOK><CODE>16-105</CODE><CATEGORY>ASP</CATEGORY><RELEASE_DATE>1998-05-
10</RELEASE_DATE><SALES>297311</SALES><TITLE>Instant Active Server
Pages</TITLE></BOOK></BOOKLIST>
```

Internet Explorer 5 parses the file to extract the implicit XML structure, and breaks it up into a more logical format by adding line breaks in appropriate places, and by indenting the code. This is what many early XML-parsing applications did, and it proves that IE5 knows what it is doing.

Version and Update References

This book was written using Internet Explorer 5, build number 5.00.2014.0216. You can check the current build number of your browser in the Help | About box. Remember that installing new software, such as Microsoft Office or development tools, may provide the option to upgrade this to a newer version. You can check the latest information about IE5 versions and the new features on the Microsoft web site at http://www.microsoft.com/windows/ie/.

The standards for XML and XSL are published by the World Wide Web Consortium (W3C). Their web site at http://www.w3.org/ contains the latest proposals, working drafts, and ratified recommendations. It also contains links to many other sites that provide information and resources for XML and XSL.

What XML Features Does IE5 Support?

In the remainder of this book, we'll be examining the different ways that Internet Explorer 5 supports XML, XSL and related technologies. In some cases, we'll also be comparing this with the support that was available in IE4, so that you can judge the way it has changed. The topics you'll see, together with the chapter number where that topic is covered in more depth, are listed next.

Defining XML documents using document type definitions

IE5 supports the W3C Document Type Definition (DTD) standards for creating definitions of the structure of XML documents that can be read by all kinds of other XML applications. It will read and display such documents in a structured and intuitive collapsible tree format automatically, and can also verify the structure against the DTD. This is covered in Chapters 2 and 3.

Building data structures using XML-Data schemas and data types

Internet Explorer 5 supports industry-wide proposals for a new way of defining the document structure. Rather than using a DTD, the new proposals call for a simpler and more extensible standard called XML-Data schemas. Part of the proposal consists of the definition of XML data types and a data content model to allow the data content of an XML document to be parsed and formatted in a more intelligent way, depending on the type of data it contains. And, because the schema itself is written in XML, it can be parsed, read and manipulated just like any other XML document. This is covered in Chapter 3.

Embedding XML as a data island in an HTML document

XML data can be embedded into an existing HTML document directly (as part of the document), indirectly (from a linked XML data file), or through an embedded parser object. All these techniques create **XML data islands**, which can be accessed in a range of ways by script or other objects within the page. This is covered in Chapter 4.

Using embedded XML data in data binding or client-side script

XML in a data island is automatically exposed to the browser as a recordset that can be used in data binding, or manipulated directly with client-side script code and ADO. The XML data-binding feature provides the same table paging and master/detail recordset presentation as existing RDS techniques, plus it adds new events and methods.

The opportunity to access the recordsets using script code also allows the programmer to build completely customized solutions that can display and manipulate the data in any way that is required. This is covered in Chapter 4.

Accessing embedded XML using the XML Document Object Model

XML in a data island is also exposed to the browser via the **XML Document Object Model** (DOM). There is a range of new functions available in IE5 that can access and manipulate the data, even if it isn't in the form of a structured recordset. These allow programmers to edit and update existing XML documents, or to even create new ones from scratch, within the browser. It means that building applications that handle XML data is easier than ever before. This is a big topic, and it's covered in Chapters 5 and 6.

How CSS styles can be used with XML to format individual elements

Cascading style sheets can be used with XML in much the same way as they are used with HTML. We can use them to format and layout documents that are partially or entirely composed of XML. In particular, the recent CSS2 standard provides wide-ranging control over the placement and styling of individual elements or groups of elements. This is covered in Chapter 7.

How XSL can be used to format XML data in a document

Once XML data is embedded into a document, or once the browser has loaded a pure XML document, it can be displayed to the user in a number of ways. The Extensible Stylesheet Language (XSL) is an emerging standard that provides a whole new range of techniques for formatting the data content to provide a more controlled and precise display. The W3C are still working on producing a recommendation for XSL, but IE5 does support the main 'transformation' part of the working draft. This is also covered in Chapter 7.

How the XQL extensions to XSL can be used to query and link documents

As well as using XSL to format XML data, we can apply extensions to XSL called XQL (XML Query Language). These extensions allow the data in an XML document or data file to be modified, sorted, and selected for inclusion in the output in a whole range of ways. This is covered in Chapter 7 as well.

How XML elements can be used with, and as part of, behaviors

Behaviors are a new technique for separating script code in a page from the HTML and XML document content. Code stored in a separate file defines how elements of a particular style class will behave, and it can affect both HTML and XML elements. There are default behaviors built into IE5, and these are generally instantiated by using XML syntax and namespaces to create custom elements within an HTML or XML page. It is also possible to create your own custom behaviors, and the simplest way to do this is with a new XML-based language that can be used within the *definition* of a behavior to specify the type of behavior, the methods and properties it exposes, and the way it reacts to events. This is covered in Chapter 8.

Using XML to provide data or state persistence in the browser

IE5 includes a set of predefined behaviors that can be used to 'persist' (or store) data on the local (client's) hard disk so that it can be reloaded automatically or on demand when the user returns to that page. The storage is via a hierarchically structured XML file held on the client's disk, and this can be accessed using the same techniques as you would with XML documents loaded over the Web.

There are also methods available to work with the Favorites list, the History list, and to access the data in a free-form way for customized local data storage. This is also covered in Chapter 8.

> *IE5 also provides extra features for the **Channel Definition Format** (CDF) and **Open Software Distribution** (OSD) file formats. These are XML-based and were introduced in IE4, but due to their specialist nature we won't be covering them in this book.*

Some Example XML Pages

Next, we'll take a look at some of the ways that XML can be used within Internet Explorer 5. This section of the chapter will briefly demonstrate some of the topics I've listed above, and help you to get a feel for what the remainder of the book covers. You'll find each of the examples in sample files that you can download from our web site at http://webdev.wrox.co.uk/books/1576/. You can also run many of the samples directly from the site.

Embedded XML Data with Data Binding

We can embed XML data within an HTML page, a useful technique for working with XML data in a client-side application. The data can be embedded directly — that is, it can be written in the page within an <XML> element:

```
<XML ID="dsoBookList"> ...XML data goes here... </XML>
```

Alternatively, we can embed a separate XML file into an HTML page by using the SRC attribute of the opening <XML> tag:

```
<XML ID="dsoBookList" SRC="booklist.xml"></XML>
```

*It's important to remember that <XML> is actually an HTML element, and **not** an XML element. Hence we cannot use the shorthand syntax < . . . />
for closing empty elements mentioned earlier, but must use a 'proper' closing
tag instead.*

Once we've embedded the XML data, it is automatically exposed as a recordset by the
IE5 browser, in much the same way as it is with the traditional (IE4) RDS **Data Source
Objects** like the **Remote Data Service Control (RDS)** and the **Tabular Data Control
(TDC)**. This means that we can use normal data-binding techniques to bind and
display it within elements in the page. Here's the result of doing this with our simple
booklist.xml file, and you'll see more of this technique (including how this page
works) in Chapter 4:

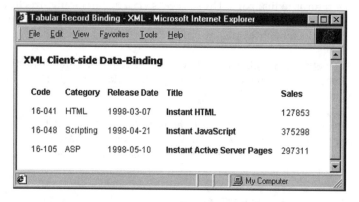

This page, named xml_tabular.htm, *is available with the sample files that
can be run or downloaded from our web site at
http://webdev.wrox.co.uk/books/1576/*

Embedded XML Data with Client-side Script

Once we can get our XML data into a client-side recordset, as we did in the previous
example, we can access this recordset directly using script code. This is a common
technique when working with RDS, and operates in the same way with an XML data
island. In the next example, we are using the <XML> element to embed data into the
page from a more comprehensive list of books.

The HTML page itself displays a text box, a button and a list box. When the button is
clicked, we access the data in the recordset directly using script code (instead of
binding it to HTML controls) and search for records that match the criterion entered
into the text box. Each one that does match is added to the list box. The next screenshot
shows the results of a search for titles containing "html" — you'll meet this example
again in Chapter 4:

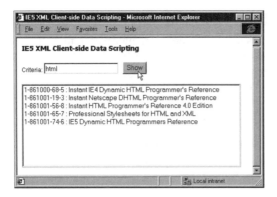

This page, named findtitle.htm, *is also available with the sample files that can be run or downloaded from the Wrox web site.*

Embedded XML and the Document Object Model

XML data embedded into a document can also be accessed directly, rather than through a recordset. This is more appropriate for data that doesn't fit the concept of individual 'records', as would be stored in a database. To access it, we use script and methods that are defined by W3C standards. The XML data is exposed as a structured series of objects called the **Document Object Model**, or **DOM**.

We'll be looking at this topic in much more detail in Chapters 5 and 6. As a simple example (which you'll meet again later on), we can use script code that accesses the DOM to get at the root node, and then call a recursive function that enumerates all the nodes that contain data. This provides a way of listing the entire content of the XML document as though it was a tree structure. For each node in the tree we can extract the name, type and value. This is the result with another list of books:

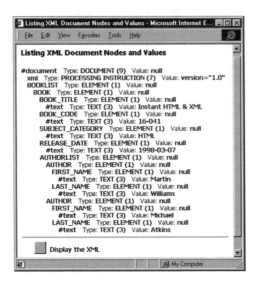

The filename of this sample HTML document is parsewithvalues.htm.

Simple Presentation of XML

One of the simplest ways to add presentation information to XML data is through the application of a normal cascading style sheet (CSS). This technique is part of the W3C XML recommendation, allowing us to apply predefined styles to XML document elements. This works even if we don't have an HTML document to host the XML (as a data island), because special XML elements can be used to link a CSS to a 'pure' XML document.

In the style sheet, we specify the style attributes for each element type in the same way as we would when using CSS styles in an HTML document:

```
ITEM            { display:block; margin:15px }

CODE            { display:inline;
                  font-family:Tahoma,Arial,sans-serif;
                  font-size:10pt;
                  font-weight:bold }

CATEGORY        { display:inline;
                  font-family:Tahoma,Arial,sans-serif;
                  color:darkgray;
                  font-size:12pt;
                  font-weight:bold }
...
```

Here's the result of applying this style sheet to our sample `booklist.xml` file. You'll see this example described in more detail in Chapter 7:

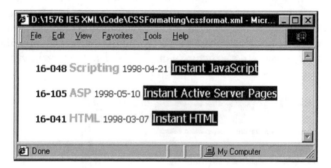

The filename of this sample XML document is `cssformat.xml`.

Formatting and Displaying XML Data with XSL and XQL

You've just seen how we can format XML elements directly by using Cascading Style Sheets. However, it's also possible to use the XML equivalent: stylesheets written using the **Extensible Stylesheet Language** (XSL). All we need to do is link an XSL stylesheet to our XML document instead of a CSS style sheet.

XSL is a very powerful language: it can do a lot more than just formatting element contents, and you'll be seeing a lot more about it in Chapter 7. For the moment, this screenshot shows how an XSL stylesheet can re-order and format the data in the same simple `booklist.xml` file that we used in the previous (CSS) example page:

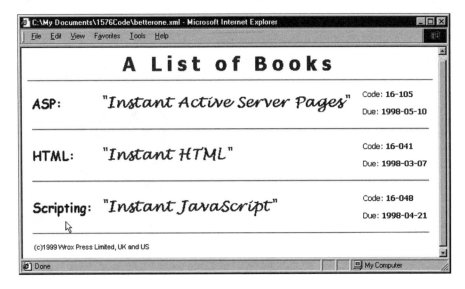

Like the previous XML document, this is available from the Wrox web site; its filename is `betterone.xml`.

XSL works by applying **templates** to each element that define the output that is sent to the browser for display. To display the book title, for example, the following template is used to specify the style to apply to the text. The template then inserts the text using the special XSL element `<xsl:value-of />`, enclosing it in double-quotes as seen in the screenshot above:

```
<xsl:template match="TITLE">
   STYLE="font-family:Lucida Handwriting Italic, Arial, sans-serif;
         font-size:18pt; font-weight:bold; color:darkred">
   "<xsl:value-of />"
</xsl:template>
```

If you compare the contents of this page with the previous (CSS) example, you can see that the books now appear with the 'fields' in a different order, and that the books themselves (the 'records') are sorted into a different order as well. In this example, they are listed alphabetically by category. Although more complex and harder to learn than CSS, XSL (and the associated query language XQL) can achieve all kinds of effects that just aren't possible with the older technology. You'll see some more examples in Chapter 7.

Using XML with Behaviors

In the introduction to this chapter, I briefly mentioned **behaviors**. This is a new feature in IE5 that allows page authors to separate the script code that does the work in a dynamic page completely from the HTML that creates the physical appearance of the page.

In its most basic form, the feature simply involves a new CSS selector attribute named `behavior`. This can specify a separate file containing the code that will be attached to elements in the page. To make the connection, you just apply the style that contains the `behavior` selector to the appropriate HTML or XML elements. The following page, which is available on our web site at http://webdev.wrox.co.uk/books/1576/, shows how a simple behavior component can be used to provide dynamic effects. As you move your mouse pointer over the words, they glow with random colors.

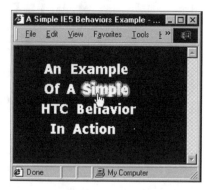

XML is used to build the interface and definition of the behavior component. We'll see how this example works using XML in Chapter 8, when we come to examine behaviors in more detail.

So, having seen some examples of what is possible with XML in IE5, I hope that you're excited about the prospects that it offers. You don't need to have grasped fully all the intricacies of the samples that we've looked at, because we'll be coming back to examine all the techniques in more detail throughout the remainder of the book. However, it should have helped you appreciate the many different, XML-based features that are available, most of which are unlike anything you've seen in earlier versions.

Building Applications that use XML

Earlier in this chapter, we discussed how XML offers us a chance to create global formats for data transfer. This universality is one of the main reasons why XML is an ideal subject for applications that may have to work across disparate platforms and operating systems. And this is, of course, one of the inherent properties of the Internet. A topic that is regularly aired in the XML world is the way that XML can be used to build **applications** — particularly web-based applications that work in a browser or a custom interface program.

Universal Data Formats

To achieve anything approaching a universal data format will be very difficult, and may never be a reality. However, XML starts off with a couple of major advantages over most other data formats. Firstly, (disregarding the small matter of character encoding schemes) the transmitted data is pure text, not a binary format that has to be translated from standard 8-bit bytes into the 7-bit format that is required with HTTP. Secondly, the data content can be made self-descriptive, and is easily validated through the use of a document type definition. This means that all applications can verify the structure and content of an XML file.

Of course, there are disadvantages with XML as well. It is a highly verbose format, with a lot of repeated information that describes the structure of the data. It may also require additional metadata to be set up to make searching over XML efficient. Other data formats generally dispense with this repeated information, using smaller files that take up less bandwidth. In many situations, however, the benefits of XML generally outweigh the disadvantages.

To see why the universality of format is so important, consider an Internet-based application that passes data between different clients and different servers. This may be the situation in many industries, where data is shared for all kinds of reasons. The next diagram shows how (as long as all clients and servers can make the translation from their own native format into XML) data can be passed from any server to any client, and vice versa:

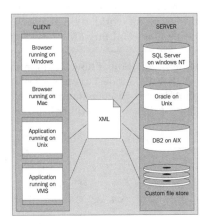

Building XML-based Applications

So, how can an application convert data to and from XML? One simple answer is to use an XML parser that can take an XML document and expose it as a structured set of elements and values. Of course, this is just what Internet Explorer 5 does, as we saw in the example of parsing an XML document using recursion earlier in this chapter. Each element and value is available in a tree-like structure, and script code running in IE5 can access a loaded XML document and extract or update the content. (We'll be looking in detail at how this is done in Chapters 5 and 6.) An alternative is a specialized component that can read XML data and use it to interact with the application or data store directly.

Assuming that we have such a parser or component available, we can use it to convert our application data from one format to another. On the client we might use IE5 to do this, although on other platforms and operating systems, and with other applications, we may have to use a separate parser. Certainly, this will generally be the case on the server. There are many different parser components available, for almost all platforms and operating systems, and it's just a matter of setting up the plumbing so that your applications can access them.

This means that we can drop parser components in as required to perform our data translation. The next diagram shows data from a database being parsed into XML to pass over the network, after which another parser translates it back into an appropriate format to be used in the client application:

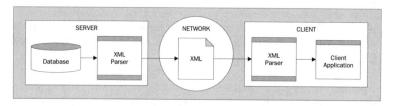

XML Application Structure in the Microsoft World

It's hard to say anything about how the various parts of a process like that described above would fit together in general terms. However, if we look at a particular example, we can fill in a little more detail. In the Microsoft world, technologies like Active Server Pages and client-side data binding make building XML-based applications easy.

The figure that follows is a schematic representation of how we might construct such an application. When the client makes an initial request to our server, an ASP page accesses the database and retrieves an ADO recordset containing the required data. It converts this to XML by adding the appropriate tags and other instructions, and returns it to the client.

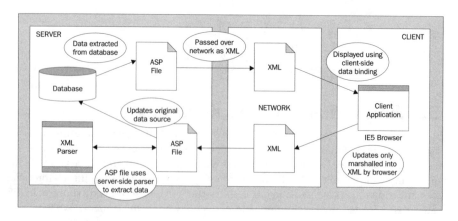

On the client — in this case, IE5 — the XML data is embedded in a data island, which automatically exposes it as an ADO-type recordset again. The remainder of the page defines a set of HTML controls that are bound to this recordset, and which allow the user to browse, edit and update the data. This last stage could also be achieved by attaching a relevant XSL stylesheet to the XML document/recordset sent to the client.

Once the user has finished editing the data, the changes alone are marshaled into an XML document, and this is posted back to the server. There, another ASP page can create an instance of a parser component and load the XML document into it. This exposes it as individual elements and values, which ASP code can extract and use to update the original data source.

Using Specialist Components

There are several new, third-party components appearing that are specially designed to make the work of updating server-based data stores easier, and it's likely that Microsoft and others will add specialist support for XML updates to their server operating systems and databases in the future.

One component that you might like to try is ASP2XML, which is designed to make it easy to fetch XML formatted data from any data store that supports SQL statements through an ODBC or OLE DB driver, and pipe changes back to the data store in the same way. You can try this component out for yourself from the Gallery page of the Web-Developer web site, or direct from http://webdev.wrox.co.uk/resources/gallery/components/asp2xml/:

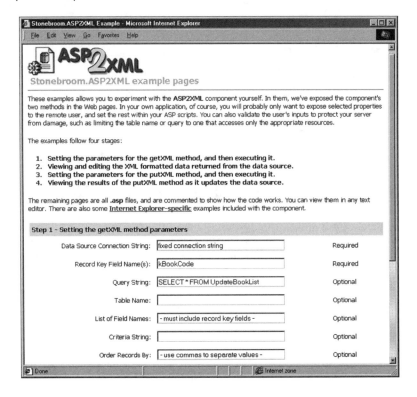

Alternatively, a component based on the principles used in XPointers (which you'll see more about in Chapter 3) might prove useful. The ASPointer component is designed to access XML and other types of text files on the server's disk directly, and return or update specific sections only. You can try this component out for yourself from the Gallery page of the Web-Developer web site, or direct from http://webdev.wrox.co.uk/resources/gallery/components/aspointer/:

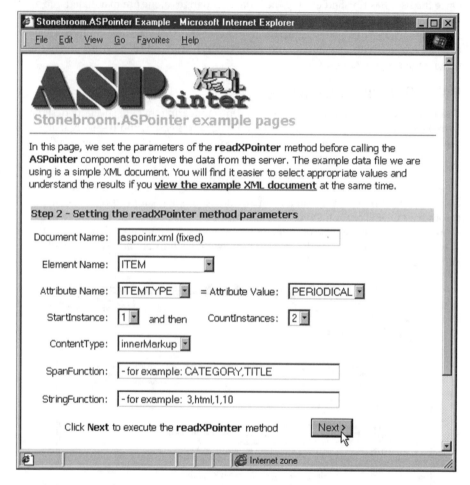

Of course, these are only simple examples, and there are lots of other ways that XML can be used to build applications and to transmit, store and manage data. However, this should be enough to start you thinking about why, and how, XML will probably play a very substantial part in the future of distributed application design.

> *To learn more about building applications that are based on XML, look out for* XML Applications *(ISBN 1-8651001-52-5), also from Wrox Press.*

Summary

The aim of this chapter was to introduce you to XML and its related technologies, and to help you to see where they come from and where they are going. In particular, you should now appreciate why they are such important topics, and why they will, without a doubt, form the basis for many new applications that will be coming our way in the future.

I also presented an overview of the ways that XML is supported in Internet Explorer 5. This should help to clarify the different topics that we will be covering, and show you how they are related to each other. Throughout the remainder of this book, you'll see them in action in a range of ways.

Then, we looked at some simple examples of XML at work in IE5. These examples are designed to reinforce the different ways that XML can be used, but in reality you'll find that they often become blended together in more complex applications. You'll find some more detailed discussion of how the client-side might be implemented in Chapter 4.

Finally, you saw briefly how we might use XML-formatted data within distributed applications so as to achieve platform and operating system independence. Overall, this is probably the main reason why XML is proving to be such a compelling new technology. In summary, then, we've looked at:

❑   The foundations, development, and future of XML

❑   The differences between HTML and XML

❑   The ways that XML is supported in Internet Explorer 5

❑   Some simple but practical uses of XML and behaviors in IE5

❑   How web-based applications might be constructed to use XML

In the next chapter, we'll examine the theory, structure and syntax of XML in more depth. I'll admit that it's not the most exciting of topics in itself, but you need to have a firm grasp of these basics before we go on to see how XML can be used to build more complex pages and applications.

2

Creating XML Documents

In the previous chapter, we looked briefly at what XML is, and saw some of the ways that it can be used in Internet Explorer 5. You can carry on just using the simple techniques we saw there without knowing any more about XML, but this will mean that you won't be able to take full advantage of the features of XML that allow you to build real applications.

In this chapter, we'll tackle the whole concept of XML as a language, and see how it is built up of a series of elements. You'll see how the elements are defined with a **document type definition (DTD)**, and how associated standards and proposals such as **XML Schemas and Data Types**, **Extensible Stylesheet Language (XSL)** and **XML Query Language (XQL)** fit into the picture.

However, the bulk of the chapter is concerned with document type definitions, as these are currently the standard for defining XML documents. It's possible that other proposals may eclipse DTDs over time, and circumvent the need to learn the rather obtuse and unintuitive syntax they use. For now, however, you really do need to have a good grasp of them, and we'll be using them throughout the book as well.

So, this chapter covers:

- ❏ How XML and its related technologies fit together
- ❏ How to define a well-formed and valid XML document
- ❏ The XML declaration and version information for an XML document
- ❏ The structure of XML documents, and how they can represent data
- ❏ How we declare and use namespaces in an XML document
- ❏ How to create a DTD to define the structure of a document

The first step is to take an overview of the whole structure of the XML-related technologies to see how they fit together. After that, we'll move on to look at individual topics in greater detail. In the final section of the chapter, we'll study how DTDs are constructed.

We'll leave the study of XML Schemas and Data Types, and all the associated acronyms, until the next chapter — there's just not enough room to do justice to all these topics in one chapter.

XML and Related Technologies

After reading through Chapter 1, you should have a reasonably good idea of what XML is, what it looks like, and some of the ways in which it can be used. However, like all new technologies, having only a couple of new three-letter acronyms really isn't good enough — we need a few more to make it a serious proposition for future development. In this first section of the chapter, we'll look at the different languages and definitions that make up the umbrella term, "XML".

The World of XML

Over the last year or so, XML seems to have been developing in a parallel universe from the traditional web programming languages like HTML and scripting. Much of this enforced isolation was because there were no widely used applications available that supported XML — probably because there was no widely accepted, standard format for many of the features that add functionality to the core XML standard. All this is now changing, and XML is finding its way into many new applications.

An Overview of XML Technologies

In this book our concern is really for the XML capabilities of Internet Explorer 5, but we'll look first at the complete picture. This will help you to get an overall feel for how the various technologies fit together. The following diagram demonstrates the basic relationships:

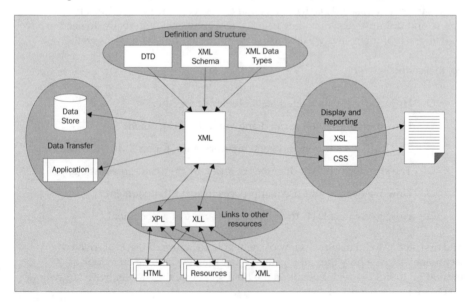

At the heart of these technologies is the real cause of all the excitement: XML. With the standard having been set for version 1.0, through a recommendation from the W3C as far back as February 1998, this is firmly established. Internet Explorer 5 supports the XML 1.0 specification in full, as well as many of the supporting specifications like those for the document object model (DOM), CSS, and (partially) XSL and XQL.

The supporting specifications clustered around XML are the other languages, definitions and technologies that make it much more useful. Without them, XML is limited in its functionality. I'll explain that contentious statement and work through the acronyms in the next section.

XML Technologies in More Detail

XML is purely a way of describing and structuring data, which is why I said that its functionality is limited without the supporting languages, definitions and technologies. In contrast to this, consider HTML. When we create HTML documents, we know that (in most cases) the browser reading it will understand what each element actually 'means', and render the document and any associated content as a web page.

XML tags, as we've already discovered, have no intrinsic meaning. When we send an XML document to a browser, at best we'll just get the data displayed as text; in some browsers, we'll see nothing at all. To get the most out of XML, we have to do three things:

❑ Define the structure of the document, and hence define what makes a document valid

❑ Define the meaning of the individual elements in some way, so that we know what the data they contain represents

❑ Define ways in which the information in the document can be stored, manipulated, processed by an application, communicated, displayed or presented

These definitions are closely interrelated, to the extent that in practice it is almost impossible to carry out any one of them alone without also performing the other two to some degree. I have separated them out here simply for the purposes of explanation.

In order to define these aspects of documents and the way they are used, we must take advantage of some of the technologies that have been submitted to the W3C in various proposals — the ones that were indicated in the earlier schematic diagram.

DTD (Document Type Definition)

The standard way to define the structure of an XML document is through a document type definition. In fact, the DTD syntax is an integral part of the core XML 1.0 standard. By specifying a matching DTD for an XML file, we allow a parser or other application to retrieve the definitions for the format and structure that apply to the file, and use them to ensure that the file is valid — in other words, that it has the correct structure.

The DTD helps the parser to interpret the contents in a pre-defined way. For example, we can tell the parser that each book in a list of books must have a title and an ISBN, and that it may optionally contain a list of author names.

Internet Explorer 5 supports the XML 1.0 standard DTDs, and allows us to specify either inline definitions (where the content of the DTD is within the XML file itself) or external, linked DTDs (where the URL or identifier of the DTD file is provided in the XML file). We'll be looking at DTDs in depth later on in this chapter.

XML Schemas and Data Types

DTDs are fine for defining the structure of an XML file, but they do suffer from a few limitations. Several industry leaders, including Microsoft, Inso, ArborText and DataChannel, have proposed a different system for defining the structure of an XML document called **XML-Data Schemas**. These are designed to be easier to learn and to use than DTDs, they provide extra features, and they allow reuse of element definitions through inheritance. Unlike DTDs, they define the structure of the document using the *same syntax* as the rest of the document, allowing the use of a single parsing engine for the whole process of reading the document and validating its structure.

Another idea included within the proposals for XML-Data Schemas is for the use of **data types** in XML. In a DTD, and in the actual XML document structure, all data content is made up of text strings (usually called **character data**). This makes it harder to specify whether, for example, a string of numbers represents a date or a number. Data types are designed to allow the type of data to be defined, while still keeping it as plain text for easy cross-platform transmission. The W3C is considering these two proposals at present (along with a number of others), but in the meantime IE5 implements support for what Microsoft refers to as a "preview version" called **XML Schemas and Data Types**. We'll be looking at these in more detail in Chapter 3.

XSL, XQL and CSS

We came across the Extensible Stylesheet Language (XSL) and Cascading Style Sheets (CSS) in Chapter 1. CSS is an existing standard, currently at version 2, and it's used in HTML as well as XML. XSL is a new proposal that is purpose-built for use with XML. Both are designed with the same end in mind, though the methods and syntax they use are very different. The XML Query Language (XQL) is connected with XSL: it provides ways to manipulate XML in order to create new documents, to control the content of existing documents, and to manage the ordering and presentation of these documents along with XSL.

It all sounds a bit complicated, but the theory is simple enough. As I said earlier, XML is really just plain text that has a meaningful structure only when used in context with a DTD, or in an application that recognizes the individual elements. For general-purpose applications, like a web browser, there is no pre-defined structure for XML elements. Without guidance, the application can make no sensible decisions about how to display the data.

We can define the way that we want the data within each type of element to appear by using XSL or CSS that's specific either to a single document, or to a document type.

Adding a STYLE block (in CSS) or inserting an xsl:template definition (in XSL) to the document does this by specifying presentation information for each element type. However, XSL and XQL go further than this — they allow an XSL template to do things like filter or sort repeating data, or to make decisions about the display based on the values of the data. Internet Explorer 5 supports the W3C recommendations for CSS and XSL transformations (transforming XML documents into HTML, or other XML documents), but not for direct formatting with XSL. In Chapter 7, we'll look at the way that CSS and XSL are used in more detail.

XLink (XML Linking Language) and XPointer (XML Pointer Language)

One of the problems with HTML is the difficulty you face in providing accurate and useful links between resources. While hyperlinks can be created and used in a range of ways, they all have one major disadvantage: they point to a single resource. This link is fixed in the HTML of the page, and does not usually depend on the nature of the document containing the link.

The one exception to this is the <LINK> element, which can be used in HTML to relate documents together in a few limited ways, such as linking to a style sheet or to a table of contents. However, this is still a long way from the ideal of being able to refer to documents in relation to each other as part of a structured set of resources.

The W3C is working on standards to define two related technologies that will solve this problem. The basic technique is defined in a new proposal called **XML Linking Language** (or just **XLink**), which provides a way to relate a series of documents together. XLink can then be extended using **XML Pointer Language** (also known as **XPointer**), which allows links into the internal structures of other documents.

Internet Explorer 5 does not support either XLink or XPointer at present, though it may do in future versions. Indeed, the continuing evolution of the core XML standards and the associated proposals like XSL, XQL and XML Schemas may make the current proposals obsolete. However, we will be looking at XLink and XPointer in Chapter 3 on the grounds that whatever *does* become the standard will without doubt adopt many of the existing proposals in one form or another.

XML as a Format for Application Data Exchange and Storage

Finally, in the schematic diagram you saw earlier, I included a section intimating that XML can be used as a protocol for transferring data between an application and a data store. Of course, this is exactly what happens when we load an XML document into a web browser or some other parsing application to view it. XML provides the structure for the data within the page.

When it comes to transmitting data that is not actually a 'viewable' page, we do exactly the same thing. The XML syntax provides no inherent formatting instructions, and we can mold it to fit any data structure we want. Then we can transmit this data from one place to another as pure text — ideal for situations such as HTTP over the Internet, or in applications such as EDI (Electronic Data Interchange), where we want to pass something such as an invoice from one application to another. If we use a multi-byte character set such as Unicode or the Universal Character Set (2 or 4 bytes per character), we can represent any letter or character from any of the world's languages.

So, as I suggested in Chapter 1, XML can replace custom data formats and thereby provide a cross-platform and application-neutral communication method. Even non-character data can quite easily be transmitted, because each value is reduced to its text equivalent. For example, we can transmit binary numbers by using the characters one and zero, just as we do when we write it down:

```
<BINARY_VALUE>100110100010101</BINARY_VALUE>
```

Alternatively, we might have blocks of numeric data, such as the pixel values that make up an image. We could transmit these as long string of hexadecimal value pairs:

```
<NUMERIC_VALUE>10FF7C88153D780C104589A5AAC0...</NUMERIC_VALUE>
```

As long as the receiving application knows the meaning of the element, it can read and decipher the value. The next step for us, however, is to take a closer and more detailed look at the way we create and structure XML documents.

The Structure of XML Documents

In their simplest form, XML elements and their content look very similar to HTML. To make the most of XML, we need to provide more information with the file about its structure and its content, since the element types and their meanings are not given in some external, standardized specification as they are for HTML. In XML, we can make our own rules. One way to provide this extra information is with a document type definition that specifies the structure of the XML document exactly. In this section of the chapter, we'll start by looking at how to structure legitimate XML documents, and by examining the difference between valid and well-formed documents.

Valid and Well-Formed Documents

Two topics that I have referred to but not really looked into in depth are those of document **validity** and '**well-formedness**'. While we can create our own elements and document structure using XML, as I have been suggesting so far in this book, there are some restrictions on what we're permitted to do.

What are Well-Formed Documents?

We looked at the most obvious of these restrictions in Chapter 1 — the ones concerned with the syntax of the document. For example, XML elements always have a closing tag:

```
<ITEM>Element Content Here</ITEM>
```

However, we can use an abbreviated syntax if there is no element content; this usually occurs when the element is used to carry a value in an attribute, rather than as content:

```
<ITEM TYPE="PERIODICAL" />
```

We also noted that elements must nest *completely*, or not at all. The 'partial' nesting that is generally acceptable in HTML cannot be used — for example, this is not allowed in XML:

```
...
<CODE>16-048<CATEGORY>Scripting</CODE>for beginners</CATEGORY>
...
```

If you break the code up into separate lines and try to indent it, the problem is easily visible:

```
...
<CODE>16-048
   <CATEGORY>Scripting
</CODE>for beginners
   </CATEGORY>
...
```

Another requirement is that an XML document can only have one root element, and that all other elements in the document must be properly nested within it. A complete document like this, therefore, is not well-formed:

```
<BAD>
   <NESTED_BAD_STUFF />
</BAD>
<BAD>
   <NESTED_BAD_STUFF />
</BAD>
```

To make this well formed, we can wrap the structure in a single root element:

```
<GOOD>
   <OK>
      <NESTED_WELL />
   </OK>
   <OK>
      <NESTED_WELL />
   </OK>
</GOOD>
```

So, to qualify as a well-formed document, the XML it contains must follow these simple syntax rules laid down in the standards.

What are Valid Documents?

An XML document can be well formed but still not be **valid**. To understand why, let's go back to our previous and regularly voiced assertion that the elements in XML can mean whatever we want them to mean. You've seen this in all the examples we've looked at so far, and you've also seen that there is no pre-defined structure for an XML document, other than the requirement that it is well-formed and follows the syntax prescribed by the XML standards.

In most cases, we will want to pre-define a structure for our XML documents. If we are using them in a browser to display information, or in a custom application that manipulates the data contained in the document, we will want to be sure that the structure of the document is correct for our display or application requirements.

HTML uses a DTD to define what constitutes a valid web page. For example, it insists that the page content is enclosed in an <HTML> element, and that the displayable content is in a <BODY> element that is contained within the parent <HTML> element.

While most browsers are pretty relaxed about these requirements, and will display content that isn't enclosed between these elements, the standards for strict HTML insist that they be present.

In fact, the tighter the structure requirements for the document are, the easier it is to build applications that can correctly parse the data, without having to make assumptions about what the author intended. XML is a tightly controlled language, and variations from the structure specified in a DTD should not really be permissible (although IE5 does allow some relaxation to maintain compatibility with changes to the standards as they evolve).

So, a DTD can define the entire structure of an XML document. If we decide to include one with our document, any application can compare the definition in the DTD with the actual document, and discover whether the document conforms to the rules. If it does, it is a **valid** document. We can summarize the distinction thus: *well-formed* documents obey the rules defined in the XML standard, while *valid* ones also obey the rules defined in the DTD.

The XML Declaration

As all XML documents must do, the XML document we saw in Chapter 1 began with a special line referred to as the **XML declaration**. It declares the version of XML that the file's syntax conforms to (at the time of writing, there is only a version 1.0 of the XML standard):

```
<?xml version="1.0"?>
```

The declaration may optionally include the character encoding being used for the document. To specify UTF-8 encoding (an 8-bit encoding of 16-bit Unicode), for example, you'd do this:

```
<?xml version="1.0" encoding="UTF-8"?>
```

The specification of the encoding type helps other applications to decipher the content of the document, and is particularly useful in mixed-platform or mixed-language environments.

If the document requires declarations given in an external DTD, or in some other definition or support files, the special instruction standalone can be added to the prolog, with the value "no":

```
<?xml version="1.0" standalone="no"?>
```

Alternatively, if the document requires no other files, the attribute can be set to "yes" or more usually just omitted completely.

Notice that the single XML declaration is identified by being enclosed in the '<?xml' and '?>' delimiter pair, and by having a version attribute, and that the word xml *must* be in lower case.

Simple XML Documents

In Chapter 1, we used an XML document called booklist.xml that describes some fictitious Wrox books:

```
<?xml version="1.0"?>
<BOOKLIST>
   <BOOK>
      <CODE>16-041</CODE>
      <CATEGORY>HTML</CATEGORY>
      <RELEASE_DATE>1998-03-07</RELEASE_DATE>
      <SALES>127853</SALES>
      <TITLE>Instant HTML</TITLE>
   </BOOK>
   <BOOK>
      <CODE>16-048</CODE>
      <CATEGORY>Scripting</CATEGORY>
      <RELEASE_DATE>1998-04-21</RELEASE_DATE>
      <SALES>375298</SALES>
      <TITLE>Instant JavaScript</TITLE>
   </BOOK>
   <BOOK>
      <CODE>16-105</CODE>
      <CATEGORY>ASP</CATEGORY>
      <RELEASE_DATE>1998-05-10</RELEASE_DATE>
      <SALES>297311</SALES>
      <TITLE>Instant Active Server Pages</TITLE>
   </BOOK>
</BOOKLIST>
```

The complete document is enclosed in a <BOOKLIST> element, and each book is itself enclosed in an <BOOK> element. The names we use for the elements are not critical at this stage because — as you'll recall from the previous chapter — we can use any names that we like provided that they conform to the overall syntax rules of XML. Each element means whatever we want it to mean, because XML is a way of describing *data*. It isn't a predefined formatting or presentation language like HTML.

XML Elements

Like HTML elements, XML elements are the items that make up the structure of the file. Elements can contain either data content or a mixture of data content and other (sub-)elements. Remember that the word **element** describes the complete item, usually consisting of an opening tag, any attributes within the opening tag, any content between the opening and closing tags, and the closing tag itself.

> **Valid XML element names must start with an unaccented alphabetic character ('A' to 'Z' or 'a' to 'z') or an underscore '_'. The remainder of the name can consist of letters, digits, hyphens, underscores, or periods. However, names beginning with the string "xml" or "XML" (or any combination of upper and lower case) are reserved and should not be used. Case is significant so, for example, <BOOKLIST> is different from <booklist>.**

Element Attributes

As in HTML, we can use **attributes** within an opening tag to attach specific values to an element. Note that unlike HTML attributes, XML attribute values are case-sensitive, and *must* be contained within quotes. For example, we could have a list of publications, <PUBLIST>, that may contain articles and periodicals as well as books. We could specify the type of each item in the list by using an attribute within the <ITEM> tag:

```
<?xml version="1.0"?>
<PUBLIST>
   <ITEM ITEMTYPE="BOOK">
      <CODE>16-048</CODE>
      <CATEGORY>Scripting</CATEGORY>
      <RELEASE_DATE>1998-04-21</RELEASE_DATE>
      <SALES>375298</SALES>
      <TITLE>Instant JavaScript</TITLE>
   </ITEM>
   <ITEM ITEMTYPE="ARTICLE">
      <CODE>20-105</CODE>
      <CATEGORY>HTML</CATEGORY>
      <RELEASE_DATE>1998-10-07</RELEASE_DATE>
      <SALES></SALES>
      <TITLE>Building Compatible Pages</TITLE>
   </ITEM>
   <ITEM ITEMTYPE="PERIODICAL">
      <CODE>24-041</CODE>
      <CATEGORY>ASP</CATEGORY>
      <RELEASE_DATE>1998-06-14</RELEASE_DATE>
      <SALES>357835</SALES>
      <TITLE>ASP Today Magazine</TITLE>
   </ITEM>
</PUBLIST>
```

Where Do We Put the Data?

Notice that the <SALES> element in the second item — the article entitled *Building Compatible Pages* — has no content. We don't want to record the sales, so we include the element but leave it empty. This is important if we are going to treat the document as a data source, because it preserves the structure. However, as you'll see later, it is not mandatory for all elements to appear like this in every case. It all comes down to how you define the structure for the document.

However, each <ITEM> element now has two possible sources of data: the content of the element (the book/periodical/article details) and an attribute named ITEMTYPE. And in theory, if we wanted to record the sales of an item, we could use an attribute named SALES instead of a child <SALES> element:

```
<ITEM ITEMTYPE="PERIODICAL" SALES="357835">
   <CODE>24-041</CODE>
   <CATEGORY>ASP</CATEGORY>
   <RELEASE_DATE>1998-06-14</RELEASE_DATE>
   <TITLE>ASP Today Magazine</TITLE>
</ITEM>
```

There is no hard and fast rule about whether data should reside in an attribute or as the content of an element. It really depends on how you view the data, and how you intend to use it. If you are processing the XML document using custom script, it's easier to pull out the values of the element attributes (as we'll see in Chapter 6).

On the other hand, if the data itself consists of nested elements, it can only be included as the content of another element. Only a character string can be used as an attribute value.

Building Data Structures

The previous example is a very simple XML document, but we can make the structure of the document as complex as is necessary to store our information. For example, we may want to store the name of the author(s). We could do this in a number of ways:

```
<ITEM ITEMTYPE="BOOK">
    <CODE>16-048</CODE>
    <CATEGORY>Scripting</CATEGORY>
    <RELEASE_DATE>1998-04-21</RELEASE_DATE>
    <AUTHOR>Marvin Williams</AUTHOR>
    <SALES>375298</SALES>
    <TITLE>Instant JavaScript</TITLE>
</ITEM>
```

Or perhaps:

```
<ITEM ITEMTYPE="BOOK">
    <CODE>16-048</CODE>
    <CATEGORY>Scripting</CATEGORY>
    <RELEASE_DATE>1998-04-21</RELEASE_DATE>
    <AUTHOR>
        <FIRST_NAME>Marvin</FIRST_NAME>
        <LAST_NAME>Williams</LAST_NAME>
    </AUTHOR>
    <SALES>375298</SALES>
    <TITLE>Instant JavaScript</TITLE>
</ITEM>
```

In the second case, we isolate the first and last names, making it possible for an application that uses the data to parse out the two names more easily. It's rather like the decisions you have to make when creating a database table for storing information. It helps to know what you will actually want to be able to extract in the future.

If there is more than one author for a book, however, the previous structure will not work unless the definition of the document allows multiple <AUTHOR> elements to exist within an <ITEM> element. A better plan would probably be to nest the list of authors within an <AUTHORLIST> element:

```
<ITEM ITEMTYPE="BOOK">
    <CODE>16-048</CODE>
    <CATEGORY>Scripting</CATEGORY>
    <RELEASE_DATE>1998-04-21</RELEASE_DATE>
    <AUTHORLIST>
        <AUTHOR>
            <FIRST_NAME>Marvin</FIRST_NAME>
            <LAST_NAME>Williams</LAST_NAME>
        </AUTHOR>
        <AUTHOR>
            <FIRST_NAME>Cheryl</FIRST_NAME>
            <LAST_NAME>Caprialdi</LAST_NAME>
        </AUTHOR>
        <AUTHOR>
            <FIRST_NAME>Luigi</FIRST_NAME>
            <LAST_NAME>Pressaldo</LAST_NAME>
        </AUTHOR>
    </AUTHORLIST>
```

43

```
        <SALES>375298</SALES>
        <TITLE>Instant JavaScript</TITLE>
    </ITEM>
```

This example begins to demonstrate the power of XML for storing information in ways that relational database management systems have never been able to do efficiently. In a database table, repeated groups of information need to be lifted out and placed in separate tables, and then each item has to be linked back to the original through a key value. XML allows us to nest repeated information in the way that is most natural, and closest to the 'real-life' format of the data. Of course, when it comes to retrieving and working with complex nested data outside XML, the problems tend to return to haunt us!

XML Documents as Data Trees

Because XML supports complex nested structures with such ease, it's often easier to think of the data that they contain as a **tree**, rather than as a database-style **table**. For example, given the following extract from a list of books:

```
<BOOKLIST>
    <ITEM>
        <CODE>16-048</CODE>
        <CATEGORY>Scripting</CATEGORY>
        <RELEASE_DATE>1998-04-21</RELEASE_DATE>
        <AUTHORLIST>
            <AUTHOR>
                <FIRST_NAME>Marvin</FIRST_NAME>
                <LAST_NAME>Williams</LAST_NAME>
            </AUTHOR>
            <AUTHOR>
                <FIRST_NAME>Cheryl</FIRST_NAME>
                <LAST_NAME>Caprialdi</LAST_NAME>
            </AUTHOR>
        </AUTHORLIST>
        <SALES>375298</SALES>
        <TITLE>Instant JavaScript</TITLE>
    </ITEM>
    ...

</BOOKLIST>
```

We can describe the information very intuitively as a tree:

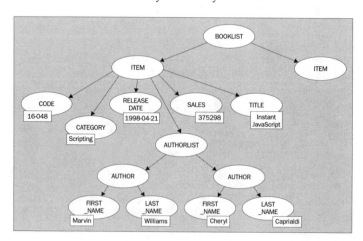

You can see that even a simple data file soon becomes a large and complex-looking tree. However, understanding this kind of structure is of vital importance. In Chapters 5 and 6, we'll look in detail at the way in which the standards defined by the W3C for the Document Object Model allow us to access the data in a tree directly, rather than by exposing it as an ordered recordset.

XML Namespaces

One problem that had to be tackled in defining standards for XML was something we came across back in Chapter 1. We used an element named <CODE> for our book code number, but as you saw when we viewed the XML document in IE4, this 'collided' with the built-in HTML <CODE> element.

While this is not really a problem in XML-aware applications, which will ignore this kind of XML/HTML name collision, it is more serious within XML itself. Remember that we are completely free to give an element any name we like. I might create an XML document that describes a cycle race, and include in it a <FINISH> element with a value that describes the location of the finishing line:

```
...
<FINISH>Main Street Park</FINISH>
...
```

However, you might have a document describing the different shifts that members of your staff work. This could use a time value within a <FINISH> element:

```
...
<FINISH>18:30PM</FINISH>
...
```

And to make matters worse, a furniture manufacturer may have a totally different idea about what a <FINISH> element should contain. When describing a dining table, for example, they might use this:

```
...
<FINISH>Polished African Teak</FINISH>
...
```

While each document stays physically separate, there is no problem. However, if you are organizing a cycle race for your local furniture manufacturer whose staff works shifts, you can see that a conflict is likely between identically named elements.

I know this is a contrived example, but it illustrates why we need a way of identifying elements with a unique definition that *doesn't* just depend on the element name. The technique we use is called **namespaces**.

The W3C Namespaces Recommendation

At the time of writing this book, the W3C had just released recommendations for namespaces in XML (REC-xml-names-19990114, published on 14th January 1999). This defines the way that they expect to see namespaces developing, and Internet Explorer 5 fully supports these recommendations.

The xmlns Attribute

In an XML document, we can define a **namespace** within an opening XML element tag. The namespace then applies to the entire contents of this element, unless it's overridden by another namespace declaration. Each namespace requires a **Universal Resource Identifier (URI)** that identifies it, so that homonymous elements defined by two different namespaces can be differentiated by applications reading a document. While any word will do, the most obvious unique identifier for a company is the URL of their web site. However, if there are separate divisions working on namespaces, you may prefer to add a further path (or extra characters) to the URL. Alternatively, you might use e-mail addresses or other unique identifiers.

To define the namespace, and to associate it with a unique identifier, we specify it in the xmlns attribute:

```
<mydocument xmlns="http://www.wrox.com/ns/">
    ...namespace applies to this element and all content here...
</mydocument>
```

Note that at present there is no mechanism defined to connect the URL with a namespace definition at that location, though this may appear in a future version.

Qualified Namespaces

Rather than defining a **default namespace** by using the xmlns attribute with a unique URI, we can specify local identifiers that are associated with the namespace purely in the context of this single document. This is done by defining a prefix that is applied to any elements or attributes that are to be considered part of that namespace. The combination of the prefix and the element or attribute name places it in a qualified namespace defined by the URI that the prefix is standing in for.

In the following snippet, for example, we're defining a prefix called wrox as a stand-in or **qualifier** for our namespace:

```
<mydocument xmlns:wrox="http://www.wrox.com/ns/books/">
    ...namespace applies to elements with the "wrox" prefix only...
</mydocument>
```

We can then use the prefix that we've defined as an identifier with each XML element. Note that in this next XML example, the <code> element is *not* within the wrox namespace:

```
<mydocument xmlns:wrox="http://www.wrox.com/ns/books/">
    <wrox:booklist>
        <wrox:title>Instant JavaScript</wrox:title>
        <code>16-038</code>
    </wrox:booklist>
</mydocument>
```

Of course, if we had defined a default *and* a qualified namespace, like this:

```
<mydocument xmlns="http://www.wrox.com/ns/"
            xmlns:wrox="http://www.wrox.com/ns/books/">
    <wrox:booklist>
        <wrox:title>Instant JavaScript</wrox:title>
```

```
      <code>16-038</code>
   </wrox:booklist>
</mydocument>
```

then the `<code>` element would have been in the default namespace defined with the
first `xmlns` attribute. This gives us a way to override default namespaces by using
qualified namespace prefixes, so we can be assured that any other definitions of lists of
books that use the same element names can be differentiated from ours.

If we are using qualified namespaces, they only apply to the *content* of the element
where they are declared. They don't apply to the element itself unless it is bound to the
namespace with a qualifier prefix. Hence, the following is perfectly legal:

```
<wrox:mydocument xmlns:wrox="http://www.wrox.com">
    ...namespace now applies to this element as well...
</wrox:mydocument>
```

Attribute Namespaces

The W3C namespaces recommendation says that namespaces also apply to attributes
that appear within opening element tags. The same rules apply to these as to elements,
so (for example) all the attributes inside an element or its child elements that are within
a default namespace will exist in the same namespace as those elements:

```
<mydocument xmlns="http://www.wrox.com/ns/">
    ...namespace applies to all elements and attributes...
    <booklist listdate="1998-01-14">
       ...etc...
    </booklist>
</mydocument>
```

However, if we are using a qualified namespace, we have to apply that prefix to
attributes as well if we want to place them in the same namespace:

```
<mydocument xmlns:wrox="http://www.wrox.com/ns/books/">
    <wrox:booklist wrox:listdate="1998-01-14">
       ...etc...
    </wrox:booklist>
</mydocument>
```

The namespace applied to an attribute doesn't have to be the same as the one applied
to the element. You can override default namespaces, or use different qualifier
prefixes, for the elements and all their attributes if you wish:

```
<mydocument xmlns="http://www.wrox.com/ns/"
            xmlns:wrox="http://www.wrox.com/ns/books/">
    ...the default namespace applies to all elements and attributes here...
    <wrox:booklist wrox:listdate="1998-01-14">
       ...but the 'wrox' namespace requires that prefix...
    </wrox:booklist>
</mydocument>
```

Removing Namespaces

There are a few other details of namespaces that are worth remembering. We can
remove the default namespace from a subset of child elements by setting it to an empty
string, or by specifying a different namespace:

```
<mydocument xmlns="http://www.wrox.com/ns/">
   <booklist>
      <book xmlns="http://www.wrox.com/ns/books/">
         <title>Instant JavaScript</title>
         <refdetail xmlns="">
            <category>Scripting</category>
            <code>16-038</code>
         </refdetail>
         <code>16-038</code>
      </book>
   </booklist>
</mydocument>
```

Here, the `<mydocument>` and `<booklist>` elements are in the http://www.wrox.com/ns/ namespace, the `<book>` and `<title>` elements are in the http://www.wrox.com/ns/books/ namespace, and the `<refdetail>`, `<category>` and `<code>` elements aren't actually in any namespace at all.

There are, however, overall default namespaces that come into effect if you don't specify one. The namespace defined by the letters xml (in any combination of case) is bound by default to http://www.w3.org/XML/1998/namespace, so any element using this prefix will automatically be bound to this namespace.

Now that we have seen how to structure and create well-formed XML documents that conform to the XML specification, we'll consider how to create document type definitions, so that we can also create documents that are valid — that is, they obey the rules laid out in the DTD.

XML Document Type Definitions

The W3C XML 1.0 standard provides a way to define the structure of an XML document through a document type definition. Internet Explorer 5 supports the W3C standard, and it also provides support for the alternative technique of XML Schemas and Data Types.

XML Schemas are designed to be easier to learn and to use, and to provide more extensibility than DTDs in the definition of an XML document structure. However, DTDs are part of XML 1.0, and have widespread support in the industry and in the XML applications that are currently available.

We'll look at DTDs first, and come back to XML Schemas in the next chapter. In fact, just describing the way that XML and DTDs work is a huge subject if you delve right down to the finest detail, and whole books have been written about it. In this chapter, I'll introduce you to the topic and show you enough to get on and work with XML.

If you want to learn more, look out for other books that have chapters devoted solely to this topic, such as Professional XML Applications *(ISBN 1-861-001-52-5) from Wrox Press. Alternatively, check out the XML specifications at* http://www.w3.org/TR, *and Microsoft's own XML site at* http://www.microsoft.com/xml/.

Creating and Using DTDs

The XML 1.0 standard defines a special declaration, DOCTYPE, which is used to place a **document type declaration** within an XML document. The document type declaration can contain the DTD (document type *definition*) that we've been talking about so far in this book. The syntax of such a DOCTYPE declaration is:

```
<!DOCTYPE documentname [ document_type_definition ]>
```

This assumes that the DTD is present in the XML document, and in this case it is placed within the square brackets in the DOCTYPE statement. The documentname is the outermost or 'root' element of the XML document. We'll come back to the actual syntax of the definition shortly.

External DTDs

Rather than specifying the DTD within the XML document, we can instead use a DTD that is stored in a separate file by providing the URL or location within the DOCTYPE statement:

```
<!DOCTYPE documentname PUBLIC "public_identifier" "url_of_dtd">
<!DOCTYPE documentname SYSTEM "url_of_dtd">
```

The public_identifier used within the PUBLIC section of the DOCTYPE declaration is a text string that the parser will attempt to use to find the DTD within some kind of internal or external repository or document store. If it can't be found, the parser uses the URL provided instead. When a SYSTEM section is used, the parser goes straight to the URL specified to retrieve the DTD.

> *Public identifiers consist of a text string divided into four sections by double slash characters, for example:*
>
> "-//wrox//TEXT booklist//EN".
>
> *The '-' at the start indicates that this is a 'non-registered' identifier — that is, the identifier might not be unique. For an identifier that has been registered (usually by the W3C), the '+' character is used, and for an ISO standard document the character string 'ISO' is used. The second part of the entry is an identifier for the author or organization, and the third section is a keyword indicating the content format (in this case 'TEXT ') followed by the document name or some other descriptor. The final section is the language code, in this case 'EN' for English. The actual use of these identifiers with respect to the storage, distribution and access of DTDs is not specified in the standards at present.*

Using a separate DTD is useful, as it means that you only have to write one DTD that you can then apply to a set of documents. It allows you to build repositories of your own DTDs, or to use standard DTDs defined (and even stored) elsewhere.

The Syntax of a DTD

In simple terms, we use a DTD to define the structure of the XML file by using special characters that indicate what elements are required, optional or repeating, and by specifying the nesting pattern for these elements. As an example, assume we have a single-element XML document of this form:

```
<book>Instant JavaScript</book>
```

The DTD for this document uses the outermost element name (the only one in this example) as the name of the document:

```
<!DOCTYPE book [<!ELEMENT book (#PCDATA)>]>
```

The DOCTYPE declaration is made up of the document name, and the document type definition. Here, the single element is defined by an ELEMENT declaration that provides the name of the element and a definition of its **content model** (what the element in the document is allowed to contain). In this case, the definition is just #PCDATA; we'll look at the meaning of this term in the section on *Character Data Types* later on.

The complete XML document with an inline declaration is therefore:

```
<?xml version="1.0" encoding="UTF-8"?>
<!DOCTYPE book [<!ELEMENT book (#PCDATA)>]>
<book>Instant JavaScript</book>
```

If we have a separate DTD, stored at the URL booklist.dtd, we could use the following instead of an inline declaration:

```
<?xml version="1.0" encoding="UTF-8"?>
<!DOCTYPE book SYSTEM "booklist.dtd">
<book>Instant JavaScript</book>
```

The separate file booklist.dtd is then just this:

```
<?xml version="1.0" encoding="UTF-8"?>
<!ELEMENT book (#PCDATA)>
```

If an XML document declares both an inline (the **internal subset**) and an external DTD (the **external subset**), the declarations within the internal subset of the DTD take preference over any external ones where they refer to the same element type. There are two reasons for this, both dictated by the XML 1.0 specification:

❑   The parser works with the first definition it is given for an element type

❑   In the case where the document has both internal and external DTD subsets, although the reference to the external subset is given before the square brackets containing the internal subset, the parser doesn't insert the contents of the external subset till after those of the internal subset

Building XML Structures in a DTD

The previous example showed a very simple, single-element XML document. To be able to build complex structures in our DTDs that reflect the structure of the XML data we want to manipulate, we use a series of declaration elements:

Element	Description
DOCTYPE	Declares the document entity that is the root of the element tree, and the 'starting point' of the XML document. Also defines the root of the DTD declarations.
ELEMENT	Declares an element type within the DTD. Encloses a content model of all elements and content that will nest within it.
ATTLIST	Declares attributes of element types. It specifies the element type in which the attribute appears, the type of values that the attribute can accept, and optionally a default value.

For example, given this XML document:

```
<PUBLIST>
   <ITEM ITEMTYPE="BOOK">
      <CODE>16-048</CODE>
      <AUTHORLIST>
         <AUTHOR>
            <FIRST_NAME>Cheryl</FIRST_NAME>
            <LAST_NAME>Caprialdi</LAST_NAME>
         </AUTHOR>
      </AUTHORLIST>
      <SALES>375298</SALES>
      <TITLE>Instant JavaScript</TITLE>
   </ITEM>
</PUBLIST>
```

We might use a DTD like this:

```
<!DOCTYPE PUBLIST [
   <!ELEMENT PUBLIST (ITEM)>
   <!ELEMENT ITEM (CODE, AUTHORLIST, SALES, TITLE)>
      <!ATTLIST ITEM ITEMTYPE CDATA #REQUIRED>
   <!ELEMENT CODE (#PCDATA)>
   <!ELEMENT AUTHORLIST (AUTHOR)>
   <!ELEMENT SALES (#PCDATA)>
   <!ELEMENT TITLE (#PCDATA)>
   <!ELEMENT AUTHOR (FIRST_NAME, LAST_NAME)>
   <!ELEMENT FIRST_NAME (#PCDATA)>
   <!ELEMENT LAST_NAME (#PCDATA)>
]>
```

You can see that the DOCTYPE entry declares a series of ELEMENT and ATTLIST entries. The first ELEMENT describes what a <PUBLIST> element actually consists of — in this case it just contains an <ITEM> element. The next line shows that an <ITEM> element consists of one each of the <CODE>, <AUTHORLIST>, <SALES> and <TITLE> elements, in that order. The <ITEM> element also has a single attribute ITEMTYPE, which is of type CDATA and is required (not optional).

In the remainder of the DTD, each of the <CODE>, <SALES> and <TITLE> elements is declared just to contain data of type #PCDATA.

However, the <AUTHORLIST> element contains an <AUTHOR> element, which in turn contains a <FIRST_NAME> and a <LAST_NAME> element, each of which is declared to contain just #PCDATA. The terms CDATA and #PCDATA both represent character data types; the difference between them will be explained a little further on in the chapter.

Repeated and Optional Elements

So, using this system, we can define any XML structure that consists of single, discrete elements. In our earlier examples, however, we had more than one book (ITEM), and each book could have more than one author. This DTD doesn't allow for that — it says that each element will appear once and only once. To get round this, we need to add special suffix characters to the content model definitions of elements:

- ❑ A plus sign (+) means that an element can appear one or more times
- ❑ An asterisk (*) means that an element can appear zero or more times
- ❑ A question mark (?) means that an element can appear zero or one time
- ❑ A vertical bar (|) is used to separate elements in a list where any one of the listed elements can appear

So, if we had to cope with a <PUBLIST> XML document like the one above, but which allowed multiple <ITEM> elements and optional repeating <AUTHOR> entries, we would modify the DTD like this:

```
<!DOCTYPE PUBLIST [
  <!ELEMENT PUBLIST (ITEM*)>
  <!ELEMENT ITEM (CODE, AUTHORLIST, SALES, TITLE)>
    <!ATTLIST ITEM ITEMTYPE CDATA #REQUIRED>
  <!ELEMENT CODE (#PCDATA)>
  <!ELEMENT AUTHORLIST (AUTHOR*)>
  <!ELEMENT SALES (#PCDATA)>
  <!ELEMENT TITLE (#PCDATA)>
  <!ELEMENT AUTHOR (FIRST_NAME, LAST_NAME)>
  <!ELEMENT FIRST_NAME (#PCDATA)>
  <!ELEMENT LAST_NAME (#PCDATA)>
]>
```

This would allow the following XML document still to be accepted as valid:

```
<PUBLIST>
  <ITEM ITEMTYPE="BOOK">
    <CODE>16-048</CODE>
    <AUTHORLIST>
      <AUTHOR>
        <FIRST_NAME>Marvin</FIRST_NAME>
        <LAST_NAME>Williams</LAST_NAME>
      </AUTHOR>
      <AUTHOR>
        <FIRST_NAME>Cheryl</FIRST_NAME>
        <LAST_NAME>Caprialdi</LAST_NAME>
      </AUTHOR>
    </AUTHORLIST>
    <SALES>375298</SALES>
    <TITLE>Instant JavaScript</TITLE>
  </ITEM>
```

```
<ITEM ITEMTYPE="PERIODICAL">
    <CODE>24-041</CODE>
    <AUTHORLIST></AUTHORLIST>
    <SALES>357835</SALES>
    <TITLE>ASP Today Magazine</TITLE>
</ITEM>
</PUBLIST>
```

Alternatively, if we wanted to allow an <AUTHORLIST> to include a list of names *or* a single reference to another book *or* an indication that it is anonymous, we could change the DTD to look like this:

```
    ...

<!ELEMENT AUTHORLIST (AUTHOR* | REFERENCE | ANON)>
<!ELEMENT SALES (#PCDATA)>
<!ELEMENT TITLE (#PCDATA)>
<!ELEMENT AUTHOR (FIRST_NAME, LAST_NAME)>
<!ELEMENT FIRST_NAME (#PCDATA)>
<!ELEMENT LAST_NAME (#PCDATA)>
<!ELEMENT REFERENCE (#PCDATA)>
<!ELEMENT ANON EMPTY>
]>
```

The EMPTY keyword indicates that the element has no content; it is often used when the data for the element is held in an attribute. Now, as well as the previous list of author names, we can use the following kinds of <AUTHORLIST> elements:

```
<AUTHORLIST>
    <REFERENCE>Computing for Nerds 1-861001-79-7</REFERENCE>
</AUTHORLIST>
```

Or:

```
<AUTHORLIST>
    <ANON />
</AUTHORLIST>
```

There is also a keyword ANY, which indicates that the element can accept any type of content:

```
<!ELEMENT ANON ANY>
```

Having this definition in the DTD permits us to include any content we like within the <ANON> element, so all the following are legal (providing that any child elements are also defined in the DTD):

```
<ANON />
```

```
<ANON>Anonymous</ANON>
```

```
<ANON>
    <DETAIL>Anonymous</DETAIL>
</ANON>
```

```
<ANON>
    <SUBMITTED_BY>James Mason</SUBMITTED_BY>
    <EDITED_BY>Enricho Gonzales</EDITED_BY>
    <PROOFED_BY>Susie Wong</PROOFED_BY>
</ANON>
```

Further Options for Element and Attribute Declarations

In the earlier code, we specified that the ITEMTYPE attribute was required by including the #REQUIRED keyword in the ATTLIST entry in the DTD:

```
<!ATTLIST ITEM ITEMTYPE CDATA #REQUIRED>
```

We can alternatively use #IMPLIED to indicate that the attribute is optional and that there is no default value provided (it implies that the processing system will provide a value), or #FIXED to indicate that only a specific value is acceptable, whether supplied as input or as the default value. Note that we can only use one of these three modifiers (#REQUIRED, #IMPLIED, #FIXED) at a time, as they either conflict or are mutually redundant. Internet Explorer 5 produces an error if more than one is supplied.

If we only ever published periodicals, for example, we could change the ITEMTYPE attribute declaration to:

```
<!ATTLIST ITEM ITEMTYPE CDATA #FIXED "PERIODICAL">
```

We limit the values that an element or an attribute can take by using a list, and we can also specify a default value. The acceptable values for an element or an attribute are separated by a vertical bar (|) and are not enclosed in quotes. The default value must be one of the values in the list, and must also be enclosed in either single or double quotes:

```
<!ELEMENT COVERTYPE (hardback | softback | none)>
    <!ATTLIST COVERTYPE GRAPHICALIGN (left | center | right) "center">
    <!ATTLIST COVERTYPE CAPTION CDATA "none">
```

In the definition of the GRAPHICALIGN attribute, we are specifying that the default value is center if the attribute is not included in the element. The CAPTION attribute has the value none, which is its default if the attribute is not present with some other value. The following examples are all legal with respect to this DTD fragment:

```
<COVERTYPE GRAPHICALIGN="left" CAPTION="The author">
    <hardback />
</COVERTYPE>
```

```
<COVERTYPE GRAPHICALIGN="right">
    <softback />
</COVERTYPE>
```

```
<COVERTYPE CAPTION="A picture">
    <none />
</COVERTYPE>
```

Acceptable values can also be specified together with the #REQUIRED keyword, so that the attribute *must* be provided with one of the specified values. As we saw in the previous section, we can also specify that an element must be empty (that is, it has no content) using the EMPTY keyword:

```
<!ELEMENT SPINE EMPTY>
    <!ATTLIST SPINE TEXTALIGN (vertical | horizontal) #REQUIRED>
```

The only two possible versions of this XML element are now:

```
<SPINE TEXTALIGN="vertical" />
<SPINE TEXTALIGN="horizontal" />
```

The 'Whitespace' Instruction

One further useful attribute that can be added to the definition of an element within the DTD is xml:space. This controls whether whitespace (space, tab, return, line feed characters, etc.) is preserved or ignored.

In HTML, unless we specify otherwise with a <PRE> element, browsers ignore whitespace characters by default, replacing any combination with a single space in the rendered document. In XML, the implied default is also to ignore whitespace, but we can add the special optional attribute xml:space within an ATTLIST entry to indicate to the client application whether whitespace should be ignored or preserved by setting the attribute to default or preserve respectively. Thus, if we want to prevent the browser or application from removing whitespace characters from the content of an element when rendering it, we can set xml:space to preserve:

```
<!ATTLIST COVERTYPE xml:space (default | preserve) "preserve">
```

Character Data Types

In the declarations above, we used the term #PCDATA to define the content type of various elements. #PCDATA means **parsed character data**, and indicates that the element's content consists of text characters. #PCDATA strings cannot contain characters that are part of the markup, such as the element delimiters '<' and '>', or the ampersand character '&'. Instead, where required, the entity references <, > and & are used.

XML allows a string for attribute values to be enclosed in either single or double quotes, allowing any given string to contain the 'other type' of quote, for example:

```
"The company's name contains an apostrophe."
'We use the name "this string" for this string.'
```

However, for compatibility, it is better to use the replacement character entities ' and ":

```
"The company&apos;s name contains an apostrophe."
'We use the name &quot;this string&quot; for this string.'
```

There is also a special construct, the CDATA section, which has content that is treated as plain text. No parsing operations are performed on the content, so CDATA sections can contain characters that are not permitted in #PCDATA strings, such as the element delimiters '<' and '>', the ampersand character '&', the apostrophe character and the double-quote character:

```
You can get a list of low-priced Wrox books by using the SQL query:
<![CDATA[SELECT * FROM BOOK WHERE
                    BOOK.PRICE<15.00 AND BOOK.PUBLISHER="WROX"]]>
```

This allows us to 'escape' blocks of text that contain large numbers of characters that are not legal in element content. For example, we can define a string that contains characters that are not valid in XML:

```
<ASP_CODE_ELEM>
    <![CDATA[<FORM ACTION="<% = Request("SCRIPT_NAME") %>" METHOD="POST">]]>
</ASP_CODE_ELEM>
```

As you've seen, CDATA sections are also used for attribute values. The PUBLIST DTD that we looked at earlier, for example, contained this entry:

```
<!ATTLIST ITEM ITEMTYPE CDATA #REQUIRED>
```

Because attributes can only ever have string-type values that are not parsed, they are declared as being of type CDATA. Any illegal HTML characters that the attribute's value contains, such as '<' or '&', will always be treated as plain text.

Definitions of Some Important Terms

At this point, it might be useful to give definitions for a few terms that we've been using, or that we'll come to later. They all have very precise meanings when referring to DTDs:

Term	Definition
text	The entire content of the document, including elements, entities, character data and comments.
markup	The characters that make up the elements themselves — the tags and attributes but not the actual element content.
literal	A string of characters enclosed in single or double quotes.
character data	All the text that is not markup.
character reference	A direct reference to a specific character in the ISO/IEC 10646 character set — usually one not directly accessible from the available input devices.
entity	A storage unit of no fixed value, similar to a variable and identified by a name. Often referred to as a **general entity**.
parsed entity	An entity that has content that is parsed and replaced with actual literal values. The result is called the **replacement text**.
unparsed entity	An entity that has content that is not XML, and may not even be text. It has an associated notation, declared separately, which provides information about the type of content of the entity.
entity reference	The reference to an entity within the document or DTD indicating where it will be inserted.

Term	Definition
replacement text	The literal value that is the result of parsing the content of an entity.
notation	Notations identify the format of the content of unparsed entities by name.

The XML standards can appear confusing at first in the way that they refer to the various types of entities. To help you understand the differences, a summary of the way each type is usually used is shown below:

❑ **Standard entities** (such as <) are used to insert characters that have a special meaning in XML into the document as plain text that will not be parsed. The browser defines these internally, in the same way as it does for HTML, and replaces them with the actual character or value when they are rendered for display.

❑ **Character entities** (such as &#202A;) are used to insert characters that are not available within the 7-bit ASCII character set, or that don't appear on most keyboards, into the document.

❑ **Internal entities** are generally used for text such as a version number, a publication date, a name or some other character string that appears in several places throughout this document alone. It allows you to change all the occurrences by changing the definition in just one place in the DTD.

❑ **External entities** are generally used for blocks of boilerplate text, such as a standard copyright statement, that apply across all documents that share the DTD.

❑ **External unparsed entities** are used for inserting non-text items such as graphics (with the caveat that it's largely up to your application what happens to these — don't expect the parser to cope with them).

❑ **Parameter entities** provide the ability to take advantage of entity replacements within the DTD — for the situation where several elements have the same internal structure or the same attributes, for example.

Declaring and Using Entities and Character References

We use entity references and character references to put the literal value, or **replacement text**, of an entity or a character into the document. An entity reference or character reference is simply the name of the entity preceded by an ampersand and followed by a semicolon. This is familiar from HTML, where we use a similar technique with the predefined entities that specify special illegal symbols. For example, if we define an entity called wrox like this:

```
<!ENTITY wrox "Wrox Press Limited">
```

We can insert the string "Wrox Press Limited" into our document using this **entity reference**:

```
&wrox;
```

Entities can also be declared by using an external definition, in which case either a URL or a public identifier is used to locate the value for the entity, in the same way that external DTDs are defined:

```
<!ENTITY wrox SYSTEM "http://www.wrox.com/defs/wroxdef.txt">
<!ENTITY wrox PUBLIC "-//wrox//TEXT booklist//EN"
                     "http://www.wrox.com/defs/wroxdef.txt">
```

An entity can also be declared as a **parameter entity**. In this case, a percent character (%) is used in the declaration:

```
<!ENTITY % wrox "Wrox Press Limited">
```

And we also use the '%' character in the **parameter entity reference** in the DTD:

```
%wrox;
```

Note that there is a space between the '%' character and the entity's name in the declaration, whereas the entity reference consists of the '%' character, the entity name and a semicolon without spaces.

The major difference between a parameter entity and an ordinary parsed entity is that the parameter entity can only be referenced (expanded) within the DTD, while an ordinary entity can only be referenced in the XML document itself. This means that parameter entities can be used to simplify complex DTDs by defining sections that are repeated. One restriction is that in the internal subset of a DTD, parameter entity references can only be made *between* declarations, and not within them. Parameter entities can therefore only be used to simplify the DTD in external DTDs.

For example, this section from another fictitious BOOKLIST DTD (of the external type) declares a <SHELF_OPTIONS> element that can have multiple nested <CATEGORY> and <SHELF_ORDER> elements. The parameter entity named prefertype allows us to apply the value list and default value to the ATTLIST declarations without having to type them in full again:

```
...
<!ELEMENT SHELF_OPTIONS (CATEGORY+, SHELF_ORDER+)>
<!ENTITY % prefertype "PREFERENCE (PRIME | SECOND | OTHER) 'PRIME'">
<!ELEMENT CATEGORY (#PCDATA)>
   <!ATTLIST CATEGORY %prefertype;>
<!ELEMENT SHELF_ORDER (#PCDATA)>
   <!ATTLIST SHELF_ORDER %prefertype;>
...
```

The matching XML document might look like this. The PREFERENCE attribute is optional, and so the first <SHELF_ORDER> element will assume the value "PRIME":

```
<SHELF_OPTIONS>
   <CATEGORY PREFERENCE="PRIME">Scripting<CATEGORY>
   <CATEGORY PREFERENCE="SECOND">ASP<CATEGORY>
   <CATEGORY PREFERENCE="OTHER">Computing<CATEGORY>
   <SHELF_ORDER>3</SHELF_ORDER>
   <SHELF_ORDER PREFERENCE="OTHER">5</SHELF_ORDER>
</SHELF_OPTIONS>
```

Character references are also familiar from HTML; they are used when we want to use non-standard characters in a document. For example, the character code 169 (decimal) is the copyright character '©'. We can refer to this using the character reference © in our document. If we want to use hexadecimal values, we include an 'x' in the definition, like this: ©.

Declaring and Using Notations

It might be the case that we want to define and associate certain names with particular actions — an executable file, perhaps, or a definition of a term. We can do this using a combination of NOTATION declarations and notation-type attributes. First, we provide our NOTATION declarations with references to URLs or public identifiers, as we did when declaring external DTDs or entities:

```
<!NOTATION bmp SYSTEM "file://Wrox/Bitmap.exe">
<!NOTATION jpg SYSTEM "file://Oursystem/JPEGs.cat">
<!NOTATION gif PUBLIC "-//Wrox//NOTATION Gifs OurWay//EN"
                      "http://www.wrox.com/notations/gif">
```

And now we can use them, for example, in the content model for an attribute:

```
<!ATTLIST GRAPHIC IMAGE_FORMAT NOTATION (bmp | jpg | gif)>
```

In effect, we have used the NOTATION declarations to create labels that link an image format with an application or resource that matches that image format — for displaying it, perhaps. Typically, the data values for NOTATION attributes are external, non-XML data formats.

We can then apply our NOTATION types in the following way to provide information about non-XML data included in or appended to the document:

```
<!NOTATION bmp SYSTEM "file://Wrox/Bitmap.exe">
<!NOTATION jpg SYSTEM "file://Oursystem/JPEGs.cat">
<!NOTATION gif PUBLIC "-//Wrox//NOTATION Gifs OurWay//EN"
                      "http://www.wrox.com/notations/gif">
<!ELEMENT GRAPHIC EMPTY>
   <!ATTLIST GRAPHIC IMAGE_FORMAT NOTATION (bmp | jpg | gif)>
...
```

Then, in the XML document, we can use the GRAPHIC element:

```
<GRAPHIC IMAGE_FORMAT="gif"/>
```

For validity, all the notation names must first have been declared using NOTATION declarations, and then the value of the notation-type attribute must match one of the notation names declared in the ATTLIST declaration for the element.

Including and Excluding DTD Sections

Two special entries can be used to define sections within an external subset of a DTD that are ignored or included. This is useful when building and testing DTDs, or when allowing for future expansion or evolution of the DTD and the XML document. To mark a section of a DTD that is to be ignored when parsing, we use the IGNORE entry:

```
<![IGNORE[anything here will be ignored when parsing]]>
```

The FUTURE_USE element in the following section of a DTD will be ignored, for example:

```
...
<![IGNORE[
   <!ELEMENT FUTURE_USE (#PCDATA)>
]]>
...
```

An INCLUDE section has a very similar syntax, and can contain declarations in the same way as the IGNORE section:

```
<![INCLUDE[anything here will be included when parsing]]>
```

Then, to switch over the sections that are included or ignored, we simply have to change the keyword at the start of the appropriate section.

XML Processing Instructions

We saw in Chapter 1 that we can add a style sheet to a document in Internet Explorer 5. For a CSS style sheet, we use:

```
<?xml-stylesheet type="text/css" href="filename.css"?>
```

And for an XSL stylesheet, we use:

```
<?xml-stylesheet type="text/xsl" href="filename.xsl"?>
```

This is just one example of an XML **processing instruction**. Processing instructions pass data to the XML parser or application, and can be used to provide information about how the document should be interpreted and used. They are integral parts of the document that are counted as nodes in the document's tree structure, and are identified by being enclosed in the '<?' and '?>' delimiter pair.

Processing instructions can be used to pass process-specific information between two applications. For example, an application that uses XML to display book information might add a processing instruction to the file to indicate the time that the list was last updated. Alternatively, they might be used to define formatting instructions, for example:

```
<?WroxAutoFormat FormatStyle="ChapterStart"?>
```

They are often used to include vendor- or application-specific information within the document in a way that won't affect the data content if the XML document is passed over to another client application for a different use. However, it is there for use when required in the particular environment that the instructions were aimed at. Notice that no custom processing instructions may use the xml keyword, which is reserved for the XML Declaration.

Adding Comments

Like HTML, XML supports the inclusion of comments that are not visible to the parser or to the application:

```
<!-- this is a comment -->
```

Comments are permitted anywhere *in between* markup — that is, anywhere outside the < and > enclosing delimiters. As the contents of a comment are completely ignored by XML parsers, they can contain characters that are not allowed elsewhere in the document. However, the combination -- should not be included in comments, to avoid confusion with the closing --> delimiter.

Summary

You may not have found this chapter as exciting as you'll find the ones to follow. It probably seems a little 'dry' because it focuses on the standards and techniques for creating XML documents. It's important to understand the basics of the syntax and structure of XML, and the way it interacts with connected technologies like XSL and namespaces, before we go on to build more complex pages and applications that use XML.

We still have a couple more XML definition technologies to look at yet, and we'll do that in the next chapter. The good news, though, is that you have now covered the worst of it by understanding how DTDs work. After a short discourse on XML Schemas and Data Types in the next chapter, you'll have sufficient knowledge to be able to get on and build those pages and applications. And we'll be doing just that in the remainder of this book.

In this chapter, we studied the world according to XML by looking at how the various technologies such as XSL, XQL, XLink, XPointer and CSS fit into the big picture. We also examined more deeply the reasons why XML is such a useful new concept.

We learned more about the structure of XML, how to build complex documents using it, and the requirements for those documents to be both well-formed and, if necessary, valid. Finally, we ended with a look at how to define the structure using a document type definition. In summary, we looked at:

- ❑ How XML and its related technologies fit together
- ❑ What defines a well-formed and valid XML document
- ❑ The XML declaration and version information for an XML document
- ❑ The structure of XML documents, and how they can represent data
- ❑ How we define namespaces for an XML document

3

XML Schemas, Links and Pointers

In the previous chapter, we looked at the basics of XML and saw how the structure of data can be determined by the structure and ordering of the individual elements that make up an XML document. We also looked at how we can define this structure using a document type definition (DTD), and how to use this to check the 'well-formedness' and validity of the XML documents associated with it.

Before we begin to discuss some practical applications of XML in the next chapter, we need to spend a little time in this one to introduce a couple of technologies for which IE5 has limited support at present. However, just like the standard itself, Internet Explorer will continue to evolve after its initial release, and it's likely that support for the things we'll talk about here (or developments of them) will be included or extended in future versions of IE.

It turns out that there are ways to define the structure of a document without using a document type definition. In this chapter, we'll look at the reasons why we might want to use a different method, before examining Microsoft's proposal for **XML Schemas and Data Types**. This technology allows programmers to define another way for the parser, browser or application to interpret the values in the XML elements and attributes. At the time of writing, some parts of this proposal have been implemented in IE5 — Microsoft calls it a "Technology Preview".

Another topic that we'll be considering here is the way to link documents together in XML, and how we can also point links to *specific sections* of a document or some other resource. While this topic is still very much "up in the air" (IE doesn't support it at all at present), we'll examine the current state of play. At the time of writing, it involved two W3C working drafts: the **XML Linking Language** (XLL or **XLink**) and the **XML Pointer Language** (XPL or **XPointer**).

In brief, then, this chapter focuses on:

❑ Alternative ways of defining an XML document, using XML Schemas and Data Types

❑ How we can define the way that data should be interpreted using the same technique

❑ How the proposed XML Link Language can define links between XML documents

❑ How the proposed XML Pointer Language can define pointers to parts of other resources

XML Schemas and Data Types

In this section of the chapter, we'll look at an alternative to DTDs for defining the structure of XML documents and XML data. The techniques you'll see described here have not yet reached the level of a recommendation by the W3C, but they are very close to the current working drafts. There has been some considerable reshuffling on this issue since the initial proposals for the **Document Content Description** language (DCD), **XML-Data** and others were put forward.

As there is no standard at the time of writing, we can't be sure what the final outcome of the W3C's discussion process will be. In the meantime, however, Microsoft has put forward a proposal for a technology called **XML Schemas**. Internet Explorer 5 contains limited support for XML Schemas in the form of a technology preview, and it's this that we'll discussing in the pages to come.

Why Not Just Use DTDs?

XML Schemas were initially proposed by Microsoft, and you might think that they're just another attempt to commandeer the standards and drive them in the direction that it wants to go. On this occasion, however it's not the case that Microsoft is defending an existing set of standards that it already implements in other applications. XML Schemas do seem to be a real attempt to create a technique that is better suited to the users' actual requirements.

However, all that is just politics. Based on your range of target platforms, it's up to you and the other parties that you'll interchange data with to decide whether to follow this technique in your documents and applications. The first question to ask yourself is, "What's wrong with using DTDs, and why do we need a different technique at all?" According to its documentation, Microsoft's reasons for promoting XML Schemas are:

❑ They are easier to learn and use than DTDs

❑ They support the specification of element data types

❑ They simplify application design

❑ They provide better support for namespaces

- ❑   They allow reuse of elements via inheritance
- ❑   They are extensible, allowing new features to be added easily over time
- ❑   They are a natural development of DTDs

Later on, we'll look at these areas in more depth as we work through the way that XML Schemas are used. However, let's briefly consider some background to the first of these suggestions — that XML Schemas are easier to learn and use than DTDs.

Why are DTDs so Complex?

Like so many things, DTDs aren't difficult once you've got the hang of using them. That doesn't disguise the fact, though, that they *are* a lot more complex than the actual XML data they define. The syntax used is often arbitrary and confusing, and some of the concepts, such as parameter entities, are stretched to perform many different functions. This doesn't make for easy understanding.

Sometimes, for example, parts of an element or attribute declaration require quotation marks when the same thing written elsewhere in the same declaration does not — look at the following to see what I mean:

```
<!ATTLIST COVERTYPE GRAPHICALIGN (left | center | right) "center">
```

The declaration of entities also takes some getting used to. For example, an entity defined like this:

```
<!ENTITY % wrox "Wrox Press Limited">
```

is inserted into a DTD with %wrox;. However, an entity defined like this:

```
<!ENTITY wrox "Wrox Press Limited">
```

we insert into the document with &wrox; (using an ampersand). Why isn't it declared like this instead?

```
<!ENTITY & wrox "Wrox Press Limited">
```

And what about the definition of a character data section using CDATA? Who dreamed this one up, you might be tempted to ask:

```
<![CDATA["This is the value of the entity"]]>
```

Where DTDs Came From

This is not a blanket attack on DTDs; there is a very good reason why they look the way they do. Remember that XML is a subset of SGML, and that HTML (an application of SGML) has a DTD that is every bit as complex as any XML DTD we might use. When we build web pages, however, we don't have to worry about that — we're depending on the browser knowing what all the elements mean, and we don't have to provide a DTD. In XML, where the free-form nature of the structure allows us to specify our own meanings for the elements in our documents, we have to be able to create definitions for these documents. Freedom, it seems, comes at a price.

SGML is a fiendishly complex language definition framework that allows the markup to be defined down to the smallest detail, including such things as the characters used to define element tag delimiters, text delimiters, and operators. If they had *really* wanted to make developers' lives harder, the originators of XML could have used characters that were completely unlike HTML and yet still complied with SGML, for example:

```
{*BOOK* BOOKTYPE@$PERIODICAL$ }
   {*TITLE*}
      Instant JavaScript
   {*#TITLE*}
{*#BOOK*}
```

We should really be thankful that XML is at least like HTML in appearance and basic structure. DTDs, however, have to be written in a way that complies with SGML syntax, and they involve a step up in complexity for precisely that reason. As a by-product, this enables people with a lot of legacy data tied up in SGML markup to convert it to the 'lite' version of SGML (that is, XML) with ease. Ultimately, XML will enable faster processing of this data because it doesn't have to support the weightier syntax of SGML that's overkill for most purposes.

The Basics of XML Schemas

According to the current documentation, Microsoft provides a "preview" of its XML Schemas and Data Types technology in Internet Explorer 5. We'll look at this in some detail here, and discover just how different it is from the DTDs we met in the previous chapter. While this *is* only a preview technology, it is likely to be quite close to the final recommendations of the W3C working parties, and so the knowledge you gain will prove useful in understanding the final standards.

While DTDs use syntax taken from SGML to define XML documents, XML Schemas use *XML* syntax to define other XML documents. This makes it more natural to use, because you don't have to learn a new syntax — it all looks quite familiar. However, the underlying principle of XML Schemas is very much the same as it is for DTDs: the definition of each element includes pointers to the definitions of the contained elements and attributes.

A Sample XML Document

To see this more clearly, and give you an idea what XML Schemas look like, we'll start with a familiar XML document. The following document, `publist.xml`, is a modified version of the list of books, articles and periodicals that we've been toying with in the previous chapters. It contains three items, and provides a range of information about each one:

```
<?xml version="1.0"?>

<PUBLIST>

  <ITEM ITEMTYPE="BOOK">
     <CODE>16-048</CODE>
     <CATEGORY>Scripting</CATEGORY>
     <RELEASE_DATE>1998-04-21</RELEASE_DATE>
     <TITLE>Instant JavaScript</TITLE>
```

```
        <AUTHORLIST>
          <AUTHOR>
            <FIRST_NAME>Marvin</FIRST_NAME>
            <LAST_NAME>Williams</LAST_NAME>
          </AUTHOR>
          <AUTHOR>
            <FIRST_NAME>Cheryl</FIRST_NAME>
            <LAST_NAME>Caprialdi</LAST_NAME>
          </AUTHOR>
        </AUTHORLIST>
        <SALES>375298</SALES>
      </ITEM>

      <ITEM ITEMTYPE="ARTICLE">
        <CODE>20-105</CODE>
        <CATEGORY>HTML</CATEGORY>
        <RELEASE_DATE>1998-10-07</RELEASE_DATE>
        <TITLE>Building Compatible Pages</TITLE>
        <AUTHORLIST>
          <AUTHOR>
            <FIRST_NAME>Susie</FIRST_NAME>
            <LAST_NAME>Wong</LAST_NAME>
          </AUTHOR>
        </AUTHORLIST>
      </ITEM>

      <ITEM ITEMTYPE="PERIODICAL">
        <CODE>24-041</CODE>
        <CATEGORY>ASP</CATEGORY>
        <RELEASE_DATE>1998-06-14</RELEASE_DATE>
        <TITLE>ASP Today Magazine</TITLE>
        <SALES>357835</SALES>
      </ITEM>

    </PUBLIST>
```

By comparing the three items, you can see that some elements are optional, and others are repeated. Only one element (<ITEM>) has an attribute, and there are a variety of types of data — character strings, dates and numbers.

A Sample DTD

To define this document with a DTD, we might use the following:

```
<!DOCTYPE PUBLIST [
  <!ELEMENT PUBLIST (ITEM+)>
  <!ELEMENT ITEM (CODE, CATEGORY, RELEASE_DATE, TITLE, AUTHORLIST?, SALES?)>
    <!ATTLIST ITEM ITEMTYPE (BOOK | ARTICLE | PERIODICAL) "BOOK">
  <!ELEMENT CODE (#PCDATA)>
  <!ELEMENT CATEGORY (#PCDATA)>
  <!ELEMENT RELEASE_DATE (#PCDATA)>
  <!ELEMENT TITLE (#PCDATA)>
  <!ELEMENT AUTHORLIST (AUTHOR*)>
  <!ELEMENT SALES (#PCDATA)>
  <!ELEMENT AUTHOR (FIRST_NAME, LAST_NAME)>
  <!ELEMENT FIRST_NAME (#PCDATA)>
  <!ELEMENT LAST_NAME (#PCDATA)>
]>
```

You can see that this meets the requirement for the repeated <ITEM> element, which must occur at least once as it is defined with a plus sign (+). The DTD also specifies the <AUTHORLIST> and <SALES> elements as being optional (using a question mark) so they can appear once only or not at all. You can also see that the ITEMTYPE attribute of the <ITEM> element can only take one of the three values we've used in the XML document, with "BOOK" as the default. Among the remaining lines in the DTD is the specification of the <AUTHORLIST> element content — the repeated but optional <AUTHOR> element (defined with an asterisk).

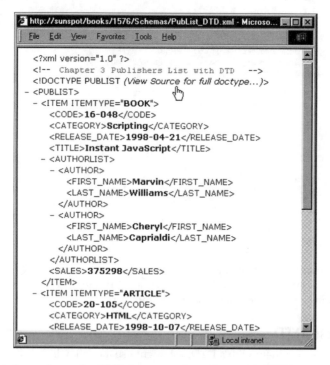

The screenshot above shows the XML document (complete with DTD) open in Internet Explorer 5. To see the DTD, you have to view the page's source code. You should make careful note, however, that IE5 currently *doesn't* validate the document against the DTD when opened this way — it only checks for well-formedness. To validate the document, you have to load it using script, as we'll see in Chapter 5.

> *To help remedy this situation, Microsoft provides a useful tool called the **XML Validator**, an HTML page that validates XML documents and provides a limited amount of debug information. It displays error messages that are useful when you are trying to develop a schema or an XML document bound to a DTD:*

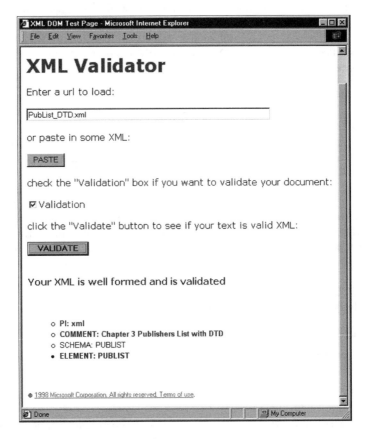

You can run or download this page from
http://www.microsoft.com/downloads/samples/Internet/xml/
xml_validator/Default.asp

I know: we covered DTDs in the last chapter, and you're keen to see an XML Schema. That's coming next, and as you've probably guessed, we'll be developing one to match the document shown above. It will also be broadly equivalent to the DTD we've just looked at, so you will easily be able to see how they relate.

An Equivalent XML Schema

The first step in the process is to provide the 'envelope' for our schema. In much the same way as a DTD uses a DOCTYPE instruction, our XML Schema uses a <Schema> element. This encloses the entire schema, and accepts attributes that define the schema name and the namespaces that the schema inhabits:

```
<Schema name="listSchema"
        xmlns="urn:schemas-microsoft-com:xml-data"
        xmlns:dt="urn:schemas-microsoft-com:datatypes">

  ...contents of the schema...

</Schema>
```

71

The name of the schema does not have to be the same as the document name, but IE5 *is* very particular about the namespaces you use. While you can change the prefix for the 'datatypes' namespace if you want to, you *must* use the identifiers shown here. These are Universal Resource Names (URNs) that identify and define the meaning of the schema element types.

The Root Element

To define elements within the schema, we use <ElementType> elements. Each one defines the content type for an individual element, in a similar way to the <!ELEMENT ... > entry in a DTD. However, in the current release of IE5, there is a restriction that does not appear in DTDs. An <ElementType> element can only use definitions of other elements and attributes that occur *before it* in the schema.

It is likely that this limitation will be removed in the final implementation of schemas, but you should certainly bear it in mind. In our example, to make it easier to assimilate the way schemas work, we're going to start with the outermost element. Remember, though, that in the actual schema file, this entry appears *after* all the other element definitions.

As in our DTD, we define the outermost element of the document, named PUBLIST, and then declare the content that the element can accept:

```
<ElementType name="PUBLIST" content="eltOnly" model="closed">
    <description>The root element of the publications list</description>
    <element type="ITEM" minOccurs="1" maxOccurs="*" />
</ElementType>
```

We've used special attributes of the <ElementType> element to specify that the only permitted content is other elements ("eltOnly" means no text or other entities). We've also specified that the model is "closed", so there can be no optional content placed within the element, as would be the case if we declared it as "open".

> *The* model *attribute defines whether the element can accept content (such as text or other elements) that is not defined in the schema. The value* "open" *allows undefined content to appear, while the value* "closed" *allows only content defined in the schema to appear.*

Inside the <ElementType> element is the **content model**. The first entry here is a <description> element, which is intended primarily for the human reader — perhaps a document author or programmer who wants to know what a PUBLIST is for. However, software tools could also use it, so it might appear when a user clicks a help button in an XML browser for example. Remember though that this is *within the schema*, so elements here won't be visible to an application designed to read only the XML document.

The important part of the <ElementType> content model is the specification of the XML document content itself — in this case, a single element named <ITEM>. The instance shown in our schema (above) uses the minOccurs and maxOccurs attributes to specify that it must appear at least once, and that it can be repeated. This is the equivalent of the DTD entry:

```
<!ELEMENT PUBLIST (ITEM+)>
```

The Repeated ITEM Element

We now know that our document will consist of repeated <ITEM> elements. Before we continue, remember that in reality the <PUBLIST> definition appears *after* all the other definitions that it depends on. We're working our way backward, 'up' the schema, rather than forwards as we would with a DTD.

To define the content model for the <ITEM> element, we use another <ElementType> element in our schema. However, the <ITEM> element has an ITEMTYPE attribute, so we need to define this before we can define the element and its content. In the code below, the attribute definition appears in the <AttributeType> element that precedes the <ElementType> element. ITEMTYPE has the data type "enumeration", and a list of values and a default value are also specified (the data type attributes come from the secondary namespace we defined in the opening <Schema> element):

```
<AttributeType name="ITEMTYPE" dt:type="enumeration"
                dt:values="BOOK ARTICLE PERIODICAL" default="BOOK" />
<ElementType name="ITEM" content="eltOnly" model="closed">
   <description>Repeated element that describes each item</description>
   <attribute type="ITEMTYPE" />
   <group order="seq">
      <element type="CODE" />
      <element type="CATEGORY" />
      <element type="RELEASE_DATE" />
      <element type="TITLE" />
      <element type="AUTHORLIST" minOccurs="0" />
      <element type="SALES" minOccurs="0" />
   </group>
</ElementType>
```

Beneath this is the definition of the <ITEM> element itself, with a list of the child elements declared within <element> schema elements. I've enclosed these in a <group> schema element with the attribute order="seq", which means that the enclosed elements can appear once only, and in the specified sequence. This is equivalent to enclosing a series of elements in parentheses in a DTD.

Two of the elements are optional, so I've added the minOccurs attribute to them. The default value for this attribute is "1" and so elements will occur once only if the attribute is omitted. In this case, setting the values to zero means that the elements do not have to appear. The previous section of code is therefore equivalent to the DTD lines:

```
<!ELEMENT ITEM (CODE, CATEGORY, RELEASE_DATE, TITLE, AUTHORLIST?, SALES?)>
<!ATTLIST ITEM ITEMTYPE (BOOK | ARTICLE | PERIODICAL) "BOOK">
```

The Elements within Each ITEM

The elements within each <ITEM> contain information about the publications. The first of these elements holds the product code, which consists of a mixture of alphanumeric characters. We specify that this is a simple string type in the element definition, and set the content attribute to textOnly so that the element can only contain text and no other elements:

```
<ElementType name="CODE" content="textOnly" model="closed" dt:type="string">
    <description>Defines a code number for the publication</description>
</ElementType>
```

The DTD entry that we are aiming to emulate with this schema entry is:

```
<!ELEMENT CODE (#PCDATA)>
```

In fact though, we've provided a more constrictive definition in our schema, because unlike #PCDATA (which does not specify the type of data to be included) we have limited our content to a text string. No content other than that defined in the schema can be included in this element (model="closed"), and the schema says it can only accept *only* a string value (dt:type="string").

In the DTD, we also define the <CATEGORY> element as of type #PCDATA:

```
<!ELEMENT CATEGORY #PCDATA>
```

However, in our schema we would like to restrict its content to one of four string values. The documentation claims that we can do this by using another enumeration:

```
<ElementType name="CATEGORY" content="textOnly" model="closed"
            dt:type="enumeration"
            dt:values="HTML Scripting ASP Components">
    <description>Indicates the category for the publication</description>
</ElementType>
```

This again would give us the ability to extend our control over document content when compared with using a DTD. At the time of writing, though, the technology preview implemented by IE5 does not support enumerations for elements, only for attributes. At the moment, we therefore have the same restrictions as for DTDs, although hopefully the level of support for data types will increase as Internet Explorer continues to evolve. For the moment, we just have to write:

```
<ElementType name="CATEGORY" content="textOnly" model="closed"
            dt:type="string">
    <description>Indicates the category for the publication</description>
</ElementType>
```

Using the 'date' Data Type

The <RELEASE_DATE> element holds a string (#PCDATA) in the DTD, but in the schema we can improve on that by specifying a proper 'date' data type:

```
<ElementType name="RELEASE_DATE" content="textOnly"
            model="closed" dt:type="date">
    <description>Shows the date the publication was released</description>
</ElementType>
```

While we will still use the same format for the content of the element in the XML document (yyyy-mm-dd, the ISO 8601 preferred format for dates), an application receiving the document will *know* that it's a date, and that it should be handled as such. This allows a platform-neutral format to be used when exchanging data between applications, and allows each one to format the date as appropriate.

All this is in contrast to the DTD, which defines the type as #PCDATA and so gives no hint to the receiving application as to how to handle it:

```
<!ELEMENT RELEASE_DATE (#PCDATA)>
<!ELEMENT TITLE (#PCDATA)>
```

After the release date (as seen above) comes the <TITLE> element, which is again just a simple #PCDATA in the DTD and a string type in our schema:

```
<ElementType name="TITLE" content="textOnly"
             model="closed" dt:type="string">
  <description>Indicates the title of the publication</description>
</ElementType>
```

The Optional Repeated AUTHORLIST Element

In the DTD, we specified that the <AUTHORLIST> element should appear once or not at all, because it was declared with a question mark suffix. This element encloses <AUTHOR> elements that are defined as being optional and repeated — in other words, they can appear zero, one or more times. Each <AUTHOR> element contains only one <FIRST_NAME> and one <LAST_NAME> element, in that order:

```
<!ELEMENT ITEM (CODE, CATEGORY, RELEASE_DATE, TITLE, AUTHORLIST?, SALES?)>
...
<!ELEMENT AUTHORLIST (AUTHOR*)>
...
<!ELEMENT AUTHOR (FIRST_NAME, LAST_NAME)>
<!ELEMENT FIRST_NAME (#PCDATA)>
<!ELEMENT LAST_NAME (#PCDATA)>
```

To demonstrate the flexibility of XML Schemas over DTDs, we'll offer a more 'open' approach with this element and its content. The following definition of the <AUTHORLIST> element has its content attribute set to "mixed", which means that the content can consist of any mixture of text and other elements. It also has model set to "open", so that the content can vary from the definition if required — in other words, it can include other elements and nodes that are not shown in the schema.

The <ElementType> element also supports the order attribute, which defines how many times the content of that element can appear. The default if omitted is "one", but here we've specified "many" so that the enclosed element instances within this element can appear in any order, as many times as required (including not at all):

```
<ElementType name="AUTHORLIST"
             content="mixed" model="open" order="many">
  <description>Contains none, one or more author details</description>
    <element type="AUTHOR" />
</ElementType>
```

So, the content of the <AUTHORLIST> element is just zero or more <AUTHOR> elements. Note the difference between the <ElementType> definition of an element, and the instance of that element described by <element type="...">. Given the similarity of the names, they can easily be confused until you become more familiar with schemas.

Of course, before we can define the <AUTHORLIST> like this, we must have already defined the content element <AUTHOR>. From what you've already seen, this is reasonably simple and should require no further explanation:

```
<ElementType name="FIRST_NAME" content="textOnly"
             model="closed" dt:type="string">
  <description>Contains the author's first name</description>
</ElementType>

<ElementType name="LAST_NAME" content="textOnly"
             model="closed" dt:type="string">
  <description>Contains the author's last name</description>
</ElementType>

<ElementType name="AUTHOR" content="eltOnly" model="closed">
  <description>Contains details of one author</description>
  <element type="FIRST_NAME" />
  <element type="LAST_NAME" />
</ElementType>
```

Using a Numeric Data Type

The one remaining element that we've yet to define is <SALES>. This contains a numeric value, and so we can specify the data type and control the permissible content to a high degree in our XML Schema. Again, this is unlike the DTD in which it could really only be defined as #PCDATA — that is, a text string.

In our schema definition, we'll add some fictional (and unrealistic) limitations to demonstrate another aspect of XML Schemas. The documentation allows the use of the <datatype> schema element to specify the range of values that are allowed for an element, as well as its data type. Here, we're only going to allow values greater than 1000 and up to and including 999000 to be placed in the <SALES> element:

```
<ElementType name="SALES" content="textOnly" model="closed">
  <description>Specifies the number of sales</description>
  <datatype dt:type="i4" dt:max="999000" dt:minExclusive="1000" />
</ElementType>
```

The data type i4 means a 4-byte integer, and the max and minExclusive attributes should be self-explanatory. There are also <datatype> attributes called maxExclusive and min, plus maxlength which restricts the length of the data (in characters if it's a string, or bytes for a numeric value). You'll find more details in later sections of this chapter, and a list of all the data types in Appendix C.

However, just as the "technology preview" of XML Schemas in IE5 does not support restricting the possible values of elements through enumerations, neither does it support restricting the values through these numerical and string operation attributes. However, we are allowed to specify that the value must be a four-byte integer:

```
<ElementType name="SALES" content="textOnly" model="closed">
  <description>Specifies the number of sales</description>
  <datatype dt:type="i4" />
</ElementType>
```

With that, we now have a complete XML Schema that is broadly equivalent to the DTD we saw earlier, but provides extra opportunities to control the content of the document. In particular, we can specify the data types of the values contained in each element more carefully, and we can expect even greater control in this area as standards solidify and IE5 evolves. Here then is the complete, working schema:

```
<Schema name="listSchema"
        xmlns="urn:schemas-microsoft-com:xml-data"
        xmlns:dt="urn:schemas-microsoft-com:datatypes">

  <ElementType name="SALES" content="textOnly" model="closed">
    <description>Specifies the number of sales</description>
    <datatype dt:type="i4" />
  </ElementType>

  <ElementType name="FIRST_NAME" content="textOnly"
               model="closed" dt:type="string">
    <description>Contains the author's first name</description>
  </ElementType>

  <ElementType name="LAST_NAME" content="textOnly"
               model="closed" dt:type="string">
    <description>Contains the author's last name</description>
  </ElementType>

  <ElementType name="AUTHOR" content="eltOnly" model="closed">
    <description>Contains details of one author</description>
    <element type="FIRST_NAME" />
    <element type="LAST_NAME" />
  </ElementType>

  <ElementType name="AUTHORLIST"
               content="mixed" model="open" order="many">
    <description>Contains none, one or more author details</description>
    <element type="AUTHOR" />
  </ElementType>

  <ElementType name="TITLE" content="textOnly"
               model="closed" dt:type="string">
    <description>Indicates the title of the publication</description>
  </ElementType>

  <ElementType name="RELEASE_DATE" content="textOnly"
               model="closed" dt:type="date">
    <description>Shows the date the publication was released</description>
  </ElementType>

  <ElementType name="CATEGORY" content="textOnly" model="closed"
               dt:type="string">
    <description>Indicates the category for the publication</description>
  </ElementType>
  <ElementType name="CODE" content="textOnly" model="closed"
               dt:type="string">
    <description>Defines a code number for the publication</description>
  </ElementType>

  <AttributeType name="ITEMTYPE" dt:type="enumeration"
                 dt:values="BOOK ARTICLE PERIODICAL" default="BOOK" />
  <ElementType name="ITEM" content="eltOnly" model="closed">
    <description>Repeated element that describes each item</description>
    <attribute type="ITEMTYPE" />
```

```
      <group order="seq">
         <element type="CODE" />
         <element type="CATEGORY" />
         <element type="RELEASE_DATE" />
         <element type="TITLE" />
         <element type="AUTHORLIST" minOccurs="0" />
         <element type="SALES" minOccurs="0" />
      </group>
   </ElementType>

   <ElementType name="PUBLIST" content="eltOnly" model="closed">
      <description>The root element of the publications list</description>
      <element type="ITEM" minOccurs="1" maxOccurs="*" />
   </ElementType>

</Schema>
```

Validation and Linked Schemas

Now we have our schema, we have to get our XML file to be validated against it. In order to do that, we have to **link** the schema to the document by placing a special value in the xmlns attribute of the outermost ('root') element of the document:

```
<?xml version="1.0" ?>
<!-- Chapter 3 Publishers List with XML Schema -->
<PUBLIST xmlns="x-schema:listschema.xml">
   <ITEM ITEMTYPE="BOOK">
   ...
```

The xmlns value "x-schema:listschema.xml" indicates that we want to link the schema file named listschema.xml to this document, and use it to validate the document. The listschema.xml file itself is simply our complete schema with an XML version element added at the top:

```
<?xml version="1.0"?>
<Schema name="listSchema" xmlns="urn:schemas-microsoft-com:xml-data"
        xmlns:dt="urn:schemas-microsoft-com:datatypes">
   ...
   ...
</Schema>
```

The screenshot below shows the result: it contains the complete XML file with the reference to the external schema in line three, and the data types listed as if they were element attributes (these are colored green when you view this in IE5):

```
H:\BOOKS\1576.IE5XML\chapter.03\code\PubList_Schema.xml - Microsoft I...    ▯□▯
  File   Edit   View   Favorites   Tools   Help

<?xml version="1.0" ?>
<!-- Chapter 3 Publishers List with XML Schema    -->
- <PUBLIST xmlns="x-schema:alsschema.xml">
  - <ITEM ITEMTYPE="BOOK">
      <CODE dt="string">16-048</CODE>
      <CATEGORY dt="string">Scripting</CATEGORY>
      <RELEASE_DATE dt="date">1998-04-21</RELEASE_DATE>
      <TITLE dt="string">Instant JavaScript</TITLE>
    - <AUTHORLIST>
      - <AUTHOR>
          <FIRST_NAME dt="string">Marvin</FIRST_NAME>
          <LAST_NAME dt="string">Williams</LAST_NAME>
        </AUTHOR>
      - <AUTHOR>
          <FIRST_NAME dt="string">Cheryl</FIRST_NAME>
          <LAST_NAME dt="string">Caprialdi</LAST_NAME>
        </AUTHOR>
      </AUTHORLIST>
      <SALES dt="i4">375298</SALES>
    </ITEM>
  - <ITEM ITEMTYPE="ARTICLE">
      <CODE dt="string">20-105</CODE>
      <CATEGORY dt="string">HTML</CATEGORY>
      <RELEASE_DATE dt="date">1998-10-07</RELEASE_DATE>
      <TITLE dt="string">Building Compatible Pages</TITLE>
    - <AUTHORLIST>
      - <AUTHOR>
          <FIRST_NAME dt="string">Susie</FIRST_NAME>
          <LAST_NAME dt="string">Wong</LAST_NAME>
        </AUTHOR>
      </AUTHORLIST>
      <SALES dt="i4" />
    </ITEM>
  - <ITEM ITEMTYPE="PERIODICAL">
      <CODE dt="string">24-041</CODE>
      <CATEGORY dt="string">ASP</CATEGORY>
      <RELEASE_DATE dt="date">1998-06-14</RELEASE_DATE>
      <TITLE dt="string">ASP Today Magazine</TITLE>
      <AUTHORLIST />
      <SALES dt="i4">357835</SALES>
    </ITEM>
  </PUBLIST>

 Done                                              Local intranet
```

*The complete schema (listschema.xml) and XML document
(publist_schema.xml), plus the XML document with in-line DTD
(publist_dtd.xml) are included in the samples for this book available from
http://webdev.wrox.co.uk/books/1576/. You can also view the schema and
the DTD online there.*

79

Remember, however, that the XML parser in IE5 is a *non-validating* parser, which means that although the XML document and the external schema are both checked for well-formedness, they are not checked for validity. The XML document can be validated against the schema through script (as we shall see in Chapter 6), or through Microsoft's XML Validator, which we saw earlier in the chapter.

The Structure of XML Schemas

Having seen an example of XML Schemas in use, you should now have a firm grasp of the principles. The schema we developed above is known to work with the latest build of IE5 available at the time of writing, but there are many more features described in Microsoft's documentation for XML Schemas that were not implemented in that build, and I touched upon one or two of them in the discussion.

In this section, we're going to look in more detail at *all* of the elements that can be used in schemas, according to Microsoft's documentation. There is also a reference section at the back of the book that you will find useful once you start writing your own schemas. It is impossible to guarantee immediate support in Internet Explorer 5 for all of these features, but it is likely that support will increase with successive versions as standards become more fixed.

XML Schema Elements

There are eight special XML elements that are used to create schemas, which the browser recognizes through the default namespace that must be used when you define the schema. We'll look at the overall structure of a schema first, then see the elements in more detail. The following code shows the broad outline of an XML Schema. The elements are shown with just their names, to make the overall structure clearer:

```
<Schema ... >

    <AttributeType>                 <!-- globally available attribute -->
        <description />
        <attribute ... />
        <datatype ... />
    </AttributeType>

    <ElementType ... >

        <AttributeType ... >        <!-- local attribute for this element-->
            <description />
            <attribute ... />
            <datatype ... />
        </AttributeType>

        <description />
        <datatype ... />
        <element ... />
        <attribute ... />

        <group ... >
            <element ... />
            <attribute ... />
        </group>

    </ElementType>

</Schema>
```

The Schema Element

The `<Schema>` element is the base element that encloses the entire schema. It accepts attributes that define the schema name and the namespaces that the schema inhabits:

Attribute	Description
name	Defines a name by which the schema will be referred to
xmlns	Specifies the default namespace identifier or Uniform Resource Identifier (URI) for the elements and attributes in the schema.
xmlns:*prefix*	Specifies the namespace URI for the `datatype` attributes in the schema. The common prefix is `dt`.

The namespaces of the schema for this version of IE5 *must* be as shown here:

```
<Schema name="myschema"
        xmlns="urn:schemas-microsoft-com:xml-data"
        xmlns:prefix="urn:schemas-microsoft-com:datatypes">
```

Using the common `dt` prefix, as we have done elsewhere in this chapter, the last line of the above would be:

```
xmlns:dt="urn:schemas-microsoft-com:datatypes">
```

Inside the schema element there can be zero or more `<AttributeType>` and `<ElementType>` elements. We'll look at `<ElementType>` elements first.

The ElementType Element

An `<ElementType>` element is used to define a type of element that is used within the schema, and hence in the XML document. Instances of child elements within this element are indicated using the `<element>` element. Here's a list of the attributes that `<ElementType>` can take:

Attribute	Description
content	Defines the type of content that the element can contain. `"empty"` means no content, `"textOnly"` means it can contain only text (unless the `model` is `"open"`), `"eltOnly"` means it can contain only other elements and no free text (other than white space), and `"mixed"` means it can contain any mixture of content.
dt:type	Indicates the data type of the text appearing within the element: one of the specific or primitive data types listed in Appendix C. The datatypes prefix here is assumed to be `dt`.

Table Continued on Following Page

Attribute	Description
model	Defines whether the element can accept content that is not defined in the schema. The value "open" allows undefined content to appear, while the value "closed" allows only content defined in the schema to appear.
name	A unique string that identifies the element within the schema, and provides the element name.
order	Defines how sequences of the element can appear. The value "one" means that only one of the set of enclosed <element> elements can appear; "seq" means that all the enclosed elements must appear in the order that they are specified; "many" means that none, any or all of the enclosed elements can appear in any order.

The following code defines an element named <AUTHOR> that contains two child elements, <FIRST_NAME> and <LAST_NAME>. Each <AUTHOR> element will also contain one (and only one) of the elements defined in the <group> element:

```
<ElementType name="AUTHOR" content="eltOnly" model="closed" order="seq">
    <description>Details of one author</description>
    <element type="FIRST_NAME" />
    <element type="LAST_NAME" />
    <group order="one">
        <element type="STAFF_NUMBER" />
        <element type="TEMPORARY_EMPLOYEE_CODE" />
        <element type="CONTRACT_REFERENCE" />
    </group>
</ElementType>
```

All of the child elements of the <AUTHOR> element must be defined in <ElementType> elements earlier in the schema, before they are used in <element> elements. For example:

```
<ElementType name="LAST_NAME" content="textOnly"
             model="closed" dt:type="string" />
```

The element Element

The <element> element is used to define instances of the child element types that may appear within the parent element type. For an example, look back at the previous code. The <element> element can take the following attributes:

Attribute	Description
type	The name of an element type defined in this or another linked schema, and of which this element is an instance.
minOccurs	Defines whether the element is optional in instances of the parent element type. "0" denotes that it is optional and does not need to appear, while "1" denotes that the element must appear at least once. The default if omitted is "1".

Attribute	Description
maxOccurs	Defines the maximum number of times that the element can appear in instances of the parent element type. "1" means only once, while "*" means any number of times. The default if omitted is "1".

The AttributeType Element

The <AttributeType> element is used to define a type of attribute that is used within elements in the schema.

Attribute	Description
dt:type	One of the specific or primitive data types listed in the appendix at the back of book. The datatypes prefix here is assumed to be dt.
dt:values	A set of values that form an enumerated type, for example "rose carnation daisy". The datatypes prefix here is assumed to be dt.
default	The default value for the attribute. If the attribute is an enumerated type, the value must appear in the list. This and required are mutually exclusive — you can use one or the other.
name	A unique string that identifies the <AttributeType> element within the schema and provides the attribute name.
model	Defines whether the attribute can accept content that is not defined in the schema. The value "open" allows undefined content to appear, while the value "closed" allows only content defined in the schema to appear.
required	Specifies whether a value for this attribute is required. Can be either "yes" or "no". This and default are mutually exclusive when required is "yes".

If the <AttributeType> element appears within an <ElementType> element, the attribute definition is available only for that element. If it appears outside all <ElementType> elements, and within the root <Schema> element, this attribute definition is available to all elements that follow it in the schema.

Instances of an attribute based on the `<AttributeType>` definition are then specified within `<ElementType>` elements by using `<attribute>` elements. For example:

```
<Schema ...>

    <!-- This attribute type is globally available -->
    <AttributeType name="COLOR" dt:type="string" />

    <ElementType name="HORIZ_RULE" content="empty" model="closed">

        <!-- This attribute type is available for use -->
        <!-- only within elements of type HORIZ_RULE. -->
        <AttributeType name="WIDTH" dt:type="string" />

        <!-- These are instances of our two attribute types -->
        <!-- they can be used when we use this element type -->
        <attribute type="WIDTH" />
        <attribute type="COLOR" />

    </ElementType>

    <!-- Finally, we use the HORIZ_RULE element in our other -->
    <!-- element definitions. Here it is in the root element -->
    <ElementType name="THEROOT">
        <element type="HORIZ_RULE" maxOccurs="*" />
    </ElementType>

</Schema>
```

So, we could use this schema with a rather unexciting document that simply consisted of horizontal rule elements of different colors and varying widths:

```
<?xml version="1.0" ?>
<THEROOT>
    <HORIZ_RULE WIDTH="200" COLOR="red"/>
    <HORIZ_RULE WIDTH="50" COLOR="blue"/>
    <HORIZ_RULE WIDTH="10" COLOR="green"/>
</THEROOT>
```

The `dt:type` and `dt:values` attributes are used in the same way as in the `datatype` element, which we'll cover in more detail shortly:

```
<AttributeType name="flowername" default="rose"
               dt:type="enumeration" dt:values="rose carnation daisy" />
```

The attribute Element

As we saw in the previous section, the `<attribute>` element is used to specify instances of an attribute that has been defined within an `<AttributeType>` element. The `<attribute>` element is used within an `<ElementType>` element.

Attribute	Description
default	The default value for the attribute, used when `required` is `"no"`. If `required` is `"yes"`, then `default` cannot be used.
required	Specifies whether a value for this attribute is required. Can be either `"yes"` or `"no"`. This and `default` are mutually exclusive when `required` is `"yes"`.
type	Specifies the `<AttributeType>` of which the attribute is an instance.

The description Element

The `<description>` element is used to provide information about an attribute or an element. It does not have any attributes.

The datatype Element

The `<datatype>` element is used to define the type of data that an attribute or element can contain. At the time of writing, however, support for this element in IE5 was limited.

Attribute	Description
dt:max	The maximum *inclusive* value that the element or attribute can accept. The datatypes prefix here and for the other attributes in this table is assumed to be dt.
dt:maxExclusive	The maximum *exclusive* value that the element or attribute can accept — that is, the value supplied must be less than this value.
dt:maxlength	The maximum length of the element or attribute value. For strings this is the number of characters. For number and binary values it is the number of bytes required to store the value.
dt:min	The minimum *inclusive* value that the element or attribute can accept.
dt:minExclusive	The minimum *exclusive* value that the element or attribute can accept — the value supplied must be more than this value.
dt:type	One of the specific or primitive data types listed in the appendix at the back of book.
dt:values	For an `enumeration`, the list of values in the enumeration.

Some of the more common data types are:

Type	Description
string	Represents a generic 'string' data type — a string of characters
number	Any kind of number, with no limit on the number of digits, which can have a leading sign and a fractional part if required.
int	An integer (whole) number, with an optional sign, such as 17 or -42

Table Continued on Following Page

Type	Description
float	A floating point number that can have a fractional part, such as $2.46E+3$
boolean	A true/false value — either "1" or "0" — where "1" is 'true'
date	A date in yyyy-mm-dd format
enumeration	An enumerated type — that is, a list of permissible values

As an example, this code defines an element named <HORIZ_RULE> that accepts three optional attributes: SIZE, WIDTH and COLOR:

```
<AttributeType name="COLOR">
   <description>Only one of these five colors is supported</description>
   <datatype dt:type="enumeration" dt:values="red blue green white black"
           default="black" model="closed" />
</AttributeType>

<ElementType name="HORIZ_RULE" content="empty" model="closed">
   <description>Creates a horizontal rule in the page</description>
   <AttributeType name="SIZE" dt:type="int" default="5" required="no" />
   <AttributeType name="WIDTH" dt:type="string"
                   default="90%" required="no" />
   <attribute type="COLOR" />
   <attribute type="SIZE" />
   <attribute type="WIDTH" />
</ElementType>
```

So, we could use this element in our document in any of the following forms:

```
<HORIZ_RULE />
<HORIZ_RULE SIZE="10" />
<HORIZ_RULE WIDTH="50%" />
<HORIZ_RULE COLOR="red" SIZE="3" />
<HORIZ_RULE SIZE="3" COLOR="red" WIDTH="75%" />
```

The group Element

The group element is used to collect series of <element> elements together so that they can be assigned a specific sequence in the schema. This can precisely control their order and appearance in documents that are based on this schema.

Attribute	Description
minOccurs	Defines whether the group is optional in documents based on the schema. "0" denotes that it is optional and does not need to appear, while "1" denotes that the group must appear at least once. The default if omitted is "1".
maxOccurs	Defines the maximum number of times that the group can appear at this point within documents based on the schema. "1" means only once, while "*" means any number of times. The default if omitted is "1".

Attribute	Description
order	Defines how sequences of the groups and element types contained in this group can appear. The value `"one"` means that only one of the set of enclosed groups or element types can appear, `"seq"` means that all the enclosed groups or element types must appear in the order that they are specified, and `"many"` means that none, any or all of the enclosed groups or element types can appear in any order.

This example shows some of the ways that groups and element types can be used to define the ordering and appearance of elements in a document:

```
<ElementType name="first" content="empty" />
<ElementType name="second" content="textOnly" dt:type="string" />
<ElementType name="thirdEqual" content="empty" />

<ElementType name="third" content="eltOnly" order="many">
   <element type="thirdEqual" />
</ElementType>

<ElementType name="fallen" content="empty" />
<ElementType name="unplaced" content="empty" />
<ElementType name="last" content="empty" />

<ElementType name="raceorder" order="seq">

   <element type="first" />
   <element type="second" />
   <element type="third" />

   <group minOccurs="1" maxOccurs="1" order="one">
      <element type="fallen" />
      <element type="unplaced" />
      <element type="last" />
   </group>

</ElementType>
```

Because the main element raceorder has the attribute order="seq", the <first>, <second> and <third> elements must appear at least once in the order shown. This also applies to the group element; however, of the three elements that are defined within the group, only one can occur in the document. So, the following combinations are some of the legal and valid possibilities:

```
<first />
<second>too slow again</second>
<third />
<fallen />
```

```
<first />
<second />
<third>
   <thirdEqual />
</third>
<unplaced />
```

```
<first />
<second>still too slow</second>
<third>
   <thirdEqual />
   <thirdEqual />
   <thirdEqual />
</third>
<last />
```

Schema Element Scope

There are a couple of topics that were introduced in the first **Document Content Declaration** proposals, and which may well find their way into the final standards for Schemas and Data Types. The first is the concept of **scope**, or having local elements and attributes.

This just means elements and attributes defined within another element definition are 'local' to that element, and cannot be referenced from other elements in the schema.

For example, take the following definition of an element with two attributes. The first attribute definition is within the `<ElementType>` definition, so it's *local* to that element definition. The other attribute definition is outside the element definition, at the global `<Schema>` level scope. So this attribute, COLOR, can be reused in other elements while the WIDTH attribute cannot:

```
<Schema ...>
   <AttributeType name="COLOR" dt:type="string"
                  default="red" required="no" />

   <ElementType name="HORIZ_RULE" content="empty" model="closed">
      <AttributeType name="WIDTH" dt:type="string"
                     default="90%" required="no" />
      <attribute type="WIDTH" />
      <attribute type="COLOR" />
   </ElementType>
   ...
</Schema>
```

Note that Internet Explorer 5 only supports local *attribute* definitions. You cannot use an `<ElementType>` element anywhere except at the global Schema level.

Inheritance and Sub-classing in XML Schemas

XML Schemas are designed to allow inheritance and sub-classing of elements. As an example of what this means, take the following definition of a simple horizontal line with a single attribute, WIDTH:

```
<AttributeType name="WIDTH" dt:type="string" default="90%" required="no" />
<ElementType name="HORIZ_LINE" content="empty" model="closed">
   <attribute type="WIDTH" />
</ElementType>
```

If we now define another type of horizontal line element, which only differs from the simple one by the addition of a COLOR attribute, we can sub-class the simple line and inherit its properties:

```
<AttributeType name="COLOR" dt:type="string" default="red" required="no" />
<ElementType name="COLOR_LINE" content="empty" model="closed">
    <extends type="HORIZ_LINE" />
    <attribute type="COLOR" />
</ElementType>
```

Now, we can use the new <COLOR_LINE> element in our XML documents like this:

```
<COLOR_LINE WIDTH="50%" COLOR="green" />
```

The other nice thing about this technique is that we can use the two elements interchangeably in places where either one is acceptable. For example if we have an advert block in our page, which is defined like this:

```
<ElementType name="ADVERT_BLOCK" content="mixed" model="closed">
    <element type="HORIZ_LINE" minOccurs="0" maxOccurs="*" />
</ElementType>
```

We can use both types of element in it:

```
<ADVERT_BLOCK>
    <HORIZ_LINE WIDTH="100%" />
    Visit Our Sponsors
    <COLOR_LINE WIDTH="100%" COLOR="blue" />
    Advertising by Wrox
    <HORIZ_LINE WIDTH="100%" />
</ADVERT_BLOCK>
```

Again, much of this is theoretical, and not supported in the first release of Internet Explorer 5. However, you should find that it is implemented more fully in future upgrades and fixes that will no doubt be issued as some of the still-fluid XML standards begin to solidify into Recommendations.

XML Links and Pointers

We've now completed our study of the ways that the structure of an XML document can be defined. However, one of the things we haven't really thought about are the ways that these XML documents might be used. The areas of application for XML are many and varied, and in the remainder of this book we will explore several of them.

Ways of Using XML

There are two distinct categories of application for XML that we need to consider. You saw in Chapter 1 that XML files can be parsed directly by Internet Explorer 5 when we load them as a document. In the same vein, we can load and validate an XML document using script. What's important is that we are loading a file that starts with an XML version instruction something like this:

```
<?xml version="1.0"?>
```

The point is that this file contains no traditional HTML code. It will usually have the .xml file extension, although if it were generated dynamically the MIME type "text/xml" would be used to identify it.

> When we create HTML web pages dynamically (by using Active Server Pages
> or CGI scripts, for example), the browser doesn't get to see the file extension.
> On the server, an .asp or .pl file is transformed into a stream of text and
> HTML and sent to the browser. The browser only knows that it's HTML
> because the server appends a MIME-type HTTP header of "text/html" to
> the stream when it is created.

The XML file (possibly with an inline or externally linked DTD or schema) provides
the complete content of the page. Don't forget that the client can be *any* suitable
browser, parser or application designed to receive XML, and formatting and
content/layout control of the XML is achieved by linking a CSS or XSL style sheet to it.

The second way that XML may be used is as *part* of an HTML document, or as data
that is to be used within another web page or application. In both these cases, the XML
content is most likely to be pure data, operated on by code or a style sheet defined
elsewhere in the page or application. What's important is that in this case, the XML is
acting as a resource for another page or application, rather than the entire content.

Freedom Comes at A Price

In this section, we're interested exclusively in the first case, where the XML document
forms the entire content. In this situation, we have to think about how we are going to
cope with some of the features that we have lost by discarding the cozy and familiar
surroundings of HTML.

XML brings freedom to creating structured documents — each element's meaning is
defined by the author of the document, and not by some faceless application
manufacturer or committee (as is the case with HTML). Freedom, however, comes at a
price: we can no longer depend on the facilities that we took for granted in the
browser.

A perfect example of such a facility is the **link**. The fundamental nature of the Web is
that it consists of documents linked together, generally with the ubiquitous <A>
element. Now that we've discarded all the baggage associated with HTML and pre-
defined document and element meanings, how are we going to link our shiny new
XML documents together?

In fact it is possible to display 'ordinary' links when viewing an XML document. We
can do this using XSL (described in Chapter 7) to transform some element that we
want to be a link into normal HTML <A> elements that the browser will recognize and
react to. We can even embed script in XSL to actuate the links. Alternatively, if the
XML is embedded in an HTML page, we can use the Document Object Model (DOM)
with script, or normal HTML data binding, to wrap the values in <A> tags for display.

However, none of these get round the issue of there being no generic element that
XML applications or browsers recognize by default as a link. This is where **XLink** and
XPointer come in.

What are XLink and XPointer?

XLink and **XPointer** are languages designed to allow us to implement links between XML documents and resources. XLink is the **XML Linking Language** (XLL), and XPointer is the **XML Pointer Language** (XPL).

XPointers provides a syntax for specifying individual parts of an XML document, such as the third `<BOOKTITLE>` element, or even the 3 characters after the second instance of the word 'computer' in the element with the ID of `Description`. On top of this technology is built XLink. **XLinks** can use **XPointers** to specify the destination of a link.

While you can think of XLink as being the XML equivalent of the HTML `<A>` element, the foundation of XPointer adds a whole new set of features that are not available in HTML.

At the moment, IE5 offers no support for XLink and XPointer. In fact, the original W3C proposals as described here are likely to change fundamentally or even disappear altogether before reaching the level of recommendations. So why are we talking about them here? Well, there are several good reasons, as we'll see next.

What can XLink and XPointer Do?

XLink and XPointer may be unlikely to surface as full W3C Recommendations in their current form, but some emergence of the techniques they encompass is inevitable. And, because of the amount of work already done on these two technologies, there's a good chance that much of the content and syntax will continue to be valid. Therefore, a working knowledge, or at least a broad appreciation of their approach to linking XML documents together will be useful in the future.

XLink and XPointer attempt to solve some of the faults inherent in HTML linking as it stands today. For example:

❏ HTML is notoriously bad at providing real information about the navigation opportunities available in any page. At best, you get pop-up text descriptions of the target resource.

❏ HTML links are extremely wasteful of bandwidth when only a portion of a document is required. The browser has to load the whole target page and then scroll to the relevant position.

❏ HTML links can only return a single target resource, and therefore cannot provide overviews of information that is available. Compare this to many Help files or other applications that pop up a 'related topics' window.

❏ HTML links cannot be specified in enough detail to return just single subsections of an element's content. Again, you get the whole page and have to locate the part of this page you want yourself.

❏ HTML links carry no concept of the structure of the document, depending entirely on the physical location of anchor elements to span the target resource. Hence, changes to the document can easily render the link invalid, or useless.

❑ HTML links demand that the author of the target document be continually aware of the requirements of the author of the source document. In other words there have to be specific anchors placed in the target document before a link to that point in the document is possible. Updating a target document often means updating the source documents that link to it as well, and vice versa.

All these issues mean that we really could do with a better way to provide inter-document links in HTML, never mind XML. You can probably see now why the work being done to create these standards is so important if XML is to supercede HTML in the future as the language of choice for creating web pages and applications.

Whether you wish to 'get involved' now, and learn about XLink and XPointer as they stand today, is entirely your decision. I've included the information here because the overall concepts and techniques it describes will no doubt be useful in the future. If you're in a hurry to get on and start working with the Document Object Model (DOM), feel free to skip to the next chapter and come back to this section another time.

> If you decide to experiment with the **ASPointer** component that is available from our web site, you will find the section on XPointers useful. Although the component doesn't follow the syntax exactly, it does absorb the bulk of the principles that XPointer is based upon.

About XLink (XLL)

XLink, or XLL, is designed to allow an XML document to include broadly the same kinds of links that are available in HTML, plus a range of extra abilities. In particular an **extended link** can be defined. Extended links are application-specific, and they can identify different types of resources, such as multimedia files and other non-document resources. They can also be used to provide filtering of the targets of a link, depending on the kind of application in use. The standards are rather vague about this aspect, as the precise meaning depends on the application in question.

About XPointer (XPL)

XPointer, or XPL, is a language that can be used to specify single or multiple locations of a target document, each of which can encompass any section of that document. They can be used as the target for XLink elements, to provide flexible ways of linking between documents. As we saw, one of the problems with both HTML-style <A> links and the equivalent XLink links is that they generally target a single specific document or resource. However, the HTML <A> element *can* be used to define an **anchor** within a page (its original use, and why, in fact, we use A as the element name). The following HTML defines an anchor named Ch5_Start in a page:

```
<A NAME="Ch5_Start"><H1>Chapter 5</H1></A>
```

We can provide a link to jump to this position from elsewhere in the page by using the other form of the <A> element:

```
<A HREF="#Ch5_Start">Jump to Chapter 5</A>
```

This will only work if the anchor is in the same page as the link, but we can tell the browser to open a different page by including its address in the link's HREF attribute:

```
<A HREF="/books/thebook.htm#Ch5_Start">Jump to Chapter 5</A>
```

Link Limitations

Being able to jump to a specific point in a document is very useful, but it has some fundamental problems in HTML, the most obvious of which is that there must be an `<A NAME=" . . . ">` element at the destination point. This means that we have to be able to define all the places that we'll want to be able to jump to when we create the document. If the document is on a different site, or otherwise out of our control, we can't do much about it.

Secondly, the single target point is a distinct limitation. It would be nice if we could specify a selection of the document, or even multiple selection areas. This could offer the opportunity for features like highlighting all the relevant passages in a document in response to a query.

The XPointer language provides solutions to these and the other problems we noted in previous sections of the chapter (see *What can XLink and XPointer Do?*). XLink and XPointer combined allow you to specify the target of a link within the current document *or* a different document as being a specific element, a set of elements, or even parts of elements and their content. These elements can be identified by name, by ID, by type, by value, or by their absolute or relative position within the document. In all, this provides a real boost in capabilities for linking resources together.

Defining Links with XLink

One of the aims of the XLink language is to allow more complex types of links than the simple HTML-style `<A HREF=" . . . ">` link to be defined in an XML document. However, it does also support these simple links so that an XML page can perform exactly the same kind of role as a traditional HTML page.

The Reserved xml:link Attribute

Because XML elements have no implicit meaning, creating a link element that can be universally understood by all applications presents a problem. The solution in XLink is a fixed (or *reserved*) attribute name that can be attached to any element to indicate that it is a link. This attribute is `xml:link` (which helps to illustrate why you should never use the word `xml` as part of your own custom attribute names).

All XML applications should (in time) recognize this attribute, and provide appropriate actions for elements that contain it. For example, they should provide methods for **traversing** the link (actuating it, or opening the target resource), and perhaps even default formatting for the contents of the link element.

Types of Links

In XLink, the various types of links are formalized into two groups:

- **Simple links**, where the target of the link is a single document or resource and the link can only be traversed in one direction. The HTML equivalent is the <A HREF=" ... "> syntax.

- **Extended links**, where the target can be several documents or resources, and the links can define a relationship between those resources. This relationship allows the links to be bi-directional; the nearest equivalent in HTML is the <LINK> element.

In both cases, XLink defines a standard set of attributes that are used to specify the parameters of the link.

Inline and Out-Of-Line Links

XLink also allows the definition of **inline** or **out-of-line** links:

- For an **inline link**, the target is part of the local resource of the link

- For an **out-of-line link**, the target is *not* part of the local resource of the link

In HTML, the equivalent of an **inline link** is the use of the <A> element as a hyperlink that specifies another point in the same resource or page, for example:

```
<A HREF="#anchor_name">This is the hyperlink text</A>
```

The nearest HTML equivalent of an **out-of-line link** is the use of the <A> element as a hyperlink to another resource or page. This can be to the start of the page or to an anchor within that page, for example:

```
<A HREF="another_page_url">Hyperlink Text</A>
<A HREF="another_page_url#anchor_name">Hyperlink Text</A>
```

Simple Links

If we have an element named <mylink>, we could use it to place a link in an XML document with:

```
<mylink xml:link="simple" inline="false" href="mydoc.xml">
   Go to My Document
</mylink>
```

When value of the xml:link attribute is "simple", we can provide a value that indicates the target of the link, using the reserved attribute name href. If we are linking to a separate file (rather than to an anchor in the same page), we also need the inline="false" attribute.

However, if we decide to define our own <mylink> element in a DTD attached to the document, we can fix the default behavior of the xml:link attribute so that it can be omitted, and provide a default for the inline attribute as well:

```
<!ELEMENT mylink ANY>
<!ATTLIST mylink xml:link CDATA #FIXED "simple">
<!ATTLIST mylink inline (true | false) "false">
```

Note that the definition of the content (ANY) allows the element to contain any other type of content, such as nested elements, text, or nothing at all if this is appropriate.

Now we only need to provide 'normal', HTML-style syntax for the link in the XML document:

```
<mylink href="mydoc.xml">Go to My Document</mylink>
```

Both of these examples produce hyperlink elements (the kind that browsers usually underline, and often color blue, in HTML). For a simple HTML-style anchor (that is, the equivalent to <A NAME="...">) we don't need to specify an href, but instead provide a role attribute:

```
<myanchor xml:link="simple" role="Ch5_Start">
    <heading>Chapter 5</heading>
</myanchor>
```

The role attribute acts as the equivalent to the NAME attribute in an HTML opening <A> tag, and can be used by the application or browser to identify the purpose of the link as we'll see next.

The XLink Reserved Link Attributes

The XLink specification provides other reserved attributes that mirror other functions that we use in HTML links. The full list is:

Attribute	Description
href	Specifies the URI, URL or location of the target resource.
inline	Specifies if the link is an inline link (to the same resource) or an out-of-line link (to a different resource). Accepts the value true or false.

Table Continued on Following Page

95

Attribute	Description
show	Specifies how the target resource will be displayed, in a similar way to the TARGET attribute in an HTML <A> element. Can be one of:
	replace — the target resource or document is loaded into the current window, or replaces the current data for processing or display purposes. As in HTML, this will usually be the default behavior when no target is specified.
	embed — the target resource or document is embedded within the current resource or data. There is no equivalent in HTML for this process.
	new — the target resource or document is loaded into a new window, or into a new context, and does not replace or affect the current data or display. This is similar to the HTML behavior when a non-existing window name is specified.
actuate	Specifies when the link should be traversed — that is, when the resource that the link points to is retrieved or accessed. Generally used only in extended links (see later) where there is more than one target resource defined in the link. Can be one of:
	user — the target resource is only accessed when the user or other outside action specifically requests this.
	auto — the target is accessed when any other resource in the same link is accessed, perhaps to open a series of related documents or resources from a single mouse-click.
behavior	Specifies a set of instructions that are not defined in XLink or in the XML document, but which control the behavior of the link in the way that the content is displayed, or the link is traversed. Allied to using the behavior property in a CSS style sheet to link an element to a scriptlet or code function.
role	Specifies to the application what role the target resource plays in the link, equivalent to the NAME attribute in an HTML <A> element. This is also useful for creating relationships between documents that assist in intelligent traversal, such as "NextPage" or "Author". This use is roughly equivalent to the REL attribute in an HTML <LINK> element.

Attribute	Description
title	Specifies a caption or a text description that is displayed to the user for this link. It differs from the role in that it plays no part in the application's view of the way that the link should be used.
content-role	An alternative place for the role of a link to be specified. The way that this information is used is not specified in the XLink standards.
content-title	An alternative place for the title of a link to be specified. The way that this information is used is not specified in the XLink standards.
steps	Specifies how many 'levels deep' to go when accessing resources from a link. For example, if the target page of a link specifies other resources as the targets of links in that page, whose actuate property is set to auto, the application could be overloaded when trying to access all the links. An integer value for steps prevents this by controlling the number of links in a chain that are followed.

So, for an element that acts as a hyperlink to another document, we might use:

```
<mylink xml:link="simple" inline="false" href="books/thisbook.xml#Ch5_Start"
                          show="new" title="Opens Chapter 5 in a new window">
   Go to Chapter 5
</mylink>
```

Extended Links

When the xml:link attribute is "extended", we can provide more than one value for the target of the link. This is unlike any existing HTML equivalent, and more like a Related Topics button, or the drop-down menu that you find in Help windows.

The xml:link Attribute Values for Extended Links

To define extended links, we have to have a way of specifying a set of target resources or documents. This is done using three special values for the reserved xml:link attribute:

Value	Description
"locator"	Specifies that this link points to one of the resources or documents within an extended link.
"group"	Indicates that the link is itself a group of document links, and the link element encloses a list of these links.

Table Continued on Following Page

97

Value	Description
`"document"`	Indicates that this is a link to a document or resource within a group.

To give you a general idea of what extended links look like, here are some examples of the XML that might be used to define them. Firstly, we can define a series of pages using a set of `locator` links. These are enclosed inside an `extended` link element:

```
<mylink xml:link="extended" inline="false">
    <mytarget xml:link="locator" inline="false" role="Font"
            title="How to specify different fonts"
            href="http://mysite.com/help/fonts.xml" />
    <mytarget xml:link="locator" inline="false" role="Color"
            title="How to specify different colors"
            href="http://mysite.com/help/colors.xml" />
    <mytarget xml:link="locator" inline="false" role="Text Size"
            title="How to specify different text sizes"
            href="http://mysite.com/help/textsize.xml" />
</mylink>
```

The resources listed in the `locator` link elements will usually be presented to the user as a list of available targets. This is useful for providing a **Related Topics** feature, or for allowing a choice to be made from a set of other documents or resources. In some cases, we may have a list or set of documents that we want to access in one go, as a single process. To define a group of documents like this, we use a `group` link element, and embed the `document` link elements inside it:

```
<mylink xml:link="group" inline="false">
    <mytarget xml:link="document" href="http://mysite.com/docs/doc1.xml" />
    <mytarget xml:link="document" href="http://mysite.com/docs/doc2.xml" />
    <mytarget xml:link="document" href="http://mysite.com/docs/doc3.xml" />
</mylink>
```

Simplifying Link Construction

In some cases, creating links using XLink is much the same as it is when using HTML, and this is particularly true for simple unidirectional links. However, even here there are several attributes that we often won't want to provide specific values for, and for which we would like to assume sensible defaults. The easiest way to do this is by including a DTD within the XML document, or as an attached file.

Overruling Default Definitions with a DTD

You saw earlier how it's possible to overrule the application's default definition of a link element by using a DTD. The following example defines a `<mylink>` element as always being a simple, unidirectional link that points to a single document or resource:

```
<!ELEMENT mylink ANY>
<!ATTLIST mylink xml:link CDATA #FIXED "simple">
<!ATTLIST mylink inline (true | false) "false">
```

But there's nothing to stop us from specifying default attribute values for the other attributes. For example, we might use:

```
<!ELEMENT open_in_new_win ANY>
<!ATTLIST open_in_new_win href CDATA #REQUIRED>
<!ATTLIST open_in_new_win xml:link CDATA #FIXED "simple">
<!ATTLIST open_in_new_win inline CDATA #FIXED "false">
<!ATTLIST open_in_new_win show CDATA #FIXED "new">
<!ATTLIST open_in_new_win title CDATA #IMPLIED>
<!ATTLIST open_in_new_win actuate CDATA #FIXED "user">
<!ATTLIST open_in_new_win behavior CDATA #IMPLIED>
```

This will allow us to provide links in our document that are automatically out-of-line simple links, and which open the target resource in a new window (or context, as appropriate to the resource type). For example:

```
<open_in_new_win href="page1.xml" title="View Page One">
   Page One
</open_in_new_win>
<open_in_new_win href="page2.xml" title="View Page Two">
   Page Two
</open_in_new_win>
<open_in_new_win href="page3.xml" title="View Page Three">
   Page Three
</open_in_new_win>
```

This is rather like having a list of HTML <A> tags with the target set to different window names:

```
<A HREF="page1.htm" TARGET="new_win_1" TITLE="View Page One">
   Page One
</A>
<A HREF="page2.htm" TARGET="new_win_2" TITLE="View Page Two">
   Page Two
</A>
<A HREF="page3.htm" TARGET="new_win_3" TITLE="View Page Three">
   Page Three
</A>
```

Creating and Using XPointers

Now that we've seen how we can create links to other documents and resources through XLink, we need to look at a related topic that deals with building links that can access *individual sections* of a document or resource, rather than referring to it as a whole. The technology in question is an extension of XLink called the XPointer language, or just XPL.

Document Fragments

In the previous section of the chapter, we examined how XML can create links and anchors that mimic the <A> element we use in HTML. For example, the following loads the document referred to in the href attribute:

```
<mylink xml:link="simple" inline="false" href="/books/thebook.htm">
   Read the book
</mylink>
```

To load the document and go to a given point in it, we have to create an anchor in the target document:

```
<myanchor xml:link="simple" role="Ch5_Start">
   <heading>Chapter 5</heading>
</myanchor>
```

and then specify this anchor name in the hyperlink in the original document:

```
<mylink xml:link="simple" inline="false" href="/books/thebook.htm#Ch5_Start">
   Read Chapter 5 of the book
</mylink>
```

In this case, the document thebook.htm is the **containing resource**, and the
<heading> element within it is a **document fragment**. The question now is how to
specify this document fragment as the target for an XML link without having to wrap
the content of the fragment in a link element that uses the xml:link attribute, like we
have to do in HTML? As you can probably guess, this is where **XPointers** come into
play.

Linking to Document Fragments in XML

The XLink standard contains a specification for the **locator** of a link, which we've so far
rather carelessly referred to as the "target resource". The locator is placed in the href
attribute of a link, and can specify both the containing resource (the document to be
loaded), and the document fragment (the equivalent of an HTML anchor) that should
be selected or displayed.

The familiar '#' syntax of HTML is also used in XML links to indicate that the thing
following it is an XPointer. However, we can also use a new syntax: the vertical bar
character (|) indicates that the thing following *it* is also an XPointer. XPointers can
define the document fragment in a whole range of ways, which we'll look at briefly
later on in this section.

Just like an <A> element in HTML, XPointers can be used with or without a resource
URI or URL:

```
href="#xpointer"
href="/books/thebook.xml#xpointer"
href="|xpointer"
href="/books/thebook.xml|xpointer"
```

*XML prefers the term **URI** (Uniform Resource Indicator) to **URL** (Uniform
Resource Locator). In this book we tend to use both, depending on the context.*

The difference between the '#' and '|' syntax is that the former will always retrieve the
entire resource first, then locate the document fragment within it. This is the way that
HTML works with document anchors. However, it is extremely wasteful of bandwidth
and processing cycles if we only want to display, for example, the last paragraph in a
document.

Instead, the '|' syntax will allow suitably equipped clients and servers to retrieve just
the required section and transmit only that across the network. How this is achieved is
not specified in the standards, but is likely to be addressed in new versions of web
server software and by component suppliers.

XPointer 'Name' Links

There are a few ways that XPointers can be used to mimic HTML-style syntax closely, making links to an HTML document from an XML document easier to implement. The first of these is by using an element name as the XPointer. This name must be the value of the `id` attribute of the element that we want to link to. For example, if a document named `thebook.xml`, in the `books` directory, contained this element:

```
<myelement id="thisone">My Element Content</myelement>
```

we could link directly to that element using either of these `href` values:

```
href="/books/thebook.xml#thisone"
href="/books/thebook.xml|thisone"
```

And if the target element is in the same page as the link — in other words, it is an *inline* link — we can use the following for the `href`:

```
href="#thisone"
href="|thisone"
```

Alternatively, as you'll see later, there is a special kind of XPointer that locates a document fragment by searching for an `<A>` element that has a `NAME` attribute of a specified value. This XPointer is named `html`, and acts just like an HTML-style hyperlink created with the `<A>` element:

```
href="#html(anchorname)"
href="/books/thebook.xml#html(anchorname)"
href="|html(anchorname)"
href="/books/thebook.xml|html(anchorname)"
```

So, if we have an HTML document named `thebook.htm`, which contains this anchor:

```
<A NAME="Ch05_Start"><H1>Chapter 5</H1></A>
```

We can load the document from an XML page, and locate the anchor, using this XML element:

```
<mylink xml:link="simple" inline="false"
        href="/books/thebook.htm#html(Ch05_Start)">
   Read Chapter 5
</mylink>
```

Creating XPointer Locators

Having seen how we use XPointers, we'll finish off this chapter with a look at how to create them. The syntax of an XPointer is quite simple, but it looks complex when you come to examine all the possible combinations of parameters. XPointers depend on the specification of an absolute starting location within a document, followed by optional instructions that define how the required 'target' element is related to this starting location.

Defining the Absolute 'Start' Location

The starting location must be an absolute location. If it is omitted, the root of the containing resource is used instead — in XML, this will be the root element of the document. We can specify the absolute location using:

Attribute	Description
root()	The default. Specifies the root of the containing resource, usually the root element of the document.
origin()	Used only when the target location is within the same document as the link. Specifies the element that contains the link.
id(elementid)	Specifies the element that has the value elementid for its id attribute. All id attribute values must be unique in the target document.
html(anchorname)	Specifies the HTML <A> anchor that has the value anchorname for the NAME attribute. All NAME attribute values must be unique in the target document.

Note that the empty parentheses after root *and* origin *are mandatory.*

To select or locate the following element, which has an id value of "thiselement":

```
<myelement id="thisone">Some content here</myelement>
```

we could use an XML link containing an XPointer, like this:

```
<mylink xml:link="simple" inline="false" href="mydoc.xml#id(thisone)">
    Go to this individual element
</mylink>
```

Defining Relative Locations

It is recommended practice to include unique id attribute values in *all* the elements in *all* your XML documents. If all document authors did this, we could use the simple technique you've just seen to jump to the appropriate place in any document. Unfortunately, this is not likely to happen any time soon.

Furthermore, there will be cases where we want to select or locate *sets* of elements, or just individual parts of the document such as single words or fragments of elements.

For both these reasons, XPointers provides a technique for locating parts of a document that are relative to an absolute starting position. The relative terms that can be used in such expressions are:

Term	Description
child	Elements that are direct descendants of the current element at the next level down — that is, children only
descendant	Elements at any level below the current element — child, grandchild, etc.
ancestor	Elements at any level above the current element — parent, grandparent, etc.
psibling	Elements at the same level as the current element (siblings) and that appear before the current element in the source of the document
fsibling	Elements at the same level as the current element (siblings) and that appear after the current element in the source of the document
preceding	Elements that have an opening or closing element tag coming before the current element in the source of the document
following	Elements that have an opening or closing element tag coming after the current element in the source of the document

To visualize the way that these relative terms work, you really need to look at both the source of the document and the tree structure that it creates. Have another look at this document extract that we met in Chapter 2:

```
<BOOKLIST>
   <ITEM>
      <CODE>16-048</CODE>
      <CATEGORY>Scripting</CATEGORY>
      <RELEASE_DATE>1998-04-21</RELEASE_DATE>
      <AUTHORLIST>
         <AUTHOR>
            <FIRST_NAME>Marvin</FIRST_NAME>
            <LAST_NAME>Williams</LAST_NAME>
         </AUTHOR>
         <AUTHOR>
            <FIRST_NAME>Cheryl</FIRST_NAME>
            <LAST_NAME>Caprialdi</LAST_NAME>
         </AUTHOR>
      </AUTHORLIST>
      <SALES>375298</SALES>
      <TITLE>Instant JavaScript</TITLE>
   </ITEM>
...

</BOOKLIST>
```

You'll remember that we can represent this document as a tree like the one in the following diagram:

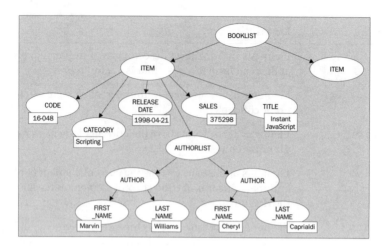

From this figure, it's clear that:

- ❑ The `<AUTHORLIST>` element has two `child` elements, both of type `<AUTHOR>`.

- ❑ The `<AUTHORLIST>` element has six `descendant` elements, of types `<AUTHOR>`, `<FIRST_NAME>` and `<LAST_NAME>`.

- ❑ The `<AUTHORLIST>` element has two `ancestor` elements, of types `<BOOKLIST>` and `<ITEM>`.

- ❑ The `<AUTHORLIST>` element has three `psibling` elements, of types `<CODE>`, `<CATEGORY>` and `<RELEASE_DATE>`. They are defined before it in the source document.

- ❑ The `<AUTHORLIST>` element has two `fsibling` elements, of types `<SALES>` and `<TITLE>`. They are defined after it in the source document.

The `preceding` and `following` terms are the hardest to assimilate until you get used to them. Remember the descriptions from the table above, here expanded a little:

`preceding`	All elements that have an opening *or* a closing element tag coming before the current element in the source text of the document, i.e. above it in a listing of the document.
`following`	All elements that have an opening *or* a closing element tag coming after the current element in the source of the document, i.e. below it in a listing of the document.

So, from this, you should be able to see that:

❑ The <AUTHORLIST> element has five preceding elements, of types <BOOKLIST>, <ITEM>, <CODE>, <CATEGORY> and <RELEASE_DATE>. All these have an opening or closing tag that comes before it in the source document. The opening <BOOKLIST> and <ITEM> tags come before the <AUTHORLIST> element even if the closing one does not.

❑ The <AUTHORLIST> element has at least four following elements, of types <SALES>, <TITLE>, <ITEM> and <BOOKLIST> (remember, the closing </ITEM> and </BOOKLIST> tags come after the <AUTHORLIST> element). All elements for any other books that follow this one (repeated <ITEM> elements) will also be following elements. All these have an opening or closing tag that comes after it in the source document.

Defining Relative Location Arguments

The relative location terms we've just seen are only part of the equation. They simply specify which set of elements are **candidate elements** for the XPointer to select from. If we want to select or locate all the candidate elements, we use the parameter keyword all:

```
root().child(all)
```

However, we can instead provide a numeric 'offset' value that indicates which of the candidates we want to select. For example, to select the <AUTHORLIST> element, we could use this XPointer:

```
root().child(1).child(4)
```

This selects the element that is the first child of the outermost element, and then the fourth child of that element. And, because root() is optional and assumed to be the default, we could just use:

```
child(1).child(4)
```

We could select the <CATEGORY> element relative to the <AUTHORLIST> element, using:

```
child(1).child(4).psibling(2)
```

However, just to make it confusing, the numbering sequence isn't as obvious as you might think. To select the <CODE> element instead, for example, we would substitute the value 3 for psibling, and not 1 as you might expect.

This is because for psibling, preceding and ancestor, the elements are counted *in reverse*. And to make it even more interesting, we can also specify negative values, so that the count starts at the 'opposite end'. You might like to read the following paragraphs a couple of times...

❑ For child, descendant, fsibling and following, we start at the current element and count *forwards* (down through the document source), with 1 as the next element. If the value is negative, we start at the end of the set of candidate elements and count *backwards* (up through the document source). The value -1 indicates the last of the candidate elements — that is, the one nearest the *end* of the document source.

❑ Conversely, for ancestor, psibling and preceding, we start at the current element and count *backwards* (up through the document source), with 1 as the previous element. If the value is negative, we start at the beginning of the set of candidate elements and count *forwards* (down through the document source). This time, the value -1 indicates the first of the candidate elements — that is, the one nearest the *start* of the document source.

Defining Candidate Element Types

The specification of candidate elements using relative terms locates an element by default. For example, this XPointer:

```
root().child(1).child(4)
```

selects or locates the AUTHORLIST element in the document we used in the previous section. However, we can also select elements by *type*, and the example above is equivalent to specifying the type as #element — the default if the type is omitted. We would get the same result with:

```
root().child(1).child(4, #element)
```

The element selector types that are available are:

Type	Description
#element	The default. Selects the element itself, irrespective of type or name.
#comment	Selects only elements that are comments, for example <!-- comment -->.
#cdata	Selects regions that are within CDATA sections only.
#text	Selects regions that are within the text content of elements and CDATA sections.
#pi	Selects only processing instructions, for example <? instruction ?>.

Type	Description
#all	Selects entire elements and regions that are within the text content of elements and CDATA sections.
element-name	Selects only elements that have a specified name.

So, we can select the third comment in an XML document using:

```
root().child(3, #comment)
```

To select the text content of the first previous sibling of the first child element in an XML document, we might use:

```
root().child(1).psibling(1, #text)
```

We can also select using the element name, so the following would select the third <MYELEMENT> element in an XML document:

```
root().child(3, MYELEMENT)
```

Defining Candidate Attribute Names and Values

The next option allows us to select elements depending on the attributes that they contain. This is only applicable to selections that specify whole elements, and cannot be used with XPointers that specify parts of elements or just the text that they contain. In other words, it is only appropriate when the element type selector is #element, #all, a valid element name, or when it is omitted altogether.

We define the attribute in the third parameter of the relative selector, after the element type selector, and the value to match in the fourth parameter. An asterisk (*) specifies any value. For example the following XPointer selects the third <MYELEMENT> element in the document which has a COVERTYPE attribute of any value:

```
root().child(3, MYELEMENT, COVERTYPE, *)
```

If the COVERTYPE attribute is optional (#IMPLIED in the DTD), we can include it in the set of candidate elements by using:

```
root().child(3, MYELEMENT, COVERTYPE, #IMPLIED)
```

If we want to specify an attribute value, but we aren't interested in the element type, we can use #element, #all, or omit the element type selector altogether. The following are all functionally equivalent:

```
root().child(3, #element, COVERTYPE, *)
root().child(3, #all, COVERTYPE, *)
root().child(3, , COVERTYPE, *)
```

107

To indicate a specific matching value for an attribute, we include it as the fourth parameter:

```
root().child(3, MYELEMENT, COVERTYPE, hardback)
root().child(3, #element, PAGECOUNT, 370)
```

Remember that all attribute values are text strings. We don't need to use quotation marks within the XPointer to indicate which attribute match values are strings and which are numbers. We can, however, use quotation marks to specify if the match should be case sensitive. This XPointer:

```
root().child(3, MYELEMENT, COVERTYPE, "EasyFold")
```

will match an element like this:

```
<MYELEMENT COVERTYPE="EasyFold">
```

but not this element:

```
<MYELEMENT COVERTYPE="easyfold">
```

If we omit the quotation marks in the XPointer, it will match both elements.

Finally, if we want to specify a value for an element attribute, but we're not worried what the actual attribute name is, we can use an asterisk for the attribute name. The following selects the third element of any type for which any attribute has the value "hardback":

```
root().child(3, #element, *, hardback)
```

Spanned Elements Selections

Rather than selecting or locating a set of candidate elements, we can select contiguous areas of an XML document. One way of doing this is with a **spanning location term**. This is just an XPointer that specifies the start and end points within the document, using the span keyword:

```
span(root().child(3), root().child(5))
```

or:

```
span(id("element14id"), id("element17id"))
```

The first of these two examples selects the regions from (and including) the third to the fifth child of the root element of the document. The second of the examples selects the regions from (and including) the element with an id attribute value "element14id" to the one with an id value of "element17id".

The two elements within the span don't have to be specified in the same way, so (for example) the following is equally valid:

```
span(root().child(3), id("element17id"))
```

Selecting Strings in Text Regions

It's also possible to use a **string location term** to select or locate a region of a document by specifying particular text strings. For example, the following XPointer locates the second instance of the string "find this string" in the entire document, and then selects the word "this" (by starting at the sixth character of the matched string and selecting the next four characters):

```
root().string(2, "find this string", 6, 4)
```

We can search within only a subset of candidate elements by specifying an expression like this in the XPointer's element selector section. For example, the following code selects the same string only if it is in an element that is a descendant of the third <P> element in the document:

```
root().descendant(3, P).string(2, "find this string", 6, 4)
```

If we omit the 'start' and 'length' arguments from the string location term, we can achieve another effect. The next example selects the single point immediately before the first character of the match string because the 'start' parameter defaults to one, and the 'length' parameter defaults to zero:

```
root().string(2, "find this string")
```

Using an empty string for the 'match string' parameter means selecting just the point immediately to the left of the text content of the candidate element(s). In this case, the first parameter specifies the position within the text content of the element. For example, given this root element:

```
<MYELEMENT>This is the content</MYELEMENT>
```

we can select the point just before the word "is" using:

```
root().string(5, "")
```

Note that the string location term automatically ignores any text that is within an element tag, and only operates on the text region between the opening and closing tags. When character offsets exceed the number of characters within a text region, the count continues the other side of any element tags. For example, in this XML fragment:

```
<MYELEMENT>
    This is the text content of element one
    <ANOTHERELEMENT>
       This is the text content of element two
    </ANOTHERELEMENT>
</MYELEMENT>
```

the XPointer:

```
root().string(1, "one", 1, 10)
```

would return text from the child element as well, giving "oneThis is".

The numeric character offsets can also be negative, and in this case they start at the end of the matched text and count backwards through it. So, the following code would select the second instance of the string `"find this string"` in the document, and return just the string `"tri"`:

```
root().string(2, "find this string", -5, 3)
```

Attribute Location Terms

The final task that we can achieve with XPointers is to select or locate an element based purely on its attributes. We can select all the elements in a document that have a COVERTYPE attribute using this syntax:

```
root().child(all, #element, COVERTYPE, *)
```

Alternatively, we can specify an **attribute location term** by using the attr keyword. The following also selects all the elements in a document that have a COVERTYPE attribute:

```
root().attr(COVERTYPE)
```

Likewise, if we only want elements that are descendants of the fourth BOOK element and have a COVERTYPE attribute, we might use:

```
root().child(4, BOOK).descendant(all).attr(COVERTYPE)
```

Summary

In this chapter, we've finally completed our exploration of the ways that XML documents are structured and defined. In the previous chapter, we looked at how to build data and document structures using XML elements, and how to create a document type definition. In this chapter, we continued the topic with a look at XML Schemas and Data Types.

We also went on to look at how we might provide links between XML documents using the XLink (XLL) and XPointer (XPL) languages. These are still only proposals, and they are not implemented in Internet Explorer 5. However, they do provide one of the features that we lose when we abandon the pre-defined structure and semantics of HTML. Furthermore, in keeping with the advance in complexity of documents and the need to provide better linking abilities between them, they also give us a whole range of new ways to define these links.

XPointer allows us to link to specific parts of a document or some other resource on demand, without having to pre-define the targets when we create each document. Internet Explorer, on the other hand, implements the links between XML documents using a very different technique. This is bound up with the latest versions of XML and XSL, and we'll be looking at these topics in more detail in Chapter 7.

To recap, this chapter looked at:

❑ Alternative ways of defining an XML document, using XML Schemas and Data Types

❑ How we can define the way that data should be interpreted, using the same technique

❑ How the proposed XML Link Language can define links between XML documents

❑ How the proposed XML Pointer Language can define pointers to parts of other resources

Our look at the various XML technologies and standards has been by no means exhaustive. There is a lot to these standards, and we have omitted some of the finer details due to limitations of space. However, this book is aimed at showing you the possibilities for XML in Internet Explorer, and you now have enough information to build and understand the kinds of XML documents that we'll be using throughout the remainder of the book.

And now that we are all becoming experts on XML syntax and structure, in the next chapter we'll move on to look at how we can embed XML documents and data into existing HTML pages, and some of the things we can do with them once we get them there.

> For a comprehensive study of all aspects of the XML standards, you should visit the W3C site at *http://www.w3.org*. This contains all the latest documentation on XML standards (both recommendations and working drafts), plus a host of links to other sites that contain information about XML. Also check out the Microsoft Workshop site for XML, at *http://www.microsoft.com/workshop/xml/* to see the latest developments and support for XML in IE5.

4

Using XML in HTML Documents

Now that we've got the necessary theory of XML out of the way, and seen the different ways of defining the structure of XML documents and data files, it's time to get our hands dirty and look at what we can do with this new-found knowledge. In this chapter, we'll examine how XML can be used *within* HTML documents — we'll be looking at using stand-alone XML documents in Chapter 7.

Why would you want to use XML in an HTML document? This chapter will answer that question by showing you some of the things that make it a compelling technique. They include displaying the content of data files that are in XML format, as well as using XML in a much more limited and simple way to pass small volumes of data from server to client.

The point is not that XML brings a whole world of *new* techniques as such; rather it provides better opportunities for working with *existing* techniques of manipulating data on the client. The application format-independence of XML makes it a strong candidate for data transmission in all kinds of circumstances, especially where existing techniques are made more complex and difficult by the need to connect disparate platforms or operating systems. In this chapter, you'll see:

- ❑ What **remote data access** means, and some of the techniques available for doing it

- ❑ What **data source objects** (**DSOs**) are, and how to transfer data to the client

- ❑ How we can use **data binding** to display or access data in a DSO

- ❑ How we can use **client-side scripting** to access and work with XML data

We'll start off with a look at data transmission scenarios in web applications and web pages, before moving on to see in more detail how we can insert data into HTML pages, and what we can do with it once we get it there.

Remote Data Access Techniques

Almost since its inception, one of the prime requirements of the Web has been to take data from a database of some kind, and display it in a web page. In the early days, this was usually done with CGI executables. Later on, Perl and IDC scripts were used for the task. More recently still, Active Server Pages and Java servlets have become popular ways of doing the job.

All these techniques have one thing in common. They retrieve the data from the database and manipulate it on the server to produce an HTML page. In other words, all decisions about the data that is to be included, the way that it is filtered, and the sort order, are determined by the server-side application. All that gets sent to the client browser are the results, in plain HTML.

This is fine if, for example, you only want to view one or two records from a database table containing several thousand. If you just want details of customer number 47301, there's no point in sending details of the other customers across the network as well. All that does is waste processing cycles and bandwidth.

But what if you want to see all the customers in, say, San Francisco? Then you might get a list of a few hundred people, and yet the sort order is still determined by the server-based application. If you want to sort the resulting list into a different order, or just view a subset of it, you have to go back to the server again and get a new HTML page built up. And the user just has to wait.

Microsoft Remote Data Services

During the last couple of years, a better way to achieve this kind of task has been under development. In Internet Explorer 4, Microsoft introduced a set of **remote data access** techniques, based around ActiveX controls that were installed on the client with the browser. These allowed IE4 to download a set of records from a database or delimited text file and cache them on the client. The data could then be manipulated there, without having to go back to the server when you wanted to sort the records into a different order, or view a subset of them.

This magic was achieved through a range of client-side ActiveX components, most notably the **Remote Data Service Control** (RDS, formerly known as the Advanced Data Connector), and the **Tabular Data Control** (TDC, sometimes known as the Text Data Control). Controls of this type are known collectively as **Data Source Objects** (DSOs).

Remote Data and XML

The RDS and TDC controls are also supplied with IE5, and so pages that use them will still work in the new browser. However, these controls aren't a lot of help when the data we want to use is in XML format, rather than stored in a database on the server or in a delimited text file. The RDS control uses a SQL query or a stored procedure to extract data from a database, while the TDC demands a text file (or data stream) that is in a delimited format. Neither RDS nor TDC will work with an XML file directly, because each only understands its own, specific data structure.

The possibility of transmitting data in a globally recognized, standard format is our aim, and XML is the way we're going to achieve it. This means, though, that we need a technology for caching XML-formatted data on the client, so that we can use it in the same way as we can use the RDS and TDC controls. And yes, Microsoft is way ahead of us here, because Internet Explorer 5 includes just such a technology. In fact, the browser has built-in components that can cache and parse XML data without the need for *any* add-in controls.

Using these facilities, we will be able to arrange for an HTML page to reference an XML data file, and have this data sent to the client and cached there for use as required. The client will not need to connect to the server again to filter or sort the data, or otherwise to manipulate it. The data can also be modified on the client, with existing values being changed or new ones added.

Updating the Source Data

One area where the RDS control excels is that it can not only download data to the client, but also marshal together any changes that are made to the data on the client, and send just the changed records back to the server. There, they can be used to update the original data source automatically. Of course, this assumes the presence of a suitable web server — basically, it has to be Internet Information Server (IIS) version 3 or above.

This technique provides a simple way to build efficient and highly responsive applications that modify data — you don't need to keep going back to the server and produce a new page for the user with each change to the records. The bad news is that the technique isn't available when we use XML through the IE5 browser.

Instead, we have to do a lot of the work on the client and the server ourselves, by packaging up the changes and sending them across the network, and then unpacking them and updating the data source with custom code when they reach their destination. However, because many of the applications you build are likely to be used just for displaying data (rather than updating it), the update limitation tends not to be a critical one.

> *The ability to implement updates to XML data requires quite a lot of programming on the server — a topic that is outside the scope of this book. However, we did see briefly at the end of Chapter 1 how source data can be updated through the use of server-based parsers or specialist components.*

Getting Data to the Client

In the previous section, I gave you a quick overview of the techniques for **remote data access**, or **data remoting** as it's sometimes called. In this part of the chapter, we'll look into how this is achieved in IE5 with XML, and compare it to the techniques that were available in IE4. If your pages simply have to be compatible with both IE4 and IE5, you can't use the latest techniques that we'll be concentrating on later, and I'll point out what is and is not possible as the subjects arise.

About Data Source Objects

There are actually three kinds of data source objects that we can expose in HTML code, and we'll look briefly at all of them in this section. First, we'll skim over the techniques for using the RDS and TDC Data Source Objects; then we'll look at the Microsoft Java XML DSO; and finally we'll see how to achieve the same effect using **XML data islands** through the DSO built into Internet Explorer 5.

The RDS and TDC Controls

In IE4, we can persuade an HTML page to download and cache data from a data store (such as a relational database) using the RDS control. To do so, we insert the control into a web page using an HTML <OBJECT> element. For example, to connect to a database with the DSN "books" on a server with the address www.yourserver.com, we could use the following code:

```
<OBJECT CLASSID="clsid:BD96C556-65A3-11D0-983A-00C04FC29E33"
        ID="dsoBookList" HEIGHT=0 WIDTH=0>
  <PARAM NAME="Server" VALUE="http://www.yourserver.com">
  <PARAM NAME="Connect" VALUE="DSN=books;UID=anon;PWD=">
  <PARAM NAME="SQL" VALUE="SELECT * FROM BookList">
</OBJECT>
```

> Note the SQL property, which specifies the SQL query or stored procedure that extracts the data from the data source.

Alternatively, if the source data is in a delimited text file, we can use the TDC instead. If this is a text file named booklist.txt:

```
tCode:String;tCategory:String;dRelease:Date;nSales:Int;tTitle:String
16-041;HTML;1998-03-07;127853;Instant HTML
16-048;Scripting;1998-04-21;375298;Instant JavaScript
16-105;ASP;1998-05-10;297311;Instant Active Server Pages
...etc...
```

We can use the following code to cache it locally on the client as a recordset:

```
<OBJECT CLASSID="clsid:333C7BC4-460F-11D0-BC04-0080C7055A83"
        ID="dsoBookList" WIDTH=0 HEIGHT=0>
  <PARAM NAME="DataURL" VALUE="booklist.txt">
  <PARAM NAME="UseHeader" VALUE="true">
  <PARAM NAME="FieldDelim" VALUE=";">
  <PARAM NAME="Sort" VALUE="tCategory; -dRelease">
  <PARAM NAME="Filter" VALUE="tCode=16-1*">
</OBJECT>
```

Both of these methods create a client-based recordset containing the data. By using script on the client, or by binding the recordset to controls on the page, we can manipulate and display the data. By using a different SQL query with the RDS control, we can change the way that the data is filtered and sorted. With the TDC, we can dynamically amend the values for the Sort and Filter properties with script to change the way that the data is filtered and sorted, without having to go back to the server to reload the data.

The Java XML DSO and Other XML Parsers

As XML started to gain prominence, the browser manufacturers looked for ways to use XML within web pages. The theory was all there — as we discovered for ourselves earlier in this book — but the technology was trailing behind. Until a new browser could be released, Microsoft filled the gap by producing a Data Source Object in Java that could read XML files.

In fact, they were not alone in producing components for reading XML documents, and nor were they the first to do so. Several other manufacturers were (and still are) building components that can read and parse XML, and make it available within another application. For the purposes of this discussion, however, we're interested in components that can act as DSOs — and the only obvious ones are the MSXML components from Microsoft. Other parser components don't expose the XML data as a recordset.

The Microsoft Java XML Data Source Object

The Microsoft XML DSO is supplied as a Java applet for use in IE4 and (through backward compatibility) IE5. It is supplied as part of the updated Microsoft **Java Virtual Machine** (VM), which can be downloaded from http://www.microsoft.com/java/. Once you've installed it, you can use it as a Data Source Object to read and parse an XML data file. Here's our trusty sample file, `booklist.xml`:

```
<?xml version="1.0"?>
<BOOKLIST>
   <BOOK>
      <CODE>16-041</CODE>
      <CATEGORY>HTML</CATEGORY>
      <RELEASE_DATE>1998-03-07</RELEASE_DATE>
      <SALES>127853</SALES>
      <TITLE>Instant HTML</TITLE>
   </BOOK>
   <BOOK>
      <CODE>16-048</CODE>
      <CATEGORY>Scripting</CATEGORY>
      <RELEASE_DATE>1998-04-21</RELEASE_DATE>
      <SALES>375298</SALES>
      <TITLE>Instant JavaScript</TITLE>
   </BOOK>
   <BOOK>
      <CODE>16-105</CODE>
      <CATEGORY>ASP</CATEGORY>
      <RELEASE_DATE>1998-05-10</RELEASE_DATE>
      <SALES>297311</SALES>
      <TITLE>Instant Active Server Pages</TITLE>
   </BOOK>
</BOOKLIST>
```

The code to instantiate the Java XML DSO uses the normal HTML <APPLET> element:

```
<APPLET CODE="com.ms.xml.dso.XMLDSO.class"
       ID="dsoBookList" WIDTH=0 HEIGHT=0 MAYSCRIPT=true>
   <PARAM NAME="URL" VALUE="booklist.xml">
</APPLET>
```

The CODE attribute specifies the Java package in which the code is implemented, which is defined in the user's registry. Once instantiated, the control loads an XML-format data file from the location specified in the URL parameter, parses it, and makes the data available as a locally cached recordset.

117

The Java XML DSO also provides several methods that you may find useful if you need to build pages that are backward-compatible with IE4, so that you have to use this DSO rather than a data island (our topic for the next section). For example, it can save the XML to a local file on the client's disk, and dynamically reload the data on demand. You can also use it to create new documents, modify existing ones, and retrieve the XML as a string. This provides an opportunity for building applications that can modify their source data back on the server.

> It's worth downloading the documentation for the complete SDK
> (sdkjdoc.exe) from the Microsoft Java site at
> http://www.microsoft.com/java/, as it contains several useful examples and a
> full list of the methods and features of the Java XML DSO.

IE5 as a Data Source Object

If we can ditch the requirements for backward compatibility with IE4 and other browsers, we can use IE5 itself (or to be more precise, the C++ XML DSO built into IE5) as an XML DSO. This is far easier and more efficient than using the Java applet or indeed any other technique. All we have to do is create a **data island** within our HTML page by using the new <XML> element that is supported in IE5.

Note that <XML> is in fact an *HTML* element, and *not* an XML element. It is used in an HTML page to denote a section of the page that the browser should treat as being XML, rather than HTML. In other words, it acts as the interface that exposes the XML data. The data can then be used in exactly the same way as it would with other DSOs — either bound to controls in the page, or manipulated using script code.

Creating a Data Island

Getting XML data into IE5 as part of an HTML document is easy: we use the new <XML> element that we have just been discussing. Here, I've set the ID attribute to "dsoBookList". This element then becomes our DSO, which we can reference via its ID and use with scripting or data binding:

```
<XML ID="dsoBookList">
   <?xml version="1.0"?>
   <BOOKLIST>
      <ITEM>
         <CODE>16-041</CODE>
         <CATEGORY>HTML</CATEGORY>
         <RELEASE_DATE>1998-03-07</RELEASE_DATE>
         <SALES>127853</SALES>
         <TITLE>Instant HTML</TITLE>
      </ITEM>
      <ITEM>
         ...
         ...rest of the XML data here
         ...
      </ITEM>
   </BOOKLIST>
</XML>
```

Linking to XML Data Files

Rather than embedding the data directly into the HTML page, however, it generally makes a lot more sense to link to it. This makes it far easier to update the XML data without having to edit the HTML page, which could contain a lot of peripheral content such as presentation information and script code.

To link to an XML file, we use the SRC attribute of the <XML> element:

```
<XML ID="dsoBookList" SRC="booklist.xml"></XML>
```

*Remember that the <XML> element is an HTML element, and not an XML element, so it must have a 'proper' closing tag. The XML shorthand syntax will not work, so you **cannot** use:*

```
<XML ID="dsoBookList" SRC="wontwork.xml" />
```

About DSO Recordsets

Once the DSO has loaded and parsed its source data, it exposes it as a recordset. This recordset can be accessed through script code, so (for example) we can iterate through the records, retrieve individual field values, and do pretty much whatever we like with them. I'll demonstrate some ways of doing this later in the chapter.

We can also use a separate feature of IE4 and IE5 to bind the data in the recordset to HTML controls or elements on the page. These will display the data and — provided that the DSO exposes it as an updateable recordset — allow us to update the content as well.

The process of binding the data to the controls in the page is carried out by a component of Internet Explorer called the **DataBinding component**. Even though we can't use it to update our XML data on the server directly (as is possible when using the RDS control with a SQL statement), it is a very useful way of displaying read-only data and exposing it to script in the page. We'll be examining this technique a little later on, too.

Filtering and Sorting XML Data

One point to note with the XML DSO and the data islands in IE5 is that we don't have any opportunity to filter or sort the XML data, as we did with the RDS and TDC DSOs. There is a very good reason for this: SQL queries and delimited text files usually return or contain data that is in the form of a **symmetric table**. In other words, the recordset that they expose has the same number of fields or columns for each record.

XML data isn't always like that — the whole point is that we should be able to structure the XML file in the way that best describes the data that it contains. This will often be more like a tree than a symmetric table, and so there is no obvious context for filtering or sorting it as there is with a recordset.

Instead, we use **XSL**, or Extensible Stylesheet Language. This provides techniques for sorting and filtering XML data within the client. We'll be looking at XSL in Chapter 7.

Recordset Heuristics and DTDs

When we send a data file to a DSO, it interprets the data and builds up a symmetric recordset automatically. To decide what the fields are for each record, it uses built-in **heuristics**, or rules. With data created by a SQL statement, this will generally be a simple task, as the database will usually return a symmetric recordset. As we've discussed, however, this isn't always the case with XML.

We'll look at the concepts of using **master/detail recordsets** with a DSO when we come to examine tabular data binding. For the time being, it's enough to be aware of the ways that we can give the DSO a hint as to how we want our data to appear. *All* DSOs *always* expose the data as a recordset, irrespective of the inherent structure it may have, so tabular data binding is a useful technique if you want to be sure that the data will be correctly interpreted.

As you know, to provide information about the structure of an XML file, we use a Document Type Definition or an XML Schema. The XML parser will validate the data against the definition and from this build up the structure in the required format. Only data that is valid and well formed will be parsed and exposed by the DSO.

The DSO can easily identify a simple XML file (like our list of book information) as being a symmetric recordset, because it has repeated records that all have the same format:

```
<?xml version="1.0" ?>
<BOOKLIST>
   <ITEM>
      <CODE>16-041</CODE>
      <CATEGORY>HTML</CATEGORY>
      <RELEASE_DATE>1998-03-07</RELEASE_DATE>
      <SALES>127853</SALES>
      <TITLE>Instant HTML</TITLE>
   </ITEM>
   <ITEM>
      <CODE>16-162</CODE>
      <CATEGORY>Java</CATEGORY>
      <RELEASE_DATE>1998-06-18</RELEASE_DATE>
      <SALES>148224</SALES>
      <TITLE>Instant Java</TITLE>
   </ITEM>
   <ITEM>
      . . .
      ...more books here
      . . .
   </ITEM>
</BOOKLIST>
```

However, to be absolutely sure that it will be interpreted correctly, we can add a DTD to it to confirm the structure we intended:

```
<?xml version="1.0" ?>

<!DOCTYPE BOOKLIST [
   <!ELEMENT BOOKLIST (ITEM+)>
   <!ELEMENT ITEM (CODE, CATEGORY, RELEASE_DATE, SALES, TITLE)>
   <!ELEMENT CODE (#PCDATA)>
   <!ELEMENT CATEGORY (#PCDATA)>
   <!ELEMENT RELEASE_DATE (#PCDATA)>
```

```
    <!ELEMENT SALES (#PCDATA)>
    <!ELEMENT TITLE (#PCDATA)>
]>

<BOOKLIST>
   <ITEM>
   ...
```

Client-side Data and ADO

Before we move on to look at how we might use the XML data that we've now got cached on the client, I want briefly to mention the core data-manipulation technologies that you'll see being used in this and subsequent chapters. Microsoft is standardizing their data access technologies around a relatively recent development called **ActiveX Data Objects** (**ADO**).

ADO provides techniques for working with data from all kinds of different sources in a uniform way. As long as the data can be exposed as a recordset — something that ADO is designed to achieve — we use the same code to work with that data irrespective of where it came from.

However, ADO cannot work directly with XML data unless it falls into a symmetrical pattern, as we discussed in the previous section. When we embed a data source such as a DSO into a web page (or any other application), the data is exposed as an ADO `recordset` object (albeit with limited functionality). This has methods and properties that can be used to work with that data. All the DSOs we've looked at provide this feature, and it means that we can interchange DSOs almost at will. The script in the page, or the bindings to controls in the page, should still work seamlessly.

> *ADO is used in most Microsoft applications, and is fast becoming the standard way to work with data. To learn more about ADO, look out for* **ADO 2.0 Programmer's Reference** *(ISBN 1-861001-83-5) also from Wrox Press. This book also contains a chapter showing how the Remote Data Service works in more detail.*

Data Binding in IE4 and IE5

Once our XML data has been retrieved and cached locally by a DSO, we can use it to populate HTML controls in a web page in a process called **data binding**. This process involves the **DataBinding component** that is part of IE4 and higher, which can provide two types of data binding: **tabular** data binding or **single record** data binding (often called **current record** data binding). All DSOs can take part in tabular data binding or single record data binding.

In the coming sections, I'll briefly summarize the HTML controls that are used in web pages, and then go on to look at the two types of data binding, so that you can see how they can be used. If you're not familiar with the technique of data binding, you can find a full reference in the Wrox Press book *Professional IE4 Programming* (ISBN 1-861000-70-7). This section summarizes the process, and concentrates on the new features that have been added in Internet Explorer 5.

Elements Used in Data Binding

The HTML elements that can be bound to a DSO recognize special attributes that provide the connection information they need. These are:

- ❑ DATASRC — the ID of the DSO that will supply the data, prefixed by a '#' character

- ❑ DATAFLD — the name of the field in the DSO's recordset to which this control should be bound

- ❑ DATAFORMATAS — either 'TEXT' (the default if omitted) to display the field value as plain text, or 'HTML' to specify that the browser should render any HTML content within the value.

Here is the full list of controls that can participate in data binding in Internet Explorer 4 and onwards. The columns indicate the name of the HTML element, the properties that are bound to the data in the DSO, whether the element allows the data to be updated, and whether tabular binding and HTML formatting are supported.

HTML element	Bound property	Update Data	Tabular binding?	Display as HTML?
A	href	No	No	No
APPLET	param	Yes	No	No
BUTTON	innerText and innerHTML	No	No	Yes
DIV	innerText and innerHTML	No	No	Yes
FRAME	src	No	No	No
IFRAME	src	No	No	No
IMG	src	No	No	No
INPUT TYPE=CHECKBOX	checked	Yes	No	No
INPUT TYPE=HIDDEN	value	Yes	No	No
INPUT TYPE=LABEL	value	Yes	No	No
INPUT TYPE=PASSWORD	value	Yes	No	No
INPUT TYPE=RADIO	checked	Yes	No	No
INPUT TYPE=TEXT	value	Yes	No	No

HTML element	Bound property	Update Data	Tabular binding?	Display as HTML?
LABEL	innerText and innerHTML	No	No	Yes
MARQUEE	innerText and innerHTML	No	No	Yes
OBJECT	param	Yes	No	No
SELECT	text of selected option	Yes	No	No
SPAN	innerText and innerHTML	No	No	Yes
TABLE	none	No	Yes	No
TEXTAREA	value	Yes	No	No

So, as an example, we could bind a SPAN element to the value in a field named tTitle in a recordset exposed by a DSO that has the ID dsoBookList, using:

```
<SPAN DATASRC="#dsoBookList" DATAFLD="tTitle"></SPAN>
```

The value of the tTitle field in the current record in the recordset would then be displayed in the page within the SPAN element as plain text (the default). If the tTitle field contained HTML formatting within the value, we could cause the browser to render it as such using:

```
<SPAN DATASRC="#dsoBookList" DATAFLD="tTitle" DATAFORMATAS="HTML"></SPAN>
```

However, HTML markup cannot be included 'unescaped' in an XML document, so either the content would have to be included in a CDATA section in the element declaration:

```
<tTitle><![CDATA[<B><I>Instant HTML</I></B>]]></tTitle>
```

Or else the angled brackets would have to be escaped individually:

```
<tTitle>&lt;B&gt;&lt;I&gt;Instant HTML&lt;/I&gt;&lt;/B&gt;</tTitle>
```

We can also use client-side script to set up or change the bindings once the page has loaded, by changing the dataSrc, dataFld and dataFormatAs properties of the appropriate elements. To remove the bindings, we just set the properties to an empty string. To change the binding of elements within a bound *table*, we must remove the binding of the table first (in the <TABLE> tag), change the bindings of the elements in the table, and then reset the binding of the table. The reason why that could be important is coming up in the next section.

123

Tabular Data Binding

Tabular data binding depends on the ability of the <TABLE> element to repeat the contents of the <TBODY> section once for each record. It's important to recognize that this use of the word *tabular* — in the sense of the way the data is bound to controls — is entirely unconnected with the name of the Tabular Data Control.

The data source object is identified within the opening <TABLE> tag, and the column or field name for each bound control is identified within each table cell. Note that the <TD> element itself does not take part in the data binding process. Instead, a bound element is placed within each cell. This could be a <SPAN> or a <DIV> element, or one of the other HTML controls. For example:

```
...
<!-- Definition of XML DSO named dsoBookList elsewhere in page -->
...
<TABLE DATASRC="#dsoBookList">
   <THEAD>
      <TR>
         <TH>Code</TH>
         <TH>Category</TH>
         <TH>Release Date</TH>
         <TH>Title</TH>
         <TH>Sales</TH>
      </TR>
   </THEAD>
   <TBODY>
      <TR>
         <TD><SPAN DATAFLD="CODE"></SPAN></TD>
         <TD><SPAN DATAFLD="CATEGORY"></SPAN></TD>
         <TD><SPAN DATAFLD="RELEASE_DATE"></SPAN></TD>
         <TD><B><SPAN DATAFLD="TITLE"></B></SPAN></TD>
         <TD><SPAN DATAFLD="SALES"></SPAN></TD>
      </TR>
   </TBODY>
</TABLE>
...
```

The use of a <TBODY> element is not mandatory. Internet Explorer will repeat all bound elements (one for each record) automatically, even if there is no <TBODY> element.

The code we've just seen produces this result:

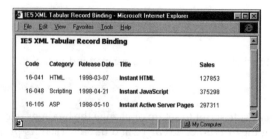

The code for this example, xml_tabular.htm, is available in the samples that can be downloaded for this book from our web site at http://webdev.wrox.co.uk/books/1576/. You can also run many of the samples directly from there.

Table Paging with Tabular Data Binding

ADO recordsets support **paging**, which is useful if there are a lot of records to display. When tabular data binding is used, the <TABLE> element is bound to the DSO that provides the source recordset, and displays the records in that recordset. The DSO properties are exposed through the bound <TABLE> element, and this includes the dataPageSize property. In IE4 and above, this property is mapped to the DATAPAGESIZE attribute of the table as well:

❏   DATAPAGESIZE — sets the maximum number of records that will be displayed within the body of a table.

By setting this attribute in the opening HTML <TABLE> tag, we can create a table that displays only a specified number of records:

```
<TABLE DATASRC="#dsoBookList" DATAPAGESIZE=10>
```

Then we can move through the recordset by using the nextPage and previousPage methods. Furthermore, in Internet Explorer 5 two new methods have been added — firstPage and lastPage — which allow us to go directly to the first or last page of records. The bound table also exposes the recordNumber property of the underlying data set for each element within the table.

Multiple Recordset Data Binding

It's possible to use a DSO to embed data into a web page where that data *doesn't* fit neatly into a single table. This is the case with data that has repeating groups of records for each master record — generally referred to as **master/detail recordsets**.

Given a list of books, for example, each may have more than one author. We can't express this relationship neatly within a single table, so we usually lift out the repeating group into a separate table, and link (or **join**) it to the master table:

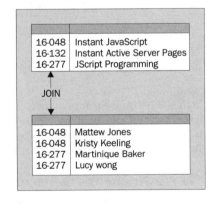

In IE4, we can try to express this data as a **hierarchical recordset** by using a nested table. However, don't expect too much when using XML data, as the XML DSOs generally fail to expose it as a master/detail recordset successfully unless it follows a specific format. As an example, the following data file, named nonsymbooks.xml, has repeating groups (within AUTHORLIST elements).

Because there could be zero or more authors in each list, the recordset is not symmetrical in terms of the definition we used earlier in this chapter:

```
<?xml version="1.0" ?>

<!DOCTYPE BOOKLIST [
   <!ELEMENT BOOKLIST (ITEM+)>
   <!ELEMENT ITEM (CODE, TITLE, AUTHORLIST, SALES)>
   <!ELEMENT CODE (#PCDATA)>
   <!ELEMENT TITLE (#PCDATA)>
   <!ELEMENT AUTHORLIST (AUTHOR*)>
   <!ELEMENT SALES (#PCDATA)>
   <!ELEMENT AUTHOR (FIRST_NAME, LAST_NAME)>
   <!ELEMENT FIRST_NAME (#PCDATA)>
   <!ELEMENT LAST_NAME (#PCDATA)>
]>

<BOOKLIST>
   <ITEM>
      <CODE>16-048</CODE>
      <TITLE>Instant JavaScript</TITLE>
      <AUTHORLIST>
         <AUTHOR>
            <FIRST_NAME>Martin</FIRST_NAME>
            <LAST_NAME>Williams</LAST_NAME>
         </AUTHOR>
         <AUTHOR>
            <FIRST_NAME>Cheryl</FIRST_NAME>
            <LAST_NAME>Caprialdi</LAST_NAME>
         </AUTHOR>
      </AUTHORLIST>
      <SALES>375298</SALES>
   </ITEM>
   <ITEM>
      <CODE>23-177</CODE>
      <TITLE>JavaScript Today</TITLE>
      <AUTHORLIST>
         <AUTHOR>
            <FIRST_NAME>Angela</FIRST_NAME>
            <LAST_NAME>Millania</LAST_NAME>
         </AUTHOR>
      </AUTHORLIST>
      <SALES>118524</SALES>
   </ITEM>
   ...
</BOOKLIST>
```

There are two authors for the first <ITEM>, but only one for the second. The DTD also permits <ITEM> elements to appear in the data that have no authors listed. An attempt to instantiate a DSO and display master/detail records such as these from an HTML file will fail: the repeated author names will not appear.

XML File Structure for Master/Detail Record Binding

The reason for the problem is that the repeated data (the list of authors) is not *directly* within each <ITEM> element. There is an intermediate <AUTHORLIST> element containing them, very much in the 'tree structure' style that I have been advocating for XML files. What we need here is a data file that contains the repeated elements directly within the parent 'record'. Look at this rewrite of the above listing to see instead how the <AUTHOR> element can be repeated within the <ITEM> element:

```
<?xml version="1.0" ?>

<!DOCTYPE BOOKLIST [
  <!ELEMENT BOOKLIST (ITEM+)>
  <!ELEMENT ITEM (CODE, TITLE, AUTHOR*, SALES)>
  <!ELEMENT CODE (#PCDATA)>
  <!ELEMENT TITLE (#PCDATA)>
  <!ELEMENT AUTHOR (FIRST_NAME, LAST_NAME)>
  <!ELEMENT SALES (#PCDATA)>
  <!ELEMENT FIRST_NAME (#PCDATA)>
  <!ELEMENT LAST_NAME (#PCDATA)>
]>
<BOOKLIST>
  <ITEM>
    <CODE>16-048</CODE>
    <TITLE>Instant JavaScript</TITLE>
    <AUTHOR>
      <FIRST_NAME>Martin</FIRST_NAME>
      <LAST_NAME>Williams</LAST_NAME>
    </AUTHOR>
    <AUTHOR>
      <FIRST_NAME>Cheryl</FIRST_NAME>
      <LAST_NAME>Caprialdi</LAST_NAME>
    </AUTHOR>
    <AUTHOR>
      <FIRST_NAME>Michael</FIRST_NAME>
      <LAST_NAME>Atkins</LAST_NAME>
    </AUTHOR>
    <SALES>375298</SALES>
  </ITEM>
  <ITEM>
    <CODE>23-177</CODE>
    <TITLE>JavaScript Today</TITLE>
    <AUTHOR>
      <FIRST_NAME>Angela</FIRST_NAME>
      <LAST_NAME>Millania</LAST_NAME>
    </AUTHOR>
    <SALES>116489</SALES>
  </ITEM>
  ...etc...
</BOOKLIST>
```

Master/Detail HTML Tables

To use this data file in IE4 and IE5, we must first create an instance of a DSO, as shown earlier in this chapter (using the Java XML DSO or an <XML> element). Then we can perform master/detail tabular data binding using this code:

```
<TABLE DATASRC="#dsoBookList" CELLSPACING=0 WIDTH=100%>
  <THEAD>
    <TR>
      <TH ALIGN="LEFT">Code</TH>
      <TH ALIGN="LEFT">Title</TH>
      <TH ALIGN="LEFT">Author(s)</TH>
      <TH ALIGN="LEFT">Sales</TH>
    </TR>
  </THEAD>
  <TBODY>
    <TR><TD COLSPAN=4><HR></TD></TR>
    <TR VALIGN="TOP">
      <TD><SPAN DATAFLD="CODE"></SPAN></TD>
      <TD><SPAN DATAFLD="TITLE"></SPAN></TD>
      <TD>
        <TABLE DATASRC="#dsoBookList" DATAFLD="AUTHOR" CELLSPACING=0>
          <TBODY>
            <TR>
              <TD>
```

127

```
                        <SPAN DATAFLD="FIRST_NAME"></SPAN> 
                        <SPAN DATAFLD="LAST_NAME"></SPAN>
                    </TD>
                </TR>
            </TBODY>
          </TABLE>
        </TD>
        <TD><SPAN DATAFLD="SALES"></SPAN></TD>
      </TR>
    </TBODY>
    <TFOOT>
      <TR><TD COLSPAN=4><HR></TD></TR>
    </TFOOT>
</TABLE>
```

This listing contains a definition of a table that is bound to the DSO named
dsoBookList. Within one of the table cells is a nested <TABLE> element that is also
bound to dsoBookList. This table has the AUTHOR field specified in the binding,
through the DATAFLD attribute. Within this nested table are the bindings to the
FIRST_NAME and LAST_NAME elements. Here's the result:

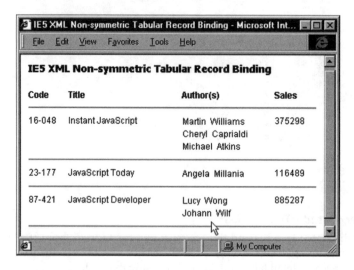

The code for this example is contained in the files xml_tab_nonsym.htm
and nonsymbooks.xml, *both of which are included with the samples for
this book that can be downloaded from our web site.*

If the data contained another level of 'nesting' — that is, another layer of repeated
elements (such as multiple first names), we would handle this in exactly the same way
by adding a further bound table within the existing one.

Fixed Layout Tables

One other point to remember is that IE5 now supports 'fixed layout' tables, which can
considerably reduce the perceived load time of a page. By adding the table-
layout:fixed property to the CSS style definition of the table, and specifying the
absolute width of each column, the browser knows up front how wide to make the
table and the columns without having to read all the content and decide for itself.

As a result, not only is processing overhead reduced, but also the data in table can be rendered *as it arrives*, rather than having to wait for all the content to arrive. This HTML code, for example, defines a table with three columns of fixed width:

```
<TABLE style="table-layout:fixed" width=600>
   <TR>
      <TD width=25%>cell content here</TD>
      <TD width=40%>cell content here</TD>
      <TD width=35%>cell content here</TD>
   </TR>
</TABLE>
```

Single Record Data Binding

Tabular display is fine for simply displaying data, but to edit it we really need to be able to display the values from *one record at a time* within HTML controls. As soon as a recordset is created by a DSO, the first record becomes the **current record**, exactly as it does when the recordset is created directly with ADO (if the recordset is empty, the EOF and BOF properties are both `True` at this point). We can display the values from the current record in any of the bindable HTML elements listed earlier by setting their DATASRC and DATAFLD properties. For example:

```
...
<!-- Definition of XML DSO named dsoBookList elsewhere in page -->
...
Code: <INPUT ID="Code" TYPE="TEXT"
            DATASRC="#dsoBookList" DATAFLD="CODE" SIZE=5><P>
Title: <INPUT ID="Title" TYPE="TEXT"
            DATASRC="#dsoBookList" DATAFLD="TITLE" SIZE=40><P>

Category: <SELECT ID="Category"
                DATASRC="#dsoBookList" DATAFLD="CATEGORY" SIZE=1>
            <OPTION VALUE="HTML">HTML
            <OPTION VALUE="Scripting">Scripting
            <OPTION VALUE="ASP">ASP
         </SELECT><P>
Release date: <SPAN ID="Release"
                DATASRC="#dsoBookList" DATAFLD="RELEASE_DATE"></SPAN><P>
Sales to date: <SPAN ID="Sales"
                DATASRC="#dsoBookList" DATAFLD="SALES"></SPAN><P>
...
```

This code produces the following page. The buttons at the bottom of the page allow users to move around the recordset, and they work by calling the appropriate move methods of the underlying recordset object, as we'll see next.

The code for this example, which once again makes use of the booklist.xml *data file, can be found in* xml_current.htm.

Moving Around and Updating the Data

If we're only displaying a single record, then we need a way to move to another record. We also need a way to update the source data (if this is appropriate, depending on the DSO we are using) by adding, deleting and editing records. And we will probably also need to cancel updates, and refresh the data displayed in the controls at some stage.

All these tasks are accomplished using the standard methods of the DSO that are exposed via ADO. As far as XML in the Java parser or a data island is concerned, the most common methods are:

Method	Description
move moveFirst moveLast moveNext movePrevious	Moves the current record pointer within the cached recordset
cancelUpdate	Cancels all changes made to cached records
delete	Removes the current record from the cached recordset
addNew	Adds a new record to the cached recordset

So, to move around the recordset of our previous example, we can use an HTML button control to call the exposed methods of the DSO. This is the code that creates the four buttons shown in the previous screenshot:

```
...
<button onclick="dsoBookList.recordset.moveFirst()"
        title="First Record"> |&lt; </button>

<button onclick="if(!dsoBookList.recordset.BOF)
                    dsoBookList.recordset.movePrevious()"
        title="Previous Record"> &lt; </button>

<button onclick="if(!dsoBookList.recordset.EOF)
                    dsoBookList.recordset.moveNext()"
        title="Next Record"> &gt; </button>

<button onclick="dsoBookList.recordset.moveLast()"
        title="Last Record"> &gt;| </button>
...
```

Notice how we're checking the BOF property of the recordset before attempting to move backwards, and the EOF property before attempting to move forwards. This prevents errors being caused by moving beyond the limits of the recordset.

Data Binding Events

Both a DSO embedded within the page and the browser itself raise events that can be trapped and used in script on the client. They can be divided into two groups: those raised by the browser or the controls on the page (when the user navigates to another page or edits the data in the HTML controls), and those raised by a DSO as the user edits the data it exposes.

Events Raised by HTML Elements and the Browser

When a page containing a DSO is unloaded, or when the user edits the data in HTML controls that are bound to a DSO, various events are raised. Some of them can be canceled by returning the value `false` from the event handler routine:

Event	Cancel?	Description
onbeforeupdate	Yes	Occurs before the data in the control is passed to the DSO
onafterupdate	No	Occurs after the data in the control has been passed to the DSO
onerrorupdate	Yes	Occurs if an error prevents the data being passed to the DSO
onbeforeunload	No	Occurs before the current page is unloaded

The `onbeforeunload` event is raised by the `window` object, while the remainder are raised by the HTML controls on the page. With the exception of the `onbeforeunload` event, they all bubble up through the document hierarchy, so we can display a message when the user changes the value in a control with:

```
<INPUT ID="txtTitle" DATASRC="#dsoBookList" DATAFLD="TITLE">
...
<SCRIPT LANGUAGE="JavaScript">
   function txtTitle.onbeforeupdate()
   {
      return confirm("Are you sure you want to change this value?");
   }
</SCRIPT>
```

Events Raised by the Data Source Object

The data source object itself raises events as various actions take place. The first four entries in the table below are concerned with indicating the current state of the DSO as it loads the data. The others are fired when the 'current record' changes as the user moves through the recordset, or when records are inserted, deleted or changed:

Event	Cancel?	Description
ondataavailable	No	Occurs periodically while data is arriving from the data source.
ondatasetcomplete	No	Occurs when all the data has arrived from the data source.
ondatasetchanged	No	Occurs when the data set changes, such as when a filter is applied.
onreadystatechange	No	Occurs when the readyState property of the DSO changes.
onrowenter	No	Occurs for a record when it becomes the current one during navigation of the recordset.
onrowexit	Yes	Occurs for a record before another record becomes the current one during navigation of the recordset.
onrowsdelete	No	New in IE5. Occurs when rows are about to be deleted from the current recordset.
onrowsinserted	No	New in IE5. Occurs after rows are inserted into the current recordset.
oncellchange	No	New in IE5. Occurs when the data in a bound control or table cell changes, and the focus moves from that cell.

Of these, only the onrowexit event can be canceled by returning false from the event handler routine. This time, *all* the events bubble up through the document hierarchy. It's usual to take advantage of the ondatasetcomplete event for any script that you want to run once the data has arrived. Here, we're using an INPUT element named txtStatus to display appropriate messages:

```
<INPUT ID="txtStatus" VALUE="Initializing, please wait...">
...
<SCRIPT LANGUAGE="JavaScript">
   function dsoBookList.ondatasetcomplete()
   {
      txtStatus.value = "Data arrived OK";
   }
</SCRIPT>
```

The DHTML Event Object and Data Binding

We've seen how a DSO in a web page can raise events that are passed to the page, where they can be linked to script code. In IE5, this feature has been extended by adding new properties to the event object that provide extra information about events that are raised by a DSO. The new properties are:

Property	Description
bookmarks	A collection of ADO bookmarks that identify the records being inserted or deleted, or which contain the cells that are being changed.
boundElements	A collection of all the elements in the page that are bound to the DSO that raised the event.
dataFld	The name of the column (or field) in the recordset that was affected by an oncellchange event, and hence the dataFld property of the element(s) bound to that field.
recordset	A reference to the recordset that is bound to the DSO that raised the event, and in which the event occurred. (A DSO can support master/detail or parent/child recordsets, and so may itself reference more than one.)

To show these at work, we can add some events to the XML DSO element. These define the functions that will be called when records are added (inserted), deleted or changed. This is the new <XML> element definition:

```
<XML ID="dsoBookList" SRC="booklist.xml"
                      onrowsdelete="deleteAction()"
                      onrowsinserted="insertAction()"
                      oncellchange="cellchangeAction()">
</XML>
```

We can also add a couple of extra buttons to the page that allow the user to add a new record or delete an existing one:

```
<button onclick="dsoBookList.recordset.addNew()"
        title="Add New Record"> Add </button> 
<button onclick="dsoBookList.recordset.Delete()"
        title="Delete Record">Delete</button>
```

Now we can add some script code to implement the functions listed in the <XML> element. The first two of these functions, which run when a new record is inserted or an existing one is deleted, look like this:

```
<SCRIPT LANGUAGE="JavaScript">

  function deleteAction()
  {
    alert('You DELETED the record with bookmark ' + event.bookmarks(0));
  }
```

```
function insertAction()
{
    alert('You INSERTED a record with bookmark ' + event.bookmarks(0));
}
...
```

These use the `bookmarks` collection that is exposed by the `event` object, and simply display the unique 'bookmark' string of the record that was inserted or deleted.

The third function runs when a record is changed. In this case, we create a message that contains the names of all the elements bound to the DSO that raised the event (from the `boundElements` collection of the `event` object), and then add the name of the field that was changed using the `dataFld` property of the `event` object:

```
...
function cellchangeAction()
{
    strMesg = 'The following elements are bound to the DSO:\n';
    for(i = 0; i < event.boundElements.length; i++)
        strMesg += 'ID=' + event.boundElements[i].id + ' ';

    strMesg += '\nThe name of the field you changed is: ' + event.dataFld;
    alert(strMesg);
}

</SCRIPT>
```

In JavaScript or JScript, we can refer to the `event` *object directly, as in the code above. In VBScript, we have to prefix it with the* `window` *object because* `event` *is a previously reserved word:*

```
window.event.boundElements[i].id
```

Here's the result when we edit the value of the CATEGORY field:

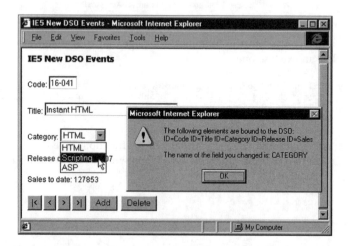

Once again, the code for this example can be downloaded from our web site; the name of the file in question is `newevents.htm`.

134

XML Data Binding in IE5 with Attributes

If you adopt data binding in IE5 through a data island, one issue that you may come across is that it all seems to fall apart if there are any attributes within the opening element tags. Unfortunately, the DataBinding component in IE5 does not parse the XML data in the same way as the Java parser component used with IE4 or IE5, and it fails to see or display the values of elements with attributes.

In this situation, you can continue to use the parser component instead of a data island in Internet Explorer 5, but as data islands are more efficient and don't need a parser to be pre-installed by the user, it's worth looking at the workarounds that are available.

The problem arises because the IE5 DataBinding component treats an attribute in an element as a separate element, so this:

```
<myElement myAttribute="attr_value">element_value</myElement>
```

is treated as though it were this:

```
<myElement><myAttribute>element_value</myAttribute></myElement>
```

To get round the problem, we have to use a data-bound table within the data-bound element to 'get at' the nested element's value, rather than the outer element's value (which is an empty string). The text value of the element can be obtained from the default $TEXT property:

```
<TABLE DATASRC="#dsoData" DATAFLD="myElement">
   <TR>
      <TD>
         <INPUT TYPE="TEXT" DATASRC="#dsoData" DATAFLD="$TEXT">
      </TD>
   </TR>
</TABLE>
```

If we're using tabular data binding, we already have a table to hold the element values. In this case, we have to place a nested table inside each existing table cell:

```
<TABLE DATASRC="#dsoData">
   <TR>
      <TD>
         <TABLE DATASRC="#dsoData" DATAFLD="firstColumnName">
            <TR>
               <TD><SPAN DATAFLD="$TEXT"></SPAN></TD>
            </TR>
         </TABLE>
      </TD>
   </TR>
   <TR>
      <TD>
         <TABLE DATASRC="#dsoData" DATAFLD="nextColumnName">
            <TR>
               <TD><SPAN DATAFLD="$TEXT"></SPAN></TD>
            </TR>
         </TABLE>
      </TD>
   </TR>
...etc...
</TABLE>
```

This also means that if we need to access the values using script, via the recordset created by the data island, we have to refer to the $TEXT property of the nested element as well.

For example, we would have to use:

```
var objDI = document.all('dsoData');
strValue = objDI.recordset.fields('column_name').value.fields('$TEXT');
```

Instead of the more usual:

```
var objDI = document.all('dsoData');
strValue = objDI.recordset.fields('column_name').value;
```

Client-Side Script and XML

In the previous section of this chapter, we looked at the ways that we can use data binding to display data from an XML file or a data island within a web page. However, there are often times when we want to do more than just list the data or present it in HTML controls. For example, we may want to provide users with the opportunity to search through the data for particular values. Alternatively, we may want to use the data in the background to create dynamic pages, rather than just displaying the values to the user.

Scripting Opportunities

We've already seen that the data embedded in a web page through a DSO is exposed as a recordset, and that this recordset can be used in data binding. However, the DSOs go further than this. Each one has a recordset property, which provides us with a reference to the recordset that is cached on the client. And, because this is a normal ADO recordset (albeit with limited functionality), it can be accessed using ADO techniques in script code running in the client page.

As we've seen, though, this really only makes sense if the recordset is symmetrical — in other words, if it looks like a set of normal database tables with the same number of fields in each record. The DSO will always attempt to expose it as such, but with irregular XML-formatted data, this isn't necessarily going to produce something useful. In particular, if there are different numbers or types of child elements in each record, IE5 may create a recordset that bears no relation to what you expect.

In such cases, we will usually access this kind of data using a different technique involving the **Document Object Model** (DOM), which exposes all the objects in the page as a tree and a series of collections. In particular, it exposes the XML content of the page (or a linked XML file) as a structure that we can access using special scripting techniques. Of course, we can access *any* XML data using the DOM if we wish — it doesn't *have* to be in an 'irregular' format.

In the remainder of this chapter, we'll be looking at how to use script code to access the DSO's recordset with ADO. In the next chapter, we'll look at accessing embedded XML data through the DOM.

Accessing XML Recordsets with ADO

To end this chapter, we'll look briefly at two ways of using script code with ADO to access the contents of embedded XML data through the recordset exposed by a DSO. The first provides custom, client-side manipulation of the recordset data, allowing users to search through it and display selected values. This is a useful technique for building interfaces to a database or other type of data store.

The second example uses XML in the background, transmitting data to the client that the user doesn't actually see. Instead, this data is used behind the scenes — in this case to set the display preferences for a particular user. This scenario may arise in all kinds of situations where you need to pass just a few values to the client that do not form a structured recordset in the usual sense of the term.

Searching Through and Presenting Recordset Data

Once data binding has been completed, the data in our XML document is exposed as a standard ADO client-side (or **disconnected**) recordset, irrespective of the kind of DSO and data file we use. We can get a reference to this recordset from the DSO's `recordset` property:

```
myRecordset = dsoMyDSO.recordset;        // JavaScript or JScript
Set myRecordset = dsoMyDSO.recordset     ' Same thing but in VBScript
```

Once we have a reference to the recordset, we can access the fields to get their values:

```
theValue = myRecordset('FIELD_NAME');     // JavaScript or JScript
theValue = myRecordset("FIELD_NAME")      ' Same thing but in VBScript
```

Of course, we can access all the other properties or methods of the recordset as well. To see how we've done it in this example (which you originally met as a Chapter 1 sample called `findtitle.htm`), we'll look first at the HTML code for the page.

The Book Search Page Form

We want a simple form with a text box for entering the search criterion, and a button to start the process. There's also a list box in which we'll display the results:

```
<FORM>
    Criteria: <INPUT TYPE="TEXT" NAME="txtCriterion">  
    <INPUT TYPE="BUTTON" VALUE="Show" ONCLICK="showBooks()"><P>
    <SELECT NAME="selListBox" STYLE="width:450" SIZE="10">
        <OPTION>Enter a criterion to search for a title, then click 'Show'...
    </SELECT>
</FORM>
```

Next comes the DSO that loads our list of books. Here, it's the `<XML>` element in IE5 (for both IE4 and IE5 support, we could use the MSXML Java DSO instead):

```
<XML ID="dsoBookList" SRC="booklist_dtd.xml"></XML>
```

The XML Data File and DTD

In this case, the XML file named `booklist_dtd.xml` lists around 30 books, and contains — among other things — the ISBN and title of each. It also has a separate DTD, as you can see from the `DOCTYPE` element:

137

```
<?xml version="1.0" standalone="no" ?>
<!DOCTYPE BOOKLIST SYSTEM "booklist_dtd.dtd">
<BOOKLIST>
   <BOOKINFO>
      <ISBN>1-861000-44-8</ISBN>
      <BOOK_TITLE>Instant VBScript Programming</BOOK_TITLE>
      <RELEASE_DATE>1996-12-01</RELEASE_DATE>
      <CATEGORY>Client-side Scripting</CATEGORY>
      <COVER_IMAGE_URL>
         http://webdev.wrox.co.uk/webdev/wd_images/0448.gif
      </COVER_IMAGE_URL>
      <MORE_INFO_URL>
         http://www.wrox.co.uk/Store/Details.asp?Code=0448
      </MORE_INFO_URL>
   </BOOKINFO>
   ...
   ...other book details here
   ...
</BOOKLIST>
```

This is the DTD for the file, showing the way that the BOOKINFO elements are repeated:

```
<?xml version="1.0" ?>
<!ELEMENT BOOKLIST (BOOKINFO)+>
<!ELEMENT BOOKINFO (ISBN, BOOK_TITLE, RELEASE_DATE,
                        CATEGORY, COVER_IMAGE_URL, MORE_INFO_URL)>
<!ELEMENT ISBN (#PCDATA)>
<!ELEMENT BOOK_TITLE (#PCDATA)>
<!ELEMENT RELEASE_DATE (#PCDATA)>
<!ELEMENT CATEGORY (#PCDATA)>
<!ELEMENT COVER_IMAGE_URL (#PCDATA)>
<!ELEMENT MORE_INFO_URL (#PCDATA)>
```

Note that in IE4, where you must use the Java XML DSO, you may have to change the XML data file and the DTD slightly (depending on the version of the DSO that you have installed). At the time of writing, the DSO was part of build 3165 of the Microsoft Java Virtual Machine. You may have to remove the standalone="no" *attribute from the data file's* <?xml..?> *declaration, and the complete* <?xml..?> *declaration from the linked DTD file.*

So, the user can now load the page and enter a word to search for in the book titles. Of course, this is a very simple approach designed purely to demonstrate the ways that we can access the XML data using script:

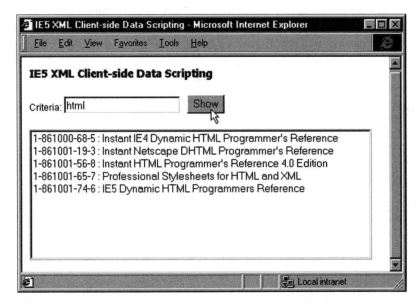

The Script to Run the Search

When the Show button is clicked, as shown in the previous screenshot, a script function named showBooks() is executed. This is shown below:

```
function showBooks()
{
    strCriterion = document.forms[0].txtCriterion.value.toLowerCase();
    objListBox = document.forms[0].selListBox;
    objListBox.options.length = 0;
    recBooks = dsoBookList.recordset;          // The XML recordset
    while(!recBooks.EOF)
    {
        strTitle = '' + recBooks("BOOK_TITLE");
        strTitle = strTitle.toLowerCase();
        if(strTitle.indexOf(strCriterion) >= 0)
        {
            objListBox.options.length += 1;
            objListBox.options[objListBox.options.length - 1].text =
                        recBooks("ISBN") + " : " + recBooks("BOOK_TITLE");
        }
        recBooks.moveNext();
    }
}
```

The code collects the search criterion and converts it to lower case in the variable strCriterion, gets a reference to the list box into objListBox, and empties the list by setting the length property to zero. Then it gets a reference to the DSO's recordset, and iterates through all the records by calling the moveNext method until the EOF property returns true.

139

For each record, it extracts the title from the BOOK_TITLE element as a string (by appending it to an empty string), converts it to lower case, and then checks to see if it contains the criterion using the JavaScript indexOf() function. If it does, it adds a new option to the list box, and sets it to the ISBN and title of the book from the current record.

You could turn this into a more useful application by adding some code to retrieve the cover images and display them as books are selected. You could even use the URLs in the data file to provide links direct to the appropriate books on our web site.

Using XML Data in the Background

Using a DSO to fetch data and expose it in an HTML page as a recordset implies that the data will always follow a strict and symmetrical (or perhaps master/detail) format. This isn't always the case with XML data, so we need other ways to 'get at' the exposed XML *without* using the recordset exposed by a DSO.

This is largely the subject of the next chapter, but here I'll just demonstrate a simple case where we can get at the data from a DSO quite easily, and use it in the background. In other words, the data is not something that the user will see, but information to be used solely within the page, via scripting.

The User Preferences Page

The HTML code shown next creates a simple page with a button that, when clicked, executes a function named setOptions(). The page also includes an <XML> element that creates our data island through the DSO built into IE5. Again, if we need to support both IE4 and IE5, we could use the Java DSO instead:

```
<XML ID="dsoOptions" SRC="userpref.xml"></XML>
...
<DIV ID="divMain">
    This page demonstrates how you can use XML
    to persist a user's display preferences.
</DIV><P>
<SPAN CLASS=intro>
    Click  <BUTTON onclick="setOptions()">Here</BUTTON> 
    to retrieve your preferences.
</SPAN>
```

Here's the page when it first loads:

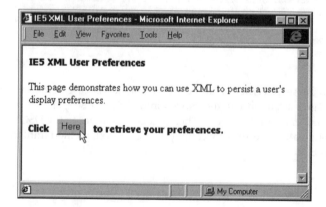

The XML Data File and DTD

Our XML data file is a 'flat file' structure with a single record that contains a list of fields. These fields are the values that we want to pass to our page (in reality, of course, they would be different for each user):

```
<?xml version="1.0"?>
<PREFERENCES>
   <USERPREF>
      <FONTFAMILY>Courier New</FONTFAMILY>
      <FONTWEIGHT>bold</FONTWEIGHT>
      <FONTSIZE>24</FONTSIZE>
   </USERPREF>
</PREFERENCES>
```

The structure can be as simple or as complex as required, provided that the DSO can expose it as a recordset. We can, of course, create the values dynamically and even change them once the page has loaded. In effect, we've got an easy and extensible way of getting data from server to client on demand, without having to keep creating complete new pages on the server.

The Script to Retrieve the User's Preferences

The script to set the user's preferences is basic enough. We just have to change the appropriate properties of the `style` object — in this case, the main `<DIV>` element that fills the central part of the page:

```
function setOptions()
{
   recOptions = dsoOptions.recordset;          // The XML recordset
   divMain.style.fontFamily = recOptions("FONTFAMILY");
   divMain.style.fontWeight = recOptions("FONTWEIGHT");
   divMain.style.fontSize = recOptions("FONTSIZE");
}
```

And here's the result with the values in the sample XML file we saw above:

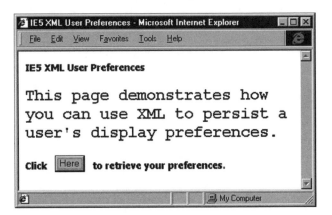

Once again, the code for this, the final example in the chapter, is available for download from our web site. The name of the file is userpref.htm.

Summary

In this chapter, we've taken a decisive step from theory into practice by looking at some real code for working with XML. We looked at the application of **data source objects** and **data binding** in both IE4 and IE5, and how we can apply the same techniques to XML data as we do to data in more traditional formats.

In fact, we saw that XML provides a really useful way to transfer data from the server to the client, to be manipulated there. Not only can we display it as a table and in HTML controls for editing, we can also use the data in client-side script to build all kinds of dynamic pages.

The particular advantages of client-side data caching are the increased responsiveness of pages and the reduction in network traffic. However, this does depend on the amount of data that you need to transfer, and there will always be a trade-off if you have very large data files.

In the next chapter, we'll move on to look at another way that we can access and work with XML data in a data island — this time using the **Document Object Model**.

5

The XML Document Object Model

The previous chapter demonstrated how it's possible to use a data island in IE5 to embed or link an XML document into an HTML page. We also looked at some of the ways that the XML content — the data — is made available for use with data binding or custom scripting techniques. However, all the ways we considered revolved around the fact that a data source object exposes the XML data as an ADO-like recordset.

This is fine if the data falls into a reasonably standard and symmetrical pattern, as is required for client-side data binding. However, there are often situations where we want to use less symmetric data sets, or access the data in a more precise and individual way. In these cases, we can use script code to manipulate the individual parts of the XML document directly.

To be able to 'get at' the data in an XML document when it's exposed through a data island within an HTML page, the application (such as a browser) has to build up some kind of 'model' of the data structure. OK, so it could just scan through the text that makes up an XML file and find elements and data on demand, but this isn't a very efficient way of doing things. Instead, the browser or application will generally build up some kind of structured internal representation of the data as it loads it. This is where the **XML Document Object Model (DOM)** comes in.

Coverage of the Document Object Model in this book is divided into two chapters, because there is a lot to discuss. The topics that we'll be looking at in this chapter are:

- ❑ What the XML Document Object Model actually is
- ❑ What the individual objects within the DOM are

Then, in the next chapter, we'll move on to look at:

- ❑ How we use the DOM to access and manipulate XML documents
- ❑ Some simple applications that you can experiment with

What is a Document Object Model?

In this chapter, we'll be looking in detail at the **Document Object Model** that is available within Internet Explorer 5 for accessing the content of XML documents. Bear in mind that the term "Document Object Model" has been applied to browsers for some time. In recent browsers, the intrinsic objects (such as `window`, `document`, `history`, etc.), as well as most of the elements in an HTML page, are part of a document object model. (In older browsers, this tends to apply mainly to the intrinsic objects and the elements on a `FORM`.) The important point is that this model is reasonably standardized, and so code to manipulate the DOM can be written that will work on all popular browsers.

The XML Document Object Model

What we are examining in this chapter isn't the document object model that holds information about the browser environment and the HTML pages it loads, but the specific area that contains information about an XML document that the browser is hosting. This may be by loading the XML document directly, but it's often likely to be through the `<XML>` element in IE5 (or a Java Applet in IE4). When an HTML page contains an XML document, a sub-tree is added to the entire HTML page object model, starting from the element or object that loads and exposes the XML document. In an HTML page, this is our **data island**:

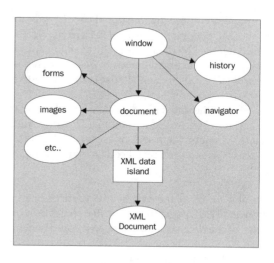

Note that we are certainly not restricted to one data island per page, and we can even have multiple data islands exposing the same XML document. This allows us to make different changes to different cached versions of the same XML file.

The final object in this diagram is our XML document. This is the root of the next object tree, which consists of the contents of the XML data file that has been parsed by the data source object that created the data island, and is now available within the page. Of course, when an XML document is loaded into the browser directly, the document itself becomes the root of the tree. Either way, this is the focus of our interest — this chapter is all about the **XML Document Object Model**.

Conceptual Views vs. Physical Objects

The simplest conceptual model for a non-symmetric XML document is as a tree, even if the application's internal representation of the document is something totally different. In many ways, the design of the objects within the browser and the way that they are physically structured is not important. All that *is* important is the programming interface that they provide — in other words, the lists of methods and properties that are available for each item in the XML document. And it would be particularly useful if every XML application provided the same conceptual view of the data, and the same programmatic methods for accessing and manipulating it.

To bring this dream closer to reality, the World Wide Web Consortium has released a Recommendation for a standard Document Object Model (DOM), which covers the ways that an XML processor (that is, a browser or an application) should expose data to the outside world. The structure of the individual objects that represent elements, attributes, and entities in the XML document, and the methods and properties available, are all documented.

> *You can read the W3C's DOM recommendations on their web site at
> http://www.w3.org/TR/REC-DOM-Level-1/. At the time of writing, this was
> at version 1.0. The W3C recommendations refer to **interfaces** rather than
> **objects** (interfaces being considered less implementation-specific), but the
> 'object' concept probably makes it easier to appreciate how the various parts fit
> together.*

Standards Compliance

The development of Internet Explorer 5 has followed the W3C DOM recommendation process, and Microsoft has announced full support — both now and into the future — for the W3C XML standards. However, it has also added a range of objects, methods and properties to the DOM in IE5 to extend the overall functionality. Some of these are tied to the particular features of IE5, such as asynchronous loading and parsing of the document, and handling custom HTTP requests for XML documents. There are also additions that make working with the XML content easier than using the W3C Recommendation's techniques.

The presence of these extensions to the W3C DOM makes it harder to be sure that you are writing code that is compatible with other browsers and applications. It's very easy to drop in a call to an IE5-specific method, or access to an IE5-specific property, without realizing it. To help you out, I've included a full reference to all the W3C DOM and IE5-specific objects, methods and properties in Appendix A, indicating which are Microsoft-specific.

The XML DOM Objects in Detail

In this section of the chapter, we'll examine the objects that are available in Internet Explorer 5 for accessing and manipulating XML documents via the XML DOM. To help you build application-independent pages, I'll also indicate which extensions to the DOM are IE5-specific as we go along.

*There is a full list of the base and high-level objects in the reference section of
this book. It includes details of all the methods and properties for each one,
together with their meaning and syntax.*

The XML DOM Base Objects

In the implementation of the Document Object Model for HTML, the objects and collections
have reasonably obvious names, such as `window`, `navigator`, `forms` and `images`. In the
XML DOM, there are also individual objects to represent the different types of content that
XML documents can contain. However, these 'high-level' objects are based on a series of
general-purpose 'base' objects that define standard characteristics of all the entries
(elements, attributes, text nodes, etc.) in XML documents.

There are three 'general-purpose' or **base objects** in Internet Explorer 5:

❑   `Node` objects are the base objects for all the entries in an XML document,
including the document object itself. The Automation implementation of this,
as exposed in IE5, is the `IDOMNode` object. This is extended by the
`IXMLDOMNode` object, which provides additional methods and properties.

❑   `NodeList` objects are the base objects for most of the ordered collections of
other nodes within the DOM, such as the collections of child elements for each
element. In IE5 this is implemented by the `IDOMNodeList` object, which is
extended by `IXMLDOMNodeList`.

❑   `NamedNodeMap` objects are the base objects for collections that can be accessed
by object names, in a similar way to a 'dictionary' object. They are mainly used
for the collection of *attributes* for each XML element, and the attributes of the
document object itself. In IE5 this is implemented by the `IDOMNamedNodeMap`
object, which is extended by `IXMLDOMNamedNodeMap`.

The XML Higher-Level Objects

As well as these base objects, there are also some higher-level objects that inherit from the
`Node` object (the `IXMLDOMNode` interface). These represent specific *types* of node; for
example, an element within the XML document is represented by an instance of the
`Element` object, the document itself by an instance of the `Document` object, etc.

The following table lists the types of node that can be accessed through the XML DOM (by
the name of the node type in the W3C Recommendation), together with the name of the
interface and a description of its purpose. As well as the Microsoft-extended interfaces
(which have names beginning `IXML...`), there are interfaces which expose only the
methods and properties listed in the W3C Recommendation (with names starting
`IDOM...`). These inherit from the `IDOMNode` interface.

Name	Interface	Description
Document	IXMLDOMDocument	Represents the root node of the XML document.
DocumentType	IXMLDocumentType	Represents the Document Type Declaration or Schema declaration of the XML document.
DocumentFragment	IXMLDocument Fragment	Represents a lightweight object used for storing sections of an XML document temporarily.
Element	IXMLDOMElement	Represents an element node. Note that the text content of an element is not held in the element node itself, but in a Text or CDATASection node which is a child of the element.
Attribute (Attr)	IXMLDOMAttribute	Represents an attribute.
Entity	IXMLDOMEntity	Represents an unparsed entity within the DTD (not the <!ENTITY...> declaration itself).
EntityReference	IXMLDOMEntity Reference	Represents a reference to an entity within the XML document, such as &myEntity;. If the document has been parsed, this may have been expanded, and the EntityReference will refer to the entity content.
Notation	IXMLDOMNotation	Represents a notation declared within the DTD.
CharacterData	IXMLDOMCharacter Data	Provides methods and properties that are inherited by Text, Comment and CDATASection nodes.

Table Continued on Following Page

Name	Interface	Description
Text	IXMLDOMText	Represents a Text node that is a child of an Element node.
CDATASection	IXMLDOMCDATA Section	Represents a CDATASection in the XML document.
Comment	IXMLDOMComment	Represents a comment in the XML document.
Processing Instruction	IXMLDOMProcessing Instruction	Represents a processing instruction.
Implementation	IXMLDOMImplementation	Provides access to methods and properties that are application-specific and independent of any specific implementation of the DOM.

The object representing attributes was named Attr rather than Attribute by the W3C to avoid clashing with existing interface definition languages.

The names of individual instances of these nodes vary according to the node type. So, for example, all Document nodes are named "#document", all Text nodes "#text", and all Element nodes have the name that is contained in their tags (so an XML element <myElement>...</myElement> would be called "myElement"). The node types also vary with regard to the values they can hold. You can find a complete list of these names and values towards the end of this chapter.

There are three IE-specific objects that do not have equivalents in the W3C Recommendation. These are: IDOMParseError, which exposes properties providing information about any errors that occurred while the XML document was loading or parsing; HttpRequest, which provides support for client-server communication through the HTTP protocol; and IXTLRuntime, which exposes methods and properties which can accessed through script in XSL stylesheets.

We'll return to discuss the methods, properties and events of all these objects later in the chapter, after we've looked at the base objects in rather more detail.

Why Nodes instead of Elements?

One of the major differences between the DOM for HTML and the DOM for XML is the flexibility of structure. In an HTML document, for example, there is *always* a single images collection and a single forms collection — even if they are actually empty. They are *always* child objects (direct descendants) of the single document object — which is itself a direct descendant of the window object. There might be several form objects in the page that each contain a selection of controls, but each form is a member of a single document.forms collection, and has its own single elements collection.

In an XML document, we don't have anything like this kind of advance knowledge of the structure of a document until we receive and parse it. We know that there will be a single root element object, but there could be any combination of objects and collections within that element. And, unlike HTML, we don't even know what the object names will be.

The obvious solution is to think of the document as a tree, and of each item within the tree as a generic **node**. Some will be leaf nodes (child nodes with no children of their own), and others will be parent nodes that do have their own collection of child nodes. The point is that if a standard object that can store any kind of XML item is provided, XML documents that have any kind of structure can be dealt with.

An Example of an XML Tree

The next diagram shows an XML document that we first came across in Chapter 2, displayed as a tree. You can see that there is a node at the top of the diagram, which is our <BOOKLIST> element. Within this are two child nodes, each one being an element named <ITEM>. Each <ITEM> element has its own series of child nodes, in this case the elements <CODE>, <CATEGORY>, <RELEASE_DATE>, <AUTHORLIST>, <SALES> and <TITLE>:

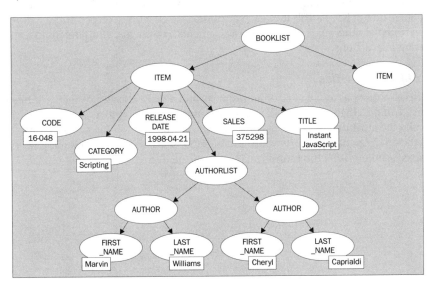

Going further down the tree, you can see that the <AUTHORLIST> node has two child nodes of its own, of type Element and named <AUTHOR>, each of which has child element nodes called <FIRST_NAME> and <LAST_NAME>.

Element Node Values

The XML tree diagram shows the elements as having individual values 'attached' to them, so (for example) the <CATEGORY> of the first <ITEM> is 'Scripting'. However, the actual structure is more complicated than this. The text string between the opening and closing XML element tags defines the 'value' of our XML elements in the original document:

```
<CATEGORY>Scripting</CATEGORY>
```

In the XML DOM, this string *is itself a Node object* — but of type Text rather than type Element. The *value* of the <CATEGORY> node is null, and it has a child node with the value 'Scripting'. We will cover this subject in more depth when we look at the properties and methods of Node objects in the next section.

The XML Node Object

A Node object can be used to represent any of the nodes in the document, and provides standard properties and methods that are useful for working with all types of node. Each node can have only a single parent node object, and may also have a single collection of child node objects. The one exception to this is the root node of the document, which cannot have a parent and can have only a *single*, Element-type child node (this latter being the actual outermost element of the document — <BOOKLIST> in the earlier diagram).

Some types of nodes can also have attributes. In general, these only appear for the document and for element nodes. Other nodes, such as comments, entity references and processing instructions, do not have attributes. Each attribute is itself a Node object, but of a different subtype from the other node objects such as elements, comments, entity references and processing instructions.

Node Object Properties

Every Node object has an attributes property and a childNodes property. If the node has any attributes, the attributes property returns a reference to a NamedNodeMap containing the attribute node objects; otherwise it returns null. If the node has any child nodes, the childNodes property returns a reference to a NodeList containing the child node objects; otherwise it too returns null.

Property	Description
attributes	For nodes that have attributes, this returns a NamedNodeMap object containing all the Attribute (or Attr) object nodes of this node.
childNodes	For nodes that have child nodes, this returns a NodeList object containing all the child nodes of this node.

Both NodeList and NamedNodeMap are collection-like structures that provide their own methods and properties for accessing and manipulating the nodes that they contain. We'll look at these objects in more detail shortly. In the meantime, every node also exposes properties that allow direct access to certain nodes within its childNodes collection. Each property returns a Node object, or null if there is no matching node:

Property	Description
firstChild	Returns a reference to the first child node of this node.
lastChild	Returns a reference to the last child node of this node.
previousSibling	Returns a reference to the previous sibling node of this node — the previous node in the source file at the same level of the hierarchy.
nextSibling	Returns a reference to the next sibling node of this node — the next node in the source data file at the same level of the hierarchy.

We can also use two more properties of every node to access nodes higher up the tree. Again, each property returns a Node object, or null if there is no matching node:

Property	Description
ownerDocument	Returns the root node of the document that contains the node (this property returns null for the document node itself).
parentNode	Returns the parent node of this node. The document root node, DocumentFragment nodes and Attribute nodes return null.

Once we've got a reference to a node, we can get a reference to a child or the parent of that node. We can then use this node's `childNodes` or `parentNode` property to walk up or down the tree to get to *any other node*. For example, given an XML document with a structure like this:

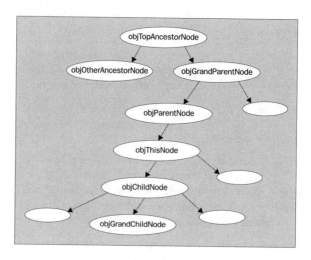

We can reference the various nodes in relation to each other using the Node object's properties:

```
objChildNode = objThisNode.firstChild;
objGrandChildNode = objChildNode.lastChild.previousSibling;
objParentNode = objThisNode.parentNode;
objGrandParentNode = objParentNode.parentNode;
objTopAncestorNode = objThisNode.ownerDocument;
objOtherAncestorNode = objTopAncestorNode.firstChild;
```

Once we've got a reference to a node, we can use other properties to examine it. For example, we can retrieve the name, the node type, and the value. Remember that the *value* of an Element node is not the *content* of that element. The latter is stored in the `nodeValue` property of an element's text-type child node; the value of the Element node itself is `null`:

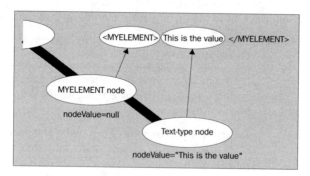

Property	Description
nodeName	Returns the name of the node, depending on the node type.
nodeType	Returns the node type as a number.
nodeValue	Sets or returns the value of the node as plain text.

IE5-Specific Node Object Properties

As well as the IDOMNode object, which provides the standard W3C-recommended DOM properties described above, IE5 also implements the IXMLDOMNode interface, which extends the list of methods and properties of the IDOMNode interface. The extension provides three properties that support namespaces:

Property	Description
nameSpace	Returns the URI for the namespace as a string. For example, in the namespace declaration xmlns:name="uri" it returns the "uri" part.
baseName	Returns the node name with any namespace removed. For example, in a node declared as <nspace:elemname> it returns the "elemname" part.
prefix	Returns the element namespace prefix as a string. For example, in a node declared as <nspace:elemname> it returns the "nspace" part.

IXMLDOMNode also provides a property that gives access to the Document Type Definition or Schema:

Property	Description
definition	For an EntityReference node, this returns the node containing the definition for the entity referenced — that is, <!ENTITY entityname "Entity Text">. For other nodes, it returns null.

There are also three properties that provide access to the data type for a node, and indicate if the current value of the node was derived from a default value for that node:

Property	Description
dataType	Sets or returns the data type for this node.
nodeTypedValue	Sets or returns the value of the node, expressed in its defined data type.
specified	Indicates whether the node value is explicitly specified or derived from a default value in the DTD or schema. Normally only used with attribute nodes.

Finally, there are three properties that expose the type of the node, and the content of the node and all its descendants:

Property	Description
nodeTypeString	Returns the node type as a string, depending on the node type. For example "element" or "entityreference". Note that these strings are only composed of lower-case characters, regardless of the actual type name.
text	Returns the entire text content of this node and all descendant nodes of this node.
xml	Returns the entire XML of this node and all descendant nodes of this node.

We'll see the way that some of these properties can be used later in this chapter.

> Direct knowledge of the 'internal' interface structure is really only important if you are programming in a language like C++. When you're programming the DOM with script, you don't need to worry about which interface object (IDOMNode or IXMLDOMNode) provides the particular methods and properties you are using.

Node Object Methods

When we want to change the content of a loaded XML document using the DOM, we can do so by setting the read/write properties that are exposed — such as the nodeValue property. However, to change the *structure* of the document, we have to be able to create new nodes, insert them into the XML tree, and remove nodes that we no longer want.

The Node object provides a set of methods for use when editing an XML document. The cloneNode() method creates a new Node object by copying an existing node, and optionally copying all its descendant nodes as well:

Method	Description
`cloneNode(recurse_children)`	Creates a new node object that is an exact clone of this node, optionally including all descendant nodes depending on the value of the Boolean parameter `recurse_children`.

There are also four methods that allow us to add a new node, or replace or remove an existing node:

Method	Description
`appendChild(new_node)`	Appends the node object new_node to the end of the list of child nodes for this node.
`replaceChild(new_node, old_node)`	Replaces the child node old_node with the new child node object new_node, and returns the old child node.
`insertBefore(new_node, this_node)`	Inserts a new node object new_node into the list of child nodes for this node, before this_node or at the end of the list if this_node is omitted.
`removeChild(this_node)`	Removes the child node this_node from the list of child nodes for this node, and returns it.

For example, assuming that we already have a reference to an `Element`-type node named `<REVIEWED>`, which has a child `Text`-type node containing the review date, we can append a copy of this node to the parent element's `childNodes` collection using this code:

```
objNewReview = objThisElem.cloneNode(true);
objParentNode = objThisElem.parentNode;
objParentNode.appendChild(objNewReview);
objReviewDate = objNewReview.firstChild;
objReviewDate.nodeValue = '1998-10-28';
```

We can also check to see if the current node has any child nodes by calling the `hasChildNodes()` method:

Method	Description
`hasChildNodes()`	Returns true if this node has any child nodes.

There are other ways to create new nodes that don't involve cloning an existing node. The higher-level `Document` object adds several methods to the base `Node` object that are designed to create different types of nodes from scratch. We'll look at these when we come to examine the various individual object interfaces in detail later in this chapter.

IE5-Specific Node Object Methods

The `IXMLDOMNode` interface implemented in Internet Explorer 5 adds four methods to the `IDOMNode` object that implements the W3C Recommendation for the `Node` object. The first of these allows us to determine whether parts of a document have been parsed when the document is being loaded:

Method	Description
`parsed()`	Returns `true` if this node and all its descendants have been parsed and instantiated.

The other three methods are used in conjunction with XSL stylesheets. We'll be looking at what **XML patterns** are, and how to create them, in Chapter 7 when we come to examine how XSL works in IE5 as a whole.

Method	Description
`selectNodes (pattern)`	Applies a specified pattern to this node's context and returns a node list object containing matching nodes. The string `pattern` specifies the XSL pattern-matching operation to be used.
`selectSingleNode (pattern)`	Applies a specified pattern to this node's context and returns just the first node object that matches. The string `pattern` specifies the XSL pattern-matching operation to be used.
`transformNode (stylesheet)`	Processes this node and its children using an XSL stylesheet specified in the `stylesheet` argument, and returns the resulting transformation.
	The stylesheet must be either a `Document` node object (in which case the document is assumed to be an XSL stylesheet) or a `Node` object in the `xsl` namespace (in which case this node is treated as a standalone stylesheet fragment).

The XML NodeList Object

In the previous section, we saw that each node can expose a collection of child nodes via its `childNodes` property. This returns `null` if there are no child nodes, or a `NodeList` object containing existing child nodes. A `NodeList` is rather like an array or a collection, and allows us to access the node objects by index, starting from zero for the first node.

The `NodeList` (and `NamedNodeMap`) objects are 'live' references. This means that when we create a `NodeList` (or `NamedNodeMap`) object by accessing the DOM, any changes that occur to the original nodes (the nodes in the document that the node objects in our list or map reference) are reflected in the objects in the list or map. In other words, the list or map contains collections of *references* to the original objects, not copies of the objects themselves.

NodeList Object Property

A NodeList has just one property, the length of the list:

Property	Description
length	Returns the number of nodes in the node list (not including descendant nodes).

NodeList Object Method

In the W3C Recommendation, there is a single method named item():

Method	Description
item(index)	Returns the node at position index in the node list, where the first node is indexed zero.

In fact, the item() method is the default method of this interface, which means that in line with normal scripting-style collections, we can access a child node using either of the following:

```
objChildNode = objThisNode.childNodes.item(3);
objChildNode = objThisNode.childNodes(3);
```

To iterate through a NodeList, we can use the following JScript or JavaScript code:

```
for (i = 0; i < objThisNode.childNodes.length; i++)
{
    // Do something with objThisNode.childNodes(i);
}
```

Or we can do the same with VBScript:

```
For intNode = 0 To objThisNode.childNodes.length - 1
    ' Do something with objThisNode.childNodes(intNode)
Next
```

IE5-Specific NodeList Object Methods

The IXMLDOMNodeList object implemented by IE5 adds two methods to the IDOMNodeList interface that implements the W3C Recommendation for the NodeList object:

Method	Description
reset()	Resets the internal pointer to the point before the first node in the node list. Prepares the list for iteration with the nextNode() method.
nextNode()	Returns the next node object in the node list, or null if there are no more nodes.

These make it possible to iterate through a `nodeList` using a different technique:

```
objThisNode.childNodes.reset();
objCurrentNode = objThisNode.childNodes.nextNode();
do
{
    // Do something with objCurrentNode;
    objCurrentNode = objThisNode.childNodes.nextNode();
} while(objCurrentNode != null);
```

Or in VBScript:

```
objThisNode.childNodes.reset
Set objCurrentNode = objThisNode.childNodes.nextNode
Do While Not IsNull(objCurrentNode)
    ' Do something with objCurrentNode
    Set objCurrentNode = objThisNode.childNodes.nextNode
Loop
```

The XML NamedNodeMap Object

Earlier, I mentioned the fact that rather than being 'ordinary' child nodes, the nodes that make up attributes of other nodes are referenced through the `attributes` property of their parent node. This is generally the case for the attributes within an element, and for the attributes applied to an XML document object through a processing instruction. It also applies to the version number in the XML declaration, and to the file name of an external DTD in the `DOCTYPE` declaration.

Like the `NodeLists`, the `NamedNodeMap` objects are 'live' references. When we create a `NamedNodeMap` object using the DOM, any changes to the original nodes that these objects reference are reflected in the objects in the map.

While the `childNodes` property of all `Node` objects returns a `NodeList` object, the `attributes` property returns a `NamedNodeMap` object. The diagram here attempts to make the distinction clearer by showing three nodes that are referenced by a `NodeList`. One of the nodes has three attributes, and these are referenced by a `NamedNodeMap` object. Remember, however, that `Attribute` (or `Attr`) objects are still classed as nodes, although they cannot be accessed in the same way as other nodes.

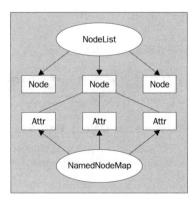

As far as programming is concerned, a `NamedNodeMap` is similar to a `NodeList`, except that it provides direct access to the objects it contains using their names, as well as via their index positions within the list.

NamedNodeMap Property

The `length` property is the same as for a `NodeList` object:

Property	Description
`length`	Returns the number of nodes in the named node map.

NamedNodeMap Methods

The `item()` method is also the same as for a `NodeList` object:

Method	Description
`item(index)`	Returns the node at position `index` in the named node map, where the first node is indexed zero.

The other three methods that are specified in the W3C Recommendation are:

Method	Description
`getNamedItem(name)`	Retrieves the node object with the specified `name`. Typically used to retrieve attributes from an element.
`setNamedItem(new_node)`	Inserts the node object `new_node` into the named node map, updating the XML document. Any existing node with the same name is replaced with the new node. Typically used to update attribute values for an element.
`removeNamedItem(name)`	Removes the node object with the specified `name` from the named node map. Typically used to remove attributes from an element.

These methods allow us to access individual members of the list directly, without having to iterate through it examining each object's `nodeName` property:

```
strAttrValue = objThisNode.attributes.getNamedItem("Date");
objRemovedNode = objThisNode.attributes.removeNamedItem("Date");
```

IE5-Specific NamedNodeMap Methods

Internet Explorer 5 adds four methods to the W3C Recommendation for the `NamedNodeMap` object through the `IXMLDOMNamedNodeMap` interface. The first two allow us to iterate through the list 'node by node', in the same way as shown with the `NodeList` object earlier:

Method	Description
`reset()`	Resets the internal pointer to the position before the first node in the named node map. Prepares the list for iteration with the `nextNode()` method.
`nextNode()`	Returns the next node object in the named node map, or `null` if there are no more nodes.

The other two IE5-specific methods are used to access individual nodes within the `NamedNodeMap` when they have a namespace qualification. Each method accepts the base name of the node and the URI that identifies the namespace:

Method	Description
`getQualifiedItem(base_name, namespace_uri)`	Returns the node object with the specified `base_name` and `namespace_uri` values.
`removeQualifiedItem(base_name, namespace_uri)`	Removes the node object with the specified `base_name` and `namespace_uri` values from the named node map.

The Higher-Level XML DOM Objects

In the previous sections, we've seen the base objects that are used to create a structured representation of an XML document within Internet Explorer 5 (and in other environments that follow the W3C Recommendation for the XML DOM). Now we can move on to see the higher-level objects that add extra features to the object model.

The Node Structure of XML Documents

An XML document is represented as a structure that starts with a `Document` node. This node can have a collection of child objects, and a collection of attributes. The child objects can include only a single `Element`-type object, plus a selection of other objects such as processing instructions, comments, and the document type definition (DTD) or schema:

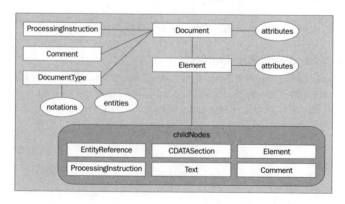

The DTD or schema is represented by the DocumentType object, which has its own collections of entities and notations that represent the NOTATION and ENTITY items in the DTD.

The single Element object descendant of Document is the outermost element of the document, whose tags enclose all the other elements in the document. For example, in a simple document defined like this, the outermost element is <BOOKLIST>:

```
<?xml version="1.0" ?>
<!DOCTYPE BOOKLIST [
   <!ELEMENT BOOKLIST (BOOKINFO*)>
   <!ELEMENT BOOKINFO (ISBN, BOOK_TITLE)>
   <!ELEMENT ISBN (#PCDATA)>
   <!ELEMENT BOOK_TITLE (#PCDATA)>
]>

<BOOKLIST>
   <BOOKINFO>
      <ISBN>1-861000-46-4</ISBN>
      <BOOK_TITLE>ActiveX Database Programming</BOOK_TITLE>
   </BOOKINFO>
   <BOOKINFO>
      <ISBN>1-861000-44-8</ISBN>
      <BOOK_TITLE>Instant VBScript Programming</BOOK_TITLE>
   </BOOKINFO>
</BOOKLIST>
```

This element can have an attributes collection, and a childNodes collection that contains the next level in the XML document tree. In this code, the root <BOOKLIST> element has no attributes but it does have two child nodes, both of type <BOOKINFO>.

The Individual DOM Object Interface Types

Each of the DOM objects that we use when accessing an XML document, as shown in the previous diagram and example code, is based on one of the **base objects** that we discussed earlier. In most cases they are derived directly from the Node object, but the Text, Comment, ProcessingInstruction and CDATASection objects are based on the CharacterData object, which is itself derived from the Node object.

Each derived object inherits the methods and properties of the base object, and may add additional methods and properties of its own. For a list of the higher-level objects exposed by the XML DOM, see the table earlier in the chapter.

Document (the IXMLDOMDocument object)

The Document object is the root object for an XML document. In IE5, it is the object that is instantiated by an <XML> element in the HTML page, by creating a new ActiveX object with the identifier "Microsoft.XMLDOM", or by loading an XML document directly into the browser. The IE5 IXMLDOMDocument object extends the W3C DOM Recommendation for the Document interface to include parser-specific functions. These include the ability to load documents asynchronously and control validation. The IXMLDOMDocument object also provides access to other IE5-specific objects such as IDOMParseError.

What follows is a summary of the properties that are added to the base `Node` object properties for the `Document` object. The first three are as per the W3C Recommendation, and provide information about the document by allowing access to parts of the DTD or schema, direct access to the root element, and details of any application-specific functions that are available:

Property	Description
doctype	Returns a reference to the `DocumentType` node specifying the DTD or schema for this document.
documentElement	Returns a reference to the outermost element of the document.
implementation	Returns a reference to the `Implementation` object for the document. This object provides methods that are application-specific and independent of the DOM implementation.

IE5-Specific Document Object Properties

The `IXMLDOMDocument` object in IE5 adds four extra properties to those available through the `IDOMDocument` interface:

Property	Description
async	Sets or returns whether asynchronous download of the XML data is permitted. Values are `true` or `false`.
validateOnParse	Sets or returns whether the parser should validate the document. Takes the value `true` to validate or `false` to check only for well-formedness.
parseError	Returns a reference to the `IDOMParseError` object that contains information about any errors encountered while parsing the document. We'll come back to this object in more detail later in this chapter.
readyState	Indicates the current load state of the XML document (see below).

The value of the `readyState` property changes as the document is loaded. It returns the value 0 or "uninitialized" when the XML parser object or data island has been created but the document has not yet begun to load, and 1 or "loading" while the load() method is executing (see below). Once the XML document has completed loading, the property returns 2 or "loaded", followed by 3 or "interactive" after enough of the data has been parsed to reveal and make available the document object model.

At this point, however, the data set is still only partially retrieved, and is read-only. After the document has been *completely* loaded and parsed, the `readyState` changes to 4 or "`completed`". If the load was successful the data is available on a read/write basis; if not, the error information is available. You'll see two events that are used in conjunction with the `readyState` property shortly.

> *The string values are returned when the XML document has been instantiated through a data island, the numerical values when it has been instantiated as an ActiveX object and loaded through script code.*

W3C Recommended Methods for the Document Object

There are also several methods available specifically for the `Document` object. The W3C Recommendation provides eight methods that can be used to create new nodes:

Method	Description
`createAttribute(attr_name)`	Creates an `Attribute` node with the specified name.
`createCDATASection(text)`	Creates a `CDATASection` node containing text.
`createComment(text)`	Creates a `Comment` node containing text as the comment between the `<!--` and `-->`.
`createDocumentFragment()`	Creates an empty `DocumentFragment` node that can be used to build independent sections of a document.
`createElement(tag_name)`	Creates an `Element` node with the specified name.
`createEntityReference(ref_name)`	Creates an `EntityReference` node with the supplied name for the reference.
`createProcessing Instruction(target, text)`	Creates a `ProcessingInstruction` node containing the specified target and data.
`createTextNode(text_data)`	Creates a `Text` node containing the specified text data.

Creating and Manipulating Elements in a Document

As an example of several of the Document properties and methods, the following code creates a new node in an XML document. It assumes that the document is exposed by a data island defined like this:

```
<XML ID="diXMLData" SRC="mydocument.xml"></XML>
```

If you're using a parser component, the code is exactly the same provided that you use the same ID attribute in the definition of the parser object. The code gets a reference to the XML document itself from the data island, then uses this to get a reference to the root element through the documentElement property:

```
// Get the XML document object
theXMLDoc = document.all.diXMLData;

// Get the outermost element
theRoot = theXMLDoc.documentElement;
```

Now we can use the Document object to create a new element node called <REVIEWED>:

```
// Create a new child element
newElem = theXMLDoc.createElement("REVIEWED");
```

Next, we get a reference to the element we want to place our new element in front of (that is, the element that will become its nextSibling in their parent's childNodes node list):

```
// Get reference to new sibling element
nextElem = theRoot.firstChild.firstChild;
```

Then, we insert the new element before the element we've just found by adding it as a child of the latter's parent node (in other words, into this element's parent's childNodes collection). Notice that the method returns a reference to the new node after inserting it, which we store back in newElem:

```
// Insert into document
newElem = theRoot.firstChild.insertBefore(newElem, nextElem);
```

Finally, we can create a new Text node with the value "1998-10-28", and append it to the childNodes collection of our newly inserted <REVIEWED> Element node:

```
// Create a new text-type node
newText = theXMLDoc.createTextNode("1998-10-28");

// Append to <REVIEWED> element
newElem.appendChild(newText);
```

In addition, the Document object provides a single method that can be used to build a NodeList of Element objects that have a specified tag name:

Method	Description
getElementsByTagName (tag_name)	Returns a NodeList object containing all the elements in the document having the specified tag name. If tag_name is "*", it returns all elements.

166

This can be useful if we have a large number of elements of a certain type to which we wish to assign a set of new values. For example, to set all the values throughout the document of an element entitled <REVIEWED> to the current time and date, we might use the following code:

```
<XML ID="domBooks" SRC="books.xml"></XML>
<SCRIPT LANGUAGE="JavaScript">
   nodeXMLDoc = document.all("domBooks").XMLDocument;
   objNodeList = nodeXMLDoc.getElementsByTagName("REVIEWED");
   for(i = 0; i < objNodeList.length; i++)
   {
       objNodeList.item(i).firstChild.nodeValue = Date();
   }
</SCRIPT>
```

IE5-Specific Document Methods

In addition to these, Internet Explorer 5 adds a single method through the IXMLDOMDocument interface that can create a new node object of *any* type:

Method	Description
createNode(node_type, node_name, namespace_uri)	Creates any type of node using the specified node_type, node_name, and namespace_uri parameters.

It also provides three methods that control loading of documents into the parser object or data island:

Method	Description
load(url)	Loads an XML document from the location in url.
loadXML(string)	Loads a string that is a representation of an XML document.
abort()	Aborts a currently executing asynchronous download.

Rather than working with a data island that is explicitly defined using an <XML> element, we can create an instance of the IE5 DOM parser object using the ActiveXObject() method in JavaScript or JScript. Then, we can use the load() or loadXML() methods to load the appropriate XML document:

```
// Create ActiveX parser object and assign to myDocument variable
var myDocument = new ActiveXObject("microsoft.XMLDOM");

// Load an XML file into the new ActiveX parser object
myDocument.load("myxmlfile.xml");
```

The `IXMLDOMDocument` object also contains a method that provides a quick way to get a reference to any node in the document, if you know its `ID` attribute value:

Method	Description
`nodeFromID(id_value)`	Returns the node object whose `ID` attribute matches the supplied value.

IE5-Specific Document Object Events

The `IXMLDOMDocument` object also adds two special properties to the `Document` object that define the names of functions to be executed in response to certain events:

Event	Description
`ondataavailable`	The `ondataavailable` event occurs when data becomes available through an asynchronous data loading process, allowing processing of the page in parallel with the XML document download.
`onreadystatechange`	The `onreadystatechange` event occurs when the value of the `readyState` property changes. This provides an alternative way of monitoring the arrival of XML data when asynchronous loading is used. The possible stages of the process (not all may occur every time) are:

0 (`"uninitialized"`) — the object has been created but the `load()` has not yet been executed.

1 (`"loading"`) — the `load()` method is executing.

2 (`"loaded"`) — loading is complete and parsing is taking place.

3 (`"interactive"`) — some data has been read and parsed and the object model is now available. The data set is only partially retrieved, and is read-only.

4 (`"completed"`) — document has been completely loaded. If successful, the data is available read/write; if not, the error information is available. |

Using the Document Object Events

We can assign our own custom functions to these event properties, and have the code executed each time the document raises these events. The following example demonstrates this. We have a simple HTML page containing a <DIV> element into which we'll insert our results. The opening <BODY> tag also specifies a function named loadXMLFile(), which will be executed once the page has finished loading:

```
<BODY ONLOAD="loadXMLFile()">

<!-- To insert the results of parsing the object model -->
<DIV ID="divResults"></DIV>
```

The page also contains some JavaScript code that defines two global variables and the loadXMLFile() function. This function creates a new instance of the MSXML parser object, and then assigns two function names, availFunction() and changeFunction() to the event properties we met earlier:

```
var objXMLData;
var objResults;

function loadXMLFile()
{
    // Get a reference to the results DIV element
    objResults = document.all('divResults');

    // Create a new parser object instance
    objXMLData = new ActiveXObject('microsoft.XMLDOM');

    // Connect the event properties with our event functions
    // Must omit the parentheses to avoid an error on return
    objXMLData.ondataavailable = availFunction;
    objXMLData.onreadystatechange = changeFunction;
    ...
```

The next step is to set the validateOnParse and async properties, and then start the load process going by calling the load() method:

```
    ...
    // Set the other parser properties...
    objXMLData.validateOnParse = true;
    objXMLData.async = true;

    // ...and load the document
    objXMLData.load('onebook.xml');
}
```

Reacting to the Document Events

The two custom functions that are executed in response to the events come next — they just display messages in the page to indicate that they fired. However, for the onreadystatechange event, we also display the value and text equivalent of the readyState property, and check for an error:

```
function availFunction()
{
    // Add message to results DIV element
    objResults.innerHTML += '<B>ondataavailable</B> event fired<BR>';
}
```

169

```
function changeFunction()
{
   // Decode the value of the readyState property
   // NOTE: this is already a string if you use an <XML> element instead of
   //  the MSXML C++ parser object to insert the XML document into the page.
   intReadyState = objXMLData.readyState;
   switch(intReadyState)
   {
      case 1: strReadyState = "loading";
              break;
      case 2: strReadyState = "loaded";
              break;
      case 3: strReadyState = "interactive";
              break;
      case 4: strReadyState = "completed";
              break;
   }

   // Add message to results DIV element
   objResults.innerHTML += '<B>onreadystatechange</B> event fired, ' +
                           'readyState is ' + intReadyState +
                           ' ("' + strReadyState + '")<BR>';

   // Check if loading is complete
   if(intReadyState == 4)
      // Check if there was an error while loading
      if(objXMLData.parseError.errorCode != 0)
         showError();
      else
         objResults.innerHTML += 'successfully loaded and parsed<BR>';
}
```

At the end of this function, you can see how we check for an error in the XML document or load process when we're using asynchronous loading. We first test the value of the readyState property to see if it is 4 ("completed"). If so, we examine the value of the parseError object's errorCode property to see if the document was loaded and parsed successfully. showError() is a custom function defined elsewhere in the page that displays an error message — we'll look at it later on. In the meantime, here's the result of loading a valid XML document into our page:

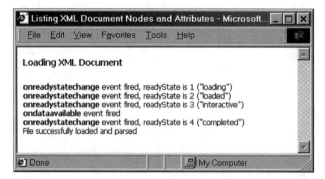

This page is named load_events.htm, *and can be run from our web site at* http://webdev.wrox.co.uk/books/1576/. *You can also download the examples to run on your own system.*

DocumentType (the IXMLDOMDocumentType object)

This object contains information about the document type declaration or schema for the document. It represents the `<!DOCTYPE>` declaration node. As well as the base `Node` object methods and properties, it provides a `name` property that returns just the name of the document type node, rather than the node object itself:

Property	Description
name	Returns the name of the document type (DOCTYPE) for this document.

The `DocumentType` represents the entire `DOCTYPE` declaration of the XML document, and as part of this task provides access to all the `ENTITY` and `NOTATION` definitions as well:

Property	Description
entities	Returns a `NodeList` containing references to all the `Entity` objects declared in the document type declaration.
notations	Returns a `NodeList` containing references to all the `Notation` objects present in the document type declaration.

DocumentFragment (the IXMLDOMDocumentFragment object)

A **document fragment** is a lightweight object that is useful for operations that insert things into trees. A new document fragment can be created, elements can be added to it, and then the entire fragment can be added to an existing document. It is also useful for storing sections of a document temporarily, such as when cutting and pasting blocks of elements. However, it provides only the methods and properties of the base `Node` object.

Element (the IXMLDOMElement object)

This object represents the elements in the document and, together with the `Attribute` and `Text` nodes, is likely to be the most common. Remember that the text content of an `Element` node is stored in a child `Text` node, and that an `Element` node always has a `nodeValue` of `null`. As well as the base `Node` object methods and properties, the `Element` object adds the `tagName` property with the specific purpose of allowing us to read and change the name of the element:

Property	Description
tagName	Sets or returns the name of the element node — that is, the text name *within* the tags.

The W3C Recommendation also provides for seven methods, six of which are specifically designed to allow access to, and manipulation of, the attributes of an element node in an XML document. These six are shown in the table overleaf:

Method	Description
getAttribute(attr_name)	Returns the value of the attribute with the specified name.
setAttribute(attr_name, value)	Sets the value of the attribute with the specified name.
removeAttribute(attr_name)	Removes the value of the attribute with the specified name, or replaces it with the default value.
getAttributeNode(attr_name)	Returns the attribute node with the specified name as an object.
setAttributeNode(attr_node)	Adds a new attribute node to the element. If an attribute with the same name exists, it is replaced and the old attribute node is returned.
removeAttributeNode(attr_node)	Removes the specified attribute node from the element and returns it. If the attribute has a default value in the DTD or schema, a new attribute node is automatically created with that default value and the specified property is updated.

The Element object also provides the getElementsByTagName() method. It provides a way of referencing just the matching elements that are descendants of this element:

Method	Description
getElementsByTagName(name)	Returns a NodeList object containing all descendant elements matching the specified name.

There is also a single method that can be used to convert several text nodes within an element into a single, contiguous one. This is useful if you have been changing the content of the element or adding and removing element nodes in the DOM using code. It can help to ensure that elements each have a single Text child node instead of several, although an intervening node (such as a comment) prevents concatenation of the Text nodes:

Method	Description
normalize()	Combines all adjacent text nodes into one unified text node for this and all descendant element nodes.

Attribute or Attr (the IXMLDOMAttribute object)

This object represents an `Attribute` of an `Element` object. In the W3C DOM Recommendation, the object name is `Attr` rather than `Attribute`, to avoid clashing with existing interface definition languages. Attributes are normally manipulated through a `NamedNodeMap` object. As well as the base `Node` object methods and properties, each `Attribute` node has a `name` and a `value` property that can be used to manipulate the attributes of an element:

Property	Description
name	Sets or returns the name of the attribute.
value	Sets or returns the value of the attribute.

Attributes also have a `tagName` property that identifies the element they belong to — useful when you are working with a set of attributes within a `NamedNodeMap`:

Property	Description
tagName	Returns the name of the element that contains this attribute.

Entity (the IXMLDOMEntity object)

This object represents a parsed entity as declared with an `<!ENTITY>` declaration in the DTD. However, it does not provide a reference to the entity declaration — version 1.0 of the W3C DOM Recommendation does not define an object that models the declaration of entities. As well as the base `Node` object methods and properties, it also provides two properties of its own which expose parts of the node content:

Property	Description
publicId	Returns the `PUBLIC` identifier value for this entity node.
systemId	Returns the `SYSTEM` identifier value for this entity node.

EntityReference (the IXMLDOMEntityReference object)

This object represents an entity reference node within the XML document. If the XML processor expands entity references while building the structure model, it's possible that no entity reference objects will appear in the tree, being replaced by the **replacement text** of the entity.

The `EntityReference` object provides only the methods and properties of the base `Node` object. The value of the replacement text is held in the `nodeValue` property of the `EntityReference` node's child `Text` node, in the same way that an `Element` node's value is held in a child `Text` node.

Notation (the IXMLDOMNotation object)

This object represents a notation declared in the DTD with a `<!NOTATION>` declaration. As well as the base `Node` object methods and properties, it provides the same `publicID` and `systemID` properties as the `Entity` object:

Property	Description
publicId	Returns the `PUBLIC` identifier value for this notation node.
systemId	Returns the `SYSTEM` identifier value for this notation node.

CharacterData (the IXMLDOMCharacterData Object)

The `CharacterData` object extends the `Node` object with additional properties and methods that make working with text content easier. These additional members are also available in nodes that inherit from the base `CharacterData` object — those of type `Text` (the child node of an `Element`), `Comment`, `ProcessingInstruction` and `CDATASection`. As well as the properties of the `Node` object, the `CharacterData` object provides two extra properties, `data` and `length`. In a node that contains text, the `data` property will return a specific section of the node's text content, depending on the type of node. In a `Comment` node, for example, it returns just the text between the `<!--` and `-->` delimiters.

Property	Description
data	Contains this node's data, which depends on the node type. Note that if you just want to get the text content of a node and all its descendants as a string, it's generally easier to use the `text` property.
length	Returns the number of characters in the `data` string of the node.

There are also five methods available in nodes that inherit from the base `CharacterData` object. These allow us to access and edit the text string stored within the node:

Method	Description
appendData(text)	Appends the string in the `text` argument to the existing string data.
deleteData(char_offset, num_chars)	Deletes a substring from the string data of the node, starting at `char_offset` (where the first character is 0) and continuing for `num_chars`.
insertData(char_offset, text)	Inserts the string in the `text` argument at the specified character offset within the data contained by the node.

Method	Description
replaceData(char_offset, num_chars, text)	Replaces the specified number of characters in the existing string data of the node, starting at the specified character offset, with the string in the text argument.
substringData(char_offset, num_chars)	Returns the specified number of characters as a string, starting at the specified character offset, from the data contained in the node.

Text (the IXMLDOMText object)

The Text object represents the text content of an element node or an attribute node. It is based on the CharacterData object, and as such has the extra properties data and length, and the five methods appendData(), deleteData(), insertData(), replaceData() and substringData() that CharacterData has. Of course, it also inherits the methods and properties of the base Node object.

However, it *also* provides an extra method that can be used to convert a node into two separate nodes:

Method	Description
splitText (char_offset)	Splits the node into two separate nodes at the specified character offset, then inserts the new node into the XML as a sibling that immediately follows this node.

CDATASection (the IXMLDOMCDATASection object)

CDATA sections are used to 'escape' blocks of text that aren't designed to be interpreted as markup. They are declared using a <![CDATA[...]]> markup declaration, and can be used anywhere in the document where character data can occur. The CDATASection object is based on the CharacterData object, and has the same properties and methods as the Text object we just discussed.

Comment (the IXMLDOMComment object)

Represents the content of an XML comment element. It has only the same properties and methods as the CharacterData object discussed above, with no extra methods or properties.

ProcessingInstruction (the IXMLDOMProcessingIntruction object)

This element represents an instruction embedded in the XML between '<?' and '?>' delimiters. It provides a way of storing application-specific information within an XML document. The text content of the node is usually subdivided into the target (the text immediately after the '<?' and up to the first whitespace character) and the data content (the remainder up to the closing '?>'). Otherwise, it has only the methods and properties of the Node object.

Implementation (the IXMLDOMImplementation object)

This object provides access to methods that are application-specific and independent of any particular instance of the document object model. It is a child of the Document object and the Element object. It was introduced by the W3C DOM working group with the intention that it would allow programs to be written that would work in any physical implementation of the DOM.

The plan is that different browsers, applications and other XML processors will allow programmers to use features of their specific DOM implementation conditionally, based on the values returned by the hasFeatures() method:

Method	Description
hasFeature(feature, version)	Returns true if the specified version of this implementation supports the specified feature.

Node Type, Node Name and Node Value Summary

The three properties you'll find yourself using most often when working with the high-level XML DOM objects are nodeType, nodeName and nodeValue. To help you appreciate the different ways that they relate to the different types of node, I've summarized them here:

Type of node	nodeType	nodeName	nodeValue
Element	1	tagName property	null
Attribute	2	name property	value property
Text	3	"#text"	content of node
CDATASection	4	"#cdata-section"	content of node
EntityReference	5	entity reference name	null
Entity	6	entity name	null
Processing Instruction	7	target property	content of node excluding target
Comment	8	"#comment"	comment text
Document	9	"#document"	null
DocumentType	10	doctype name	null
DocumentFragment	11	"#document-fragment"	null
Notation	12	notation name	null

The IE5-Specific Parser Objects

There are three other objects that are specific to IE5, and not part of the W3C Recommendation for the Document Object Model. These are:

❑   IDOMParseError

❑   IXMLHttpRequest

❑   IXTLRuntime

We'll only be looking at the first two of these — IDOMParseError and IXMLHttpRequest — in this chapter. The IXTLRuntime object implements a series of properties and methods that are available within XSL stylesheets, and allow authors to transform the contents of XML documents from one format to another without actually displaying them. We'll look at XSL stylesheets in more detail in Chapter 7.

> *There's a full list of all the base objects and DOM object interfaces in the reference section of this book. It includes lists of all the methods and properties for each one, together with their meaning and syntax.*

ParseError (the IDOMParseError object)

The properties of the ParseError object return detailed information about the last error that occurred while loading and/or parsing an XML document. This includes the line number, character position, and a text description:

Property	Description
errorCode	Returns the error number or error code as a decimal integer.
filepos	Returns the absolute character position in the file where the error occurred.
line	Returns the number of the line in the document that contains the error.
linepos	Returns the character position of the error within the line in which it occurred.
reason	Returns a text description of the source and reason for the error, and can also include the URL of the DTD or schema and the node within it that corresponds to the error.
srcText	Returns the full text of the line that contains the error, or an empty string if the error cannot be assigned to a specific line.
url	Returns the URL of the most recent XML document that contained an error.

We'll use the `errorCode` property in many of our example pages in the next chapter to make sure that the document has loaded without error before we attempt to access it. For example, the following code creates a new instance of the MSXML parser object and loads a document into it. If an error occurs, it executes our custom `showError()` function:

```
// Create a new parser object instance
objXMLData = new ActiveXObject('microsoft.XMLDOM');

// Load a document
objXMLData.load('document.xml');

// Check if there was a parser error
if(objXMLData.parseError.errorCode != 0)
   showError();

// Rest of code to use the document goes here
...
```

The `showError()` function simply accesses the various properties of the `parseError` object and displays them in an `alert` dialog:

```
function showError()
{
   // Display the error details
   var strError = new String;
   strError = 'Invalid XML file !\n\n' +
            'File URL: ' + objXMLData.parseError.url + '\n' +
            'Line No.: ' + objXMLData.parseError.line + '\n' +
            'Character: ' + objXMLData.parseError.linepos + '\n' +
            'File Position: ' + objXMLData.parseError.filepos + '\n' +
            'Source Text: ' + objXMLData.parseError.srcText + '\n' +
            'Error Code: ' + objXMLData.parseError.errorCode + '\n' +
            'Description: ' + objXMLData.parseError.reason
   alert(strError);
}
```

This page is named `load_error.htm`, *and can be run from our web site at* http://webdev.wrox.co.uk/books/1576/. *You can also download the examples to run on your own system.*

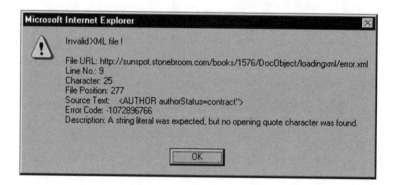

This object is also used by the Microsoft XML Validator page we used in Chapter 3 to check whether an XML document has parsed correctly, and to return descriptions of any errors that occurred.

HttpRequest (the IXMLHttpRequest object)

This object provides client-side protocol support for communication with HTTP servers. A client can use the HttpRequest object to send an arbitrary HTTP request, receive the response, and have the IE5 DOM parse that response. It has these properties:

Property	Description
readyState	Indicates the current state of the document being loaded, and changes as the download proceeds. See the Document object for more details.
responseBody	Returns the response as an array of unsigned bytes.
responseStream	Returns the response as an IStream object.
responseText	Returns the response as an ordinary text string.
responseXML	Returns the response as an XML document. For security reasons, validation is turned off during this process to prevent the parser from attempting to download a linked DTD or other definition file.
status	Returns the status code sent back from the server as a long integer.
statusText	Returns the status text sent back from the server as a string.

The HttpRequest object also provides the following methods:

Method	Description
abort()	Cancels a current HTTP request.
getAllResponseHeaders()	Returns all the HTTP headers as name/value pairs delimited by the carriage return-linefeed combination.
getResponseHeader(header_name)	Returns the value of an individual HTTP header from the response body, as specified by the header name.
open(method, url, async, userid, password)	Initializes a request and specifies the method, the complete URL, and authentication information for the request if required.
send()	Sends the HTTP request to the server and waits to receive a response.
setRequestHeader(header_name, value)	Specifies an HTTP header to send to the server.

Using the HttpRequest Object

As a simple example of the `HttpRequest` object in use, we'll load an XML document and display the results by inserting them into an HTML page that contains several `<SPAN>` elements. The opening `<BODY>` tag also references a custom function named `getPage()` that will be executed once the HTML page has finished loading:

```
<BODY ONLOAD="getPage()">
   <SPAN CLASS=intro>Using the HttpRequest Object</SPAN><P>

   status: <B><SPAN ID="rstat"></SPAN></B>      
   statusText: <B><SPAN ID="rstattx"></SPAN></B><P>
   responseText is:<BR><B><SPAN ID="rtext"></SPAN></B><P>
   responseXML: <B><SPAN ID="rxml"></SPAN></B>      
   responseXML.nodeName: <B><SPAN ID="rxmlname"></SPAN></B><P>
</BODY>
```

The `getPage()` function is shown next. All it does is create a new instance of the `XMLHTTP` object that implements the `HttpRequest` object, and then set the parameters to retrieve an XML document file. The first parameter is the method, usually either `GET` or `POST`. The second is the full (not relative) URL of the page to load, and the third specifies that we want to wait for the load to complete before running any other code. Of course, we could specify `true` for this `parameter`, then use the `readyState` property to monitor the progress of the download if required:

```
function getPage()
{
   // The URL of a document to load
   var strURL = <something appropriate>

   // Create a new parser object instance
   var objHTTP = new ActiveXObject("microsoft.XMLHTTP")

   // Set the parameters to get our page
   objHTTP.open('GET', strURL, false);
   ...
```

Once we've specified the details of the request we want to make to the server, we submit it using the `send()` method. When this returns, we display the values of the `HttpRequest` object's properties in the page. Notice that the `responseXML` property contains an object rather than a string. The returned document is parsed into the DOM automatically, as you can see from the fact that we can retrieve the `nodeName` of the root element:

```
   ...
   // And send the request to the server
   objHTTP.send();

   // Then display the results
   document.all('rstat').innerText = objHTTP.status;
   document.all('rstattx').innerText = objHTTP.statusText;
   document.all('rtext').innerText = objHTTP.responseText;
   document.all('rxml').innerText = objHTTP.responseXML;
   document.all('rxmlname').innerText = objHTTP.responseXML.nodeName;
}
```

Of course, you can use the `HttpRequest` object to fetch any kind of data or document if you wish — not just an XML document. Obviously, another type of document won't be parsed into the DOM as happens with an XML document.

This page is named httprequest.htm, *and can be run or downloaded from our web site at* http://webdev.wrox.co.uk/books/1576/.

Here's the result of loading a valid XML document into our example page:

Summary

In this chapter, we've explored what a Document Object Model (DOM) is, and why it is so useful for providing access to objects both within the browser itself, and within the pages and other documents that the browser hosts. Of course, as we're looking at XML in this book, the object model that really interests us is the XML implementation of the DOM.

The XML DOM starts at the root of the XML document, and provides a tree-like structure that holds all the entries in the XML as individual nodes. Each node is represented as generic Node object, and then extended by one of several kinds of specialist elements that provide specific properties best suited for individual types of nodes.

We looked at the base objects, Node, NodeList and NamedNodeMap, and then moved on to see what the more specialized DOM object interfaces added in the way of extra properties and methods. Many of the properties and methods, and even some of the intrinsic objects, are specific to Internet Explorer 5, and do not form part of the World Wide Web Consortium's Recommendation for the XML DOM.

However, IE5 does provide a W3C-compatible object model by including all the recommended objects, properties and methods. It just means that if you intend to write application-independent code, you have to bear in mind which of these are extensions to the W3C model.

In the next chapter, we'll move on to look at how we use the DOM to access and manipulate XML documents, and I'll provide some more simple applications that you can experiment with.

6

Using the Document Object Model

In the previous chapter, we looked at what the XML Document Object Model (DOM) actually is, and how it reflects the structure of an XML document. We also explored what the individual objects within the DOM are, and saw the lists of properties and methods that they make available to our script code.

However, reading lists of properties and methods can be tiresome, and often it doesn't provide that, "Oh, now I get it..." factor that comes from seeing the code at work. This is a reference book, and you'll find the preceding chapter extremely useful when you start to work regularly with the XML DOM. In this chapter, however, we'll take a totally different approach and see the various properties and methods provided by the DOM in use.

It's also likely that you'll want to start building your own applications that access the DOM in a range of ways, and so in this chapter I'll outline some useful techniques for doing that as well. We'll examine the working of some custom pages that I've built, and we'll build some new pages from scratch. We'll start, though, with a look at some of the common XML scripting techniques.

Common XML Scripting Techniques

In this section, we'll look at two of the common reasons for working with the XML Document Object Model, and we'll also see a couple of samples that I've provided to help you get used to using it. The two tasks that you're most likely to want to achieve, at least at first as you familiarize yourself with DOM programming, are accessing individual elements, and parsing all or part of the XML document using script.

First, we'll look at a simple example that fetches values from specific elements in an XML document. You might find that the XML we're going to use for this and the next set of examples is familiar to you; it looks like this:

```
<?xml version="1.0"?>
<BOOKLIST>
   <BOOK itemType="Reference">
      <BOOK_TITLE>Instant HTML &amp; XML</BOOK_TITLE>
      <BOOK_CODE>16-041</BOOK_CODE>
      <SUBJECT_CATEGORY>HTML</SUBJECT_CATEGORY>
```

```
        <RELEASE_DATE>1998-03-07</RELEASE_DATE>
        <AUTHORLIST>
           <AUTHOR authorStatus="contract">
              <FIRST_NAME>Martin</FIRST_NAME>
              <LAST_NAME>Williams</LAST_NAME>
           </AUTHOR>
           <AUTHOR authorStatus="retired">
              <FIRST_NAME>Michael</FIRST_NAME>
              <LAST_NAME>Atkins</LAST_NAME>
           </AUTHOR>
        </AUTHORLIST>
     </BOOK>
  </BOOKLIST>
```

This XML document provides a range of information about one book. What we're concerned with in our first example is getting information about the first author listed in the document.

The following example is a file named `getelementvalue.htm`, *which you can download or run from our web site at* http://webdev.wrox.co.uk/books/1576/.

Accessing XML Document Contents

The first step is to insert the XML data into our HTML page. As before, we'll use a data island to accomplish this task:

```
<XML ID="domBookList" SRC="onebook.xml"></XML>

...

<INPUT TYPE="BUTTON" VALUE="   "
                     ONCLICK="getAuthorName()">
   Display Details of First Author<P>
<INPUT TYPE="BUTTON" VALUE="   "
                     ONCLICK="location.href='onebook.xml'">
   Display XML Source File
...
```

This snippet also shows the two buttons that start off the process of finding the information and displaying the XML document to the user, so that they can see where the values came from.

Next comes the script code that will find our elements and retrieve the values. To help you follow it more easily, I've divided the process up into small steps rather than using long strings of properties. As an example, I use:

```
nodeBookList = nodeXMLDoc.firstChild.nextSibling;
nodeBook = nodeBookList.firstChild;
```

instead of:

```
nodeBook = nodeXMLDoc.firstChild.nextSibling.firstChild;
```

to get a reference to the <BOOK> element. (Remember that the first child node of the document is the XML declaration, so the <BOOKLIST> element is the next sibling.)

184

The Code to Find the Values

Here's the `getAuthorName()` function, with each of the steps briefly described as we go along:

```
...
<SCRIPT LANGUAGE="JavaScript">

    function getAuthorName()
    {
        // Get a reference to the embedded XML document
        nodeXMLDoc = document.all("domBookList").XMLDocument;

        // Walk down the tree to the first <AUTHOR> element
        nodeBookList = nodeXMLDoc.firstChild.nextSibling;
        ...
```

Once we've got a reference to the root of the XML document in `nodeXMLDoc`, we retrieve the `<BOOKLIST>` element by going to the second child node of the root document. The root is the `Document` node, and the first child is the `<?xml...?>` processing instruction, so we want the second child.

Now we can get the *first* child of our `<BOOKLIST>` element node — the `<BOOK>` element — and then the *last* child node of this element: the `<AUTHORLIST>` element:

```
    ...
    nodeBook = nodeBookList.firstChild;
    nodeAuthList = nodeBook.lastChild;
    ...
```

The author we want is the first one in the `<AUTHORLIST>`, and we get this with the `firstChild` property of the `<AUTHORLIST>` element. Then we can retrieve a `NamedNodeMap` from this `<AUTHOR>` element's `attributes` property:

```
    ...
    nodeAuthor = nodeAuthList.firstChild;
    mapStatus = nodeAuthor.attributes;
    ...
```

The Potential Dangers of this Approach

The technique we've just used is a little fragile, because it assumes we know exactly what the XML will contain when we write the code. An XML comment in the wrong place, for example, will cause the code to fail because the element we're seeking will no longer be in the position we expect.

An alternative (and safer) technique is to obtain a reference to the first `<AUTHOR>` element using the `getElementsByTagName()` method of the `Document` object:

```
nodeAuthor = nodeXMLDoc.getElementsByTagName("AUTHOR").item(0);
```

This method allows us to retrieve the `<AUTHOR>` element without knowing the exact structure of the document. It does mean, however, that we need to know the exact `tagName` of the element, including the case of every character.

Accessing a NamedNodeMap

Our `NamedNodeMap` contains all the `Attribute` (or `Attr`) objects for this `<AUTHOR>`
element. We want the one named `authorStatus`, and we can use the
`getNamedItem()` method to return this as an `Attribute` node object. From there,
we can use the `value` property to find the attribute value:

```
...
attrStatus = mapStatus.getNamedItem("authorStatus");
strStatus = attrStatus.value;
...
```

Alternatively, we could get the same result directly by using the `getAttribute()`
method:

```
strStatus = nodeAuthor.getAttribute("authorStatus");
```

Or, since the attribute we want is the first one, we could even access the
`NamedNodeMap` by index:

```
attrStatus = mapStatus.item(0);
strStatus = attrStatus.value;
```

Now we just need the author's first and last names. The `<AUTHOR>` element contains
two child element nodes — `<FIRST_NAME>` and `<LAST_NAME>` — which respectively
are the `firstChild` of the `<AUTHOR>` node, and its `nextSibling`:

```
...
nodeFirstName = nodeAuthor.firstChild;
nodeLastName = nodeFirstName.nextSibling;
...
```

Accessing an Element's Text Content

In the last chapter we saw that for an `Element` node, the *value* is stored in a `Text` node
object that is a child node of the element. That means we need the `nodeValue`
property of the `firstChild` of each of the elements we just discovered. Then we can
build up our message string, and display it in an `alert` dialog:

```
...
strName = nodeFirstName.firstChild.nodeValue + ' ' +
          nodeLastName.firstChild.nodeValue;
strMessage = 'First author details are:\n\nName: ' +
             strName + '\nStatus: ' + strStatus;
alert(strMessage);
}

</SCRIPT>
```

Here's the result:

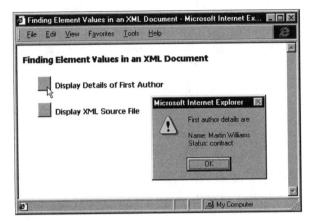

We've worked through this example in detail to show you how the tree structure looks when you access it through script code. In the next example, we'll access and display values for the entire tree of XML data.

Parsing XML Documents Using Recursion

Being able to extract values from a tree as we did in the previous example is fine if you know the exact structure of the XML document. In many cases, however, we want to produce code that can access more generic XML documents, within which the names of the elements and their relative positions within the structure aren't known beforehand. This involves 'walking' the tree, and exploring the structure as we go.

The usual way to cope with walking all kinds of data structures, especially trees, is through **recursion**. Although this is a very common technique, and is simple enough to grasp conceptually, it can become quite complex when you come to write programs that use it, and it is so important that it is worth explaining here in a little detail.

What is Recursion?

Recursion just means using a function or a section of code that calls itself repeatedly until a certain condition is reached. And until that condition *is* reached, each instance of the function is nested within the previous one that called it, as though it's a totally separate function. As each function ends (when the terminating condition is reached), the code 'unwinds' each call by completing the remaining code in the calling function, and then dropping back to the previous one. You'll see what this means in more detail when we come to look at the code.

The name of the file for this example is `simpleparse.htm`, *and as usual it can be run or downloaded from the Wrox web site.*

Apart from the script code, our sample page contains three important items. There is the usual data island to insert the XML document into the page — the same one that we used in the previous example. There's also an ONLOAD attribute in the page's opening <BODY> tag, which will execute the showBooks function as soon as the page has finished loading. Finally, there's a <DIV> element named divResults, into which we'll insert the results of parsing the document:

```
<XML ID="domBookList" SRC="onebook.xml"></XML>
...
<BODY BGCOLOR="#FFFFFF" ONLOAD="showBooks()">
...
<!-- to insert the results of parsing the document -->
<DIV ID="divResults"></DIV>
```

The Code to Walk the XML Tree

The remainder of the page just contains the style information and the page headings, plus the script code listed below. There are two script functions, the first of which — showBooks() — looks like this:

```
function showBooks()
{
    // Get a reference to the embedded XML document
    objXMLDoc = document.all("domBookList").XMLDocument;

    // Show the node and child node information
    divResults.innerHTML = showChildNodes(objXMLDoc);
}
```

This simple code just gets a reference to the XML document root, and passes this node object to a second function named showChildNodes(). The return value of this function is a string that we display in the divResults element on the page. This string contains a list of the names of the nodes in the XML document, in the order that they appear. Here's the result:

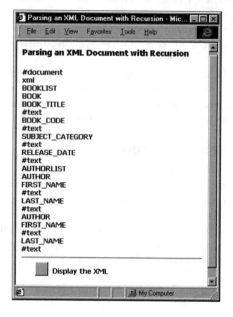

The showChildNodes() Function

The actual walking of the tree to create this string is done by the recursive function named showChildNodes(), which is listed below. All it does is read the name of the node passed to it (in the objNode parameter) from that node's nodeName property, and then examine the length of that node's childNodes property. The childNodes property, as you'll recall from the section on the XML Node object in Chapter 5, returns a NodeList that contains all the child nodes of the current node, and its length property returns the number of child nodes in the NodeList:

```
function showChildNodes(objNode)
{
    // Declare local variables for recursion
    var strNodes = '';
    var intCount = 0;
    var intNode = 0;

    // Show this node information
    strNodes += '<B>' + objNode.nodeName + '</B><BR>';

    // Count number of child nodes
    intCount = objNode.childNodes.length;
    ...
```

If childNodes.length returns a number greater than zero, we need to examine these child nodes to see what they contain. We do this by iterating through them with a for loop (we could use other techniques, such as the reset and nextNode methods, instead, but remember that these are IE5-specific). For each node in the childNodes list, we call the showChildNodes() function and pass the child node object to it. The returned string is added to the string containing the name of the original node that we created when we first entered this function (for the moment, the formatting is kept very simple, but we'll refine it a little later):

```
...
if(intCount > 0)
{
    // For each child node, display node and child node information
    for(intNode = 0; intNode < intCount; intNode++)
    {
        strNodes += showChildNodes(objNode.childNodes(intNode));
        ...
```

Here We Go Round Again

This is where we discover if you were awake, because you should have noticed that the function we just called is the same as the one we are currently executing: showChildNodes(). All that happens is that the function runs again from the beginning, but this time starting at the node that we've passed it as a parameter here. This is the first *child* node of the original node, which was the document root node.

The function will get the name of the child node, then look at the child nodes of that node. Each time the function calls itself, the names of each node are added to the result string in the order that they occur in the document — starting from the root and working down each branch in turn. Only when it reaches a leaf node with no child nodes (that is, when objNode.childNodes.length = 0) or it reaches the end of the list of child nodes does a function call return, allowing the previous call to continue where it left off with the previous node's child nodes.

```
       . . .
    }
  }
  return strNodes;
}
```

When the 'outermost' function call ends, the final outcome is a string containing the information you saw in the previous screenshot, starting with the root node and working down through the tree in order.

When you're using recursion, it is important to remember to ensure that each variable used within the function is *local* to the function. Recursion depends on the ability of each nested instance of the function to modify its own variables without changing the values in other instances of the function. In the example, we make sure of this by declaring new variables within the function, making them local to it. The current instances of the variables temporarily override the previous instances with the same name, but only while this instance of the function is executing:

```
// Declare local variables for recursion
var strNodes = '';
var intCount = 0;
var intNode = 0;
```

Displaying the Node Values

Our previous example simply displayed the name of each node as we encountered it in the tree. The display is somewhat crude, and doesn't reflect the content or structure of the XML document very well. We can do better. The next example retrieves the value of the node *and* the node type as well. It also indents the results to show the structure of the XML document more clearly.

The name of this sample file is parsewithvalues.htm.

The first step is to include a parameter that indicates the level we're at in the document tree — in other words, the number of nested elements 'deep' we are into the structure. We'll pass this value as a second parameter to our showChildNodes() function, and we start at zero with the root node:

```
function showBooks()
{
    . . .
    // Show the node and child node information
    divResults.innerHTML = showChildNodes(objXMLDoc, 0);
}
```

Indenting the Result Lines

The next step is to add the appropriate amount of indentation each time we enter the showChildNodes() function. For every nesting level, we'll add three non-breaking spaces to the result string as we enter the function. We know the current level from the new intLevel variable that appears as a parameter to the function:

```
function showChildNodes(objNode, intLevel)
{
   var strNodes = '';
   var intCount = 0;
   var intNode = 0;

   // Show this node information
   for(intIndent = 0; intIndent < intLevel; intIndent++)
   {
      strNodes += '   '
   }
   ...
```

Now we can get the extra information we want about the current node. We use the
nodeType property to get the node type, but this returns a numeric value so we need
to run it through a custom routine named getNodeType() to convert it to a string;
we'll come back to this routine later. In the meantime, we also use the nodeValue
property to get the node value:

```
   ...
   strNodes += '<B>' + objNode.nodeName +
               '</B>   Type: <B>' +
               getNodeType(objNode.nodeType) +
               '</B>   Value: <B>' +
               objNode.nodeValue + '</B><BR>';
   // Count number of child nodes
   intCount = objNode.childNodes.length;
   ...
```

One other thing that we have to remember is to increment the indent level when we
call the function recursively to display the values from the child nodes of this node:

```
   ...
   if(intCount > 0)
   {
      // For each child node, display the node and child node information
      for(intNode = 0; intNode < intCount; intNode++)
      {
         strNodes += showChildNodes(objNode.childNodes(intNode),
                                    intLevel + 1);
      }
   }
   return strNodes;
}
```

Deciphering the NodeType

The only remaining task is to implement the getNodeType() function that converts
the nodeType property value into a string. This is the code I used; it includes the
nodeType value in the resulting string as well:

```
function getNodeType(intType)
{
   switch(intType)
   {
      case 1:
         return "ELEMENT (1)";
         break;
      case 2:
         return "ATTRIBUTE (2)";
         break;
```

```
   case 3:
      return "TEXT (3)";
      break;
   case 4:
      return "CDATA SECTION (4)";
      break;
   case 5:
      return "ENTITY REFERENCE (5)";
      break;
   case 6:
      return "ENTITY (6)";
      break;
   case 7:
      return "PROCESSING INSTRUCTION (7)";
      break;
   case 8:
      return "COMMENT (8)";
      break;
   case 9:
      return "DOCUMENT (9)";
      break;
   case 10:
      return "DOCUMENT TYPE (10)";
      break;
   case 11:
      return "DOCUMENT FRAGMENT (11)";
      break;
   case 12:
      return "NOTATION (12)";
   }
}
```

*Note that the IE5-specific extensions to the W3C DOM Recommendation
include the* `nodeTypeString` *property, which returns the node type as a
string. This could be used instead of the function we've listed here, but doing
so would tie the code to IE5. Using a custom function also allows us to use our
own names, so we return* 'DOCUMENT TYPE (10)' *(with spaces) instead of
the* `nodeTypeString` *value* 'DOCUMENT_TYPE'.

Here's the result of all our efforts. I
think you'll agree that it's a lot more
informative:

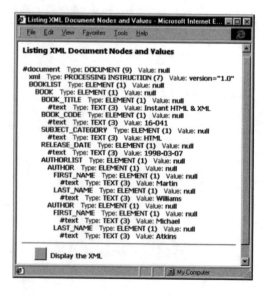

Something's Still Missing

A final improvement to our parsing example would be to make sure that we include *all* the useful information from the XML document. If you look back at the previous screenshot, you can see that there are some things missing. To be more exact, the page doesn't show the details of any of the `Attributes` in the document. Both the document itself, and all of the element nodes, can have attributes. In our example XML file, repeated below, there are attributes for the `<BOOK>` and `<AUTHOR>` elements:

```
<?xml version="1.0"?>
<BOOKLIST>
    <BOOK itemType="Reference">
        <BOOK_TITLE>Instant HTML &amp; XML</BOOK_TITLE>
        <BOOK_CODE>16-041</BOOK_CODE>
        <SUBJECT_CATEGORY>HTML</SUBJECT_CATEGORY>
        <RELEASE_DATE>1998-03-07</RELEASE_DATE>
        <AUTHORLIST>
            <AUTHOR authorStatus="contract">
                <FIRST_NAME>Martin</FIRST_NAME>
                <LAST_NAME>Williams</LAST_NAME>
            </AUTHOR>
            <AUTHOR authorStatus="retired">
                <FIRST_NAME>Michael</FIRST_NAME>
                <LAST_NAME>Atkins</LAST_NAME>
            </AUTHOR>
        </AUTHORLIST>
    </BOOK>
</BOOKLIST>
```

If we want to include details of attributes as well as the other types of nodes, we need to modify our parsing code again — and why not? `Attributes` are nodes as well, so it's not fair to leave them out. But if they *are* nodes, why didn't they appear in our tree when we walked it from top to bottom?

We don't have to look too far for the answer. We only iterated through the `NodeList` exposed by each node's `childNodes` property. Attributes are exposed through a `NamedNodeMap` that is referenced through a node's `attributes` property. We need to add some code to our example for walking through the `attributes` list as well as the `childNodes` list for each element.

Iterating Through the Attributes List

The changes to the code are not extensive, and only involve the `showChildNodes()` function. The plan is that while we've got hold of a node to retrieve its type and value, we'll iterate through its `attributes` list as well. Technically, we should allow for the situation where attribute nodes have their own child or attribute nodes (remember, each one has a `childNodes` property and an `attributes` property), but we'll assume for now that this isn't necessary.

Here's the new `showChildNodes()` function, with the added section highlighted:

```
function showChildNodes(objNode, intLevel)
{
    ...
    // Get the values for this node
    strNodes += getIndent(intLevel) + '<B>' + objNode.nodeName +
                '</B>   Type: <B>' + getNodeType(objNode.nodeType) +
                '</B>   Value: <B>' + objNode.nodeValue + '</B><BR>';
```

```
        // Check for any attributes
        objAttrList = objNode.attributes;
        if(objAttrList != null)
        {
            intCount = objAttrList.length;
            if(intCount > 0)
            {
                // For each attribute, display the attribute information
                for(intAttr = 0; intAttr < intCount; intAttr++)
                {
                    strNodes += getIndent(intLevel + 1) + '<B>' +
                                objAttrList(intAttr).nodeName +
                                '</B>   Type: <B>' +
                                getNodeType(objAttrList(intAttr).nodeType) +
                                '</B>   Value: <B>' +
                                objAttrList(intAttr).nodeValue + '</B><BR>';
                }
            }
        }

        // Check for any child nodes
        intCount = objNode.childNodes.length;
        if(intCount > 0)
        {
            for(intNode = 0; intNode < intCount; intNode++)
            {
                strNodes += showChildNodes(objNode.childNodes(intNode),
                                intLevel + 1);
            }
        }
        return strNodes;
    }
```

All this does is check if the `NamedNodeMap` exposed by the `attributes` property of each element is `null`, and if not it iterates through the attributes reading their `nodeName`, `nodeType` and `nodeValue` properties, in much the same way as we did before with ordinary child nodes. The one main difference comes from the fact that we iterate through all the attributes of this node first, adding them to the result string, then loop recursively through each of its child nodes and their descendants.

Adding the Line Indents to the Output

In fact, one other change is visible in the code above. Because we need to indent the output lines for attributes as well as child nodes, I extracted the code that adds the non-breaking spaces into a separate function:

```
function getIndent(intLevel)
{
    var strIndent = '';
    for(var intIndent = 0; intIndent < intLevel; intIndent++)
        strIndent += '     '
    return strIndent;
}
```

This function returns a string that contains the correct number of ` ` characters, and we can call it from the appropriate places in our `showChildNodes()` function.

Here's the result of all our changes to the code:

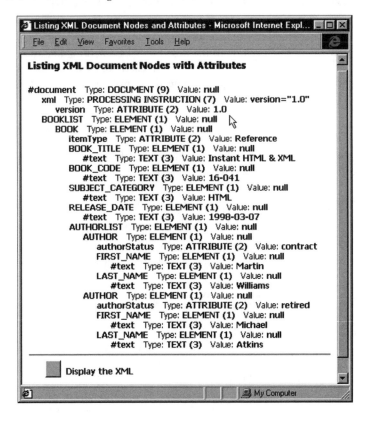

This example appears in the files that you can run or download from the Wrox web site; it's called `parsewithattr.htm`*.*

Looking at the Results

By examining the results of this example, you get a glimpse of the way that the nodes of an XML document are structured and nested. Viewing the content in this way makes it easier to visualize how all the parts of the document are arranged. For example, you can see that the root node is named #document, and has the value null, while the <?xml...?> declaration has its own attribute containing the precise version information.

Note also the final proof that each Element node has the value null. If there is a content string for an Element node, it appears within a child Text node below that element. In fact, it's worth spending some time looking at the results of parsing several documents with this simple page. All you have to do is change the SRC attribute value of the <XML> data island to load a different XML file:

```
<XML ID="domBookList" SRC="MyOwnDocument.xml"></XML>
```

Custom Tools for Experimentation

Our previous examples for parsing a document are an extremely useful aid to grasping how the XML Document Object Model can structure and store XML documents, but we're still nowhere near the limit of the possibilities. Something that can often be confusing is the large number of properties that each node exposes — many of which seem to contain the same values. We also need to consider in more depth how we go about editing an XML document, using the methods that each node provides.

We'll take a look here at two custom tools I've built to make understanding the DOM easier. You can run them directly from the Wrox web site, or download them to run on your own system. This is the XML file to be used in the first example; you can see that this time I've included a DTD as well:

```
<?xml version="1.0"?>
<!-- simple listing of one book -->
<!DOCTYPE BOOKLIST [
    <!ELEMENT BOOKLIST (BOOK+)>
    <!ELEMENT BOOK (BOOK_TITLE, BOOK_CODE, SUBJECT_CATEGORY,
                    RELEASE_DATE, AUTHORLIST)>
        <!ATTLIST BOOK itemType (Reference | Periodical | Article)
                        'Reference'>
    <!ELEMENT BOOK_TITLE (#PCDATA)>
    <!ELEMENT BOOK_CODE (#PCDATA)>
    <!ELEMENT SUBJECT_CATEGORY (#PCDATA)>
    <!ELEMENT RELEASE_DATE (#PCDATA)>
    <!ELEMENT AUTHORLIST (AUTHOR*)>
    <!ELEMENT AUTHOR (FIRST_NAME, LAST_NAME)>
        <!ATTLIST AUTHOR authorStatus CDATA #IMPLIED>
    <!ELEMENT FIRST_NAME (#PCDATA)>
    <!ELEMENT LAST_NAME (#PCDATA)>
    <!ENTITY cat_scr 'Client-side Scripting'>
    <!ENTITY cat_html 'Hypertext Markup Languages'>
    <!NOTATION bookcodes PUBLIC '-//wrox//TEXT bookcodes//EN'
                        'http://wrox/com/dummy.txt'>
]>
<BOOKLIST>
    <BOOK itemType="Reference">
        <BOOK_TITLE>Instant HTML &amp; XML</BOOK_TITLE>
        <BOOK_CODE>16-041</BOOK_CODE>
        <SUBJECT_CATEGORY>&cat_html;</SUBJECT_CATEGORY>
        <RELEASE_DATE>1998-03-07</RELEASE_DATE>
        <AUTHORLIST>
            <AUTHOR authorStatus="contract">
                <FIRST_NAME>Martin</FIRST_NAME>
                <LAST_NAME>Williams</LAST_NAME>
            </AUTHOR>
            <AUTHOR authorStatus="retired">
                <FIRST_NAME>Michael</FIRST_NAME>
                <LAST_NAME>Atkins</LAST_NAME>
            </AUTHOR>
        </AUTHORLIST>
    </BOOK>
</BOOKLIST>
```

This is the file we'll be analyzing in our discussions here, but don't forget that you can change the XML file that is used in either of the examples by editing the <XML> data island element's SRC attribute.

Displaying the XML Node's Properties

Iterating through the XML document to display a few values of each node is certainly useful, as we saw in the previous section. However, we only displayed the three common values: `nodeName`, `nodeType` and `nodeValue`. There are many more interesting ones than that, and the next example page displays almost all the available properties for each node.

The page itself is several times more complex than the simple parsing examples we've looked at so far, although much of this complexity is related to managing user navigation around the page, and displaying the node properties dynamically. As this book is about XML (not scripting techniques with Dynamic HTML), I won't be describing how the page works in great detail. We'll just examine the individual techniques that you might find useful when building your own XML applications. Of course, you can download the page (it's called `docproperties.htm`) with the rest of the samples and dissect it yourself if you wish.

The Document Node Properties

When you first open the page, it shows a listing of the nodes in the document (just like we saw earlier), but this time the root node is highlighted, and its properties are listed alongside the XML document:

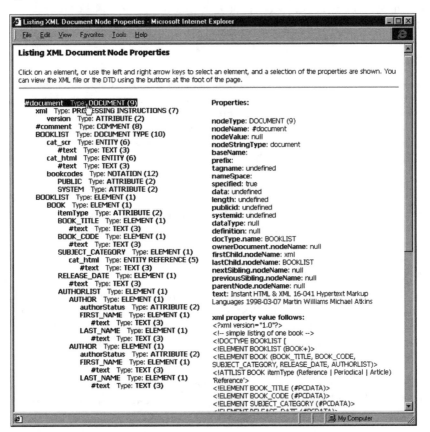

Here you can see the proof that the Document node at the root of the document actually *does* contain the whole XML structure. The text property shows the entire text (non-markup) content of the file, and the xml property contains the complete XML file content (including the DTD — you'll have to scroll the example page to see it all because we couldn't get it all on-screen in one go!).

You can also see that many of the properties return undefined or null. This is because each node is built on a generic Node object, which contains properties that are often only useful with particular kinds of nodes. However, by leaving them in the Node object, it means that we don't get an error if we try to access them. We just get null or undefined returned by our JavaScript or JScript code.

Displaying Values of Properties that Return Node Objects

Some properties of each node return a Node object, a NodeList object or a NamedNodeMap object. This makes accessing the values harder, because if we access the value of (say) the firstChild property, we'll get either null or "[object]" returned. If there are any child nodes, the property contains a Node object rather than a simple string value.

To get round this, we might be tempted to access and display the firstChild.nodeName property directly. The problem now is that an error will occur if there *isn't* a firstChild — in other words, if the firstChild property returns null. The solution is to check the property value first, and only access the nodeName (or any other) properties of the child object if the property value is not null.

Best of all, JavaScript and JScript make this task easier than you might have thought. If you weren't brought up on C or C++, you might not have come across this, so it's worth examining here. The following cryptic statement uses the '?' operator to make a choice between two values. If the condition in the first pair of parentheses is true, it returns the first value after the '?'. If the condition evaluates to false, it returns the second value — the one after the colon:

```
x = ((objNode.firstChild != null) ? objNode.firstChild.nodeName : null);
```

So, in this example, the variable x will contain either the value of the nodeName property of the first child node of objNode, or null if objNode has no child nodes. That's exactly what we want!

How Our Example Works

As you'll have guessed, the example page iterates through the XML document in much the same way as the previous examples we've looked at in this chapter. In addition, however, it collects the values of the node properties as it navigates through the document. This makes it easier to display them when required, instead of looking them up each time the user selects a different node.

To store the values, we use an array. JavaScript only supports one-dimensional arrays, so we have to cheat a little because we actually want a two-dimensional array — we want to store an array of property values *for each node*.

198

As the page is parsed, we keep a count of the line number using a global variable called intLastLine. This starts at zero and is incremented as we parse each node. We also declare a global array named arrLines:

```
var intLastLine = 0;
var arrLines = new Array();
```

As we parse each node in the XML tree, we create a new array and attach it to the current entry in the original arrLines array. This effectively gives us our two-dimensional array:

```
arrLines[intLastLine] = new Array();
```

Now we can go ahead and fill the new array with the property values we want from the current node. We build up strings that we'll use to display the property name and value when this node is selected, and insert each into the array. Notice the entry for property entry number 17, which uses the '?' operator we met earlier:

```
arrLines[intLastLine][0] = '<b>nodeType</b>: ' +
                           getNodeType(objNode.nodeType);
arrLines[intLastLine][1] = '<b>nodeName</b>: ' + objNode.nodeName;
arrLines[intLastLine][2] = '<b>nodeValue</b>: ' + objNode.nodeValue;
arrLines[intLastLine][3] = '<b>nodeStringType</b>: ' +
                           objNode.nodeStringType;
arrLines[intLastLine][4] = '<b>baseName</b>: ' + objNode.baseName;
...
...
arrLines[intLastLine][17] = '<b>firstChild.nodeName</b>: ' +
        ((objNode.firstChild != null) ? objNode.firstChild.nodeName : null);
...
...
arrLines[intLastLine][22] = '<b>text</b>: ' + objNode.text;
arrLines[intLastLine][23] = '<br><b>xml property value:</b><br>' +
                            htmlEncode(objNode.xml);
```

HTML-Encoding the XML Property Value

The final entry is also interesting, in that it uses the htmlEncode function to convert the XML string returned by the xml property into a string that can be displayed in the page. If we didn't do this, the browser would treat the '<' and '>' characters as being HTML, think that each XML element was just an HTML tag it didn't recognize — and not display anything!

If you're acquainted with Active Server Pages, you'll be familiar with the HTMLEncode method that the ASP Server object provides. However, JavaScript and JScript don't offer this function, and so instead we have to build our own. We need to convert (encode) non-legal HTML characters that can't be displayed directly in a page into their legal equivalents:

```
function htmlEncode(strInput)
{
   strCRLF = String.fromCharCode(13, 10);
   strThis = doReplace(strInput, "<", "&lt;");
   strThis = doReplace(strThis, ">", "&gt;");
   strThis = doReplace(strThis, strCRLF, "<BR>");
   return strThis;
}
```

```
function doReplace(strSource, strReplace, strWith)
{
   strIn = strSource;
   intPosn = strIn.indexOf(strReplace);
   if(intPosn >= 0)
   {
      do
      {
         if(intPosn > 0)
            strLeft = strIn.substr(0, intPosn)
         else
            strLeft = '';
         if(intPosn < strIn.length - 1)
            strRight = strIn.substr(intPosn + 1)
         else
            strRight = '';
         strIn = strLeft + strWith + strRight;
         intPosn = strIn.indexOf(strReplace);
      } while(strIn.indexOf(strReplace) >= 0);
   }
   return strIn;
}
```

This code doesn't encode (convert) *every* non-legal HTML character, only those that affect the display in a page. (We don't need to convert ampersands because they must already be escaped within the XML document, or else they would be interpreted by the parser as the beginning of an entity name.) If you want to display the results in an HTML control, such as a text box, you'll have to convert other characters as well — the double-quote, for example. However, you can easily add lines to the `htmlEncode()` function to replace any characters you require:

```
function htmlEncode(strInput)
{
   strCRLF = String.fromCharCode(13, 10);
   strThis = doReplace(strInput, "<", "&lt;");
   strThis = doReplace(strThis, ">", "&gt;");
   strThis = doReplace(strThis, '"', "&quot;");
   strThis = doReplace(strThis, "'", "&apos;");
   strThis = doReplace(strThis, "&", "&amp;");
   strThis = doReplace(strThis, strCRLF, "<BR>");
   return strThis;
}
```

Using the DocProperties Page

Let's look briefly at some of the other interesting results that our example page provides. If you select an `Element` node, such as the `<AUTHORLIST>` element, you can see that many of the properties return `undefined` or `null`. But the `text` and `xml` properties *do* provide really useful results — the entire content of the sub-tree, starting from the selected node. The one vital point to remember is that these useful properties are *not* part of the W3C DOM Recommendation. They are implemented by the `IXMLDOMNode` interface and they're IE5-specific, so if you are building cross-platform applications, you must avoid them:

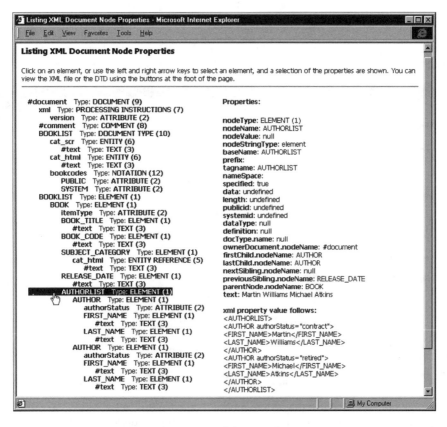

However, the xml property is also very useful in another way: it gives us access to the DTD. If you select the first BOOKLIST node (the DOCUMENT TYPE node), you'll see that (for an internal DTD) the xml property returns the entire DTD. (For an external DTD, only the DOCTYPE declaration is returned.)

```
xml property value follows:
<!DOCTYPE BOOKLIST [
<!ELEMENT BOOKLIST (BOOK+)>
<!ELEMENT BOOK (BOOK_TITLE, BOOK_CODE, SUBJECT_CATEGORY,
RELEASE_DATE, AUTHORLIST)>
<!ATTLIST BOOK itemType (Reference | Periodical | Article) 'Reference'>
<!ELEMENT BOOK_TITLE (#PCDATA)>
<!ELEMENT BOOK_CODE (#PCDATA)>
<!ELEMENT SUBJECT_CATEGORY (#PCDATA)>
<!ELEMENT RELEASE_DATE (#PCDATA)>
<!ELEMENT AUTHORLIST (AUTHOR*)>
<!ELEMENT AUTHOR (FIRST_NAME, LAST_NAME)>
<!ATTLIST AUTHOR authorStatus CDATA #IMPLIED)>
<!ELEMENT FIRST_NAME (#PCDATA)>
<!ELEMENT LAST_NAME (#PCDATA)>
<!ENTITY cat_scr 'Client-side Scripting'>
<!ENTITY cat_html 'Hypertext Markup Languages'>
<!NOTATION bookcodes PUBLIC '-//wrox//TEXT bookcodes//EN'
'http://wrox/com/dummy.txt'>
]>
```

This example should therefore help you to get a clearer picture of the kinds of information available from each node's properties, and how they relate to each other. One interesting point that you might like to investigate for yourself is the set of properties exposed by Attribute (or Attr) nodes. In the next screenshot, you can see that the firstChild and lastChild properties return the value '#text':

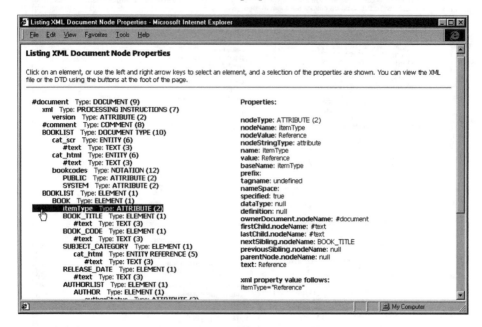

Although our code to parse the document doesn't reveal this, these values are the nodeName of the single Text child node of the Attribute node. Its nodeValue is the value of the attribute. So, our earlier assumption that Attribute nodes are leaf nodes (that they have no child nodes) is not strictly true. However, we can obtain the attribute name and value directly from the name, nodeName, value, and nodeValue properties of the Attribute node (nodeAttr.nodeValue returns exactly the same as nodeAttr.firstChild.nodeValue, for example), so we won't generally be interested in the child nodes of an attribute.

Editing the XML Document Content

Being able to *display* the values of a node's properties is great, but what about the other programmatic opportunities that are available? We can *set* the values of most properties to change the content of the XML document while it is loaded and cached on the client. On top of that, all nodes have a set of *methods*, which we used only briefly in code in the previous chapter. These too can change the content of a document as well as just retrieving objects and values from it.

Our next example is a page that allows you to execute these methods and see the results. They act on the stored representation of the XML document, and the updated document content is then displayed again so that the effects are made visible. This is a good way to get used to seeing what's actually possible, and to experiment with the various techniques.

202

This example, named editxml.htm, *can be run from our web site or downloaded to run on your own machine. However, note that this example uses a web server running Active Server Pages to 'reflect' the XML page back to the browser again. If you download the examples to run on your own system, it's important to realize that you can't run it directly as a file from your local hard drive. You have to place the pages on your web server and specify the* http:// *protocol and the server address:*

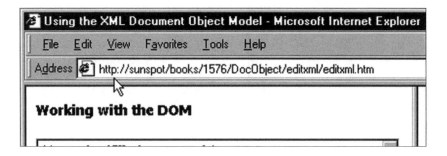

Alternatively, you can use the copy of the page on our server at
http://webdev.wrox.co.uk/books/1576/DocObject/editxml/returnxml.asp

The basic page for this example just instantiates a <frameset> consisting of two pages:

```
<frameset cols="400, *">
    <frame src="controlpanel.htm">
    <frame src="domtest.xml" NAME="fraDisplay">
</frameset>
```

The left-hand page provides a text area where you can enter a series of script commands, and a button to execute those commands. The right-hand page contains the source XML document in its original form, automatically parsed by IE5 and displayed as a collapsible tree. The XML document we're using is similar to the previous example, but has a couple of extra element nodes containing details of a third author, as you can see overleaf:

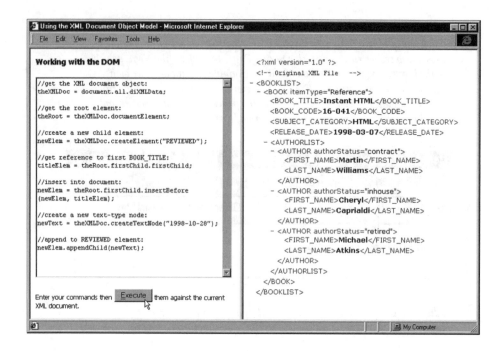

Adding an Element to the XML Document

Looking at the left-hand page of the example, you'll see that we've provided a series of default commands in the text area. These are similar to the series of commands that we used in the previous chapter to insert a new `Element` node into an XML document. The first two commands will be required every time, as they create the reference to the XML data island and its document content:

```
// Get the XML document object
theXMLDoc = document.all.diXMLData;

// Get the outermost element
theRoot = theXMLDoc.documentElement;

// Create a new element
newElem = theXMLDoc.createElement("REVIEWED");

// Get reference to first BOOK_TITLE
titleElem = theRoot.firstChild.firstChild;

// Insert into document
newElem = theRoot.firstChild.insertBefore(newElem, titleElem);

// Create a new text-type node
newText = theXMLDoc.createTextNode("1998-10-28");

// Append to REVIEWED element
newElem.appendChild(newText);
```

The remaining commands create a new Element node named <REVIEWED>, and insert it into the document as the first child of the <BOOK> element. Then they create a new Text node with the value "1998-10-28" to hold the value of the <REVIEWED> element, and insert it as the first child of that element. Here's the result of executing this code:

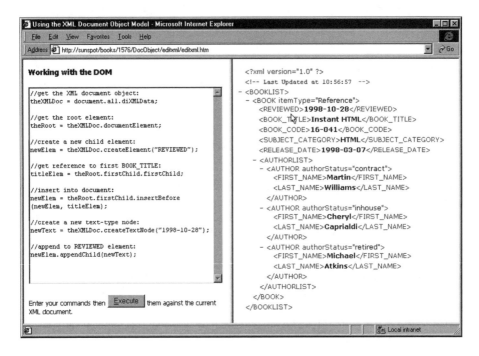

How Our EditXML Example Page Works

The left-hand page in our example is actually quite simple. It contains the now customary <XML> data island, the HTML to create and pre-fill the HTML <TEXTAREA> control, and a <FORM> containing a HIDDEN-type HTML control and the Execute button:

```
<XML ID="diXMLData" SRC="domtest.xml"></XML>
...

<BODY BGCOLOR="#FFFFFF" ONLOAD="focusSet()">
...

   <TEXTAREA WRAP="PHYSICAL" NAME="txtCmd" COLS="50" ROWS="24"
            STYLE="font-family:Courier New; font-size:12px">

      // Get the XML document object
      theXMLDoc = document.all.diXMLData;

      ...
      ...this is the default text for the text area control
      ...

      // Append to REVIEWED element
      newElem.appendChild(newText);
   </TEXTAREA>
```

205

```
<FORM NAME="frmSend" ACTION="returnxml.asp"
                 TARGET="fraDisplay" METHOD="POST">
   <INPUT TYPE="HIDDEN" NAME="hidXML">
   Enter your commands then
   <BUTTON ACCESSKEY="E" ONCLICK="executeCommands()">
       <U>E</U>xecute
   </BUTTON>
   them against the current XML document.
</FORM>
</BODY>
```

There are just two script functions. The first, executed when the page loads, merely sets the input focus to the <TEXTAREA> control. This allows the user to start typing straight away:

```
function focusSet()
{
   document.all.txtCmd.focus();
}
```

While we're on the topic of making the user's life easier, and in case you haven't seen this trick with IE4/5 and its 'enhanced forms' capability before, I've also included a 'hot-key' feature — just like in a real Windows application. The Execute button has the 'E' underlined, and pressing *Alt+E* on the keyboard clicks the button automatically (as long as this page has the focus).

Looking back at the previous code listing, in the <FORM> section, you can see that this is done using a <BUTTON> element and the ACCESSKEY attribute. The caption of the button is rendered as HTML, which is why we can use the <U> and </U> tags to underline the 'E'. You can even include a graphic by using an <IMG> element in the button face if you wish.

Executing the User's Commands

The Execute button runs the executeCommands() function when clicked:

```
function executeCommands()
{
   // Get users DOM XML commands as a string
   strCmd = '' + document.all.txtCmd.value;

   // Execute the commands
   eval(strCmd);

   // Put resulting XML into hidden control...
   document.all.hidXML.value = diXMLData.documentElement.xml;

   // ...and submit the form to our ASP 'reflector' page
   frmSend.submit();
}
```

All this does is collect the contents of the text area control as a String variable (by appending it to an empty string), and evaluate it as JavaScript code using the eval() function. This executes the commands in the string just as though they were typed into a <SCRIPT> section. In our case, these commands will update the stored XML document that is exposed by our <XML> element data island.

Next, we collect the XML content of the document from the xml property of the outermost element node (retrieved through the document's documentElement property). We place this into the HIDDEN-type HTML control named hidXML. Finally, we submit() the form to our server. The URL of the page we're submitting it to is given in the ACTION attribute of the opening <FORM> tag, and the value in the TARGET attribute means that the response will be directed to the other (right-hand) window, which we named fraDisplay in the frameset page:

```
<FORM NAME="frmSend" ACTION="returnxml.asp"
                 TARGET="fraDisplay" METHOD="POST">
```

Returning the Updated XML Document

Our server receives the contents of the form and passes it to an Active Server Pages file named returnxml.asp. All this has to do is bounce the XML back to the client browser, where it will be displayed in the right-hand frame. However, we're sending the xml property of the outermost element node, and although this contains all the XML data in the document, it's missing the <?xml version="1.0"?> line and the comment node. The xml property doesn't include any nodes that precede the outermost Element node, which in this case is our <BOOKLIST> element:

```
<?xml version="1.0"?>
<!-- Original XML File -->
<BOOKLIST>
...
```

Getting round this is easy enough: we create a new 'xml version' line and a new comment line on the server. This also allows us to change the comment to show the current processing time of the file as well. In case you're used to ASP, this is the complete returnxml.asp page:

```
<%@ LANGUAGE="VBSCRIPT" %>
<%
QUOT = Chr(34)
CRLF = Chr(13) & Chr(10)
strNow = Right("0" & CStr(Hour(Now)), 2) & ":" _
      & Right("0" & CStr(Minute(Now)), 2) & ":" _
      & Right("0" & CStr(Second(Now)), 2)
Response.ContentType = "text/xml"
Response.Write "<?xml version=" & QUOT & "1.0" & QUOT & "?>" & CRLF
Response.Write "<!-- Last Updated at " & strNow & "-->" & CRLF
Response.Write Request("hidXML")
%>
```

Although it is customary to use JavaScript/JScript on the client side for cross-browser compatibility, it is common to use VBScript on the server side because ASP only needs to be supported by the server. VBScript has some useful built-in error-handling features that JavaScript lacks.

Even if you haven't used ASP before, it should be easy to see what's happening in the code. One of the things we do is to set the ContentType of the returned XML stream (the MIME type) to "text/xml".

If you want to use the server-based ASP pages that reflect XML content back to the browser in your own pages, but don't have a server handy, you can point your <FORM> element's ACTION attribute directly at the copy on our server, and have it return the page to you. The page is at http://webdev.wrox.co.uk/books/1576/DocObject/editxml/returnxml.asp.

Using the EditXML Page

As with our previous sample, we need to come back and have a look at some of the other results that this page can provide. You can use it to experiment with any of the DOM methods and properties — adding nodes, changing their properties, removing nodes, or restructuring whole sections of the document by building new document fragments and attaching them to the existing XML tree.

This next example uses the insertData() method that is available for nodes that extend the CharacterData object. In particular, we'll access the Text-type node that holds the value of an Attribute node, and insert some data into it. This is the code we'll use:

```
// Get the XML document object
theXMLDoc = document.all.diXMLData;

// Get the root element
theRoot = theXMLDoc.documentElement;

// Get the attributes for the <BOOK> node
mapBookAttrs = theRoot.firstChild.attributes;

// Get the Text node for the first attribute
attrBookText = mapBookAttrs(0).firstChild;

// Insert the word Computer into the text
attrBookText.insertData(0, 'Computer ');
```

After getting a reference to the root document node, we retrieve a NamedNodeMap that contains the attributes of the <BOOK> node. The Text node that we want is the first child of the first (and only) Attribute node in the NamedNodeMap. Once we've got our reference to it, we can use the insertData() method to add the word 'Computer' to the attribute value. The next screenshot shows the results in our example page after executing the code listed above:

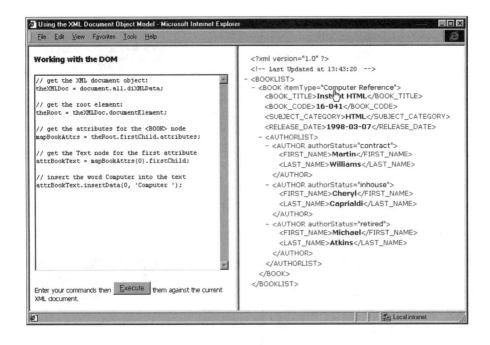

Removing Nodes and Displaying Values

You aren't limited to updating the existing XML tree. For example, if you want to get the value of a property while you're experimenting, you can use an `alert` dialog in the code. Here's a simple example that removes some nodes from the tree, and displays some results as it runs. The code we'll use is:

```
// Get the XML document object
theXMLDoc = document.all.diXMLData;

// Get the root element
theRoot = theXMLDoc.documentElement;

// Get NodeList of AUTHOR nodes
listNodes = theRoot.getElementsByTagName("AUTHOR");

// Display number found
alert('Found ' + listNodes.length + ' authors');

// Loop through list of authors
for (i = 0; i < listNodes.length; i++)
{
    // Get reference to this FIRST_NAME node...
    fNameNode = listNodes(i).childNodes(0);

    // ...and remove it from the document
    listNodes(i).removeChild(fNameNode);
}
```

Again, we start by getting a reference to our data island, and then set a variable called `theRoot` to point to the outermost XML element. This is the root `Document` element, which has a method named `getElementsByTagName()`. We can use this method to get a `NodeList` containing all the `<AUTHOR>` elements in the entire document, and then display the number we found in an `alert` dialog by querying the `length` property of the `NodeList`.

The next step is to iterate through the `NodeList` using a `for` loop. For each `<AUTHOR>` node, we get a reference to the first child `<FIRST_NAME>` node as the variable `fNameNode`, then call the `<AUTHOR>` element's `removeChild()` method to remove the `<FIRST_NAME>` node from the XML document. Here's the result in our example page after the code has been executed:

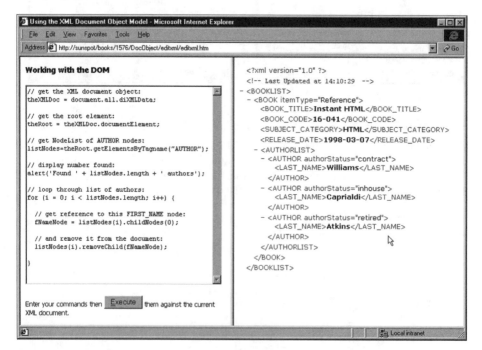

Error Messages

If you try to execute code that isn't semantically or syntactically correct, the browser displays the usual script error dialog. Of course, the line number refers to the script that is in the page, not the script that you typed into the text area control. The latter is executed as a string, using the JavaScript `eval()` method, and so it is the `eval()` method itself that will be reported as causing the error.

Summary

In this chapter, we've continued our investigation into the XML Document Object Model (DOM) by looking at some of the ways that we can use it when we build applications. Learning the theory, as we did in the previous chapter, is invaluable. However, seeing the pages parsed into lists of nodes, and the objects, methods and properties at work, makes it easier to assimilate the structure and content of the DOM.

We looked at some of the common code techniques that you'll use when working with the XML DOM, particularly how to iterate through a document using **recursion**. This powerful technique is likely to form the basis for many of your own applications.

We also looked at two custom applications that I've built to make learning about the XML DOM easier. The first displays most of the properties of each node in an XML document, allowing you to see how these relate to the document and to the other nodes in the tree. The second application allows you to execute any set of commands that use the DOM methods and properties, and view the results as an updated XML document. While these two applications are designed predominantly to be *used*, rather than held up as examples of script programming, they do contain code and techniques that you might well find useful in your own applications.

This chapter ends our study of the XML Document Object Model. In the next chapter, we move on to examine the **Extensible Stylesheet Language**, or **XSL**.

7

Using CSS and XSL with XML

This chapter covers another new XML-based programming technology: the control of presentation, style and content through the use of style sheets. This approach to controlling the appearance of web pages isn't new to experienced HTML programmers — **Cascading Style Sheets** (CSS) are at the second standards iteration, and have recently started to gain more widespread acceptance as the market share of the 'version 4' browsers has grown.

The good news is that CSS works in much the same way with XML as it does with HTML, so the time you spent learning about this technology isn't wasted. However, a far more powerful way of controlling style and content of XML documents is available: the **Extensible Stylesheet Language** or **XSL**. The current implementation of XSL in IE5 also includes much of the proposed **XML Query Language**, or XQL. When I talk about XSL in this book, you can assume that I'm talking about this XQL support as well.

In this chapter we'll look at both CSS and XSL/XQL, and see how we can use them to build attractive and functional pages. We'll also see how XSL adds a whole range of new features to traditional style sheets, by allowing the actual *content* of the document to be changed, rather than just the appearance. You'll see:

❑ The differences between CSS and XSL style languages

❑ How to use CSS to add style to XML documents

❑ An introduction to XSL and what it can achieve

❑ How we create and use XSL stylesheets

❑ A look at the future of the standards and likely changes to XSL

Like so much in the expanding world of XML, the standards are still maturing, and this is particularly true for XSL. We'll start with a look at where the various technologies stand at the time of writing, and when and how they may become standards that are widely accepted in a range of applications.

CSS, XSL and Standards

Having worked through the book to this point, you will be used to the flood of new techniques, new ideas, new proposals and recommendations that XML seems to have unleashed on an unsuspecting world. In this chapter, as they say in all the best movies, we've got some good news and some bad news. The good news is that having spent so long getting to grips with Cascading Style Sheets over the last year or so, you can continue to use them with XML. So, that's one less thing to learn from scratch.

The Difference between CSS and XSL

The bad news is that you're also going to have to learn a new (but far better) way to add style and formatting information to an XML document. The **Extensible Stylesheet Language** (XSL) is an all-new, exciting, and very different way to control the appearance of a document written in XML. Not only that, it can do a lot more than CSS will ever be able to achieve. XSL can change the *content* of the output document as well as changing the *style* of the elements in it.

To do this involves a fundamentally new approach to the way style information is applied to elements in the document. XSL requires a different mindset to understand how it works, and it's likely that many people will shy away from it at first — at least until some new development tools are available. However, the effort involved in coming to terms with XSL, although not insubstantial, is well worth it. Yes, XSL is complicated compared with many of the topics we've covered so far, but it is so incredibly useful and powerful that you really can't afford to ignore it.

Thankfully, in the way it's implemented within IE5, XSL uses HTML elements and CSS-type style properties to define the appearance of the output. This means that there is less to learn from scratch if you are already familiar with CSS techniques. In this chapter, we'll very briefly review the use of CSS with XML documents, then move on to look at XSL in more detail.

Adding Style with CSS

When we use Cascading Style Sheets with HTML documents, we can define the styles that apply to each element or class using a `<STYLE>` element, traditionally within the `<HEAD>` section of the page. For example, the following section of code defines the style for all `<P>` elements as 14pt green Arial text; and the style for all elements that have a `CLASS="myclass"` attribute as 12pt blue Courier text:

```
...
<HEAD>
   <STYLE TYPE="text/css">
      P          { font-family:Arial;   font-size:14pt; color:green }
      .myclass { font-family:Courier; font-size:12pt; color:blue  }
   </STYLE>
</HEAD>
...
```

Specifying Target Elements

CSS allows us to specify the target element for the style using the element name, as we did with the <P> element in the code above. We can be more specific about which are the target elements by indicating the nesting of the elements that we want to apply the style to. In the next example, the style is only applied to <EM> elements that lie within (are nested inside) a <P> element:

```
P EM    { font-family:Arial;   font-size:14pt; color:green }
```

Notice how this is different from the following, which separates the element names with a comma. Doing this applies the style to *all* <P> elements and *all* <EM> elements:

```
P, EM    { font-family:Arial;   font-size:14pt; color:green }
```

Specifying Target Classes

The example shown earlier also defines the style for a class named `myclass`. To indicate that this is a *custom* style class, we precede the name with a period:

```
.myclass { font-family:Courier; font-size:12pt; color:blue  }
```

We can now allocate this style to any element by using the CLASS attribute:

```
<P CLASS="myclass">Some text</P>
```

Dynamic Styles

The use of style classes is a popular technique when using Dynamic HTML, because script code can change the style of the element in response to an event. If we have different classes defined, we just set the `className` property of the element to the appropriate class using script code. This is much easier than changing each of the individual style properties one by one. In this simple example, we change the `className` property of a <P> element in response to the mouse moving over the element:

```
...
<STYLE TYPE="text/css">
   .big    { font-family:Arial;  font-size:24pt; font-weight:bold   }
   .little { font-family:Arial;  font-size:12pt; font-weight:normal }
</STYLE>

...

<P CLASS="little"  ID="myHeading"
                ONMOUSEOVER="makeBig();"
                ONMOUSEOUT="makeLittle();">
   Some text here
</P>

...

<SCRIPT LANGUAGE="JScript">
   function makeBig()
   {
      document.all('myHeading').className = 'big';
   }
```

```
    function makeLittle()
    {
        document.all('myHeading').className = 'little';
    }
</SCRIPT>
...
```

These are only simple examples of using CSS to format HTML elements, although you'll find a list of the CSS2 properties and values in the reference section of this book. If you want to learn more about CSS in general, I recommend you look out for *Instant HTML 4.0 Programmer's Reference* (ISBN 1-861001-56-8), also from Wrox Press.

Linked Style Sheets

The examples above use a <STYLE> section within an HTML document to define the style information. However, we can also link a style sheet to an HTML document using either the <LINK> element or the special @import style instruction. Both the following examples link a separate style sheet named mystyle.css to the HTML page:

```
<LINK REL="STYLESHEET" TYPE="text/css" HREF="mystyle.css">
```

```
<STYLE TYPE="text/css">
    @import url(mystyle.css);
</STYLE>
```

Adding Style to XML with CSS

In this book, what we're really interested in is how to use CSS style sheets with *XML documents*, rather than HTML documents. Here, though, a problem arises: how are we going to define the CSS style information in an XML document?

We can't use an HTML <STYLE> section, because it has no meaning in XML. In the same way, the <LINK> element means nothing in XML. For both these elements, the browser will simply display the content as data — you'll recall that this is the whole ethos behind XML. Each element means whatever the originator wanted it to mean.

The xml-stylesheet Processing Instruction

The solution to our problem is to use an XML processing instruction (PI). In Chapter 2, you learned that XML defines the special element <?xml ...?> as a processing instruction that can be used to give instructions to the XML parser. We use a special version of this PI to provide a link to a separate style sheet from within our XML documents:

```
<?xml-stylesheet type="text/css" href="mystyle.css" ?>
```

The XML parser or browser will fetch the style sheet from the location specified in the href attribute, and use it to format the content of the XML document. It's also possible to specify more than one stylesheet by using multiple xml-stylesheet instructions. In this case, the styles are merged, with those in the last style sheet taking precedence in cases of duplication.

Note that the earlier W3C proposal was for the use of a colon instead of a hyphen as the separator character:

```
<?xml:stylesheet type="text/css" href="mystyle.css" ?>
```

Internet Explorer 5 supports both versions of the syntax.

A Simple XML/CSS Formatting Example

This example shows how a simple CSS style sheet can be used to control the style and layout of an XML document. The XML document we're using is a list of three books. You can run this example from our web site at http://webdev.wrox.co.uk/books/1576/, or download it with the rest of the sample files; its name is cssformat.xml:

```
<?xml version="1.0"?>
<?xml-stylesheet type="text/css" href="booklist.css"?>
<BOOKLIST>
   <ITEM>
      <CODE>16-048</CODE>
      <CATEGORY>Scripting</CATEGORY>
      <RELEASE_DATE>1998-04-21</RELEASE_DATE>
      <TITLE>Instant JavaScript</TITLE>
      <SALES>375298</SALES>
   </ITEM>
   <ITEM>
      <CODE>16-105</CODE>
      <CATEGORY>ASP</CATEGORY>
      <RELEASE_DATE>1998-05-10</RELEASE_DATE>
      <TITLE>Instant Active Server Pages</TITLE>
      <SALES>297311</SALES>
   </ITEM>
   <ITEM>
      <CODE>16-041</CODE>
      <CATEGORY>HTML</CATEGORY>
      <RELEASE_DATE>1998-03-07</RELEASE_DATE>
      <TITLE>Instant HTML</TITLE>
      <SALES>127853</SALES>
   </ITEM>
</BOOKLIST>
```

The CSS Stylesheet

You can see that the second line of the XML document above is the processing instruction that specifies the stylesheet named booklist.css. Here is the entire content of that file:

```
ITEM          { display:block; margin:15px }

CODE          { display:inline;
                font-family:Tahoma, Arial, sans-serif;
                font-size:10pt;
                font-weight:bold }

CATEGORY      { display:inline;
                font-family:Tahoma, Arial, sans-serif;
                color:darkgray;
                font-size:12pt;
                font-weight:bold }
```

```
RELEASE_DATE { display:inline;
               font-family:Tahoma, Arial, sans-serif;
               color:red;
               font-size:10pt }

TITLE        { display:inline;
               font-family:Tahoma, Arial, sans-serif;
               font-size:12pt;
               color:white;
               background-color:black }

SALES        { display:none }
```

For each of the elements in the XML document (other than the root `<BOOKLIST>` element), we've provided a set of style properties. The style for the `<ITEM>` element is defined as `display:block`, so each `<ITEM>` element and its descendants will be separated from the others by a new line. This is similar to the use of an HTML `<DIV>` element. We've also increased the spacing between the `<ITEM>` elements by setting the `margin` property to 15 pixels.

The `<CODE>`, `<CATEGORY>`, `<RELEASE_DATE>` and `<TITLE>` elements have the `display:inline` property, so that they will all appear on the same line. This is similar to the use of an HTML `<SPAN>` element. However, each has different text properties, so that they appear in different sizes and colors. Finally, we didn't want to display the contents of the `<SALES>` element, so we just set the `display` property to none. Here's the result:

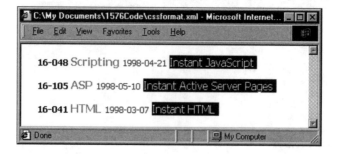

XSL Style and Content Control

We'll now move on to look at the exciting new topic of the **Extensible Stylesheet Language** (XSL), and the associated **XML Query Language** (XQL). The first thing that we must note here is that XSL as a whole is a huge topic, and at the time of writing it was not formalized into a finished W3C Recommendation. The latest working draft for XSL is available at http://www.w3.org/TR/WD-xsl; what you'll see in this chapter is the implementation of XSL within Internet Explorer 5. This closely follows the working drafts for XSL, but may not be fully compatible with forthcoming XSL Recommendations from W3C.

The XSL working drafts are expected to include techniques for styling output in a range of ways to suit different output media, such as printed output or specialist page readers. The final Recommendation is also likely to specify ways of formatting the output using other style languages, for example DSSSL (Document Style Semantics and Specification Language). However, the principal use of XSL is to style XML documents for display inside a browser such as IE5, and this is the topic area that we'll be concentrating on here.

Introducing XSL

When you first start to look at XSL, whether through the documentation or through sample stylesheets, it's often hard to grasp what is going on at even the most basic level. The trick is to understand what XSL is setting out to achieve first, and then the way that it is done will seem to fall into place more naturally.

Transforming XML for Display

XSL is often described as 'transforming XML for display'. What this is really getting at is that there is no standard way of displaying any XML elements. Because XML elements don't have any intrinsic meaning, we can never have any predetermined plan for how they should appear in the page we display.

What XSL does is to allow the author or the recipient of the XML document to specify how the content of the document should be displayed. It achieves this by transforming the content into HTML or an equivalent language that *does* have accepted display characteristics. Usually we will transform the XML elements into HTML elements — in other words, we will specify HTML code that will produce the display effect we want for each XML element. As long as the elements created are legal HTML *and* XML, they will be rendered into HTML by the browser. Because they must be legal XML as well as HTML, 'empty' HTML elements such as <HR> must be provided with XML closing slashes: <HR />. We can even include <SCRIPT> sections, which will be rendered into HTML and then run by the browser.

More than this, however, we can use XSL to create new elements or remove existing ones as we go along, so we aren't tied to the CSS model of simply applying style to existing elements. XSL provides features to copy elements from the XML source into the page, use decision structures to select only certain elements to display, create a whole range of new elements, and sort the content of the source document into a different order before displaying it.

What XSL Does

The basic principle of XSL in IE5 is that it acts as a 'processing engine' to transform any XML document into a different document. However, as you'll see, XSL stylesheets are written in XML, just like other XML technologies such as the Schemas and Data Types that we met in Chapter 3. The input to our XSL 'process' can just as easily be an XSL document itself, instead of 'normal' XML data:

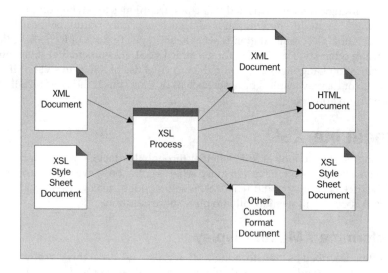

The output of the XSL 'process' is another document, but this could be in absolutely *any* format. The way that XSL works allows an XML node to be transformed into almost any text string for output, including plain ASCII text. It doesn't have to be in any kind of format that we would class as recognizable (although there's probably little point in doing this unless someone somewhere recognizes it and can use it). The big advantage is that this provides an automated technique for converting between different data or information storage formats, one of the long-held ideals of the computing fraternity.

The IE5 Default XSL Stylesheet

If you stop and think about what happens when we load an XML document into IE5, you will realize that what we're seeing is itself an XSL stylesheet at work. IE5 contains a built-in default XSL stylesheet that's used when we load an XML document that doesn't specify any other stylesheet.

The purpose of this stylesheet is to display the document in a more readable and obvious format. Back in Chapter 1, we discovered that IE5 really does 'understand' XML, because it adds line breaks, indents, and little red plus and minus signs to an XML document when we load it into the browser directly. What's happening is that IE5 is applying its default stylesheet to the XML to produce the output we see:

```
H:\BOOKS\1576.IE5XML\chapter.01\code\booklist.xml - Microsoft Internet Explorer

File  Edit  View  Favorites  Tools  Help

    <?xml version="1.0" ?>
  - <BOOKLIST>
  + <BOOK>
  - <BOOK>
      <CODE>16-048</CODE>
      <CATEGORY>Scripting</CATEGORY>
      <RELEASE_DATE>1998-04-21</RELEASE_DATE>
      <SALES>375298</SALES>
      <TITLE>Instant JavaScript</TITLE>
    </BOOK>
  - <BOOK>
      <CODE>16-105</CODE>
      <CATEGORY>ASP</CATEGORY>
      <RELEASE_DATE>1998-05-10</RELEASE_DATE>
      <SALES>297311</SALES>
      <TITLE>Instant Active Server Pages</TITLE>
    </BOOK>
  </BOOKLIST>

                                              Local intranet
```

How XSL Works

Compared with CSS, XSL requires us to adopt a different mindset toward the way that style information is applied. In general terms, CSS targets the style information at elements either by specifying an element name (such as P or EM), or through a user-defined class (such as .mystyle) that is applied to an element using the CLASS attribute.

XSL is fundamentally different. It uses special XSL processing instructions called **templates** to specify the target nodes (usually elements) that a set of style instructions will apply to. These templates specify a **pattern** or a **filter** that can accurately target the style information they contain at specific elements or groups of elements.

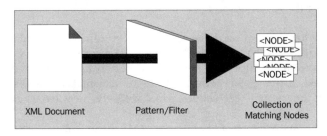

XML Document   Pattern/Filter   Collection of
                                              Matching Nodes

The matching elements do not have to have the same name, or contain specific attributes. There are many different ways of specifying a pattern so that only the appropriate elements in the XML document will **match** the filter.

XSL in the Future

While it's impossible to be absolutely sure where XSL will go in the future, the current draft recommendations give many hints. At present in IE5 (and in its own documentation), the transformation is predominantly from data stored as XML into HTML — for display in the browser. It's planned to extend this to allow transformation into other languages, particularly those better suited to purposes like printed output, spoken output, or other specialized requirements.

The W3C Working Draft for XSL also proposes techniques for formatting data using **formatting objects** (or **flow objects**) and a **formatting vocabulary**. These topics are currently changing as the standards evolve, but will eventually provide ways to specify multiple columns, floating content and other more complex layouts. At the moment, only the simplest of the objects are well defined, and even these are subject to change.

IE5 doesn't support the 'formatting objects' part of the W3C Working Draft, although it does support the transformation of XML documents into other formats. We will be concentrating mainly on the basic techniques of using XSL to transform XML documents into HTML in this chapter, though we will examine other formats as well. Overall, however, this will provide vital background for you to get started with XSL, and keep up with its continuing evolution. Once you grasp the main concepts, the finer points will come naturally and you will easily be able to absorb new standards as they appear.

Adding XSL to XML

An XSL stylesheet is purely a text file, in the same way as a normal CSS stylesheet. We can link it to our XML document using a processing instruction in very similar fashion to how we linked a CSS stylesheet earlier on in the chapter:

```
<?xml-stylesheet type="text/xsl" href="mystyle.xsl" ?>
```

We can only link one XSL stylesheet to an XML document; if you specify more than one, only the first is interpreted. And if we specify both a CSS and an XSL stylesheet, IE5 will choose the XSL stylesheet.

Another point to watch out for is that XSL stylesheets can only be loaded from the same domain (root URL) as the XML document that they are linked to. Because XSL stylesheets can contain script code, the same rules apply as for imported script sections that use the SRC attribute of an HTML <SCRIPT> element. (These rules are also the same as those for external XML entities, which were given in Chapter 2.)

So, now that we know how to add XSL to our XML document, we'll investigate exactly what that stylesheet should look like.

XSL Templates and Patterns

As we discovered earlier, an XSL stylesheet is made up of one or more special instructions called **templates**. Each of these templates specifies a **pattern** (or a **filter**) that is used to **match** the template with the target node(s) that it will be applied to. The templates also contain information about the way these matching nodes will be displayed.

A Simple XSL Stylesheet

All the instructions in an XSL stylesheet are written in XML syntax, and are referred to as **XSL elements**. Each one is really just an ordinary XML element with the xsl namespace prefix. However, the namespace defined for this prefix specifies special meanings for each of the elements. The following shows a simple XSL stylesheet containing a single template. Note that the namespace *must* be as shown here for XSL to work in IE5:

```
<?xml version="1.0"?>
<xsl:stylesheet xmlns:xsl="http://www.w3.org/TR/WD-xsl">
   <xsl:template match="/">
      <xsl:value-of />
   </xsl:template>
</xsl:stylesheet>
```

Because XSL stylesheets are XML documents, they should begin with the usual XML declaration.

The code above is just about the simplest XSL stylesheet you might ever use. It displays the entire text of the XML document exactly as it stands, in the browser's default font. (This is *not* the same as the stylesheet that is used by IE5 as the default if you don't specify a stylesheet in your XML documents.)

The code has an enclosing root <xsl:stylesheet> element, and within this a single <xsl:template> element. This template specifies a match attribute that is the pattern "/", meaning that it matches the root element. Finally, the content of the template — called the **action** — is the single XSL instruction element <xsl:value-of>. This element means, "Evaluate the content of the node and its descendants as text, and insert it into the output document'". The result with the XML BOOKLIST document file we used earlier looks like this:

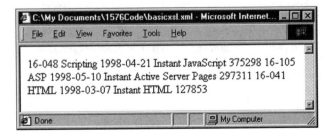

The Template and the Match Attribute

The key to the workings of an XSL stylesheet is in the way that templates are matched to elements in the XML document through the pattern in the `match` attribute. XSL uses recursion to apply the information in the **action** part of each template to the matching XML elements.

Our example above uses the `<xsl:template>` element:

```
<xsl:template match="/">
```

This specifies the simple pattern `"/"`. The forward slash character selects the root node of the XML document, so this pattern will match only that node.

The action part of the template is the single XSL element:

```
<xsl:value-of />
```

This tells the XSL processor or application to insert the text value of the matching node and its descendants. In this case it is the entire character data of the XML document, because the root node contains all the other nodes.

Applying Other Templates

Instead of just inserting the text value of a node, we can specify different templates for each node type by using an appropriate pattern that matches each node in an `apply-templates` instruction:

```
<xsl:apply-templates select="pattern" />
```

The simplest way to match a node is through its name, and this ensures that we'll match all the nodes that have that name — which is usually what we want to achieve. However, this technique lets us apply different templates to different *types* of child elements of the root element, depending on the pattern we specify in the `apply-templates` instruction. And then, by including more `apply-templates` instructions within these templates, we can apply different templates to the different types of child node for these elements as well.

So, the single template in our stylesheet will match the root node of the XML document, and the action part of the template instructs the processor to apply any matching templates to the child elements of the root node. However, through recursion, the templates in our stylesheet will match different elements and nodes in the XML document starting at the outermost (top-level) element and going down through the tree to each child element in turn. The process continues recursively until all elements have been processed. To see the effects of this, we'll add another template to our simple stylesheet:

```
<xsl:stylesheet xmlns:xsl="http://www.w3.org/TR/WD-xsl">
    <xsl:template match="/">
        <xsl:apply-templates select="//ITEM" />
    </xsl:template>
    <xsl:template match="ITEM">
        <P><xsl:value-of /></P>
    </xsl:template>
</xsl:stylesheet>
```

What we've done is to change `xsl:value-of` in the original template to `xsl:apply-templates select="//ITEM"`. This instructs the XSL processor to apply a template that matches the `ITEM` pattern to each `<ITEM>` element in the XML source document (the term `"//ITEM"` matches all `<ITEM>` elements at any level below the document node). The new template that we've added to the stylesheet will match this pattern, and so it will be executed for each `<ITEM>` element.

In the new `ITEM` template, we use `xsl:value-of` to output the text content of each `<ITEM>` in our XML file. However, if that were all that the action part of the template contained, we'd end up with the same output as the previous simple example. Instead, both so that you can see that it's doing something, and to format the output better, we've included some HTML in the template that simply places the text content of each `<ITEM>` element (complete with the text of all its child nodes) in a separate paragraph. This is the result:

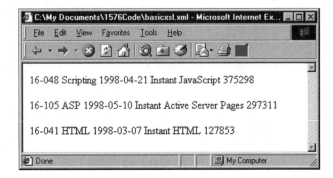

IE5 XSL Pattern Matching Syntax

The `match` attribute of a template provides a powerful set of options for specifying exactly which nodes (usually elements or attributes) in the XML document will be processed by a particular template. Our earlier example used the character `"/"` to specify the root node, but the possibilities are a lot more wide-ranging than this. In fact, there are two basic ways of specifying nodes:

❑ By the **position** of the node or nodes within the **hierarchy** of the source document

❑ By the application of a **filter** that selectively targets one or more nodes

IE5 XSL Path Operators

To select or match nodes (usually elements or attributes) through their position in the hierarchy of the source document, we use a series of **path operators** to build up a pattern string. The pattern is usually applied to select the current node and/or descendants of the current node. `BOOK`, for example, matches only `<BOOK>` elements that are descended from the current node. The exceptions from this are the patterns that explicitly reference the root node. Where no node has previously been specified, the 'current' node is taken as being the root node of the document. The path operators are:

Operator	Description
/	A forward slash is the **child** path operator. It selects elements that are direct children of the specified node, in much the same way as we would use it to specify paths in a URL, for example: `book/category` to select all `<category>` elements that are children of `<book>` elements. To indicate the root node, we place this operator at the start of the pattern, for example: `/booklist/book`.
//	Two forward slashes indicate the **recursive descent** path operator. It selects all matching nodes at any depth below the current node, so `booklist//title`, for example, would to select all `<title>` elements that are descendants at any level of the `<booklist>` element. When it appears at the start of the pattern, it indicates recursive descent from the root node, so `//title` matches all `<title>` elements at any level in the document.
.	The period is the **current context** path operator. It is used to indicate the current node or 'context', so `.//title` would select all `<title>` elements at any level below the current element. The combination `./` always indicates the current context, and is usually superfluous — `./book/category` is the same as `book/category`.
@	The 'at' operator is the **attribute** path operator. It indicates that this part of the pattern refers to attributes of the current element, so `book/@print_date` selects the `print_date` attribute of all `<book>` elements. The attribute operator/name combination can only be used at the end of the path pattern string.
*	The asterisk is a **wildcard** path operator, and is used when we want to select all elements or attributes regardless of their name, for example `book/*` to select all child elements of all `<book>` elements, or `book/@*` to select all the attributes of all `<book>` elements.

Some examples that will help to make the syntax clearer are shown next:

Pattern	Description
/	The root node only
book/author	`<author>` elements that are children of `<book>` elements
//	The root node and all nodes below it
//*	All element nodes below the root
book//author	`<author>` elements that are descendants of `<book>` elements

Pattern	Description
`.//author`	`<author>` elements that are descendants of the current element
`*`	Non-root elements, irrespective of the element name
`book/*`	Elements that are children of `<book>` elements
`book//*`	Elements that are descendants of `<book>` elements
`book/*/author`	`<author>` elements that are grandchildren of `<book>` elements
`book/@print_date`	`print_date` attributes that are attached to `<book>` elements
`*/@print_date`	`print_date` attributes that are attached to any elements

The path operators always return all elements or nodes that match the pattern. The node's **index** can be used to specify a particular node within the set (or collection) of matching nodes, and the special XSL `end()` function can be used to specify the last node:

Pattern	Description
`/booklist/book[0]`	First `<book>` node in root `<booklist>` element
`/booklist/book[2]`	Third `<book>` node in root `<booklist>` element
`/booklist/book[end()]`	Last `<book>` node in root `<booklist>` element

For example, to return the details of only the last `<book>` element in an XML document with a parent element `<booklist>`, we might use the following XSL stylesheet:

```
<?xml version="1.0"?>

<xsl:stylesheet xmlns:xsl="http://www.w3.org/TR/WD-xsl">
   <xsl:template match="/">
      <xsl:apply-templates select="//book" />
   </xsl:template>

   <xsl:template match="book[end()]">
      The last book is:<P><B><xsl:value-of /></B></P>
   </xsl:template>

</xsl:stylesheet>
```

227

Note that, like many operators, the end() instruction only applies to nodes that are children of the same parent node. For example, to find the <title> element of the last <book> element, we would have to use:

```
booklist/book[end()]/title
```

If we used:

```
booklist/book/title[end()]
```

We would get the *last* <title> element of the *first* <book> element instead.

> *A far more detailed description of the syntax and use of path operators is provided in Appendix E.*

IE5 XSL Filter Operators

An **XSL filter** has the generic form [operator pattern], where operator is an optional **filter operator** that defines how the pattern is applied, and pattern is the required XSL **filter pattern** that selects one or more elements based on a range of criteria. XSL filter patterns are very powerful, and offer an almost infinite number of pattern combinations.

We can select (matching) nodes by:

- ❑ The existence of child nodes
- ❑ The value of a node or a child node
- ❑ The existence of attribute nodes
- ❑ The value of an attribute node
- ❑ Almost any combination of these

For example, the following example uses the XSL filter [title] to select only the <category> elements of books that have a <title> child element:

```
book[title]/category
```

To find all books that have both a <category> and a <title> child element, we use two filters:

```
book[title][category]
```

To select a node by its value (for example, <book> elements that contain a <category> element whose value is "Scripting"), we could use the following:

```
book[category = 'Scripting']
```

There are also a range of comparison operators that can be used instead of 'equals':

```
book[sales > 10000]
book[release_date <= '1998-02-07']
book[title != 'Instant JavaScript']
book[title $ine$ 'Instant JavaScript']
```

The last example uses a special case-insensitive 'not equal to' operator. This is different from the example preceding it, which uses the ! = operator to test for a case-sensitive match.

A full listing of the comparison operators, with examples, is provided in Appendix E.

A filter can also use the '@' operator to specify an attribute of the current element. For example, the following filter specifies that the <book> element must have a print_date attribute:

```
book[@print_date]
```

When matching by attribute values, a filter can specify *any* attribute name by using the asterisk character. For example, while this filter will only match authors having a type attribute with the value 'contract':

```
author[@type='contract']
```

This next filter will match authors having *any* attribute with the value 'contract':

```
author[@*='contract']
```

Finally, we can build more complex filters still by using the logical operators to combine individual filter patterns. The three logical operators available are and, or and not, so the following are equivalent and filter out all elements that don't have a child <category> element with the value "Scripting", or which also have a child <category> element with the value "HTML":

```
book[category = 'Scripting' $and$ category != 'HTML']
book[category = 'Scripting' $and$ $not$ category = 'HTML']
```

A far more detailed description of the syntax and use of the various filter operators is provided in Appendix E.

When More Than One Pattern Matches an Element

If there is more than one template in a stylesheet, it's easily possible that some elements will match more than one template pattern. To prevent output duplication, the XSL processor will only allow one template to be applied to each element for a single apply-templates instruction. It decides which template to apply by checking all the templates to see which provide a match, then choosing the one that contains the most precise match. However, it is better to avoid elements matching multiple templates, since this principle does not always seem to be applied in practice.

For example, an `<author>` element that is the child of a `<book>` element would match three templates that use the patterns `"book/author"`, `"book/*"` and `"*"`. However, the processor would choose the `"book/author"` template because this is the most restrictive match. Likewise, given only the last two of the patterns, the choice would be `"book/*"`.

The Basic XSL Elements

Internet Explorer provides a range of XSL elements, or instructions, that can be used within an XSL stylesheet. The basic ones that we use to control the formatting of the XML document content are:

❑   `xsl:stylesheet`

❑   `xsl:template`

❑   `xsl:define-template-set`

❑   `xsl:apply-templates`

❑   `xsl:copy`

❑   `xsl:value-of`

xsl:stylesheet

This is the 'root' element of an XSL stylesheet, and it contains all the other elements. It can specify the scripting language used in the stylesheet, and whether to preserve any whitespace in the input document when creating the output document. It also contains a namespace declaration for the `xsl` prefix. The syntax is:

```
<xsl:stylesheet xmlns:xsl="http://www.w3.org/TR/WD-xsl"
                indent-result="yes"
                language="script_language">
   ...
</xsl:stylesheet>
```

> The namespace *must* be exactly as shown here for XSL to work in IE5.

Including the attribute `indent-result="yes"` causes whitespace to be preserved in the output. It can also be set to `"no"`, but this is the default anyway and can therefore be omitted in that case.

xsl:template

This element defines a single template within an XSL stylesheet. It uses a `match` attribute that contains a pattern to specify the XML elements that the template should match and be processed for. It also accepts an attribute that specifies the scripting language used in this template. The syntax is:

```
<xsl:template match="pattern" language="script_language">
   ...
</xsl:template>
```

xsl:define-template-set

This element is used to enclose a set of template definitions that have a different scope from the default global scope of the entire stylesheet (that is, they only apply within the particular context where the define-template-set instruction appears). It can be used within a template element or a stylesheet element, or inside the for-each element that we'll see later on. For example, the following defines two templates that are only in scope within the outer template element:

```
<xsl:template match="*">
   <xsl:define-template-set>
      <xsl:template match="book"> ... </xsl:template>
      <xsl:template match="author"> ... </xsl:template>
   </xsl:define-template-set>
   <xsl:apply-templates />
</xsl:template>
```

xsl:apply-templates

This element indicates that the processor should search for and apply any templates that match the child elements of the current element. If a pattern is provided for the select attribute, only child elements that match the pattern will be processed.

The apply-templates element also accepts an order-by attribute that defines the order in which matching elements will be displayed. It contains a semicolon-delimited set of patterns, each of which can be prefixed with a "+" or "-" to indicate ascending and descending sort order respectively. These patterns are processed in relation to the pattern in the select attribute: The syntax is:

```
<xsl:apply-templates select="pattern" order-by="pattern_list" />
```

To list books sorted alphabetically by author name, for example, we could use:

```
<xsl:apply-templates
      select="book"
      order-by="+author/last_name; +author/first_name" />
```

> If you have a template for a particular element type, but you aren't seeing that output in your result, a common reason is that the template in question has never been *invoked*.
>
> The normal technique is for the template of a parent element to use `<xsl:apply-templates />` to process the child elements of this parent, selecting the appropriate template for each one. If the parent element doesn't do this, the child elements will not be output — regardless of any templates you have defined for them. It's like having a function in a program that never gets called.

xsl:copy

This element simply copies the current node into the output as it stands. This is different from the `xsl:value-of` element, which just inserts the *text content* of the node and its descendants into the output:

```
<xsl:template match="*">
   <xsl:copy />
</xsl:template>
```

`xsl:copy` is particularly useful when your XML document contains HTML-like tags such as `<B>`, `<I>` or `<TABLE>`. You are effectively saying, "Treat these XML tags as having their usual HTML meanings." However, note that `xsl:copy` was found to be particularly unreliable during testing.

xsl:value-of

This element returns the value of an XML node (and its descendants if there are any) as text that is placed in the output of the stylesheet. An optional pattern can used in the `select` attribute to specify the elements to be included. If this attribute is omitted, the current XML element node is used. If the pattern matches more than one element, only the first one is processed. If the element has descendants, their values are concatenated into the returned text string. The syntax is:

```
<xsl:value-of select="pattern" />
```

Generating HTML Output from XSL

The XSL elements we've looked at so far are all that's needed to build a reasonably complex stylesheet that has similar capabilities to CSS. We've seen how XSL processes XML documents by matching **templates** to the original XML elements, and — within these templates — by generating output through copying the original elements or processing the information they contain. In most cases, the examples we've seen have generated HTML output that can be displayed by the browser in the usual way.

To see how we might use XSL to format an XML document, we shall produce an XSL stylesheet that gives the same result as the CSS stylesheet we met at the beginning of this chapter.

How the Stylesheet Works

In the first section of the stylesheet, shown below, you can see that the root template (which matches the pattern `"/"`) contains HTML code that will create the basic structure of an HTML page. Within the HTML is an XSL `apply-templates` element that selects each `<ITEM>` element. Each instance of this element contains the details for one book:

```
<?xml version="1.0" ?>
<xsl:stylesheet xmlns:xsl="http://www.w3.org/TR/WD-xsl">

<xsl:template match="/">
   <HTML>
      <BODY>
         <xsl:apply-templates select="//ITEM" />
      </BODY>
   </HTML>
</xsl:template>
```

This will therefore produce the following HTML output from our XML BOOKLIST document:

```
<HTML>
   <BODY>
       transformed output for first <ITEM> element
       transformed output for second <ITEM> element
       transformed output for third <ITEM> element
       ...etc...
   </BODY>
</HTML>
```

As it processes the root template, the XSL processor sees the "//ITEM" pattern and searches for all <ITEM> elements below the root node. It then looks for a matching template to apply to each of these <ITEM> elements. The best match is the one that comes next in the stylesheet, which we created especially for this purpose:

```
<xsl:template match="ITEM">
   <SPAN STYLE="display:block; margin:15px">
      <xsl:apply-templates select="CODE" />
      <xsl:apply-templates select="CATEGORY" />
      <xsl:apply-templates select="RELEASE_DATE" />
      <xsl:apply-templates select="TITLE" />
   </SPAN>
</xsl:template>
```

This template simply inserts an HTML <SPAN> element into the page at this point (for each <ITEM> element, remember), and within this <SPAN> it inserts the transformed output of each of the child elements of the <ITEM> element. It does this by applying a matching template for each one.

If you look back at the definition of the CSS stylesheet at the beginning of this chapter, you'll see that the STYLE properties we've used here are exactly the same as we specified for each <SPAN> element there. The result of this template is that the contents of each <ITEM> element (our book details) will appear on a separate line, because we've used the display:block property.

Now all that's needed are the four templates for the <CODE>, <CATEGORY>, <RELEASE_DATE> and <TITLE> elements. The <CATEGORY> template looks like this:

```
<xsl:template match="CATEGORY">
   <SPAN STYLE="display:inline;
               font-family:Tahoma,Arial,sans-serif;
               color:darkgray; font-size:12pt;
               font-weight:bold">
      <xsl:value-of />
   </SPAN>
</xsl:template>
```

Again, you can see that it's a simple HTML <SPAN> element, into which the text value of the <CATEGORY> element is inserted by the xsl:value-of instruction. The STYLE we've specified is identical to that we used in the equivalent CSS stylesheet earlier in this chapter. The other three templates do exactly the same for the <CODE>, <RELEASE_DATE> and <TITLE> elements, using the same STYLE properties as in the original CSS style sheet.

So, did we get the same result? You can judge for yourself in the next screenshot. The page `cssformat.xml` (the name is shown in the title bar) is the XML `<BOOKLIST>` document formatted with the CSS stylesheet, while the page `xslformat.xml` is the same document formatted with our new XSL stylesheet:

You can view all the pages seen in this chapter from our web site at http://webdev.wrox.co.uk/books/1576/, or download them with the rest of the sample files.

One subtle difference that isn't apparent in this example is that with CSS, the elements are displayed in the order in which they occur in the XML document, whereas with XSL they appear in the order of the `apply-templates` elements in the XSL file.

Some Things You Just Can't Do With CSS

So, having seen that XSL can quite easily achieve the same results as CSS, let's move on. XSL can do a lot more than CSS, and probably the most obvious way to appreciate this is to develop our `<BOOKLIST>` example to get something a bit more exciting. The next screenshot shows the result of applying another XSL stylesheet to the same XML `<BOOKLIST>` document. You can see that we've produced a completely different page:

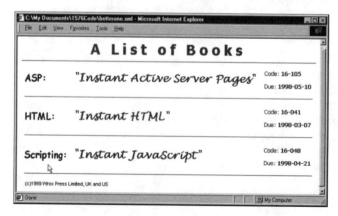

While it looks very different, much of the technique is very similar. We're still transforming the XML into HTML, but as we do so we're doing tricks like adding new elements and changing the order in which the contents of the XML file are displayed. Now, the <CATEGORY> element comes first, followed by the <TITLE> element. Admittedly, we could have done this using absolute positioning in CSS, but in fact (as you'll see shortly) these are being displayed in a normal HTML table.

If you look again, you'll see that not only are the details for each book in a different order, but the books themselves are in a different order as well — this time we've sorted them alphabetically by category. There's lots of new magic going on here, but how is it done?

How the 'Better' Stylesheet Works

As you'll no doubt have guessed, this stylesheet uses similar techniques to the simple one we saw earlier. It starts with the xsl:stylesheet element, followed by the template for the root element (that is, with match="/"):

```
<xsl:stylesheet xmlns:xsl="http://www.w3.org/TR/WD-xsl">

    <xsl:template match="/">
        <HTML>
            <BODY>
                <DIV STYLE="font-family:Tahoma,Arial,sans-serif;
                            font-size:24pt; color:green;
                            text-align:center; letter-spacing:8px;
                            font-weight:bold">
                    A List of Books
                </DIV>
                <HR />
                <TABLE WIDTH="100%" CELLPADDING="5">
                    <xsl:apply-templates select="//ITEM" order-by="+CATEGORY" />
                </TABLE>
                <DIV STYLE="font-family:Arial,sans-serif;
                            font-size:8pt; margin-left:10px">
                    (c)1999 Wrox Press Limited, UK and US
                </DIV>
            </BODY>
        </HTML>
    </xsl:template>
</xsl:stylesheet>
```

To provide the page heading, we use an HTML <DIV> element with appropriate style properties applied, then a horizontal rule. We then create a table into which we've placed the xsl:apply-templates element. This selects all of the <ITEM> elements in the XML document — in this case, the three books. The table is followed by another <DIV> that contains the 'copyright' page footer.

Coping with Empty HTML Elements

One interesting point (and one I briefly raised earlier) is that our stylesheet is an *XML* document, and so it must comply with XML syntax rules. This means that the ordinary HTML <HR> element is illegal, because it has no closing tag. We can get round this by adding a slash character to the element tag (<HR />), as we've done in the code above. The alternative is to add a 'dummy' </HR> element, which the browser will ignore.

235

Reordering the Fields in the Table

So, our root template will produce a table containing the XML document. To get each set of book details (each <ITEM> element) into a separate row on the table, we use the next template in our stylesheet:

```
<xsl:template match="ITEM">
  <TR>
    <xsl:apply-templates select="CATEGORY" />
    <xsl:apply-templates select="TITLE" />
    <xsl:apply-templates select="CODE" />
  </TR>
  <TR>
    <xsl:apply-templates select="RELEASE_DATE" />
  </TR>
  <TR><TD COLSPAN="3"><HR /></TD></TR>
</xsl:template>
```

In this template, you can see how we change the order of the elements in the output. We simply apply the specific template for each element in the order that we want them to appear — <CATEGORY> first, followed by <TITLE>, then <CODE> and <RELEASE_DATE>. This template is made more complex by the fact that we are creating a table in which the category and title cells span two rows, while the final column contains the code and release date in 'ordinary' single-row cells. This is why the extra </TR><TR> tags appear, because they force the release date to appear in the first available cell of the next row; this is the one under the book code cell. Between each book is another row that spans all three columns and contains a horizontal rule:

Category	Title	Code
		Release Date
Horizontal rule		
Category	Title	Code
		Release Date
Horizontal rule		
Category	Title	Code
		Release Date
Horizontal rule		

Building and Filling the Table Cells

To complete our stylesheet, we just need the four templates referenced above, one each for the <CATEGORY>, <TITLE>, <CODE> and <RELEASE_DATE> elements. You can see that we provide the <TD> and </TD> tags in the appropriate places, together with the ROWSPAN attributes for the <CATEGORY> and <TITLE>. We haven't reordered the templates themselves because there's no need — they are executed in the order specified in the previous <ITEM> template, so the order that they appear in our stylesheet is not important:

```
<xsl:template match="CODE">
  <TD STYLE="font-family:Tahoma,Arial,sans-serif;
             font-size:10pt">
    Code: <B><xsl:value-of /></B>
  </TD>
</xsl:template>

<xsl:template match="CATEGORY">
  <TD ROWSPAN="2" STYLE="font-family:Comic Sans MS, Arial,sans-serif;
                         color:darkblue; font-size:16pt; font-weight:bold">
    <xsl:value-of />:
  </TD>
</xsl:template>
```

```
<xsl:template match="RELEASE_DATE">
  <TD STYLE="font-family:Tahoma,Arial,sans-serif;
            font-size:10pt">
     Due: <B><xsl:value-of /></B>
  </TD>
</xsl:template>

<xsl:template match="TITLE">
  <TD ROWSPAN="2"
      STYLE="font-family:Lucida Handwriting Italic, sans-serif;
            font-size:18pt; font-weight:bold; color:darkred">
     "<xsl:value-of />"
  </TD>
</xsl:template>

</xsl:stylesheet>
```

Creating XML Nodes in the Output

XSL can create new XML nodes in the output of the stylesheet, and hence provides a way to process XML documents so that an updated XML document is returned. The XSL elements that do this are:

- ❑ xsl:attribute
- ❑ xsl:cdata
- ❑ xsl:comment
- ❑ xsl:element
- ❑ xsl:entity-ref
- ❑ xsl:pi

XSL also provides an element that returns the name of the current element node as text:

- ❑ xsl:node-name

xsl:attribute

Creates an XML Attribute (or Attr) node, with the specified name and with the contents of the attribute element as the Attribute's value:

```
<xsl:attribute name="attribute_name">attribute_value</xsl:attribute>
```

For example, to attach an attribute with the name "authortype" and the value "contract" to all of the <author> elements, we could use the following code:

```
<xsl:template match="/">
  <xsl:apply-templates select="//author" />
</xsl:template>

<xsl:template match="author">
  <xsl:copy>
    <xsl:attribute name="authortype">
       contract
    </xsl:attribute>
  </xsl:copy>
</xsl:template>
```

To add the attribute only to the last author, we would modify the last template:

```
...
<xsl:template match="author[end()]">
   <xsl:copy>
      <xsl:attribute name="authortype">
         contract
      </xsl:attribute>
   </xsl:copy>
</xsl:template>
```

We can use this element to build hyperlinks in our XML documents. To achieve this, we need to wrap our link text in HTML <A>...</A> tags and add the URL we want to link to as the attribute of this HTML anchor element. Supposing that we want to use the URL itself as the link text, and that this is contained in an XML element called <mylink>, we can build the hyperlink like this:

```
<xsl:template match="//mylink">
   <A>
      <xsl:attribute name="href">
         <xsl:value-of />
      </xsl:attribute>
      <xsl:value-of />
   </A>
</xsl:template>
```

xsl:cdata

Creates an XML CDATASection, with the value being the contents of the cdata element. The XSL processor or application does not process the value, so this can be used to create XSL elements in the output if required:

```
<xsl:cdata>CDATA_section_value</xsl:cdata>
```

xsl:comment

Creates an XML Comment node, with the value being the contents of the comment element:

```
<xsl:comment>comment_text</xsl:comment>
```

For example, this produces the node: <!--This is a comment-->:

```
<xsl:comment>This is a comment</xsl:comment>
```

xsl:element

Creates an XML Element node, with the specified name and with the value being the contents of the element element:

```
<xsl:element name="element_name">element value</xsl:element>
```

The following code, for example, produces <myelem>myvalue</myelem>:

```
<xsl:element name="myelem">myvalue</xsl:element>
```

xsl:entity-ref

Creates an XML `EntityReference` node, with the specified name and with the value being the contents of the `entity-ref` element:

```
<xsl:entity-ref name="entityref_name">entityref_value</xsl:entity-ref>
```

xsl:pi

Creates an XML `ProcessingInstruction` node, with the specified name and with the value being the contents of the `pi` element:

```
<xsl:pi name="pi_name">pi_value</xsl:pi>
```

This code produces the processing instruction `<?xml version='1.0'?>`:

```
<xsl:pi name="xml">version='1.0'</xsl:pi>
```

xsl:node-name

This element returns the name of the current XML element node as text, so that it can be inserted into the output as a text string rather than as an element node. Only element names are returned; text nodes, comments, processing instructions etc. do not return names such as `"#text"` and `"#comment"`, as they do when accessed through the DOM. To list the nodes in a document, for example, we could use:

```
<xsl:template match="/">
   <xsl:for-each select="//">
      Node Name: <xsl:node-name /><BR />
   </xsl:for-each>
</xsl:template>
```

Transforming XML into Different XML

The previous examples have looked at transforming XML into HTML so that it can be displayed in the browser. As we discovered early on in this chapter, it's also possible to transform XML into other formats — including XML. By using the various features of XSL, we can modify the structure and content of the document. We can change the order and appearance of the elements, select which data 'records' to include, and add new elements.

The next simple example stylesheet takes the BOOKLIST that we've been using so far, and creates a new XML document from it by inserting a new processing instruction and comment, and then selecting only three of the 'fields' in the original data file. It also limits the 'records' that appear, by using a pattern in the `match` attribute of the second (`<ITEM>`) template to select only those with a release date after 31st March 1998:

```
<?xml version="1.0"?>
<xsl:stylesheet xmlns:xsl="http://www.w3.org/TR/WD-xsl">

   <xsl:template match="/">
      <xsl:pi name="xml">version="1.0"</xsl:pi>
      <xsl:comment>
         A new version of the BOOKLIST document
      </xsl:comment>
```

```
    <xsl:element name="NEWBOOKS">
      <xsl:apply-templates select="//ITEM" />
    </xsl:element>
  </xsl:template>

  <xsl:template match="ITEM[RELEASE_DATE $gt$ '1998-03-31']">
    <xsl:apply-templates select="CODE" />
    <xsl:apply-templates select="TITLE" />
    <xsl:apply-templates select="SALES" />
  </xsl:template>

  <xsl:template match="CODE">
    <xsl:copy />
  </xsl:template>

  <xsl:template match="TITLE">
    <xsl:copy />
  </xsl:template>

  <xsl:template match="SALES">
    <xsl:copy />
  </xsl:template>

</xsl:stylesheet>
```

After selecting those <ITEM> elements that we want to insert into the transformed XML, we provide templates for the child elements we want to copy: <CODE>, <TITLE> and <SALES>. These templates should copy the element into the output, using the <xsl:copy> element.

The Resulting NEWBOOKS XML File

The result of applying this template is the following XML document, which has a different structure and different content:

```
<?xml version="1.0"?>
<!-- A new version of the BOOKLIST document -->
<NEWBOOKS>
  <CODE>16-048</CODE>
  <TITLE>Instant JavaScript</TITLE>
  <SALES>375298</SALES>
  <CODE>16-105</CODE>
  <TITLE>Instant Active Server Pages</TITLE>
  <SALES>297311</SALES>
</NEWBOOKS>
```

Advanced XSL Techniques

As well as simple formatting of the content of an XML document and creating new elements, XSL *also* provides ways to control the output of the XSL processor using loops and decision-making elements. This is analogous to the way SQL (Structured Query Language) works with a database. The W3C are working on proposals for a language that will define these techniques, tentatively named **XML Query Language**, or XQL. In IE5, however, they are all part of the basic XSL processing system.

XSL as implemented in IE5 also allows authors to include script code in an XSL stylesheet, which is particularly useful because it provides the only technique for including script within documents that are made up purely of XML, rather than HTML with XML data islands.

Loops and Decision Structures in XSL

XSL provides five elements that are used for loops and decision-making in stylesheets:

- ❑ xsl:for-each
- ❑ xsl:if
- ❑ xsl:choose
- ❑ xsl:when
- ❑ xsl:otherwise

xsl:for-each

This element is used to enclose a series of XSL elements that are to be repeated, and permits control of ordering without having to specify templates in a specific order, as would be the case using the apply-templates element. If a pattern is provided for the select attribute, only child elements that match the pattern will be processed.

The for-each element also accepts an optional order-by attribute that defines the order in which matching elements will be displayed. It contains a semicolon-delimited set of patterns, each of which can be prefixed with a "+" or "-" to indicate ascending and descending sort order respectively. These patterns are processed in relation to the pattern in the select attribute. The syntax is:

```
<xsl:for-each select="pattern" order-by="pattern_list">
  ...
</xsl:for-each>
```

To list author names in alphabetical order, for example, we could use:

```
<xsl:for-each select="book/author" order-by="+last_name; +first_name">
  xsl elements to be processed for each author go here
</xsl:for-each>
```

xsl:if

This element is used to include output conditionally, depending on the result of a test. The test is itself an XSL pattern:

```
<xsl:if match="pattern"> conditional_output </xsl:if>
```

The following code will only include the output "Contract Author" if the author element has a type='contract' attribute:

```
<xsl:if match="author[@type='contract']">
  Contract Author
</xsl:if>
```

xsl:choose, xsl:when and xsl:otherwise

These three elements are used together to provide a conditional branching capability in XSL. The when element takes a match attribute, which is an XSL pattern string that acts as a test. If the XML source element matches the pattern, the content of the when element is included in the output.

241

Only the first when element that matches is processed. If none of the when elements matches, the otherwise element is processed instead.

For example, given the XML file:

```
<?xml version="1.0"?>
<?xml-stylesheet type="text/xsl" href="numbertest.xsl"?>
<NUMBERTEST>
    <NUMBER>16</NUMBER>
    <NUMBER>0</NUMBER>
    <NUMBER>-48</NUMBER>
    <NUMBER>29</NUMBER>
</NUMBERTEST>
```

We can create a simple stylesheet that indicates whether a number is negative, positive or zero using the xsl:choose, xsl:when and xsl:otherwise elements:

```
<?xml version="1.0"?>
<xsl:stylesheet xmlns:xsl="http://www.w3.org/TR/WD-xsl">
    <xsl:template match="/">
        <HTML>
            <BODY>
                <H3>Number test</H3>
                <xsl:for-each select="//NUMBER">
                    <xsl:value-of />
                    <xsl:choose>
                        <xsl:when match="*[. $gt$ 0]"> POSITIVE </xsl:when>
                        <xsl:when match="*[. $lt$ 0]"> NEGATIVE </xsl:when>
                        <xsl:otherwise> ZERO </xsl:otherwise>
                    </xsl:choose>
                    <BR />
                </xsl:for-each>
            </BODY>
        </HTML>
    </xsl:template>
</xsl:stylesheet>
```

You can see that the root template creates the basic HTML page, and then within it an xsl:for-each loop is used to iterate through all the NUMBER elements. The xsl:value-of element inserts the actual number value into the output, then the xsl:choose construct that follows adds an appropriate text string.

The match values used here, "*[. gt 0]" and "*[. lt 0]", simply apply the pattern to all elements processed by the template (the '*' part). Then they compare the value of the current element (the '.' part) with zero by using a comparison operator.

*You can view this page (numbertest.xml) and all the other pages you'v
seen in this chapter on our web site at http://webdev.wrox.co.uk/
books/1576/. You can also download them with the rest of the sample files.*

Adding Script Code to XSL Stylesheets

XSL provides us with ways to manipulate and display XML documents in the browser,
so can we now abandon HTML altogether and write all our web pages in XML? One of
the things that we haven't considered so far is how we can use script code in an XML
document. In an HTML page, we use a <SCRIPT> section to define our script code. In
XML, however, the <SCRIPT> element is meaningless.

To get round this limitation, XSL provides a special element that we can use to attach
script code to an XML document by defining it within our XSL stylesheet. There is also
a special XSL instruction that is used to evaluate the script at the appropriate point in
the document:

- ❑   xsl:script
- ❑   xsl:eval

xsl:script

This element defines a section of the stylesheet that is script code, and which can be
executed on demand from anywhere in the stylesheet. It accepts a language attribute
that defines the scripting language in use:

```
<xsl:script language="scripting_language">
   ...
</xsl:script>
```

For example, we can define a function that returns today's date and time as:

```
<xsl:script language="VBScript">
   Function getDateTime()
      getDateTime = Now()
   End Function
</xsl:script>
```

xsl:eval

This element is used to evaluate a *string* that is script code, and insert the result into
the output. It accepts a language attribute that defines the scripting language in use:

```
<xsl:eval language="scripting_language">
   ...
</xsl:eval>
```

As an example, we can call the function getDateTime() that we defined previously
using:

```
<xsl:eval language="VBScript">getDateTime()</xsl:eval>
```

Alternatively, we could just call the Now() function directly from our eval element:

```
<xsl:eval language="VBScript">Now()</xsl:eval>
```

Putting It All Together

To finish off this brief look at XSL, we'll see an example that uses nearly all the available techniques to produce a sales report based on our simple XML BOOKLIST document. To make it more exciting, we'll add some images and conditional formatting. Here's what the result looks like in IE5:

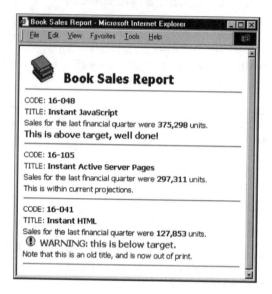

Once again, this page is available from the Wrox Press web site; its name is newbooks.xml.

How the Book Sales Report Works

Although not a very big file, we'll break the XSL stylesheet for this example down into manageable chunks and examine each in turn. By now you will appreciate how the different parts fit together. We start off with the obligatory xsl:stylesheet element, followed by the root template. As we're transforming into HTML, we can create the <HEAD> section and include inline style definitions and a title within it:

```
<?xml version="1.0"?>
<xsl:stylesheet xmlns:xsl="http://www.w3.org/TR/WD-xsl">

<xsl:template match="/">
  <HTML>
    <HEAD>
      <TITLE>Book Sales Report</TITLE>
      <STYLE TYPE="text/css">
        BODY      {font-family:Tahoma,Arial,sans-serif;
                   font-size:10pt; font-weight:normal;
                   line-height:140%}
        .heading  {font-family:Tahoma,Arial,sans-serif;
                   font-size:16pt; font-weight:bold}
```

```
            .over      {font-family:Tahoma,Arial,sans-serif;
                        font-size:11pt; font-weight:bold}
            .under     {font-family:Tahoma,Arial,sans-serif;
                        font-size:11pt; color:red;
                        font-weight:bold}
        </STYLE>
    </HEAD>
    <BODY>
        <DIV CLASS="heading">
            <IMG SRC="books.gif" ALIGN="BOTTOM" HSPACE="10" />
            Book Sales Report
        </DIV>
        <HR></HR> <!-- make legal by adding dummy end tag -->
        <xsl:for-each select="//ITEM" order-by="-SALES">
            <xsl:apply-templates select="CODE" />
            <xsl:apply-templates select="TITLE" />
            <xsl:apply-templates select="SALES" />
            <xsl:apply-templates select="RELEASE_DATE" />
            <HR></HR>
        </xsl:for-each>
    </BODY>
</HTML>
</xsl:template>
```

The `<BODY>` section contains our 'books' image and page heading, followed by an `xsl:for-each` element that will iterate through each of the `<ITEM>` elements that (as you'll surely know by now!) contain the details of each book. Notice the `order-by` attribute, which sorts the books by descending number of sales using `"-SALES"`.

We only want the `<CODE>`, `<TITLE>` and `<SALES>` elements to be displayed in the report, so we should be able to omit the others. However, we intend to do some conditional processing based on the release date of the book, so we have to include an `xsl:apply-templates` instruction for it as well.

Processing the Book Code and Title

The first step for each book is the processing of the `<CODE>` and `<TITLE>` elements. In fact, we have no specific template for these elements, so the default (or 'catch-all') template that we've included in our stylesheet will process them. This template is matched to the wildcard character `"*"`, which matches all element nodes below the root. The template simply outputs the node (element) name followed by a colon, a space, and the value of the element, enclosed in `<B>...</B>` tags to make it bold:

```
<xsl:template match="*">
    <xsl:node-name />: <B><xsl:value-of /></B><BR />
</xsl:template>
```

Including this type of template is useful, because if we change the root template to include an extra 'field', and don't add a specific template for it, this one will still catch it and output the element name and value.

Processing the SALES Element

The next template is devoted to processing the `<SALES>` element for each book. It's quite complex, because it has a lot to do. The first part inserts some text, followed by the value of the `<SALES>` element. We've formatted this with commas to separate the thousands using the `formatNumber()` method that is provided by the `IXTLRuntime` object. You'll find more details of this and other available functions in Appendix E of this book.

245

```
<xsl:template match="SALES">
   Sales for the last financial quarter were<B>
   <xsl:eval>formatNumber(this.text, "#,###,##0")</xsl:eval>
   </B>units.<BR />
   <xsl:choose>
      <xsl:when match="*[. $gt$ 350000]">
         <SPAN CLASS="over">
            This is above target, well done!
         </SPAN><BR />
      </xsl:when>
      <xsl:when match="*[. $lt$ 150000]">
         <SPAN CLASS="under">
            <IMG SRC="under.gif" ALIGN="BOTTOM" HSPACE="5" />
            WARNING: this is below target.
         </SPAN><BR />
      </xsl:when>
      <xsl:otherwise>
         This is within current projections.<BR />
      </xsl:otherwise>
   </xsl:choose>
</xsl:template>
```

After inserting the sales figure, the template then uses an xsl:choose construct to examine the sales number. If it's greater than 350000, a 'Well done!' message is inserted into the page. If it's less than 150000, the warning graphic and text are output. Otherwise, the simple 'within current projections' message is displayed.

Processing the Release Date

The remainder of the template is devoted to processing the <RELEASE_DATE> element for each book, and adding a message if the book is out of date. This uses a simple xsl:if element with the match attribute set to a pattern that selects only those with a date prior to 1st April 1998:

```
<xsl:template match="RELEASE_DATE">
   <xsl:if match="*[. $lt$ '1998-04-01']" >
      Note that this is an old title, and is now out of print.
   </xsl:if>
</xsl:template>

</xsl:stylesheet>
```

Only if the match condition evaluates to true is the content of the xsl:if element inserted into the output. Therefore, this line of text is only added to the report for books that are out of date.

Summary

In this chapter, we've covered a big topic and a lot of ground very quickly. It's likely that the first uses you'll find for XSL are similar to those we've examined here — selecting, modifying, formatting and displaying XML documents by transforming them into HTML within the browser. Just bear in mind that XSL is a hugely powerful and wide-ranging technology, and will ultimately provide a whole new set of opportunities for handling XML data and other documents.

The full XSL working draft currently under scrutiny by the W3C includes a topic that we've completely ignored in this chapter: **formatting** or **flow objects**. The reason is that IE5 doesn't implement them (yet), and so there is no way of getting any practical experience with them. But in fact, once you've grasped the intricacies of XSL transformations, as we've covered in this chapter, you'll find that the new formatting topics will be relatively simple to understand once they start to appear in a more solid form.

In the next and final chapter, we'll move on to look at another totally different topic: adding extra functionality to the browser and your web pages by using the built-in and custom XML behaviors.

8

IE5 Default and Custom Behaviors

One of the exciting new features of Internet Explorer 5 is the ability to separate programming code from display code by using **behaviors**. These are components that can be attached to the elements in a document in order to augment their meaning in a range of different ways. Behaviors can include code that is executed in response to events that occur in the document, and they can also expose properties and methods that script in the document can use.

Behavior components can be created with compiled languages such as Visual Basic, C++, J++ and Delphi. They can also be constructed using a rather strange mix of XML and script code. In fact, if you have experimented with **scriptlets** in Internet Explorer 4, you will be familiar with the principles of this technique. In IE5, however, the use of scriptlets written in HTML and script code is no longer recommended.

Instead, Microsoft suggests using **DHTML Behaviors**, which are created with script code (such as VBScript or JScript) and take advantage of Dynamic HTML techniques to manipulate the page. These are often also referred to as **HTML Components** or **HTCs**. Microsoft has submitted a proposed specification for HTCs to the W3C (see http://www.w3.org/TR/1998/NOTE-HTMLComponents-19981023).

In this chapter, we'll look at what behaviors are, why they are so useful, and how we can use them. We'll investigate how we can build our own custom HTCs, and also briefly see some of the default behaviors that are supplied as an integral part of Internet Explorer 5. The plan for this chapter, then, is to look at:

- ❑ What behaviors actually are, and why they are so useful
- ❑ The different types of behaviors, and the way they are used
- ❑ Examples of two types of custom behaviors
- ❑ The default behaviors available in IE5, and the behavior library

What Are Behaviors?

In this section of the chapter we'll look at the background to behaviors, and see why they provide us with such a neat new solution to the increasing difficulties of building dynamic web pages and sites. We'll do so by examining the ways that content development is changing as new techniques are introduced that make web pages more complex.

Content Development, Then and Now

In the early days of the Web, the language that evolved — our much-loved HTML — was designed with the same lofty ideals as those that drive XML standards today. The plan was that the elements would reflect the structure of the page's content, rather than implying any explicit formatting of that content. So, <EM> marked a word or phrase that should be emphasized, and <LI> denoted a listing of items. Other tags like <DL>, <DT> and <DD> were used to define terms, and the venerable <H1> to <H6> denoted structured heading levels.

This structure now only survives with its original meaning intact in a few places, such as research centers and colleges. Everywhere else, almost without exception, the limitations of the original HTML standards have been eased by adding various format-specific (and in many cases, browser-specific) elements. With the addition of client-side scripting abilities and cascading style sheet (CSS) support to almost all current browsers, most web pages are now a complex mixture of inline and distributed style information, HTML code, text, images, and client-side script. In fact, it's all become rather a mess.

The Present? Just Keep It Hanging Together

Most people now accept that the only way forward for efficient and cost-effective web page development is to find ways to separate the various disparate chunks of content in the page into separate areas — preferably, separate files. To some extent this change has been underway for a while, with newer browsers having the ability to load separate CSS definition files and bind them to elements in the page. In addition, it is now becoming accepted practice to use the SRC attribute within a <SCRIPT> tag to load script code from a separate file.

But this is only a partial solution. When the page creator was a scientist, as most of them were in the early days, it was quite reasonable to expect them to understand about page structure and all the other technicalities. These days we have a design consultant who creates the overall 'look' for the page, a graphic designer who creates the fancy visible parts, a programmer who creates the scripts, and an administrator who ties it all together — and who actually makes it all work when it gets onto the web server.

So, when the consultants have collected their fat pay checks and driven off in their Porsches, the programmers have moved off to work on Year 2000 compliance contracts at double the salary, and the graphics designers have been transferred to another division of the company, who looks after it all?

Yes, it's the poor old web site administrator who has to figure out what all the bits mean, remember how the whole thing fits together, and be able to maintain it. Every change to a menu list or addition of a new section to the site means digging through the pages in order to discover the links and references that are now broken.

The Future? Division of Content

The answer to all these problems is mooted to be **division of content**, and it's easy to see how this can help. If each separate aspect of creating web pages can be kept apart from each of the others, then individual specialists can create and modify their own parts of the content independently. More to the point, they can create standard routines stored in separate files that implement their part of the greater whole — and these files can be linked to many other pages.

By an unusual route, we've arrived at the essence of modern object-oriented software design and management. Change an object, and every application that uses it is automatically updated. Want an object for a specific task? There's probably a fully tested and proven one available in the library already. At last, the Nirvana of easy and bug-free software and web page development... well, that's the theory.

All we have to do now, then, is find a way to separate the different parts of the content from each other, while remaining able to bring them all together into a final product. This is where **behaviors**, together with other existing techniques, come to the fore. The following schematic shows how we can already use several existing techniques to separate a page into four distinct, individual objects:

- ❑ The physical text and HTML content
- ❑ The style and formatting information
- ❑ Standard 'modules' that are used regularly in lots of other pages
- ❑ The script code

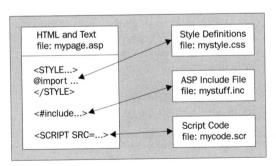

ASP include files (shown in the diagram as mystuff.inc) are server-side include (SSI) files, inserted into the page by Microsoft Internet Information Server before it is passed to the ASP engine. They can themselves contain any or all of the three other types of content.

Introducing Code Separation

Breaking the script code out of the page by placing it into a separate file, and using the SRC attribute of the opening <SCRIPT> tag to reference it, provides only part of the separation we are looking for. For example, if you want to implement a 'mouse over' effect for an element, you still have to define script routines that are attached directly to it, or to a containing element. What this means in practice is that you have to include the event handler references in the definition of the element or its container:

```
<A HREF="somepage.htm" ONMOUSEOVER="hiliteLink()" ONMOUSEOUT="loliteLink()">
...

<SCRIPT LANGUAGE="JavaScript" SRC="myscript.scr"></SCRIPT>
```

The script file itself (myscript.scr) then has to contain definitions of the two functions called hiliteLink() and loliteLink():

```
function hiliteLink()
{
  ...
}

function loliteLink()
{
  ...
}
```

Alternatively, you might use VBScript syntax and define event handlers for an element directly:

```
Sub myLinkID_onmouseover()
  ...
End Sub

Sub myLinkID_onmouseout()
  ...
End Sub
```

In the first case, the programmer has to go through the page adding event handler references to the HTML. In the second case, they have to add ID attributes to each element — in our example, the <A> tag would need to include ID="myLinkID". Whichever route you follow, it always requires the programmer and the graphical designer (or the person creating the HTML content) to work together to get it right. It also locks them both in, in the sense that each HTML element has to have a specific link to a source file that contains the page-specific code for that element.

Creating and Using Behaviors

In addition to the techniques that are currently used for separating code from content, the latest proposal to be put before the World Wide Web Consortium (W3C) for the next version of CSS includes the addition of the behavior property. In Internet Explorer 5, this is a property of the style object that is supported by all visible HTML elements. This style object can be created by a <STYLE> section in a page, a linked style sheet referenced in a <LINK> element, or an inline STYLE="..." definition for an element.

For more information about the style *object, take a look at Instant HTML (1-861001-56-8), also published by Wrox Press.*

Working with Behavior Components

The behavior property of an element's style object provides a link to a file or a resource containing code that implements the way that the element will behave in response to events. In simple terms, the style definition specifies the URL of this resource. Behaviors are assigned with CSS syntax, so the TYPE attribute of the <STYLE> element must be set to "text/css":

```
<STYLE TYPE="text/css">
   .mystyle { behavior:url(mybehav.htc); }
</STYLE>
```

The file mybehav.htc contains the code to implement the behavior of any element that has this style attached to it. The following is an extract from a simple custom behavior component that uses script code to implement the behavior of the element:

```
...
<SCRIPT LANGUAGE="JScript">

attachEvent('onmouseover', hiliteElement);
attachEvent('onmouseout', loliteElement);

function hiliteElement()
{
   ...
}

function loliteElement()
{
   ...
}

</SCRIPT>
...
```

Inside the behavior component file, we can attach custom functions that we create ourselves to any of the events that the target element might raise. For example, in the code above, we've used the new attachEvent() method that's available inside HTC components to connect our two custom functions to the normal onmouseover and onmouseout events that arise in the element that this behavior is applied to.

Attaching Behaviors to Elements

So, continuing the earlier example in which we defined a style called mystyle, specifying that it has the behavior implemented by the code above, we can attach that behavior to any element in the page simply by assigning the mystyle style to it through the CLASS attribute:

```
<A HREF="somepage.htm" CLASS="mystyle">
```

Then, because of the two attachEvent() statements in our behavior code, the onmouseover and onmouseout events will execute the code within our behavior file.

And remember that we can use CSS styles to format our XML documents as well as HTML ones, so behaviors can be used to brighten up and enliven XML documents that are loaded directly into the browser, as well as those that come in through a data island.

Using the CLASS attribute is only one way of connecting a behavior to an element. It also works if we declare the style 'inline', using the STYLE attribute of an element:

```
<A HREF="somepage.htm" STYLE="behavior:url(mybehav.htc)">
```

Behaviors can *also* be assigned to elements through script code. This can be done by assigning the name of the behavior component to the behavior style property directly:

```
objSpan = document.all('mySpanElement');
objSpan.style.behavior = 'url(mybehav.htc)';
```

Or it can be done by using the new addBehavior() method that is implemented for all visible HTML elements. This returns a unique numeric ID that can be used to remove the behavior later if required:

```
objSpan = document.all('mySpanElement');
behaviorID = objSpan.addBehavior('mybehav.htc');
```

Accessing and Removing Behaviors

There is a useful method called behaviorUrns() that allows us to access the list of behaviors that are attached to an element (elements can have more than one behavior attached). This example displays the URNs of all the behaviors attached to the mySpanElement element:

```
objSpan = document.all('mySpanElement');
collBehaviors = objSpan.behaviorUrns;
for(i = 0; i < collBehaviors.length; i++)
{
    alert(collBehaviors(i));
}
```

We can also remove a behavior from an element, and thus break the link between the element and that behavior file, by using script code. The new removeBehavior() method does this:

```
objSpan = document.all('mySpanElement');
blnWorked = objSpan.removeBehavior(behaviorID);
```

The behaviorID is the unique ID that was returned from the addBehavior() method, and the method returns true if it succeeded, or false otherwise. removeBehavior() only works when the behavior was added using the addBehavior() method, not when it was set using a <STYLE> definition section or a STYLE attribute.

Attaching and Removing Events

In the example behavior file we looked at earlier, the two events onmouseover and onmouseout were attached to target elements using the attachEvent() method inside the behavior file:

```
attachEvent('onmouseover', hiliteElement);
attachEvent('onmouseout', loliteElement);
```

This method is available for all visible HTML elements, so we can use it to attach individual events to elements dynamically. In the previous example we discarded the return value of the attachEvent() method, but we can use it to check that the event was successfully attached:

```
blnWorked = attachEvent('onmouseover', hiliteElement);
if(blnWorked == false)
   alert('Failed to attach event');
```

There is also the corresponding detachEvent() method, which requires the same two parameters but does not return a value:

```
detachEvent('onmouseover', hiliteElement);
```

These two methods allow us to control how an element behaves more precisely, by attaching only a subset of its events to the available functions in the behavior file. One behavior can therefore provide different overall effects for different elements.

Behavior File Paths, URLs and Security

The examples above use only the name of the behavior component file, assuming it to be in the same folder as the page that uses it. In most practical situations, however, you'll use the same behavior in many pages, in different parts of your site. In this case, you may prefer to centralize them and use either a relative or an absolute URL:

```
STYLE="behavior:url(mybehav.htc)"
STYLE="behavior:url(behaviors/mybehav.htc)"
STYLE="behavior:url(../code/samples/mybehav.htc)"
STYLE="behavior:url(http://mysite/behaviors/mybehav.htc)"
```

The last of the examples above may make you think about using behaviors located on other sites. However, the security model of the browser, which prevents cross-frame and cross-page script access, also applies to behavior files. This means that the page can only access a behavior file that is located in the same domain. It's fine to reference a different directory, but not a different server. The protocol must also be the same, so pages that use the HTTPS protocol cannot access behavior files via HTTP. For example, none of these pages would be permitted to access a behavior file located at http://www.wrox.com/behaviors/mybehav.htc:

http://www.anothersite.com/mypage.htm (different site)
http://webdev.wrox.com/mypage.htm (different domain)
https://www.wrox.com/mypage.htm (different protocol)

Non-Script Behaviors

Behaviors can be implemented as normal ActiveX DLL components, instead of the
script files we've been considering so far. Such 'non-script' behavior components can
be built with any language that can create COM-compliant ActiveX DLLs. This allows
a wider range of effects to be obtained, because these languages have a lot more power
and, being compiled, are more efficient than interpreted script.

To use a non-script (compiled) component, we have to insert it into the page using an
HTML <OBJECT> element. We specify the component's class ID, and (optionally) the
URL of a location from which it can be downloaded (if it's not already installed):

```
<OBJECT ID="MyBehav" CODEBASE="url_for_download"
                     CLASSID="clsid:....................">
</OBJECT>
```

We can now access the behavior(s) implemented by the ActiveX DLL in the same way
as the script-based one we used earlier. However, we specify it in the behavior style
property (and in the addBehavior() and removeBehavior() methods) by using
the ID of the <OBJECT> element instead of a URL or the automatically-assigned
behavior ID, like this:

```
<STYLE TYPE="text/css">
   .mystyle { behavior:url(#MyBehav); }
</STYLE>
```

Or like this:

```
behaviorID = objSpan.addBehavior('#MyBehav');
```

IE5 Default Behaviors

There is one other type of non-script behavior that you will probably find yourself
using quite regularly. Internet Explorer 5 comes complete with a range of **default
behaviors** built into the browser. We can use these simply by defining a style that
references them, or by specifying them in the addBehavior() method:

```
<STYLE TYPE="text/css">
   .mystyle { behavior:url(#default#behavior_name); }
</STYLE>
```

Or

```
behaviorID = objSpan.addBehavior('#default#behavior_name');
```

Here, behavior_name is the name of the default behavior we want to use. At the time
of writing, there were nine default behaviors available, though no doubt the list will
grow with future 'plug-ins' being made available from Microsoft and third-party
suppliers. We'll come back to look briefly at the default behaviors towards the end of
this chapter.

Creating Custom Behaviors

In this section of the chapter, we'll look at two custom behaviors that demonstrate two different ways in which HTML Components (HTCs) can be useful in our pages. The first is a simple behavior that reacts to events in the source document, and changes the way that elements appear. The second implements a more complex interface that a source document can use to obtain extra functionality.

Along the way, you'll see the general principles of building custom behaviors using XML and script code. We won't be getting involved with non-script (compiled) behavior components in this book.

> You'll find a full reference to the techniques and XML elements used for creating custom behaviors in Appendix F of this book.

The 'WordsGlow' Custom Behavior

One of the most common uses of Dynamic HTML is for 'mouse over' or 'roll over' effects. By way of these, the various links and other elements in a page can be made to change when the mouse pointer moves over them, indicating to the user that they are 'selected' or otherwise 'current'. This is easy enough to do — you just have to arrange a reaction to the `onmouseover` and `onmouseout` events that are supported by nearly all visible elements. This is exactly the technique I was using at the beginning of the chapter to illustrate the discussion of what behaviors are.

The Sample Page in Action

Our example page (named `wordsglow.htm`) implements the 'mouse over' effect through the medium of white text on a black background. As the mouse moves over the text, the individual words glow with random colors:

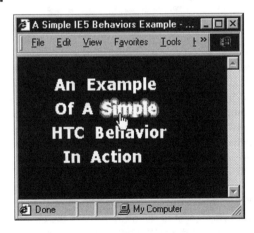

The page simply consists of a series of <SPAN> elements that are given absolute positions and assigned the `wordsglow` style:

```
<SPAN CLASS="wordsglow" STYLE="top:20; left:40"> An </SPAN>
<SPAN CLASS="wordsglow" STYLE="top:20; left:80"> Example </SPAN>

. . .
```

257

The `wordsglow` style is defined at the top of the page, and specifies the custom behavior file called `wordsbehav.htc`. It also includes the Dynamic HTML `glow` filter, which is disabled when the page loads by setting the `enabled` attribute to zero (false):

```
<STYLE TYPE="text/css">
    .wordsglow { font-family:Tahoma,sans-serif; font-size:16pt;
                font-weight:bold; color:white;
                position:absolute; cursor:hand;
                filter:glow(color=red,strength=5,enabled=0);
                behavior:url(wordsbehav.htc); }
</STYLE>
```

The 'WordsGlow' Behavior File

The behavior file `wordsbehav.htc` looks like this:

```
<COMPONENT>
    <ATTACH EVENT="onmouseover" FOR="element" HANDLER="enableGlow" />
    <ATTACH EVENT="onmouseout" FOR="element" HANDLER="disableGlow" />

    <SCRIPT language="JScript">
        function enableGlow()
        {
            intRed = (Math.round(Math.random() * 156) + 100) * 65536;
            intGreen = (Math.round(Math.random() * 156) + 100) * 256;
            intBlue = Math.round(Math.random() * 156) + 100;
            intColor = intRed + intGreen + intBlue;
            element.filters.glow.color = intColor;
            element.filters.glow.enabled = true;
        }

        function disableGlow()
        {
            element.filters.glow.enabled = false;
        }
    </SCRIPT>
</COMPONENT>
```

As you can see, it is extremely simple, and it follows the same basic outline as the theoretical one we saw earlier in the chapter. The only real differences are in the addition of the XML element <COMPONENT>, which defines it as being an HTC component, and the use of the XML <ATTACH> elements. These provide the link between the events that occur for the elements in the source document (to which this behavior is attached), and the functions in the component's <SCRIPT> section. These are an alternative to (and direct equivalents of) the `attachEvent()` method we used in earlier examples.

When the `onmouseover` event occurs, the `enableGlow()` function creates a random color, assigns it to the `glow` filter of the element that was the source of the event, and enables that filter. When the `onmouseout` event occurs, the `disableGlow()` function simply disables the filter again. The keyword `element` used in these functions provides a reference to the element that was the source of the event, in much the same way as the JScript `this` keyword.

The 'TypeText' Custom Behavior

The custom behavior we looked at in the previous example is simple, but it's just the kind of thing that many authors will want to build to enhance their pages. It simply reacts to events that occur in the source document, effectively specifying how that element will behave when the page is viewed. However, behaviors can do a lot more than that, as you'll see when we come to look at the default behaviors included in IE5.

We can build custom behaviors as HTC components that act more like **business objects** than simple 'visual controls'. In other words, they can provide features that are used from within script code to accomplish complex visible effects, carry out calculations and return results, or execute other actions that are generally more wide-ranging than those of a visual control.

The `TypeText` example is an HTC component that 'types' the text input by the user one character at a time until complete, or until stopped by the user clicking a button. Although it sounds simple, this example exposes a much more complex interface than the previous one, consisting of properties, methods and events that are raised within the component. Unlike the previous example, it does not react directly to events occurring in the source document.

Studying this sample will give us the opportunity to see how we define a custom component's interface using special XML elements. We'll examine the component first, then see how we can use it later on.

Defining an HTC Component Interface

You saw a few of the special XML elements that are used to define the interfaces of custom HTC components in the `WordsGlow` sample above, but the complete set of elements contains a few more members:

Element	Description
`<COMPONENT>`	Defines this as being an HTC component. The alternative `<HTC>` can be used instead.
`<ATTACH>`	Attaches an event in the source document to a function in the component.
`<METHOD>`	Defines a method that can be called from the source document.
`<EVENT>`	Defines an event that will be raised by the component.
`<PROPERTY>`	Defines a property that can be accessed from the source document.
`<GET>`	Defines the function that will be called when retrieving the value of a property.
`<PUT>`	Defines the function that will be called when setting the value of a property.

Microsoft recommends that the XML HTC elements should be prefixed with a custom namespace to prevent collisions between these and other elements. The examples given use a PUBLIC namespace, which indicates that we want to make them available outside the component. This namespace is defined in the opening <COMPONENT> element, which indicates that the file is an HTC component. The other XML elements define the properties, methods and events that are exposed. Then, the script section is defined with the usual <SCRIPT> element.

> Appendix F contains a general structure diagram of an HTC behavior, and a full list of the optional attributes available for each element, together with their meaning and usage.

The TypeText Component Interface Definition

To see how the XML interface definition elements are used, we'll examine the interface of our sample TypeText component. The following is the outline (with the script code removed for clarity):

```
<PUBLIC:COMPONENT URN="-/wrox:type:value/-">

   <PUBLIC:PROPERTY NAME="messageText" PUT="putMessageText" />

   <PUBLIC:PROPERTY NAME="typeStatus" GET="getTypeStatus" />

   <PUBLIC:METHOD NAME="typeText" />

   <PUBLIC:METHOD NAME="stopTyping" />

   <PUBLIC:EVENT NAME="onstatuschange" ID="typing_event" />

   <SCRIPT LANGUAGE="JScript">
      ...script code goes here...
   </SCRIPT>

</PUBLIC:COMPONENT>
```

The <PROPERTY>, <METHOD> and <EVENT> elements indicate that our component exposes two properties (messageText and typeStatus), two methods (typeText() and stopTyping()), and that it raises a single event called onstatuschange. The messageText property is write-only (there is only a PUT attribute), and the typeStatus property is read-only (there is only a GET attribute).

Once this HTC component is loaded into another page, through any of the techniques we examined earlier in this chapter, it acts as a fully COM-compliant component. It exposes the methods, properties and events defined in its interface in exactly the same way as a compiled ActiveX component would do. All this is achieved through a special COM 'wrapper' that is implemented within IE5 to host HTC components. By attaching the behavior to an element in the page, we therefore extend the element's interface to include those features implemented by our HTC component.

Inside the TypeText Component

The plan for our custom behavior is that a page author can use it to create an element in which the content appears letter by letter, as though it was being typed. The messageText property is set first, and defines the message that will be generated. The typeStatus property indicates the current status of the component.

The `typeText()` method is called each time a letter is required to be typed, probably through a timer in the source page, and the `stopTyping()` method resets the component part-way through the process if required. Finally, the `onstatuschange` event will be raised by the component every time the value of the `typeStatus` property changes.

The script section contains the functions that implement these properties and methods, and the event. It also holds a series of internal 'member' variables that we'll be using inside the component, and which aren't visible to the outside world. I've listed the entire script section below; the workings of each method are reasonably self-explanatory, but we will look at the important points in detail afterwards:

```JScript
<SCRIPT LANGUAGE="JScript">
    // Private internal 'member' variables
    var m_messageText = "_";
    var m_typeStatus = "Idle";

    // Other internal variables
    var nPosition = 0;              // Current position in string
    var nLength = 0;                // Length of string

    // Put routine for text (write only)
    function putMessageText(newString)
    {
        nPosition = 0;
        if(newString.length > 0)
        {
            // Start typing this string
            m_messageText = newString;
            nLength = m_messageText.length;
            m_typeStatus = "Typing";
        }
        else
        {
            // Reset to 'empty' string (an underscore)
            nLength = 0;
            m_messageText = "_";
            element.innerHTML = m_messageText;
            m_typeStatus = "Idle";
        }
        raiseChangedEvent();        // Raise changed event
    }

    // Get routine for typeStatus (read only)
    function getTypeStatus()
    {
        return m_typeStatus;
    }

    // Public methods for the component
    function stopTyping()
    {
        m_typeStatus = "Stopped";
        raiseChangedEvent();
    }

    function typeText()
    {
        if(nPosition < nLength)
        {
            // Not yet at end of string
            nPosition++;
            element.innerHTML = m_messageText.substr(0, nPosition);
        }
```

```
        else
        {
            // At end of string so stop
            m_typeStatus = "Complete";
            raiseChangedEvent();
        }
    }

    // Function to raise event to source page
    function raiseChangedEvent()
    {
        // Create event object and fire 'changed' event
        objMyEvent = createEventObject();
        typing_event.fire(objMyEvent);
    }
</SCRIPT>
```

What the Script Does

Looking at the code, you can see that setting the messageText property runs the putMessageText() function. This stores the message string in an internal variable called m_messageText and sets the internal m_typeStatus variable to an appropriate value — either "Typing" if there is some text to type, or "Idle" if the message string is empty. In both cases, it also calls our raiseChangedEvent() function to fire the onstatuschange event back to the source page. Notice how we're using an underscore as an 'empty' message so that the element in the source page has at least *some* content, and therefore doesn't disappear from the page.

Once the message string has been set, the source page will call the typeText() method each time it wants another character to be 'typed' (that is, added to the element content). This checks to see if it has reached the end of the string, and if not adds the next character. It then updates the source element by setting its innerHTML property:

```
element.innerHTML = m_messageText.substr(0, nPosition);
```

If the function reaches the end of the string, it sets the internal m_typeStatus value to "Complete" and calls the raiseChangedEvent() function to fire the onstatuschange event back to the source page.

The other method, stopTyping(), simply changes the value of the m_typeStatus variable to "Stopped" and calls the raiseChangedEvent() function. It's expected that whenever the source page receives this event, it will query the typeStatus property of our component. This simply returns the value of the internal m_typeStatus variable.

Method Parameters

Although we don't use any with our component, it is possible to pass parameters to a method function. The interface only defines the name of the function that is executed when the method is called, but if we define the function to accept parameters, the page author can provide values for these. For example, if we defined the typeText() function like this:

```
function typeText(strLetter)
{
    element.innerHTML = m_messageText.substr(0, nPosition);
}
```

We could call it from within our page like this:

```
object.typeText('a');
```

Firing Custom Events

As you've seen, we have defined a custom event that is fired from within our component. The interface definition that we used for the event allocates to it a name (by which it is referenced in the HTML page) and a unique ID string (by which we will access it later in the HTC script code):

```
<PUBLIC:EVENT NAME="onstatuschange" ID="typing_event" />
```

To fire the event, we have to create an `event` object. This is done with the new `createEventObject()` method that is available only within an HTC component or a compiled behavior component. In fact, the new object is an instance of the standard `window.event` object that we use in Dynamic HTML scripting to get information about any and all events that occur in the browser.

This means that we are able to create an object we can pass back to the page that hosts the behavior component, and it will appear there as a standard `event` object:

```
objMyEvent = createEventObject();
```

After creating the new `event` object, we can provide values for its properties. This means that we could set the values of the two read/write properties `reason` and `returnValue` to pass any page-specific values back to the hosting page that we want to:

```
objMyEvent = createEventObject();
objMyEvent.reason = 0;              ' Accepts only integer values
objMyEvent.returnValue = true;      ' Accepts only true or false
```

When programming in JavaScript or JScript, we can also add new properties to the `event` object ourselves. So, if we wanted to return a string value from an event, we could add a new property:

```
objMyEvent.newString = "New";
```

Finally, we send the event object off to the hosting page as a parameter to the `fire()` method of the event created by the XML `<EVENT>` element:

```
typing_event.fire(objMyEvent);
```

Other Behavior-Related Topics

One point to be aware of at all times is that behaviors are loaded *asynchronously* as the host document is loaded and parsed, or when the `addBehavior()` method is used to add a behavior to an element. To help us manage this, there are two standard events that we can use within the component:

Event	Description
oncontentchange	Occurs when the element that the behavior is attached to has been parsed on loading and each time the content of the element changes afterwards. Useful if your behavior is controlling or reacting to the element content, or managing the way it is displayed.
ondocumentready	Occurs after the complete host document that contains the element to which this behavior is attached has been loaded and parsed. Useful for running any initialization scripts in the component that need to access the document.

To use these events, you simply create an event handler function in your HTC file and attach it to the event:

```
<ATTACH EVENT="oncontentchange" HANDLER="newContent" />
<ATTACH EVENT="ondocumentready" HANDLER="docReady" />

<SCRIPT LANGUAGE="JavaScript">
   function newContent()
   {
      ...
   }

   function docReady()
   {
      ...
   }
</SCRIPT>
```

Using the 'TypeText' Behavior Component

To finish this section, I'll show you briefly how to use the component we've just described in an ordinary HTML page. The result is a page named typetext.htm, which is included in the code available for download, or can be run directly from our web site at http://webdev.wrox.co.uk/books/1576/:

In the first screenshot, the upper button has been clicked, causing the `messageText` property of the component to be set to the message in the text box, and the message to be 'typed' into the page. The status returned by the component is displayed below the message, and is currently Typing. If we now click the second button, executing the `stopTyping()` method, the status changes to Stopped:

The HTML for the TypeText page

In the HTML page, we have a `<STYLE>` section that assigns our HTC behavior component `typetext.htc` to the `typetext` class:

```
<STYLE TYPE="text/css">
  .typetext { font-family:Courier new,monospace; font-size:14pt;
              font-weight:bold; color:white; background-color:black;
              behavior:url(typetext.htc); }
  BODY { font-family:Tahoma,Verdana,Arial,sans-serif;
         font-size:12pt; font-weight:normal }
  .intro { font-family:Tahoma,Verdana,Arial,sans-serif;
           font-size:14pt; font-weight:bold }
</STYLE>
```

In the body of the page are the HTML controls and two `<SPAN>` elements. The first of these, with an ID of `mySpan`, is the one where our behavior will produce its result, because the `typetext` behavior style is attached to this element through the `CLASS` attribute. The second `<SPAN>` element, `spStatus`, is where the value of the component's `typeStatus` property will be displayed:

```
<BODY onload="showStatus()">

  <SPAN CLASS="typetext" id="mySpan"
                  onstatuschange="showStatus()">_</SPAN><P>

  Status: <B><SPAN ID="spStatus">...</SPAN></B><P>
  Message Text: <INPUT TYPE="text" ID="txtMessage"
                       VALUE="Enter some text here..."><P>

  <INPUT TYPE="button" VALUE="     "
                  onclick="setTextProperty()">
    Set the messageText property of the component<P>

  <INPUT TYPE="button" VALUE="     "
                  onclick="stopBehavior()">
    Execute the stopTyping() method of the component<P>
```

The HTML controls are the text box where you enter a value for the message, and the two buttons that set the `messageText` property and stop the typing respectively. These both call custom script functions elsewhere in this page. Notice also that the `onload` event of the document is attached to another script function in this page, `showStatus()`, through the `<BODY>` tag.

The Script in the TypeText Page

The `<SCRIPT>` section of the page defines two variables and contains four simple functions. The variables store a reference to a timer that we'll be using to control the 'typing' behavior and a reference to the `mySpan` element — because we'll be accessing this regularly throughout our script:

```
var timer = null;
var objMySpan = document.all("mySpan");
```

The functions in the page simply access the behavior component to set its properties or call its methods. When the first button is clicked, the `setTextProperty()` function in our page is called. This collects the value from the text box and places it in the component's `messageText` property. Then it starts an interval timer running and saves the reference to it in the `timer` variable. At the same time it specifies the function `nextLetter()` as the one to be called when the timer fires:

```
function setTextProperty()
{
    objMySpan.messageText = document.all("txtMessage").value;
    timer = setInterval("nextLetter()", 500);
}
```

So, the `nextLetter()` function gets called twice a second. All it has to do is call the `typeText()` method of our behavior component to display the next character in the message:

```
function nextLetter()
{
    objMySpan.typeText();
}
```

To stop the behavior, we click the second button in the page. This executes the `stopBehavior()` function, which calls the `stopTyping()` method of the behavior component. Then it stops the timer using the stored reference we placed in the `timer` variable:

```
function stopBehavior()
{
    objMySpan.stopTyping();
    clearInterval(timer);
}
```

Reacting to Events Raised by the Behavior

Our custom `TypeText` behavior raises an event each time the status changes, so instead of querying and displaying the status of the component using a timer, or each time we call the `nextLetter()` function, we can simply wait for the `onstatuschange` event to occur in the component. At this point, we know that the value of the `typeStatus` property has changed.

266

How do we connect our custom event to code in this page? We do just the same as we would with any event. If we were writing in VBScript, we could use this syntax:

```
Sub elementname_eventname()
    ' Code to handle the event
End Sub
```

For example:

```
Sub mySpan_onstatuschange()
    MsgBox "onstatuschange event fired"
End Sub
```

In JavaScript or JScript, it's more usual to add the event name and the handler function name to the element as an attribute, and this works with VBScript as well:

```
<SPAN event_name="function_name">...</SPAN>
```

For example:

```
<SPAN onstatuschange="showStatus">...</SPAN>
```

Inside the event handler code, we can access the event object to collect the returned values. In Internet Explorer 5, a new property has been added to the existing ones in the event object: srcUrn. This automatically returns the URN (as specified in the opening <COMPONENT> tag) of the behavior that fired the event. If required, this allows script in the hosting page to figure out which behavior caused the event:

```
function showStatus()
{
    intReasonValue = event.reason;
    blnReturnValue = event.returnValue;
    strSourceBehaviorURN = event.srcUrn;
}
```

In VBScript, there is one minor point to watch out for. VBScript uses event as a *property* name as well as an *object* name, so you have to specify the fact you want the object that is the child of the window object:

```
Sub mySpan_onstatuschange()
    intReasonValue = window.event.reason
    blnReturnValue = window.event.returnValue
    strSourceBehaviorURN = window.event.srcUrn
End Sub
```

Reacting to the Custom onstatuschange Event

In our page, we've used the JScript syntax to connect the onstatuschange event to the mySpan element that has the TypeText behavior attached to it. It's this behavior that raises the onstatuschange event as well as updating the element content:

```
<SPAN CLASS="typetext" ID="mySpan"
                        onstatuschange="showStatus()">_</SPAN><P>
```

Whenever this event occurs, our function named `showStatus()` will be executed (remember, it's also executed when the page first loads, through the `onload` attribute of the `<BODY>` tag). The function simply queries the `typeStatus` property of the component and displays it in the second `<SPAN>` element. It also checks to see if the status is `"Complete"`, in which case it stops the timer:

```
function showStatus()
{
    strStatus = objMySpan.typeStatus;
    document.all("spStatus").innerText = strStatus;
    if(strStatus == "Complete")
        clearInterval(timer);
}
```

Here's the result when the message has been typed in full. At this point, the `typeText()` method within our behavior component has discovered that it has reached the end of the message string. It sets the `typeStatus` property value to `"Complete"` and raises the `onstatuschange` event. Our page reacts to this event by displaying the status and stopping the timer:

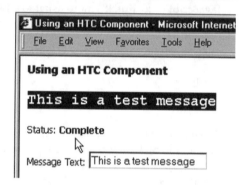

You can probably see from this example just how useful custom behaviors can be, and you probably have lots of ideas for behaviors that you want to go off and build right now. Before you do, we'll look at the behaviors that are implemented by default in IE5. This will give you a chance to see in more detail how we can use different types of behaviors in your pages. You might even find one that does exactly what you need — without having to build it yourself.

The IE5 Default Behaviors

Behaviors allow us to carry out the separation of code and content that we discussed earlier in the chapter. In effect, this is what we've been doing with the custom behaviors we've just looked at. However, IE5 also provides several *default* behaviors that are implemented internally, within the browser.

The fact that we have no idea how these behaviors are implemented doesn't matter. As far as we're concerned, in line with true object-oriented programming techniques, they are just components that provide an interface we can use in our code.

An Overview of the IE5 Default Behaviors

Internet Explorer 5 provides the following default behaviors:

Behavior	Description
saveFavorite	Allows the state of the page to be saved as a Favorites entry.
saveHistory	Allows the state of the page to be saved as a History entry.
saveSnapshot	Allows the state of the page and script variables to be saved.
userData	Can be used to save values from controls between sessions.
clientCaps	Provides information about the capabilities of the client browser.
download	Can be used to download HTML pages and other files to the client.
homePage	Allows you to query and change the user's Home Page setting.
anchorClick	Used to open a folder in Web Folder view.
httpFolder	Used to open a folder in Web Folder, DAV or WEC view (see below).

The first four of these are concerned with **data persistence** — a new topic introduced in IE5. The last two are also related, in that they achieve very similar results. They are designed to allow the client to access the server in a way that permits and supports file uploads as well as downloads.

The upload standards **Distributed Authoring and Versioning** (DAV) and **Web Extender Client** (WEC) are still evolving, although Microsoft's FrontPage Extensions use WEC technology to upload pages to a web server.

We'll look at the topic of data persistence, and the four default behaviors that provide it, later in this chapter. We'll also briefly examine the clientCaps and download behaviors. You'll find a complete reference to all the default behaviors in Appendix F at the end of this book.

The Experimental TIME Behavior

There is also an experimental behavior available in IE5 named TIME. This extends the normal < IMG> element to allow more control over the way the content is loaded, and is designed to be used to display or insert a range of different media types into a document. The behavior can be referenced through any of the internal names: animation, audio, img, media, par, seq, time and video. It provides a single implementation for all of these, so the available properties and methods are the same.

A description of the TIME behavior, and a listing of its interface members, is in Appendix F. The latest details of this behavior can be obtained from the Default Behaviors Reference *page of the Microsoft workshop site at* http://www.microsoft.com/workshop/author/behaviors/reference/ reference.asp.

The Microsoft Behaviors Library

Microsoft also makes available a range of custom behaviors in the form of script files that you can download and use or modify yourself. At the time of writing, the list consists of:

Behavior	Description
calendar	Implements a calendar control in the document.
coolbar	Implements a flat 'coolbar', as in the latest applications.
coolbutton	Implements a flat 'coolbutton' for use in a 'coolbar'.
imageRollover	Adds a 'roll over' effect to images.
mask	Adds the 'masked edit' behavior to certain HTML controls.
menu	Implements a collapsible menu in the document.
moveable	Implements a control that can be dragged and moved.
rowover	Provides alternate row shading and highlighting in HTML tables.
slider	Implements a slider control in the document.
soundRollover	Adds an audio 'roll over' effect to objects in the document.
tooltip	Implements rich 'tooltip' objects in the document with HTML.

All these behaviors are exposed as objects, and consequently they have methods, properties and events that you can use in your code. For the current list of behaviors that are available, go to http://www.microsoft.com/workshop/author/behaviors/library/behaviorslibrary.asp.

Inserting Default Behaviors into the Page

We can insert any of the default behaviors into our pages using the same techniques as we did with custom behaviors. We can specify them within a <STYLE> element:

```
<STYLE TYPE="text/css">
    .mystyle { behavior:url(#default#behavior_name); }
</STYLE>
```

Or we can specify them directly in the STYLE attribute of an opening element tag. Here, we're applying it to a <SPAN> element:

```
<SPAN STYLE="behavior:url(#default#behavior_name)">...</SPAN>
```

We can also apply the behavior using script code with the addBehavior() method, here to a <SPAN> element referenced by objSpan:

```
behaviorID = objSpan.addBehavior('#default#behavior_name');
```

Furthermore, we can apply it directly to the style object's behavior property with:

```
objSpan.style.behavior = 'url(#default#behavior_name)';
```

To Which HTML Element should they be Applied?

The examples above all apply the default behavior to an HTML <SPAN> element. However, most of the default behaviors are not specific to an element — they are designed to interact with the browser as a whole and add extra weapons to its arsenal. The clientCaps behavior, for example, returns information about the browser environment, so it is not specific to any one element on the page, or even to the page itself.

The answer to the question in the title is to switch into 'XML mode' and start dreaming up our own custom elements. The browser will generally ignore any HTML element tags that it doesn't recognize, so we can add one of our own creations to a page and it won't be visible to the viewer. However, the browser will still parse the new element into its internal representation of the page, and so we can reference it through the document object's all collection. And if we attach a behavior to this element, it will then be available to script code in the page.

Creating Custom Elements

As an example of how to create a custom element, we'll apply the clientCaps default behavior to a new element called <MYCAPS>. We use the XML syntax of a closing slash character within the tag, as we have no need for any element content or for a closing tag:

```
<MYCAPS ID="xmlCaps" STYLE="behavior:url(#default#clientCaps)" />
```

Of course, we could also connect the behavior to the element in any of the other ways we discussed earlier in this section.

Adding Custom Namespaces

If you're nervous about introducing custom elements into the document, you can add a namespace that uniquely identifies them and will prevent any chance of a collision between element names. To do this, we use the new XMLNS attribute of the <HTML> element:

```
<HTML XMLNS:MyNamespace>
```

> XMLNS **is an** *HTML* **attribute of the** <HTML> **element, so it is** *not* **case sensitive. Like XML, however, it uses a colon instead of an 'equals' sign.**

If you're as paranoid as I am, you might still think that this poses a collision risk, in that someone else might use a namespace called MyNamespace. The answer is to use a namespace prefix identifier and provide a unique URN as well:

```
<HTML XMLNS:MyNamespace="www.wrox.com/namespaces/ns">
```

The only thing to look out for now is that you have to include the namespace if you are assigning the behavior through a <STYLE> element:

```
<STYLE TYPE="text/css">
   MyNamespace\:MYCAPS { behavior:url(#default#clientCaps); }
</STYLE>
```

Notice the backslash character, which is necessary to 'escape' the colon separating the namespace prefix from the XML element name. CSS does not allow 'unescaped' colons in the selector name.

Having done this, we can insert our custom element into the page with:

```
<MyNamespace:MYCAPS ID="xmlCaps" />
```

There's a demonstration of using the clientCaps *default behavior that forms the penultimate example in this chapter.*

The Data Persistence Default Behaviors

To end this chapter, we'll look in a little more depth at some of the default behaviors available in IE5. A full list and reference to their use is provided in Appendix F. As many of the default behaviors have only a remote connection with XML, we won't be covering them all here.

Probably the most interesting of the default behaviors are those concerned with **data persistence**. This is a big topic for Internet Explorer 5, and offers a lot of new opportunities for making your pages easier and more intuitive, as well as much more user friendly.

Basically, IE5 offers four ways to persist data from a web page on the client machine, so that it can be retrieved when that page is loaded again. These techniques can be used with any page, so you can persist XML pages using the same techniques as for HTML pages:

Behavior	Description
saveFavorite	Allows the state of the page with the current values in HTML controls to be saved as a Favorites entry. It is saved in an INI file, and retrieved when the page is next loaded from the Favorites list.
saveHistory	Allows the state of the page to be saved as a History entry. The information is saved in memory, and is lost when the browser is closed.
saveSnapshot	Allows the state of the page and script variables to be saved. The values are inserted into the HTML of the page as it is saved, making them permanent in the saved copy. Note that array variables are not persisted.
userData	Can be used to save values from HTML controls between sessions. Values are saved in a local XML store that can be accessed using normal DOM scripting methods.

I've provided two samples that demonstrate these behaviors; both can be run or downloaded from the Wrox web site at http://webdev.wrox.co.uk/books/1576/. The first, named savepersist.htm, demonstrates the saveFavorite, saveHistory and saveSnapshot behaviors.

Using the saveFavorite Behavior

The savepersist.htm page demonstrates the different ways in which data in a web page can be saved. The page contains three text boxes into which you can enter data. This data persists when the page is saved in your Favorites list, in the History list, or when you opt to save the page.

The top text box illustrates the saveFavorite feature; any data entered here will be saved when this page is added to your Favorites list, and retrieved when the page is loaded from it. All you need to do is enter some text in the top text box, then add the page to your Favorites list:

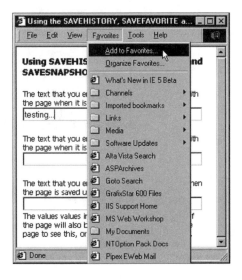

As you do so, you'll see a message box containing the value that will be saved with the page, and automatically restored when you reload the page from your Favorites list:

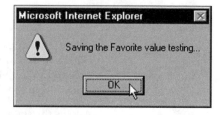

To check that it works, enter a *different* value in the text box, then select the page in your Favorites list again:

A message box indicates that the original value was retrieved, and it is then inserted back into the top text box:

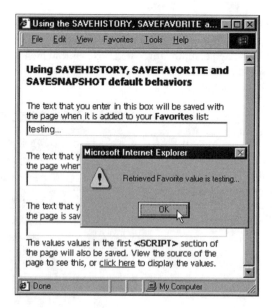

Using the saveHistory Behavior

The second section of the page allows you to specify some text that will be saved when the page is added to your History list (that is, when you open another page in the same window). To try this out, type some text into the middle text box, and then go to another page. When you come back to this page from the History list, the original value is retrieved and placed in the text box again.

Using the saveSnapshot Behavior

The bottom section of the page demonstrates how the `saveSnapshot` behavior works. This behavior is executed when you save a page locally, using the Save As... option on the File menu. Here, I've typed some text into the lower text box and saved the page:

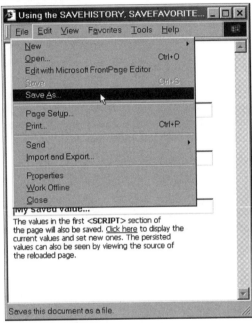

If you now reload the page from where you saved it, the values in the text box and in a couple of script variables within the page (which can be viewed by clicking on the click here link at the bottom of the page) are restored. To see how this works, open the source of the page and examine it. IE5 has actually saved its *internal representation* of the page, not the original file content. You can tell this by seeing how the HTML has been changed.

For example, this is the <BODY> tag in our original page:

```
<BODY BGCOLOR="#FFFFFF">
```

And this is what the saved version looks like:

```
<BODY bgColor=#ffffff>
```

Now, if you look at the first block of script code in the page, and the HTML that creates the lower text box, you'll see how the values are saved in the page. This is the original code:

```
<SCRIPT CLASS="saveSnapshot" LANGUAGE="JavaScript" ID="myScript">
    var myNumber = 0;
    var myString = "";
</SCRIPT>
...
    <INPUT TYPE="TEXT" ID="txtSnapshot" SIZE="40" CLASS="saveSnapshot">
```

And these are the same sections of the saved page:

```
<SCRIPT class=saveSnapshot id=myScript language=JavaScript>
    var myNumber = 26;
    var myString = "Fri 18th Dec ";</SCRIPT>
...
<INPUT class=saveSnapshot id=txtSnapshot size=40 value="My saved value...">
```

How the Persistent Page Works

The first step towards using persistence successfully is to indicate to the browser that
the page is persistent, using a <META> element. Because our page uses all three
behaviors, we have to include three <META> elements. The <STYLE> section that
defines the three behaviors then follows them:

```
<META NAME="save" CONTENT="favorite">
<META NAME="save" CONTENT="history">
<META NAME="save" CONTENT="snapshot">

<STYLE TYPE="text/css">
    .saveFavorite { behavior:url(#default#saveFavorite); }
    .saveHistory  { behavior:url(#default#saveHistory);  }
    .saveSnapshot { behavior:url(#default#saveSnapshot); }
</STYLE>
```

The page also has a <FORM> section that contains the three text boxes. Each one has the
appropriate behavior style attached to it, and the first one also has event handlers
defined for the onload and onsave events, which are fired when the page is loaded
from and saved to the **Favorites** list respectively. The saveFavorite behavior
requires the page author to handle these events in order for the values to be persisted,
while the other two behaviors do the job automatically:

```
<FORM>
    ...
    <INPUT TYPE="TEXT" ID="txtFavorite" SIZE="40" CLASS="saveFavorite"
           ONSAVE="saveFavoritesData()" ONLOAD="loadFavoritesData()">
    ...
    <INPUT TYPE="TEXT" ID="txtHistory" SIZE="40" CLASS="saveHistory">
    ...
    <INPUT TYPE="TEXT" ID="txtSnapshot" SIZE="40" CLASS="saveSnapshot">
    ...
</FORM>
```

The Script Sections

The first <SCRIPT> section in the page is the one that is persisted when the page is
saved using the saveSnapshot behavior, and it too has the saveSnapshot style
attached to it. This script section can only contain declarations of simple variables —
arrays are not persisted:

```
<SCRIPT CLASS="saveSnapshot" LANGUAGE="JavaScript" ID="myScript">
    var myNumber = 0;
    var myString = "";
</SCRIPT>
```

The remaining script code elsewhere in the page defines three functions. The first of these displays the current values of the saved variables in an `alert` dialog, creates some new values and displays them in another `alert` dialog. It runs when the Click here link at the bottom of the page is activated:

```
function setVariables()
{
    alert('Previous values are:\nmyNumber = ' +
        myNumber + '\nmyString = "' + myString + '"');
    var theDate = new Date();
    myNumber = theDate.getSeconds();
    var dateString = theDate.toString();
    myString = dateString.substr(0, 10);
    alert('New values are:\nmyNumber = ' +
        myNumber + '\nmyString = "' + myString + '"');
}
```

The other functions are the ones specified for the `onsave` and `onload` events of the first text box, and they run when the page is added to the Favorites list or loaded from it. Both of them start by getting a reference to the text box. When saving the value, it is first displayed in an `alert` dialog, and then the `setAttribute()` method is used to persist it. When retrieving the value, the `getAttribute()` method is called, and the result is displayed in an `alert` dialog and placed into the text box:

```
function saveFavoritesData()
{
    var objFavorite = document.all("txtFavorite");
    strFavorite = objFavorite.value
    alert('Saving the Favorite value ' + strFavorite);
    objFavorite.setAttribute("attrFavorite", strFavorite);
}

function loadFavoritesData()
{
    var objFavorite = document.all("txtFavorite");
    strFavorite = objFavorite.getAttribute("attrFavorite");
    alert('Retrieved Favorite value is ' + strFavorite);
    objFavorite.value = strFavorite;
}
```

The `saveHistory` and `saveSnapshot` behaviors require no script code. The values are saved automatically when the page is added to the History list, or when it is saved using the File | Save As menu option.

Using the userData Behavior

The fourth default persistence behavior, `userData`, is similar to the `saveFavorite` behavior but executed entirely in script under the page author's control. Values can be persisted and retrieved at any time, rather than just when a specific event like adding the page to the Favorites list occurs. The sample page `userdata.htm` demonstrates it in action, and its use is self-explanatory:

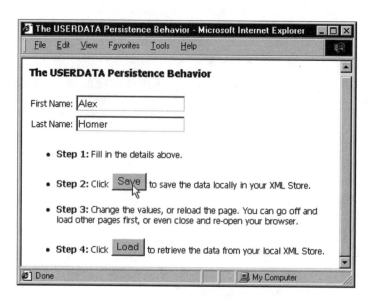

To use the `userData` behavior, we again define it in a `<STYLE>` section:

```
<STYLE TYPE="text/css">
    .userData { behavior:url(#default#userData); }
</STYLE>
```

Then we have the HTML controls that make up the page — I've omitted the descriptive text from the listing below to make it clearer. The two text boxes have the `userData` style attached to them, and the two buttons are used to execute a couple of custom script functions — `saveData()` and `loadData()`:

```
<INPUT CLASS="userData" TYPE="TEXT" ID="txtFirst"
                        VALUE="Enter your first name...">
<INPUT CLASS="userData" TYPE="TEXT" ID="txtLast"
                        VALUE="and your last name...">
...
<INPUT TYPE="BUTTON" VALUE="Save" ONCLICK="saveData()">
...
<INPUT TYPE="BUTTON" VALUE="Load" ONCLICK="loadData()">
```

The Script to Make it Work

The script section contains the two functions that make it all work. They are similar to the functions we used with the `saveFavorites` behavior, but in this case the values are saved in the XML store on the client.

When saving the values, we first get a reference to the text box and extract its value. Then we use the `setAttribute()` method to attach the value to the text box as a persisted attribute. Finally we carry out the extra step that wasn't required with the `saveFavorite` behavior — we call the `userData` behavior's `save()` method. Then we repeat the process for the other text box:

```
function saveData()
{
   objTextBox = document.all("txtFirst");
   strTheValue = objTextBox.value;
   objTextBox.setAttribute("PersistedValue", strTheValue);
   objTextBox.save("xmlFirstName");

   ...then the same for the second text box...
}
```

Retrieving the persisted value then just requires the reverse operation. First, we get our reference to the text box and load() any persisted attributes from the XML store. Then we can use the getAttribute() method to get the value, and place it in the text box. Finally, we repeat the process for the second text box:

```
function loadData()
{
   objTextBox = document.all("txtFirst");
   objTextBox.load("xmlFirstName");
   strTheValue = objTextBox.getAttribute("PersistedValue");
   objTextBox.value = strTheValue;

   ...then the same for the second text box...
}
```

The XML store is in Windows/Application data/Microsoft/Internet Explorer/UserData, *and consists of a series of XML files that are based on an element named* <ROOTSTUB>, *for example* <ROOTSTUB PersistedValue="value" />.

Other IE5 Default Behaviors

Of the remaining default behaviors, the two that are most useful when we come to build applications that use XML are clientCaps and download. The clientCaps behavior provides a lot of useful information about the capabilities and environment of the client (as opposed to the server-based Browser Capabilities component used in ASP, which only identifies the browser itself and the built in features it supports).

For example, we can do things like find out what type of network connection the client is using, whether they have disabled Java or cookie support in their browser's Options settings, what language they have selected in their operating system, and what screen resolution they are running in. We can also use a set of methods exposed by the clientCaps behavior to find out whether specific components are installed on the client.

The clientCaps Behavior

The clientCaps default behavior provides information about the capabilities of the client browser. In this example, we attach the behavior to a custom XML element that we'll name MYCAPS within our HTML page, as described earlier in the chapter (see *Creating Custom Elements*):

```
<HTML XMLNS:MyNamespace="www.wrox.com/namespaces/ns">
   <HEAD>
      <TITLE>Using the clientCaps default behavior</TITLE>
      <STYLE TYPE="text/css">
         MyNamespace\:MYCAPS { behavior:url(#default#clientCaps); }
         ...
      </STYLE>

      <MyNamespace:MYCAPS ID="xmlCaps" />
   ...
```

In the body of the page, we'll include a table to show the results. Note that the `<BODY>` tag defines a function named `getClientCaps()` that will run once the page has finished loading:

```
   ...
   <BODY BGCOLOR="#FFFFFF" ONLOAD="getClientCaps()">
      <SPAN>Using the clientCaps default behavior</SPAN><P>
      <TABLE>
         ...
         <TR>
            <TD ALIGN="RIGHT">colorDepth<TD>
            <TD ID="tdColor"></TD>
         </TR>
         <TR>
            <TD ALIGN="RIGHT">cookieEnabled:</TD>
            <TD ID="tdCookie"></TD>
         </TR>
         ...
      </TABLE>
```

The Script to Make it Work

Having created the `clientCaps` object using the XML element with the appropriate behavior attached, we can now use it to retrieve the values for the client machine. The first 'set' of these is exposed as a range of read-only properties of the component. All we have to do is get a reference to the component from the ID of the XML element to which it belongs, and place the values of the various properties into the table. Here, we're doing this by setting the `innerText` property of each of the table cell elements:

```
      function getClientCaps()
      {
         var objClientCaps = document.all("xmlCaps");
         ...
         document.all("tdColor").innerText = objClientCaps.ColorDepth;
         document.all("tdCookie").innerText = objClientCaps.cookieEnabled;
         ...
         document.all("tdWallet").innerText =
objClientCaps.isComponentInstalled(
                           "{87D3CB63-BA2E-11cf-B9D6-00A0C9083362}",
"clsid");
         document.all("tdMSJava").innerText =
objClientCaps.isComponentInstalled(
                           "MSJava", "progid");
      }
```

I've omitted most of the property retrieval lines to avoid repetition, but notice the last two statements in the function. These use the `isComponentInstalled()` method of the behavior to see if the user has installed Microsoft Wallet and the Microsoft Java runtime library on their machine.

280

The next screenshot shows the result, with the names of all the properties available from the component. This page is named `clientcaps.htm`; you can modify this file and use this technique to collect a lot of useful information about the client and its environment:

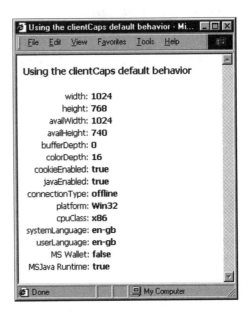

Using the clientCaps default behavior

width:	**1024**
height:	**768**
availWidth:	**1024**
availHeight:	**740**
bufferDepth:	**0**
colorDepth:	**16**
cookieEnabled:	**true**
javaEnabled:	**true**
connectionType:	**offline**
platform:	**Win32**
cpuClass:	**x86**
systemLanguage:	**en-gb**
userLanguage:	**en-gb**
MS Wallet:	**false**
MSJava Runtime:	**true**

Installing Components with clientCaps

As you saw in the previous example, the `clientCaps` behavior can be used to get details of which software and other ActiveX components are installed on the client. It can also get the version information of a component, and install or update a component. See Appendix F for more details.

The download Behavior

The `download` default behavior can be used to download HTML pages and other files to the client machine. For security reasons, the downloaded file must be in the same domain as the web page that invoked the behavior. Although this doesn't seem very useful, think about how caching works on the client. In most cases, a file that has been accessed once will be cached on the user's local machine (depending on the Options settings that they have selected in their browser).

When the same file is required again, the browser checks with the server to see if it has been updated since it cached the last copy. If not, it uses the local copy, which gives a big saving on bandwidth, as well as providing much faster response times.

We can use the `download` behavior to *force* the download of a file so that it will be pre-cached and available when the user needs it. Admittedly, when they are browsing a web site, we can't always be sure exactly when they will need that file. However, when you're building XML-based applications, it is often easier to tell ahead of time which files will be required, and use the time that the browser is idle on one page to download the files you need for the next one.

Using the download Behavior

I've produced a page that demonstrates this in a very basic way. The first part of the page specifies the namespace and style that will use the default `download` behavior, and inserts the custom element that has the `download` behavior style applied to it:

```
<HTML XMLNS:MyNamespace="www.wrox.com/namespaces/ns">
   <HEAD>
      <TITLE>Using the DOWNLOAD default behavior</TITLE>
      <STYLE TYPE="text/css">
         MyNamespace\:MYDLOAD { behavior:url(#default#download); }
         ...
      </STYLE>

      <MyNamespace:MYDLOAD ID="xmlDownload" />
      ...
```

The `<BODY>` section then provides a `<SPAN>` element that we'll use to show the progress of the download, and below this there are two buttons. The first starts off the download process, and the other opens a second page that will use the graphic we're going to download:

```
...
Download Status:
<B><SPAN ID="showStatus">
   Click the button to start the download...
</SPAN></B><P>

<INPUT TYPE="BUTTON" VALUE="     "
                     ONCLICK="doDownload('download.gif');">
 Download the graphic to your machine<P>

<INPUT TYPE="BUTTON" VALUE="     "
                     ONCLICK="location.href='showpic.htm';">
 Open the page that uses the graphic
...
```

The Script to Make it Work

Also in the page are two functions. The first of these, `doDownload()`, runs when the top button is clicked. It updates the 'status' display in the `<SPAN>` element, creates a reference to the `download` object and calls the `startDownload()` method.

`startDownload()` is a member of the `download` behavior, in the same way that `colorDepth` and `cookieEnabled` are properties of the `clientCaps` behavior. The `doDownload()` function passes it the URL of the page to download, and also the name of a function that will be executed when the download is completed. The download takes place asynchronously, so the code in the page continues to run while the download is taking place:

```
function doDownload(strURL)
{
   document.all('showStatus').innerText = 'Downloading...';
   var objDownload = document.all('xmlDownload');
   objDownload.startDownload(strURL, showComplete);
}
```

When the download is complete, our showComplete() function updates the status displayed in the page:

```
function showComplete()
{
    document.all('showStatus').innerText = 'Download completed';
}
```

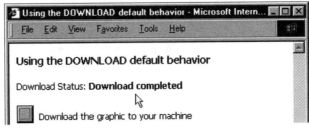

If you now click the bottom button in the page, another page opens named showpic.htm. It displays the graphic that we've just downloaded using an ordinary <IMG> element:

```
...
This is the graphic that was downloaded:<P>
<IMG SRC="download.gif"><P>
...
```

You might like to try opening the showpic.htm page without downloading the graphic file first to see the difference it makes. Of course, you'll have to delete the graphic from your browser cache before you do so, or there will be no difference at all! You can wipe the contents of the browser cache by choosing to delete your Temporary Internet files from the General page of the Tools | Internet Options dialog.

Summary

This chapter introduced the concept of behaviors, and we've looked at how they can make the management of complex pages easier by separating code and content. This is part of the ongoing process of componentization that is generally accepted by the industry as the way forward when creating ever more complicated applications. The Web is no different in this respect, as more and more applications are being moved across to run in a browser and over an intranet or the Internet as a whole.

We examined the nature of behaviors, and how we can create our own custom behaviors that offer all levels of functionality — from simple 'roll over' effects to complex components that expose properties, methods and events to the source document. And since we can use CSS styles to format XML documents as well as the HTML ones, behaviors can be used there as well. We now have the opportunity to brighten up XML documents that are loaded directly into the browser (rather than through a parser component or a data island) with rollovers and all kinds of other effects.

We also briefly focussed on the default behaviors that are supplied with Internet Explorer 5, which provide us with several useful techniques when creating code that will run on the client. The default behaviors include ways to query the capabilities of the client, manage the user's Home Page setting, and display folders on the web server in different views — including file upload and download modes. There are also four behaviors designed to make it easy to persist data on the client side, reducing the need to use complex server-side programming, or to manipulate cookies.

In brief, we looked at:

❏   What behaviors actually are, and why they are so useful

❏   The different types of behaviors, and the way they are used

❏   Examples of two types of custom behaviors

❏   The default behaviors available in IE5, and the behavior library

With this chapter, we've reached the end of the 'teaching' section of the book — and the start of the reference section. In the remaining pages, you'll find a wealth of information about how IE5 supports XML, and the various standards that it implements.

> To find out more about the way that IE5 implements Dynamic HTML generally, and the new features it provides in this area, look out for our sister book *IE5 Dynamic HTML Programmer's Reference* (ISBN 1-861001-74-6), also from Wrox Press.

IE5 XML Document Object Model

This section contains a complete reference to the **Document Object Model** that is supported in Internet Explorer 5. This includes full support for the W3C version 1.0 DOM Recommendations, plus extensions specific to IE5. It is divided into four sections:

- ❑ **The Base DOM Objects**
- ❑ **The High-level DOM Objects**
- ❑ **IE5-Specific Parser Objects**
- ❑ **The DOM NodeTypes**

The Base DOM Objects

In Internet Explorer 5, all the nodes that appear in an XML document, with a couple of minor exceptions, are based on the IXMLDOMNode object. This represents the base Node object from which the specialist node objects, such as Element, Attribute, Comment, etc, inherit. There are three other base objects as well. The full list is:

- ❑ Node (the IXMLDOMNode object)
- ❑ NodeList (the IXMLDOMNodeList object)
- ❑ NamedNodeMap (the IXMLDOMNamedNodeMap object)

Node — the IXMLDOMNode Object

The IE5 IXMLDOMNode object extends the W3C DOM recommendations (which Microsoft implements as the IDOMNode object) by adding support for data types, namespaces, DTDs, and XML schemas. In the following tables, 'Ext' indicates properties and methods that are extensions to the base W3C object model.

Node Properties

Name		Description
attributes		Returns a collection of the `Attribute` (or `Attr`) objects for this node as a `NamedNodeMap` object.
baseName	Ext	Returns the node name with any namespace removed. For example, in a node declared as `<nspace:elemname>` it returns the `"elemname"` part.
childNodes		Returns a `NodeList` containing all the child nodes of this node, for nodes that can have child nodes.
dataType	Ext	Sets or returns the data type for this node.
definition	Ext	For `EntityReference` nodes, returns the entry in the DTD or schema containing the definition for the entity, i.e. `"<!ENTITY entityname 'entity value'>"`. For other nodes, returns `null`.
firstChild		Returns a reference to the first child node of this node.
lastChild		Returns a reference to the last child node of this node.
namespaceURI	Ext	Returns the URI for the namespace as a string. For example, in the namespace declaration `xmlns:name="uri"` it returns the `"uri"` part.
nextSibling		Returns a reference to the next sibling node of this node, i.e. the next node in the source data file at the same level of the hierarchy.
nodeName		Returns the name of the node, which will depend on the node type. See the list of Node Types at the end of this appendix for more details.
nodeTypeString	Ext	Returns the node type as a string. See the list of Node Types at the end of this appendix for more details.
nodeType		Returns the node type as a number. See the list of Node Types at the end of this appendix for more details.

Name		Description
nodeTypedValue	Ext	Sets or returns the strongly typed value of the node, expressed in its defined data type. If no data type has been defined for the node, its nodeValue is returned.
nodeValue		Sets or returns the value of the node as plain text.
ownerDocument		Returns the root node of the document that contains the node.
parentNode		Returns the parent node of this node, for nodes that can have parents.
parsed	Ext	Returns true if this node and all its descendants have been parsed and instantiated.
prefix	Ext	Returns the element namespace prefix as a string. For example, in a node declared as <nspace:elemname> it returns the "nspace" part.
previousSibling		Returns a reference to the previous sibling node of this node, i.e. the previous node in the source file at the same level of the hierarchy.
specified	Ext	Indicates whether the node value is explicitly specified or derived from a default value in the DTD or schema. Normally only used with attribute nodes.
text	Ext	Sets or returns the entire text content of this node and all its descendant nodes.
xml	Ext	Returns the entire XML content of this node and all its descendant nodes.

Node Methods

Name	Description
appendChild (new_node)	Appends the node object new_node to the end of the list of child nodes for this node.
cloneNode (recurse_ children)	Creates a new node object that is an exact clone of this node, including all descendant nodes of this node if recurse_children is set to true.

Table Continued on Following Page

289

Name		Description
hasChildNodes()		Returns true if this node has any child nodes.
insertBefore(new_node, this_node)		Inserts a new node object new_node into the list of child nodes for this node, to the left of the node object this_node or at the end of the list if this_node is omitted.
removeChild(this_node)		Removes the child node this_node from the list of child nodes for this node, and returns it.
replaceChild(new_node, old_node)		Replaces the child node old_node with the new child node object new_node, and returns the old child node.
selectNodes(pattern)	Ext	Applies a specified pattern to this node's context and returns a node list object containing matching nodes. The string pattern specifies the XSL pattern-matching operation to be used.
selectSingleNode(pattern)	Ext	Applies a specified pattern to this node's context and returns just the first node object that matches. The string pattern specifies the XSL pattern-matching operation to be used.
transformNode(stylesheet)	Ext	Processes this node and its children using an XSL style sheet specified in the stylesheet argument, and returns the resulting transformation. The style sheet must be either a Document node object, in which case the document is assumed to be an XSL style sheet, or a Node object in the xsl namespace, in which case this node is treated as a standalone style sheet fragment.

NodeList — the IXMLDOMNodeList Object

This object represents a collection (or list) of Node objects. The object list is 'live', meaning that changes to the document are mirrored in the list immediately. The IE5 extensions support iteration through the list in addition to indexed access. In the following tables, 'Ext' indicates properties and methods that are extensions to the base W3C object model. (The base NodeList object is implemented in IE5 as IDOMNodeList).

NodeList Property

Name	Description
length	Returns the number of nodes in the node list.

NodeList Methods

Name		Description
item(index)		Returns the node at position index in the node list, where the first node is indexed zero.
nextNode()	Ext	Returns the next node object in the node list, or null if there are no more nodes.
reset()	Ext	Resets the internal pointer to the point before the first node in the node list. Prepares the list for iteration with the nextNode() method.

NamedNodeMap — the IXMLDOMNamedNodeMap Object

This object provides a collection of Node objects that allows access by name as well as by index. This collection is typically used with attribute objects rather than element or other node types, and is 'live' like the NodeList object. The IE5 extensions add support for namespaces, and iteration through the collection of attribute nodes. In the following tables, 'Ext' indicates properties and methods that are extensions to the base W3C object model. This base object is implemented as IDOMNamedNodeMap by Microsoft.

NamedNodeMap Property

Name	Description
length	Returns the number of nodes in the named node map.

NamedNodeMap Methods

Name		Description
getNamedItem(name)		Retrieves the node object with the specified name. Typically used to retrieve attributes from an element.
getQualifiedItem(base_name, namespace_uri)	Ext	Returns the node object with the specified base_name and namespace_uri values.

Table Continued on Following Page

Name		Description
item(index)		Returns the node at position index in the named node map, where the first node is indexed zero.
nextNode()	Ext	Returns the next node object in the named node map, or null if there are no more nodes.
removeNamedItem(name)		Removes the node object with the specified name from the named node map. Typically used to remove attributes from an element.
removeQualifiedItem (base_name, namespace_uri)	Ext	Removes the node object with the specified base_name and namespace_uri values from the named node map.
reset()	Ext	Resets the internal pointer to the point before the first node in the node list. Prepares the list for iteration with the nextNode() method.
setNamedItem (new_node)		Inserts the node object new_node into the named node map, updating the XML document. Any existing node with the same name is replaced with the new node. Typically used to update attribute values for an element.

The High-level DOM Objects

Because each type of node in an XML document differs in both obvious and subtle ways, specific objects are available for different types of nodes. Most inherit the properties and methods of the base Node (IXMLDOMNode) object, and add the specific properties and methods required for best tailoring the object to its purpose.

The specific objects are:

❑ Document (the IXMLDOMDocument object)

❑ DocumentType (the IXMLDOMDocumentType object)

❑ DocumentFragment (the IXMLDOMDocumentFragment object)

❑ Element (the IXMLDOMElement object)

❑ Attribute or Attr (the IXMLDOMAttribute object)

❑ Entity (the IXMLDOMEntity object)

- ❑ EntityReference (the IXMLDOMEntityReference object)

- ❑ Notation (the IXMLDOMNotation object)

- ❑ CharacterData (the IXMLDOMCharacterData object)

- ❑ CDATASection (the IXMLDOMCDATASection object)

- ❑ Text (the IXMLDOMText object)

- ❑ Comment (the IXMLDOMComment object)

- ❑ ProcessingInstruction (the IXMLDOMProcessingIntruction object)

- ❑ Implementation (the IXMLDOMImplementation object)

In addition to these, there are interfaces called IDOMDocument, IDOMDocumentType etc. which implement the W3C Recommendation, without the Microsoft extensions. These inherit from IDOMNode, which is the Microsoft implementation of the W3C Node object. The following tables repeat the base properties and methods, and add the node-specific ones. This provides a complete reference, with no need to check elsewhere which extra properties and methods the base objects provide in addition.

Document — the IXMLDOMDocument

The Document object is the root object for an XML document. In IE5, it is the object that is instantiated by creating a new ActiveX Object with the identifier "Microsoft.XMLDOM".

The IE5 IXMLDOMDocument object extends the base DOM document interface (implemented in IE5 by the IDOMDocument object) to include parser-specific functions. These include the ability to load documents asynchronously and control validation. The IXMLDOMDocument object also provides access to other IE5-specific objects such as parseError. In the following tables, 'Ext' indicates properties and methods that are extensions to the base W3C object model.

Document Properties

Name		Description
async	Ext	Sets or returns whether asynchronous download of the XML data is permitted. Values are true (the default) or false.
attributes		Returns a collection of the Attribute (or Attr) objects for this node as a NamedNodeMap object.
baseName	Ext	Returns the node name with any namespace removed. For example, in a node declared as <nspace:elemname> it returns the "elemname" part.

Table Continued on Following Page

Name		Description
childNodes		Returns a NodeList containing all the child nodes of this node, for nodes that can have child nodes.
dataType	Ext	Sets or returns the data type for this node.
definition	Ext	For EntityReference nodes, returns the entry in the DTD or schema containing the definition for the entity, i.e. "<!ENTITY entityname 'entity value'>". For other nodes, returns null.
doctype		Returns a reference to the DocumentType node specifying the DTD or schema for this document.
documentElement		Returns a reference to the outermost element of the document.
firstChild		Returns a reference to the first child node of this node.
implementation		Returns a reference to the Implementation object for the document. This object provides methods that are application-specific and document object model implementation independent.
lastChild		Returns a reference to the last child node of this node.
namespaceURI	Ext	Returns the URI for the namespace as a string. For example, in the namespace declaration xmlns:name="uri" it returns the "uri" part.
nextSibling		Returns a reference to the next sibling node of this node, i.e. the next node in the source data file at the same level of the hierarchy.
nodeName		Returns the name of the node, which will depend on the node type. See the list of Node Types at the end of this appendix for more details.
nodeTypeString	Ext	Returns the node type as a string. See the list of Node Types at the end of this appendix for more details.
nodeType		Returns the node type as a number. See the list of Node Types at the end of this appendix for more details.

Name		Description
nodeTyped Value	Ext	Sets or returns the strongly typed value of the node, expressed in its defined data type. If no data type has been defined for the node, its nodeValue is returned.
nodeValue		Sets or returns the value of the node as plain text.
ownerDocument		Returns the root node of the document that contains the node.
parentNode		Returns the parent node of this node, for nodes that can have parents.
parsed	Ext	Returns true if this node and all its descendants have been parsed and instantiated.
parseError	Ext	Returns a reference to the ParseError object that contains information about any errors encountered while parsing the document.
prefix	Ext	Returns the element namespace prefix as a string. For example, in a node declared as \<nspace:elemname\> it returns the "nspace" part.
preserve WhiteSpace	Ext	Specifies whether white space should be preserved. The default is false.
previous Sibling		Returns a reference to the previous sibling node of this node, i.e. the previous node in the source file at the same level of the hierarchy.
readyState	Ext	Indicates the current state of the XML document: 0 ("uninitialized") - the object has been created but the load() has not yet been executed. 1 ("loading") - the load() method is executing. 2 ("loaded") - loading is complete and parsing is taking place. 3 ("interactive") - some data has been read and parsed and the object model is now available. The data set is only partially retrieved and is read-only. 4 ("completed") - document has been completely loaded. If successful the data is available read/write, if not the error information is available.

Table Continued on Following Page

295

Name		Description
resolveExternals	Ext	Indicates whether external entities are resolved and the document is validated against external DTDs or schemas. The default is false.
specified	Ext	Indicates whether the node value is explicitly specified or derived from a default value in the DTD or schema. Normally only used with attribute nodes.
text	Ext	Sets or returns the entire text content of this node and all its descendant nodes.
url	Ext	Returns the URL of the last successfully loaded document, or null if the document was built from scratch in memory.
validateOnParse	Ext	Sets or returns whether the parser should validate the document. Takes the value true to validate or false (the default) to check only for 'well-formedness'.
xml	Ext	Returns the entire XML content of this node and all its descendant nodes.

Document Methods

Name		Description
abort()	Ext	Aborts a currently executing asynchronous download.
appendChild(new_node)		Appends the node object new_node to the end of the list of child nodes for this node.
cloneNode(recurse_children)		Creates a new node object that is an exact clone of this node, including all descendant nodes of this node if recurse_children is set to true.
createAttribute(attr_name)		Creates an Attribute node with the specified name.
createCDATASection(text)		Creates a CDATASection node containing text.
createComment(text)		Creates a Comment node containing text as the comment between the <!-- and --> delimiters.

Name		Description
createDocument Fragment()		Creates an empty DocumentFragment node that can be used to build independent sections of a document.
createElement (tag_name)		Creates an Element node with the specified name.
createEntityReference (ref_name)		Creates an EntityReference node with the supplied name for the reference.
createNode (node_type, node_name, namespace_uri)	Ext	Creates any type of node using the specified node_type, node_name, and namespace_uri parameters.
createProcessing Instruction(target, text)		Creates a ProcessingInstruction node containing the specified target and data.
createTextNode (text_data)		Creates a Text node containing the specified text data.
getElementsByTagName (tag_name)		Returns a NodeList of elements that have the specified tag name. If tag_name is "*" it returns all elements.
hasChildNodes()		Returns true if this node has any child nodes.
insertBefore(new_node, this_node)		Inserts a new node object new_node into the list of child nodes for this node, to the left of the node object this_node or at the end of the list if this_node is omitted.
load(url)	Ext	Loads an XML document from the location in url.
loadXML(string)	Ext	Loads a string that is a representation of an XML document.
nodeFromID(id_value)	Ext	Returns the node object whose ID attribute matches the supplied value.
removeChild(this_node)		Removes the child node this_node from the list of child nodes for this node, and returns it.

Table Continued on Following Page

Name		Description
replaceChild(new_node, old_node)		Replaces the child node old_node with the new child node object new_node, and returns the old child node.
save(destination)	Ext	Saves the document to the specified destination, assuming the appropriate permissions are granted.
selectNodes(pattern)	Ext	Applies a specified pattern to this node's context and returns a node list object containing matching nodes. The string pattern specifies the XSL pattern-matching operation to be used.
selectSingleNode (pattern)	Ext	Applies a specified pattern to this node's context and returns just the first node object that matches. The string pattern specifies the XSL pattern-matching operation to be used.
transformNode (stylesheet)	Ext	Processes this node and its children using an XSL style sheet specified in the stylesheet argument, and returns the resulting transformation. The style sheet must be either a Document node object, in which case the document is assumed to be an XSL style sheet, or a Node object in the xsl namespace, in which case this node is treated as a standalone style sheet fragment.

Document Events

Name		Description
ondataavailable	Ext	The ondataavailable event occurs when data becomes available. When an asynchronous data load is in progress it allows processing in parallel with the download. The readyState property changes through several states to indicate the current status of the download.
onreadystatechange	Ext	The onreadystatechange event occurs when the value of the readyState property changes. This provides an alternative way to monitor the arrival of XML data when asynchronous loading is not used.

298

Name		Description
ontransformnode	Ext	The ontransformnode event is fired when a node is transformed through the transformNode() method of the Node object using an XSL style sheet.

DocumentType — the IXMLDOMDocumentType Object

This object contains information about the document type declaration or schema for the document. It is the equivalent of the <!DOCTYPE> node. In the following tables, 'Ext' indicates properties and methods that are extensions to the base W3C object model. IE5 implements this base object as IDOMDocumentType.

DocumentType Properties

Name		Description
attributes		Returns a collection of the Attribute (or Attr) objects for this node as a NamedNodeMap object.
baseName	Ext	Returns the node name with any namespace removed. For example, in a node declared as <nspace:elemname> it returns the "elemname" part.
childNodes		Returns a NodeList containing all the child nodes of this node, for nodes that can have child nodes.
dataType	Ext	Sets or returns the data type for this node.
definition	Ext	For EntityReference nodes, returns the entry in the DTD or schema containing the definition for the entity, i.e. "<!ENTITY entityname 'entity value'>". For other nodes, returns null.
entities		Returns a node list containing references to the Entity objects declared in the document type declaration.
firstChild		Returns a reference to the first child node of this node.
lastChild		Returns a reference to the last child node of this node.

Table Continued on Following Page

299

Name		Description
name		Returns the name of the document type (!DOCTYPE) for this document.
namespaceURI	Ext	Returns the URI for the namespace as a string. For example, in the namespace declaration xmlns:name="uri" it returns the "uri" part.
nextSibling		Returns a reference to the next sibling node of this node, i.e. the next node in the source data file at the same level of the hierarchy.
nodeName		Returns the name of the node, which will depend on the node type. See the list of Node Types at the end of this appendix for more details.
nodeTypeString	Ext	Returns the node type as a string, depending on the node type. See the list of Node Types at the end of this appendix for more details.
nodeType		Returns the node type as a number. See the list of Node Types at the end of this appendix for more details.
nodeTypedValue	Ext	Sets or returns the strongly typed value of the node, expressed in its defined data type. If no data type has been defined for the node, its nodeValue is returned.
nodeValue		Sets or returns the value of the node as plain text.
notations		Returns a node list containing references to the Notation objects present in the document type declaration.
ownerDocument		Returns the root node of the document that contains the node.
parentNode		Returns the parent node of this node, for nodes that can have parents.
parsed	Ext	Returns true if this node and all its descendants have been parsed and instantiated.
prefix	Ext	Returns the element namespace prefix as a string. For example, in a node declared as <nspace:elemname> it returns the "nspace" part.

Name		Description
previousSibling		Returns a reference to the previous sibling node of this node, i.e. the previous node in the source file at the same level of the hierarchy.
specified	Ext	Indicates whether the node value is explicitly specified or derived from a default value in the DTD or schema. Normally only used with attribute nodes.
text	Ext	Sets or returns the entire text content of this node and all its descendant nodes.
xml	Ext	Returns the entire XML content of this node and all its descendant nodes.

DocumentType Methods

Name		Description
appendChild (new_node)		Appends the node object new_node to the end of the list of child nodes for this node.
cloneNode(recurse_ children)		Creates a new node object that is an exact clone of this node, including all descendant nodes of this node if recurse_children is set to true.
hasChildNodes()		Returns true if this node has any child nodes.
insertBefore(new _node, this_node)		Inserts a new node object new_node into the list of child nodes for this node, to the left of the node object this_node or at the end of the list if this_node is omitted.
removeChild (this_node)		Removes the child node this_node from the list of child nodes for this node, and returns it.
replaceChild (new_node, old_ node)		Replaces the child node old_node with the new child node object new_node, and returns the old child node.
selectNodes (pattern)	Ext	Applies a specified pattern to this node's context and returns a node list object containing matching nodes. The string pattern specifies the XSL pattern-matching operation to be used.

Table Continued on Following Page

301

Name		Description
selectSingleNode (pattern)	Ext	Applies a specified pattern to this node's context and returns just the first node object that matches. The string `pattern` specifies the XSL pattern-matching operation to be used.
transformNode (stylesheet)	Ext	Processes this node and its children using an XSL style sheet specified in the `stylesheet` argument, and returns the resulting transformation. The style sheet must be either a `Document` node object, in which case the document is assumed to be an XSL style sheet, or a Node object in the `xsl` namespace, in which case this node is treated as a standalone style sheet fragment.

DocumentFragment — the IXMLDOMDocumentFragment Object

A document fragment is a lightweight object that is useful for tree insert operations. A new document fragment can be created and elements added to it, then the entire fragment can be added to an existing document. It is also useful for storing sections of a document temporarily, such as when cutting and pasting blocks of elements. This object adds no new methods or properties to the base `IXMLDOMNode` object. In the following tables, 'Ext' indicates properties and methods that are extensions to the base W3C object model. The unextended object is implemented in IE5 by the `IDOMDocumentFragment` object.

DocumentFragment Properties

Name		Description
attributes		Returns a collection of the `Attribute` (or `Attr`) objects for this node as a `NamedNodeMap` object.
baseName	Ext	Returns the node name with any namespace removed. For example, in a node declared as `<nspace:elemname>` it returns the `"elemname"` part.
childNodes		Returns a `NodeList` containing all the child nodes of this node, for nodes that can have child nodes.

Name		Description
dataType	Ext	Sets or returns the data type for this node.
definition	Ext	For EntityReference nodes, returns the entry in the DTD or schema containing the definition for the entity, i.e. "<!ENTITY entityname 'entity value'>". For other nodes, returns null.
firstChild		Returns a reference to the first child node of this node.
lastChild		Returns a reference to the last child node of this node.
namespaceURI	Ext	Returns the URI for the namespace as a string. For example, in the namespace declaration xmlns:name="uri" it returns the "uri" part.
nextSibling		Returns a reference to the next sibling node of this node, i.e. the next node in the source data file at the same level of the hierarchy.
nodeName		Returns the name of the node, which will depend on the node type. See the list of Node Types at the end of this appendix for more details.
nodeTypeString	Ext	Returns the node type as a string, depending on the node type. See the list of Node Types at the end of this appendix for more details.
nodeType		Returns the node type as a number. See the list of Node Types at the end of this appendix for more details.
nodeTypedValue	Ext	Sets or returns the strongly typed value of the node, expressed in its defined data type. If no data type has been defined for the node, its nodeValue is returned.
nodeValue		Sets or returns the value of the node as plain text.
ownerDocument		Returns the root node of the document that contains the node.
parentNode		Returns the parent node of this node, for nodes that can have parents.

Table Continued on Following Page

Name		Description
parsed	Ext	Returns true if this node and all its descendants have been parsed and instantiated.
prefix	Ext	Returns the element namespace prefix as a string. For example, in a node declared as <nspace:elemname> it returns the "nspace" part.
previousSibling		Returns a reference to the previous sibling node of this node, i.e. the previous node in the source file at the same level of the hierarchy.
specified	Ext	Indicates whether the node value is explicitly specified or derived from a default value in the DTD or schema. Normally only used with attribute nodes.
text	Ext	Sets or returns the entire text content of this node and all its descendant nodes.
xml	Ext	Returns the entire XML content of this node and all its descendant nodes.

DocumentFragment Methods

Name	Description
appendChild(new_node)	Appends the node object new_node to the end of the list of child nodes for this node.
cloneNode(recurse_children)	Creates a new node object that is an exact clone of this node, including all descendant nodes of this node if recurse_children is set to true.
hasChildNodes()	Returns true if this node has any child nodes.

Name		Description
`insertBefore(new_node, this_node)`		Inserts a new node object `new_node` into the list of child nodes for this node, to the left of the node object `this_node` or at the end of the list if `this_node` is omitted.
`removeChild(this_node)`		Removes the child node `this_node` from the list of child nodes for this node, and returns it.
`replaceChild(new_node, old_node)`		Replaces the child node `old_node` with the new child node object `new_node`, and returns the old child node.
`selectNodes(pattern)`	Ext	Applies a specified pattern to this node's context and returns a node list object containing matching nodes. The string `pattern` specifies the XSL pattern-matching operation to be used.
`selectSingleNode(pattern)`	Ext	Applies a specified pattern to this node's context and returns just the first node object that matches. The string `pattern` specifies the XSL pattern-matching operation to be used.
`transformNode(stylesheet)`	Ext	Processes this node and its children using an XSL style sheet specified in the `stylesheet` argument, and returns the resulting transformation. The style sheet must be either a `Document` node object, in which case the document is assumed to be an XSL style sheet, or a Node object in the `xsl` namespace, in which case this node is treated as a standalone style sheet fragment.

Element — the IXMLDOMElement Object

This object represents the elements in the document, and together with the `Attribute` and `Text` nodes, is likely to be one of the most common. Note that the text content of an `Element` node is stored in a child `Text` node. An `Element` node always has a `nodeValue` of `null`. In the following tables, 'Ext' indicates properties and methods that are extensions to the base W3C object model. IE5 implements the unextended object through the `IDOMElement` interface.

305

Element Properties

Name		Description
attributes		Returns a collection of the `Attribute` (or `Attr`) objects for this node as a `NamedNodeMap` object.
baseName	Ext	Returns the node name with any namespace removed. For example, in a node declared as `<nspace:elemname>` it returns the `"elemname"` part.
childNodes		Returns a `NodeList` containing all the child nodes of this node, for nodes that can have child nodes.
dataType	Ext	Sets or returns the data type for this node.
definition	Ext	For `EntityReference` nodes, returns the entry in the DTD or schema containing the definition for the entity, i.e. `"<!ENTITY entityname 'entity value'>"`. For other nodes, returns `null`.
firstChild		Returns a reference to the first child node of this node.
lastChild		Returns a reference to the last child node of this node.
namespaceURI	Ext	Returns the URI for the namespace as a string. For example, in the namespace declaration `xmlns:name="uri"` it returns the `"uri"` part.
nextSibling		Returns a reference to the next sibling node of this node, i.e. the next node in the source data file at the same level of the hierarchy.
nodeName		Returns the name of the node, which will depend on the node type. See the list of Node Types at the end of this appendix for more details.
nodeTypeString	Ext	Returns the node type as a string, depending on the node type. See the list of Node Types at the end of this appendix for more details.
nodeType		Returns the node type as a number. See the list of Node Types at the end of this appendix for more details.

Name		Description
nodeTypedValue	Ext	Sets or returns the strongly typed value of the node, expressed in its defined data type. If no data type has been defined for the node, its nodeValue is returned.
nodeValue		Sets or returns the value of the node as plain text.
ownerDocument		Returns the root node of the document that contains the node.
parentNode		Returns the parent node of this node, for nodes that can have parents.
parsed	Ext	Returns true if this node and all its descendants have been parsed and instantiated.
prefix	Ext	Returns the element namespace prefix as a string. For example, in a node declared as <nspace:elemname> it returns the "nspace" part.
previousSibling		Returns a reference to the previous sibling node of this node, i.e. the previous node in the source file at the same level of the hierarchy.
specified	Ext	Indicates whether the node value is explicitly specified or derived from a default value in the DTD or schema. Normally only used with attribute nodes.
tagName		Sets or returns the name of the element node; i.e. the text name that appears within the tag.
text	Ext	Sets or returns the entire text content of this node and all its descendant nodes.
xml	Ext	Returns the entire XML content of this node and all its descendant nodes.

Element Methods

Name	Description
appendChild(new_node)	Appends the node object new_node to the end of the list of child nodes for this node.

Table Continued on Following Page

Name	Description
cloneNode(recurse_children)	Creates a new node object that is an exact clone of this node, including all descendant nodes of this node if recurse_children is set to true.
getAttribute(attr_name)	Returns the value of the attribute with the specified name.
getAttributeNode(attr_name)	Returns the attribute node with the specified name as an object.
getElementsByTagName(name)	Returns a node list of all descendant elements matching the specified name.
hasChildNodes()	Returns true if this node has any child nodes.
insertBefore(new_node, this_node)	Inserts a new node object new_node into the list of child nodes for this node, to the left of the node object this_node or at the end of the list if this_node is omitted.
normalize()	Combines all adjacent text nodes into one unified text node for all descendant element nodes.
removeAttribute(attr_name)	Removes the value of the attribute with the specified name, or replaces it with the default value.
removeAttributeNode(attr_node)	Removes the specified attribute node from the element and returns it. If the attribute has a default value in the DTD or schema, a new attribute node is automatically created with that default value and the specified property is updated.
removeChild(this_node)	Removes the child node this_node from the list of child nodes for this node, and returns it.
replaceChild(new_node, old_node)	Replaces the child node old_node with the new child node object new_node, and returns the old child node.

Name		Description
selectNodes (pattern)	Ext	Applies a specified pattern to this node's context and returns a node list object containing matching nodes. The string pattern specifies the XSL pattern-matching operation to be used.
selectSingleNode (pattern)	Ext	Applies a specified pattern to this node's context and returns just the first node object that matches. The string pattern specifies the XSL pattern-matching operation to be used.
setAttribute(attr_ name, value)		Sets the value of the attribute with the specified name.
setAttributeNode (attr_node)		Adds the new attribute node to the element. If an attribute with the same name exists, it is replaced and the old attribute node is returned.
transformNode (stylesheet)	Ext	Processes this node and its children using an XSL style sheet specified in the stylesheet argument, and returns the resulting transformation. The style sheet must be either a Document node object, in which case the document is assumed to be an XSL style sheet, or a Node object in the xsl namespace, in which case this node is treated as a standalone style sheet fragment.

Attribute or Attr — IXMLDOMAttribute Object

This object represents an Attribute of an Element object. In the W3C DOM recommendations, the object name is Attr rather than Attribute, to avoid clashing with existing interface definition languages. An Attribute node has a name and a value, and attributes are normally manipulated through a NamedNodeMap object. In the following tables, 'Ext' indicates properties and methods that are extensions to the base W3C object model. Microsoft implements the unextended object as IDOMAttribute).

Attribute Properties

Name	Description
attributes	Returns a collection of the Attribute (or Attr) objects for this node as a NamedNodeMap object.

Table Continued on Following Page

Name		Description
baseName	Ext	Returns the node name with any namespace removed. For example, in a node declared as `<nspace:elemname>` it returns the `"elemname"` part.
childNodes		Returns a `NodeList` containing all the child nodes of this node, for nodes that can have child nodes.
dataType	Ext	Sets or returns the data type for this node.
definition	Ext	For `EntityReference` nodes, returns the entry in the DTD or schema containing the definition for the entity, i.e. `"<!ENTITY entityname 'entity value'>"`. For other nodes, returns `null`.
firstChild		Returns a reference to the first child node of this node.
lastChild		Returns a reference to the last child node of this node.
name		Sets or returns the name of the attribute.
namespaceURI	Ext	Returns the URI for the namespace as a string. For example, in the namespace declaration `xmlns:name="uri"` it returns the `"uri"` part.
nextSibling		Returns a reference to the next sibling node of this node, i.e. the next node in the source data file at the same level of the hierarchy.
nodeName		Returns the name of the node, which will depend on the node type. See the list of Node Types at the end of this appendix for more details.
nodeTypeString	Ext	Returns the node type as a string, depending on the node type. See the list of Node Types at the end of this appendix for more details.
nodeType		Returns the node type as a number. See the list of Node Types at the end of this appendix for more details.
nodeTypedValue	Ext	Sets or returns the strongly typed value of the node, expressed in its defined data type. If no data type has been defined for the node, its `nodeValue` is returned.

Name		Description
nodeValue		Sets or returns the value of the node as plain text.
ownerDocument		Returns the root node of the document that contains the node.
parentNode		Returns the parent node of this node, for nodes that can have parents.
parsed	Ext	Returns true if this node and all its descendants have been parsed and instantiated.
prefix	Ext	Returns the element namespace prefix as a string. For example, in a node declared as <nspace:elemname> it returns the "nspace" part.
previous Sibling		Returns a reference to the previous sibling node of this node, i.e. the previous node in the source file at the same level of the hierarchy.
specified	Ext	Indicates whether the node value is explicitly specified or derived from a default value in the DTD or schema. Normally only used with attribute nodes.
tagName		Returns the name of the element that contains this attribute.
text	Ext	Sets or returns the entire text content of this node and all its descendant nodes.
xml	Ext	Returns the entire XML content of this node and all its descendant nodes.
value		Sets or returns the value of the attribute.

Attribute Methods

Name	Description
appendChild(new_node)	Appends the node object new_node to the end of the list of child nodes for this node.
cloneNode(recurse_children)	Creates a new node object that is an exact clone of this node, including all descendant nodes of this node if recurse_children is set to true.

Table Continued on Following Page

Name		Description
hasChildNodes()		Returns true if this node has any child nodes.
insertBefore (new_node, this_node)		Inserts a new node object new_node into the list of child nodes for this node, to the left of the node object this_node or at the end of the list if this_node is omitted.
removeChild (this_node)		Removes the child node this_node from the list of child nodes for this node, and returns it.
replaceChild (new_node, old_node)		Replaces the child node old_node with the new child node object new_node, and returns the old child node.
selectNodes (pattern)	Ext	Applies a specified pattern to this node's context and returns a node list object containing matching nodes. The string pattern specifies the XSL pattern-matching operation to be used.
selectSingleNode (pattern)	Ext	Applies a specified pattern to this node's context and returns just the first node object that matches. The string pattern specifies the XSL pattern-matching operation to be used.
transformNode (stylesheet)	Ext	Processes this node and its children using an XSL style sheet specified in the stylesheet argument, and returns the resulting transformation. The style sheet must be either a Document node object, in which case the document is assumed to be an XSL style sheet, or a Node object in the xsl namespace, in which case this node is treated as a standalone style sheet fragment.

Entity — the IXMLDOMEntity Object

This object represents a parsed or unparsed entity as declared with an <!ENTITY...> element in the DTD. However, it does not provide a reference to the entity declaration. The W3C DOM recommendation does not define an object in version 1.0 that models the declaration of entities. In the following tables, 'Ext' indicates properties and methods that are extensions to the base W3C object model. In IE5 the unextended object is implemented by the IDOMEntity object.

Entity Properties

Name		Description
attributes		Returns a collection of the `Attribute` (or `Attr`) objects for this node as a `NamedNodeMap` object.
baseName	Ext	Returns the node name with any namespace removed. For example, in a node declared as `<nspace:elemname>` it returns the `"elemname"` part.
childNodes		Returns a `NodeList` containing all the child nodes of this node, for nodes that can have child nodes.
dataType	Ext	Sets or returns the data type for this node.
definition	Ext	For `EntityReference` nodes, returns the entry in the DTD or schema containing the definition for the entity, i.e. `"<!ENTITY entityname 'entity value'>"`. For other nodes, returns `null`.
firstChild		Returns a reference to the first child node of this node.
lastChild		Returns a reference to the last child node of this node.
namespaceURI	Ext	Returns the URI for the namespace as a string. For example, in the namespace declaration `xmlns:name="uri"` it returns the `"uri"` part.
nextSibling		Returns a reference to the next sibling node of this node, i.e. the next node in the source data file at the same level of the hierarchy.
nodeName		Returns the name of the node, which will depend on the node type. See the list of Node Types at the end of this appendix for more details.
nodeTypeString	Ext	Returns the node type as a string, depending on the node type. See the list of Node Types at the end of this appendix for more details.
nodeType		Returns the node type as a number. See the list of Node Types at the end of this appendix for more details.
nodeTypedValue	Ext	Sets or returns the strongly typed value of the node, expressed in its defined data type. If no data type has been defined for the node, its `nodeValue` is returned.

Table Continued on Following Page

Name		Description
nodeValue		Sets or returns the value of the node as plain text.
notationName	Ext	Returns the name of the notation linked to the entity.
ownerDocument		Returns the root node of the document that contains the node.
parentNode		Returns the parent node of this node, for nodes that can have parents.
parsed	Ext	Returns true if this node and all its descendants have been parsed and instantiated.
prefix	Ext	Returns the element namespace prefix as a string. For example, in a node declared as <nspace:elemname> it returns the "nspace" part.
previousSibling		Returns a reference to the previous sibling node of this node, i.e. the previous node in the source file at the same level of the hierarchy.
publicId		Sets or returns the PUBLIC identifier value for this entity node.
specified	Ext	Indicates whether the node value is explicitly specified or derived from a default value in the DTD or schema. Normally only used with attribute nodes.
systemId		Sets or returns the SYSTEM identifier value for this entity node.
text	Ext	Sets or returns the entire text content of this node and all its descendant nodes.
xml	Ext	Returns the entire XML content of this node and all its descendant nodes.

Entity Methods

Name	Description
appendChild(new_node)	Appends the node object new_node to the end of the list of child nodes for this node.

Name		Description
`cloneNode(recurse_` `children)`		Creates a new node object that is an exact clone of this node, including all descendant nodes of this node if `recurse_children` is set to `true`.
`hasChildNodes()`		Returns `true` if this node has any child nodes.
`insertBefore(new_node,` `this_node)`		Inserts a new node object `new_node` into the list of child nodes for this node, to the left of the node object `this_node` or at the end of the list if `this_node` is omitted.
`removeChild(this_node)`		Removes the child node `this_node` from the list of child nodes for this node, and returns it.
`replaceChild(new_node,` `old_node)`		Replaces the child node `old_node` with the new child node object `new_node`, and returns the old child node.
`selectNodes(pattern)`	Ext	Applies a specified pattern to this node's context and returns a node list object containing matching nodes. The string `pattern` specifies the XSL pattern-matching operation to be used.
`selectSingleNode` `(pattern)`	Ext	Applies a specified pattern to this node's context and returns just the first node object that matches. The string `pattern` specifies the XSL pattern-matching operation to be used.
`transformNode` `(stylesheet)`	Ext	Processes this node and its children using an XSL style sheet specified in the `stylesheet` argument, and returns the resulting transformation. The style sheet must be either a `Document` node object, in which case the document is assumed to be an XSL style sheet, or a Node object in the `xsl` namespace, in which case this node is treated as a standalone style sheet fragment.

EntityReference — the IXMLDOMEntityReference Object

This object represents an entity reference node within the XML document. If the XML processor expands entity references while building the structure model, it's possible that no entity reference objects will appear in the tree, being replaced by the **replacement text** of the entity. In the following tables, 'Ext' indicates properties and methods that are extensions to the base W3C object model. The object is implemented without extensions by Microsoft as the `IDOMEntityReference` object.

EntityReference Properties

Name		Description
attributes		Returns a collection of the `Attribute` (or `Attr`) objects for this node as a `NamedNodeMap` object.
baseName	Ext	Returns the node name with any namespace removed. For example, in a node declared as `<nspace:elemname>` it returns the `"elemname"` part.
childNodes		Returns a `NodeList` containing all the child nodes of this node, for nodes that can have child nodes.
dataType	Ext	Sets or returns the data type for this node.
definition	Ext	For `EntityReference` nodes, returns the entry in the DTD or schema containing the definition for the entity, i.e. `"<!ENTITY entityname 'entity value'>"`. For other nodes, returns `null`.
firstChild		Returns a reference to the first child node of this node.
lastChild		Returns a reference to the last child node of this node.
namespaceURI	Ext	Returns the URI for the namespace as a string. For example, in the namespace declaration `xmlns:name="uri"` it returns the `"uri"` part.
nextSibling		Returns a reference to the next sibling node of this node, i.e. the next node in the source data file at the same level of the hierarchy.
nodeName		Returns the name of the node, which will depend on the node type. See the list of Node Types at the end of this appendix for more details.

Name		Description
nodeTypeString	Ext	Returns the node type as a string, depending on the node type. See the list of Node Types at the end of this appendix for more details.
nodeType		Returns the node type as a number. See the list of Node Types at the end of this appendix for more details.
nodeTypedValue	Ext	Sets or returns the strongly typed value of the node, expressed in its defined data type. If no data type has been defined for the node, its nodeValue is returned.
nodeValue		Sets or returns the value of the node as plain text.
ownerDocument		Returns the root node of the document that contains the node.
parentNode		Returns the parent node of this node, for nodes that can have parents.
parsed	Ext	Returns true if this node and all its descendants have been parsed and instantiated.
prefix	Ext	Returns the element namespace prefix as a string. For example, in a node declared as <nspace:elemname> it returns the "nspace" part.
previousSibling		Returns a reference to the previous sibling node of this node, i.e. the previous node in the source file at the same level of the hierarchy.
specified	Ext	Indicates whether the node value is explicitly specified or derived from a default value in the DTD or schema. Normally only used with attribute nodes.
text	Ext	Sets or returns the entire text content of this node and all its descendant nodes.
xml	Ext	Returns the entire XML content of this node and all its descendant nodes.

EntityReference Methods

Name		Description
appendChild (new_node)		Appends the node object new_node to the end of the list of child nodes for this node.
cloneNode(recurse_ children)		Creates a new node object that is an exact clone of this node, including all descendant nodes of this node if recurse_children is set to true.
hasChildNodes()		Returns true if this node has any child nodes.
insertBefore(new_ node, this_node)		Inserts a new node object new_node into the list of child nodes for this node, to the left of the node object this_node or at the end of the list if this_node is omitted.
removeChild(this_ node)		Removes the child node this_node from the list of child nodes for this node, and returns it.
replaceChild(new_ node, old_node)		Replaces the child node old_node with the new child node object new_node, and returns the old child node.
selectNodes (pattern)	Ext	Applies a specified pattern to this node's context and returns a node list object containing matching nodes. The string pattern specifies the XSL pattern-matching operation to be used.
selectSingleNode (pattern)	Ext	Applies a specified pattern to this node's context and returns just the first node object that matches. The string pattern specifies the XSL pattern-matching operation to be used.
transformNode (stylesheet)	Ext	Processes this node and its children using an XSL style sheet specified in the stylesheet argument, and returns the resulting transformation. The style sheet must be either a Document node object, in which case the document is assumed to be an XSL style sheet, or a Node object in the xsl namespace, in which case this node is treated as a standalone style sheet fragment.

Notation — the IXMLDOMNotation Object

This object represents a notation declared in the DTD or schema with a
`<!NOTATION...>` element. In the following tables, 'Ext' indicates properties and
methods that are extensions to the base W3C object model. The unextended object is
implemented as the `IDOMNotation` object in IE5.

Notation Properties

Name		Description
attributes		Returns a collection of the `Attribute` (or `Attr`) objects for this node as a `NamedNodeMap` object.
baseName	Ext	Returns the node name with any namespace removed. For example, in a node declared as `<nspace:elemname>` it returns the "elemname" part.
childNodes		Returns a `NodeList` containing all the child nodes of this node, for nodes that can have child nodes.
dataType	Ext	Sets or returns the data type for this node.
definition	Ext	For `EntityReference` nodes, returns the entry in the DTD or schema containing the definition for the entity, i.e. "`<!ENTITY entityname 'entity value'>`". For other nodes, returns `null`.
firstChild		Returns a reference to the first child node of this node.
lastChild		Returns a reference to the last child node of this node.
namespaceURI	Ext	Returns the URI for the namespace as a string. For example, in the namespace declaration `xmlns:name="uri"` it returns the "uri" part.
nextSibling		Returns a reference to the next sibling node of this node, i.e. the next node in the source data file at the same level of the hierarchy.
nodeName		Returns the name of the node, which will depend on the node type. See the list of Node Types at the end of this appendix for more details.

Table Continued on Following Page

Name		Description
nodeTypeString	Ext	Returns the node type as a string, depending on the node type. See the list of Node Types at the end of this appendix for more details.
nodeType		Returns the node type as a number. See the list of Node Types at the end of this appendix for more details.
nodeTypedValue	Ext	Sets or returns the strongly typed value of the node, expressed in its defined data type. If no data type has been defined for the node, its nodeValue is returned.
nodeValue		Sets or returns the value of the node as plain text.
ownerDocument		Returns the root node of the document that contains the node.
parentNode		Returns the parent node of this node, for nodes that can have parents.
parsed	Ext	Returns true if this node and all its descendants have been parsed and instantiated.
prefix	Ext	Returns the element namespace prefix as a string. For example, in a node declared as <nspace:elemname> it returns the "nspace" part.
previousSibling		Returns a reference to the previous sibling node of this node, i.e. the previous node in the source file at the same level of the hierarchy.
publicId		Sets or returns the PUBLIC identifier value for this entity node.
specified	Ext	Indicates whether the node value is explicitly specified or derived from a default value in the DTD or schema. Normally only used with attribute nodes.
systemId		Sets or returns the SYSTEM identifier value for this entity node.
text	Ext	Sets or returns the entire text content of this node and all its descendant nodes.
xml	Ext	Returns the entire XML content of this node and all its descendant nodes.

Notation Methods

Name		Description
appendChild (new_node)		Appends the node object new_node to the end of the list of child nodes for this node.
cloneNode (recurse_ children)		Creates a new node object that is an exact clone of this node, including all descendant nodes of this node if recurse_children is set to true.
hasChildNodes()		Returns true if this node has any child nodes.
insertBefore (new_node, this_node)		Inserts a new node object new_node into the list of child nodes for this node, to the left of the node object this_node or at the end of the list if this_node is omitted.
removeChild (this_node)		Removes the child node this_node from the list of child nodes for this node, and returns it.
replaceChild (new_node, old_node)		Replaces the child node old_node with the new child node object new_node, and returns the old child node.
selectNodes (pattern)	Ext	Applies a specified pattern to this node's context and returns a node list object containing matching nodes. The string pattern specifies the XSL pattern-matching operation to be used.
selectSingleNode (pattern)	Ext	Applies a specified pattern to this node's context and returns just the first node object that matches. The string pattern specifies the XSL pattern-matching operation to be used.
transformNode (stylesheet)	Ext	Processes this node and its children using an XSL style sheet specified in the stylesheet argument, and returns the resulting transformation. The style sheet must be either a Document node object, in which case the document is assumed to be an XSL style sheet, or a Node object in the xsl namespace, in which case this node is treated as a standalone style sheet fragment.

CharacterData — the IXMLDOMCharacterData Object

This object is the base for several higher-level objects including Text, CDATASection (which is inherited from the Text object) and Comment. It provides text information properties like length, and a range of text manipulation methods like substringData() that are used by these objects. The IE5 implementation of CharacterData follows the W3C recommendations for character data manipulation in the appropriate elements with the exception of those properties and methods marked with 'Ext' in the following tables. The unextended W3C CharacterData object is implemented in IE5 by the IDOMCharacterData object.

CharacterData Properties

Name		Description
attributes		Returns a collection of the Attribute (or Attr) objects for this node as a NamedNodeMap object.
baseName	Ext	Returns the node name with any namespace removed. For example, in a node declared as <nspace:elemname> it returns the "elemname" part.
childNodes		Returns a NodeList containing all the child nodes of this node, for nodes that can have child nodes.
data		Contains this node's value, which depends on the node type.
dataType	Ext	Sets or returns the data type for this node.
definition	Ext	For EntityReference nodes, returns the entry in the DTD or schema containing the definition for the entity, i.e. "<!ENTITY entityname 'entity value'>". For other nodes, returns null.
firstChild		Returns a reference to the first child node of this node.
lastChild		Returns a reference to the last child node of this node.
length		Returns the number of characters for the data, i.e. the string length.
namespaceURI	Ext	Returns the URI for the namespace as a string. For example, in the namespace declaration xmlns:name="uri" it returns the "uri" part.
nextSibling		Returns a reference to the next sibling node of this node, i.e. the next node in the source data file at the same level of the hierarchy.

Name		Description
nodeName		Returns the name of the node, which will depend on the node type. See the list of Node Types at the end of this appendix for more details.
nodeTypeString	Ext	Returns the node type as a string. See the list of Node Types at the end of this appendix for more details.
nodeType		Returns the node type as a number. See the list of Node Types at the end of this appendix for more details.
nodeTypedValue	Ext	Sets or returns the strongly typed value of the node, expressed in its defined data type. If no data type has been defined for the node, its nodeValue is returned.
nodeValue		Sets or returns the value of the node as plain text.
ownerDocument		Returns the root node of the document that contains the node.
parentNode		Returns the parent node of this node, for nodes that can have parents.
parsed	Ext	Returns true if this node and all its descendants have been parsed and instantiated.
prefix	Ext	Returns the element namespace prefix as a string. For example, in a node declared as <nspace:elemname> it returns the "nspace" part.
previousSibling		Returns a reference to the previous sibling node of this node, i.e. the previous node in the source file at the same level of the hierarchy.
specified	Ext	Indicates whether the node value is explicitly specified or derived from a default value in the DTD or schema. Normally only used with attribute nodes.
text	Ext	Sets or returns the entire text content of this node and all its descendant nodes.
xml	Ext	Returns the entire XML content of this node and all its descendant nodes.

CharacterData Methods

Name	Description
appendChild(new_node)	Appends the node object new_node to the end of the list of child nodes for this node.
appendData(text)	Appends the string in the text argument to the existing string data.
cloneNode(recurse_children)	Creates a new node object that is an exact clone of this node, including all descendant nodes of this node if recurse_children is set to true.
deleteData(char_offset, num_chars)	Deletes a substring from the string data of the node, starting at char_offset and continuing for num_chars.
hasChildNodes()	Returns true if this node has any child nodes.
insertBefore(new_node, this_node)	Inserts a new node object new_node into the list of child nodes for this node, to the left of the node object this_node or at the end of the list if this_node is omitted.
insertData(char_offset, text)	Inserts the string in the text argument at the specified character offset within the data contained by the node.
removeChild(this_child)	Removes the child node this_node from the list of child nodes for this node, and returns it.
replaceChild(new_node, old_node)	Replaces the child node old_node with the new child node object new_node, and returns the old child node.
replaceData(char_offset, num_chars, text)	Replaces the specified number of characters in the existing string data of the node, starting at the specified character offset, with the string in the text argument.

Name		Description
selectNodes(pattern)	Ext	Applies a specified pattern to this node's context and returns a node list object containing matching nodes. The string pattern specifies the XSL pattern-matching operation to be used.
selectSingleNode (pattern)	Ext	Applies a specified pattern to this node's context and returns just the first node object that matches. The string pattern specifies the XSL pattern-matching operation to be used.
substringData(char_ offset, num_chars)		Returns as a string the specified number of characters, starting at the specified character offset, from the data contained in the node.
transformNode (stylesheet)	Ext	Processes this node and its children using an XSL style sheet specified in the stylesheet argument, and returns the resulting transformation. The style sheet must be either a Document node object, in which case the document is assumed to be an XSL style sheet, or a Node object in the xsl namespace, in which case this node is treated as a standalone style sheet fragment.

Text — the IXMLDOMText Object

This object represents the text content of an element node or an attribute node. It is derived from the CharacterData object, and the CDATASection object is in turn inherited from it. In the following tables, 'Ext' indicates properties and methods that are extensions to the base W3C object model; the W3C CDATASection object is implemented in IE5 by the IDOMText object.

Text Properties

Name		Description
attributes		Returns a collection of the Attribute (or Attr) objects for this node as a NamedNodeMap object.
baseName	Ext	Returns the node name with any namespace removed. For example, in a node declared as <nspace:elemname> it returns the "elemname" part.

Name		Description
childNodes		Returns a NodeList containing all the child nodes of this node, for nodes that can have child nodes.
data		Contains this node's value, which depends on the node type.
dataType	Ext	Sets or returns the data type for this node.
definition	Ext	For EntityReference nodes, returns the entry in the DTD or schema containing the definition for the entity, i.e. "<!ENTITY entityname 'entity value'>". For other nodes, returns null.
firstChild		Returns a reference to the first child node of this node.
lastChild		Returns a reference to the last child node of this node.
length		Returns the number of characters for the data, i.e. the string length.
namespaceURI	Ext	Returns the URI for the namespace as a string. For example, in the namespace declaration xmlns:name="uri" it returns the "uri" part.
nextSibling		Returns a reference to the next sibling node of this node, i.e. the next node in the source data file at the same level of the hierarchy.
nodeName		Returns the name of the node, which will depend on the node type. See the list of Node Types at the end of this appendix for more details.
nodeTypeString	Ext	Returns the node type as a string, depending on the node type. See the list of Node Types at the end of this appendix for more details.
nodeType		Returns the node type as a number. See the list of Node Types at the end of this appendix for more details.
nodeTypedValue	Ext	Sets or returns the strongly typed value of the node, expressed in its defined data type. If no data type has been defined for the node, its nodeValue is returned.

Name		Description
nodeValue		Sets or returns the value of the node as plain text.
ownerDocument		Returns the root node of the document that contains the node.
parentNode		Returns the parent node of this node, for nodes that can have parents.
parsed	Ext	Returns true if this node and all its descendants have been parsed and instantiated.
prefix	Ext	Returns the element namespace prefix as a string. For example, in a node declared as <nspace:elemname> it returns the "nspace" part.
previousSibling		Returns a reference to the previous sibling node of this node, i.e. the previous node in the source file at the same level of the hierarchy.
specified	Ext	Indicates whether the node value is explicitly specified or derived from a default value in the DTD or schema. Normally only used with attribute nodes.
text	Ext	Sets or returns the entire text content of this node and all its descendant nodes.
xml	Ext	Returns the entire XML content of this node and all its descendant nodes.

Text Methods

Name	Description
appendChild(new_node)	Appends the node object new_node to the end of the list of child nodes for this node.
appendData(text)	Appends the string in the text argument to the existing string data.
cloneNode(recurse_children)	Creates a new node object that is an exact clone of this node, including all descendant nodes of this node if recurse_children is set to true.

Table Continued on Following Page

Name	Description
deleteData(char_offset, num_chars)	Deletes a substring from the string data of the node, starting at char_offset and continuing for num_chars.
hasChildNodes()	Returns true if this node has any child nodes.
insertBefore(new_node, this_node)	Inserts a new node object new_node into the list of child nodes for this node, to the left of the node object this_node or at the end of the list if this_node is omitted.
insertData(char_offset, text)	Inserts the string in the text argument at the specified character offset within the data contained by the node.
removeChild(this_child)	Removes the child node this_node from the list of child nodes for this node, and returns it.
replaceChild(new_node, old_node)	Replaces the child node old_node with the new child node object new_node, and returns the old child node.
replaceData(char_offset, num_chars, text)	Replaces the specified number of characters in the existing string data of the node, starting at the specified character offset, with the string in the text argument.
selectNodes(pattern) Ext	Applies a specified pattern to this node's context and returns a node list object containing matching nodes. The string pattern specifies the XSL pattern-matching operation to be used.
selectSingleNode(pattern) Ext	Applies a specified pattern to this node's context and returns just the first node object that matches. The string pattern specifies the XSL pattern-matching operation to be used.

Name		Description
`splitText(char_offset)`		Splits the node into two separate nodes at the specified character offset, then inserts the new node into the XML as a sibling that immediately follows this node.
`substringData(char_offset, num_chars)`		Returns as a string the specified number of characters, starting at the specified character offset, from the data contained in the node.
`transformNode(stylesheet)`	Ext	Processes this node and its children using an XSL style sheet specified in the `stylesheet` argument, and returns the resulting transformation. The style sheet must be either a `Document` node object, in which case the document is assumed to be an XSL style sheet, or a Node object in the `xsl` namespace, in which case this node is treated as a standalone style sheet fragment.

CDATASection — the IXMLDOMCDATASection Object

CDATA sections in a DTD or schema are used to 'escape' blocks of text that are not designed to be interpreted as markup. The are declared in the DTD using a `<!CDATA...>` element. The `IXMLDOMCDATASection` interface is inherited from the `IXMLDOMText` interface, and adds no extra methods or properties. In the following tables, 'Ext' indicates properties and methods that are extensions to the base W3C object model. IE5 implements the unextended W3C object as the `IDOMCDATASection` object.

CDATASection Properties

Name		Description
`attributes`		Returns collection of the `Attribute` (or `Attr`) objects for this node as a `NamedNodeMap` object.
`baseName`	Ext	Returns the node name with any namespace removed. For example, in a node declared as `<nspace:elemname>` it returns the "`elemname`" part.

Table Continued on Following Page

Name		Description
childNodes		Returns a NodeList containing all the child nodes of this node, for nodes that can have child nodes.
data		Contains this node's value, which depends on the node type.
dataType	Ext	Sets or returns the data type for this node.
definition	Ext	For EntityReference nodes, returns the entry in the DTD or schema containing the definition for the entity, i.e. "<!ENTITY entityname 'entity value'>". For other nodes, returns null.
firstChild		Returns a reference to the first child node of this node.
lastChild		Returns a reference to the last child node of this node.
length		Returns the number of characters for the data, i.e. the string length.
namespaceURI	Ext	Returns the URI for the namespace as a string. For example, in the namespace declaration xmlns:name="uri" it returns the "uri" part.
nextSibling		Returns a reference to the next sibling node of this node, i.e. the next node in the source data file at the same level of the hierarchy.
nodeName		Returns the name of the node, which will depend on the node type. See the list of Node Types at the end of this appendix for more details.
nodeTypeString	Ext	Returns the node type as a string, depending on the node type. See the list of Node Types at the end of this appendix for more details.
nodeType		Returns the node type as a number. See the list of Node Types at the end of this appendix for more details.
nodeTypedValue	Ext	Sets or returns the strongly typed value of the node, expressed in its defined data type. If no data type has been defined for the node, its nodeValue is returned.

Name		Description
nodeValue		Sets or returns the value of the node as plain text.
ownerDocument		Returns the root node of the document that contains the node.
parentNode		Returns the parent node of this node, for nodes that can have parents.
parsed	Ext	Returns true if this node and all its descendants have been parsed and instantiated.
prefix	Ext	Returns the element namespace prefix as a string. For example, in a node declared as <nspace:elemname> it returns the "nspace" part.
previousSibling		Returns a reference to the previous sibling node of this node, i.e. the previous node in the source file at the same level of the hierarchy.
specified	Ext	Indicates whether the node value is explicitly specified or derived from a default value in the DTD or schema. Normally only used with attribute nodes.
text	Ext	Sets or returns the entire text content of this node and all its descendant nodes.
xml	Ext	Returns the entire XML content of this node and all its descendant nodes.

CDATASection Methods

Name	Description
appendChild(new_node)	Appends the node object new_node to the end of the list of child nodes for this node.
appendData(text)	Appends the string in the text argument to the existing string data.
cloneNode(recurse_children)	Creates a new node object that is an exact clone of this node, including all descendant nodes of this node if recurse_children is set to true.

Table Continued on Following Page

Name		Description
deleteData(char_offset, num_chars)		Deletes a substring from the string data of the node, starting at char_offset and continuing for num_chars.
hasChildNodes()		Returns true if this node has any child nodes.
insertBefore(new_node, this_node)		Inserts a new node object new_node into the list of child nodes for this node, to the left of the node object this_node or at the end of the list if this_node is omitted.
insertData(char_offset, text)		Inserts the string in the text argument at the specified character offset within the data contained by the node.
removeChild(this_child)		Removes the child node this_node from the list of child nodes for this node, and returns it.
replaceChild(new_node, old_node)		Replaces the child node old_node with the new child node object new_node, and returns the old child node.
replaceData(char_offset, num_chars, text)		Replaces the specified number of characters in the existing string data of the node, starting at the specified character offset, with the string in the text argument.
selectNodes(pattern)	Ext	Applies a specified pattern to this node's context and returns a node list object containing matching nodes. The string pattern specifies the XSL pattern-matching operation to be used.
selectSingleNode(pattern)	Ext	Applies a specified pattern to this node's context and returns just the first node object that matches. The string pattern specifies the XSL pattern-matching operation to be used.

Name		Description
`splitText(char_offset)`		Splits the node into two separate nodes at the specified character offset, then inserts the new node into the XML as a sibling that immediately follows this node.
`substringData(char_ offset, num_chars)`		Returns as a string the specified number of characters, starting at the specified character offset, from the data contained in the node.
`transformNode(stylesheet)`	Ext	Processes this node and its children using an XSL style sheet specified in the `stylesheet` argument, and returns the resulting transformation. The style sheet must be either a `Document` node object, in which case the document is assumed to be an XSL style sheet, or a Node object in the `xsl` namespace, in which case this node is treated as a standalone style sheet fragment.

Comment - the IXMLDOMComment Object

Represents the content of an XML comment element. This object is derived from the `IXMLDOMCharacterData` object. In the following tables, 'Ext' indicates properties and methods that are extensions to the base W3C object model. The unextended W3C `Comment` object is implemented in IE5 by the `IDOMComment` interface.

Comment Properties

Name		Description
`attributes`		Returns a collection of the `Attribute` (or `Attr`) objects for this node as a `NamedNodeMap` object.
`baseName`	Ext	Returns the node name with any namespace removed. For example, in a node declared as `<nspace:elemname>` it returns the `"elemname"` part.
`childNodes`		Returns a `NodeList` containing all the child nodes of this node, for nodes that can have child nodes.

Table Continued on Following Page

Name		Description
data		Contains this node's value, which depends on the node type.
dataType	Ext	Sets or returns the data type for this node.
definition	Ext	For EntityReference nodes, returns the entry in the DTD or schema containing the definition for the entity, i.e. "<!ENTITY entityname 'entity value'>". For other nodes, returns null.
firstChild		Returns a reference to the first child node of this node.
lastChild		Returns a reference to the last child node of this node.
length		Returns the number of characters for the data, i.e. the string length.
namespaceURI	Ext	Returns the URI for the namespace as a string. For example, in the namespace declaration xmlns:name="uri" it returns the "uri" part.
nextSibling		Returns a reference to the next sibling node of this node, i.e. the next node in the source data file at the same level of the hierarchy.
nodeName		Returns the name of the node, which will depend on the node type. See the list of Node Types at the end of this appendix for more details.
nodeTypeString	Ext	Returns the node type as a string, depending on the node type. See the list of Node Types at the end of this appendix for more details.
nodeType		Returns the node type as a number. See the list of Node Types at the end of this appendix for more details.
nodeTypedValue	Ext	Sets or returns the strongly typed value of the node, expressed in its defined data type. If no data type has been defined for the node, its nodeValue is returned.
nodeValue		Sets or returns the value of the node as plain text.
ownerDocument		Returns the root node of the document that contains the node.

Name		Description
parentNode		Returns the parent node of this node, for nodes that can have parents.
parsed	Ext	Returns true if this node and all its descendants have been parsed and instantiated.
prefix	Ext	Returns the element namespace prefix as a string. For example, in a node declared as <nspace:elemname> it returns the "nspace" part.
previousSibling		Returns a reference to the previous sibling node of this node, i.e. the previous node in the source file at the same level of the hierarchy.
specified	Ext	Indicates whether the node value is explicitly specified or derived from a default value in the DTD or schema. Normally only used with attribute nodes.
text	Ext	Sets or returns the entire text content of this node and all its descendant nodes.
xml	Ext	Returns the entire XML content of this node and all its descendant nodes.

Comment Methods

Name	Description
appendChild(new_node)	Appends the node object new_node to the end of the list of child nodes for this node.
appendData(text)	Appends the string in the text argument to the existing string data.
cloneNode(recurse_children)	Creates a new node object that is an exact clone of this node, including all descendant nodes of this node if recurse_children is set to true.
deleteData(char_offset, num_chars)	Deletes a substring from the string data of the node, starting at char_offset and continuing for num_chars.
hasChildNodes()	Returns true if this node has any child nodes.

Table Continued on Following Page

335

Name	Description
insertBefore(new_node, this_node)	Inserts a new node object new_node into the list of child nodes for this node, to the left of the node object this_node or at the end of the list if this_node is omitted.
insertData(char_offset, text)	Inserts the string in the text argument at the specified character offset within the data contained by the node.
removeChild(this_child)	Removes the child node this_node from the list of child nodes for this node, and returns it.
replaceChild(new_node, old_node)	Replaces the child node old_node with the new child node object new_node, and returns the old child node.
replaceData(char_offset, num_chars, text)	Replaces the specified number of characters in the existing string data of the node, starting at the specified character offset, with the string in the text argument.
selectNodes(pattern) Ext	Applies a specified pattern to this node's context and returns a node list object containing matching nodes. The string pattern specifies the XSL pattern-matching operation to be used.
selectSingleNode(pattern) Ext	Applies a specified pattern to this node's context and returns just the first node object that matches. The string pattern specifies the XSL pattern-matching operation to be used.
substringData(char_offset, num_chars)	Returns as a string the specified number of characters, starting at the specified character offset, from the data contained in the node.

Name		Description
transformNode(stylesheet)	Ext	Processes this node and its children using an XSL style sheet specified in the stylesheet argument, and returns the resulting transformation. The style sheet must be either a Document node object, in which case the document is assumed to be an XSL style sheet, or a Node object in the xsl namespace, in which case this node is treated as a standalone style sheet fragment.

ProcessingInstruction — the IXMLDOMProcessingInstruction Object

This element represents an instruction embedded in the XML within the '<?' and '?>' delimiters. It provides a way of storing processor-specific information within an XML document. The text content of the node is usually subdivided into the target (the text after the '<?' and up to the first white-space character) and the data content (the remainder up to the closing '?>'. In the following tables, 'Ext' indicates properties and methods that are extensions to the base W3C object model. The W3C Recommendation for this object is implemented in IE5 by the IDOMProcessingInstruction object.

ProcessingInstruction Properties

Name		Description
attributes		Returns a collection of the Attribute (or Attr) objects for this node as a NamedNodeMap object.
baseName	Ext	Returns the node name with any namespace removed. For example, in a node declared as <nspace:elemname> it returns the "elemname" part.
childNodes		Returns a NodeList containing all the child nodes of this node, for nodes that can have child nodes.
data		Contains this node's value, which depends on the node type.
dataType	Ext	Sets or returns the data type for this node.

Table Continued on Following Page

Name		Description
definition	Ext	For EntityReference nodes, returns the entry in the DTD or schema containing the definition for the entity, i.e. "<!ENTITY entityname 'entity value'>". For other nodes, returns null.
firstChild		Returns a reference to the first child node of this node.
lastChild		Returns a reference to the last child node of this node.
length		Returns the number of characters for the data, i.e. the string length.
namespaceURI	Ext	Returns the URI for the namespace as a string. For example, in the namespace declaration xmlns:name="uri" it returns the "uri" part.
nextSibling		Returns a reference to the next sibling node of this node, i.e. the next node in the source data file at the same level of the hierarchy.
nodeName		Returns the name of the node, which will depend on the node type. See the list of Node Types at the end of this appendix for more details.
nodeTypeString	Ext	Returns the node type as a string, depending on the node type. See the list of Node Types at the end of this appendix for more details.
nodeType		Returns the node type as a number. See the list of Node Types at the end of this appendix for more details.
nodeTypedValue	Ext	Sets or returns the strongly typed value of the node, expressed in its defined data type. If no data type has been defined for the node, its nodeValue is returned.
nodeValue		Sets or returns the value of the node as plain text.
ownerDocument		Returns the root node of the document that contains the node.
parentNode		Returns the parent node of this node, for nodes that can have parents.

Name		Description
parsed	Ext	Returns `true` if this node and all its descendants have been parsed and instantiated.
prefix	Ext	Returns the element namespace prefix as a string. For example, in a node declared as `<nspace:elemname>` it returns the "nspace" part.
previous Sibling		Returns a reference to the previous sibling node of this node, i.e. the previous node in the source file at the same level of the hierarchy.
specified	Ext	Indicates whether the node value is explicitly specified or derived from a default value in the DTD or schema. Normally only used with attribute nodes.
target		Specifies the application to which this processing instruction is directed. This is the text up to the first white-space character in the node content.
text	Ext	Sets or returns the entire text content of this node and all its descendant nodes.
xml	Ext	Returns the entire XML content of this node and all its descendant nodes.

ProcessingInstruction Methods

Name	Description
appendChild(new_node)	Appends the node object new_node to the end of the list of child nodes for this node.
cloneNode(recurse_ children)	Creates a new node object that is an exact clone of this node, including all descendant nodes of this node if `recurse_children` is set to `true`.
hasChildNodes()	Returns `true` if this node has any child nodes.

Table Continued on Following Page

Name		Description
insertBefore(new_node, this_node)		Inserts a new node object new_node into the list of child nodes for this node, to the left of the node object this_node or at the end of the list if this_node is omitted.
removeChild(this_child)		Removes the child node this_node from the list of child nodes for this node, and returns it.
replaceChild(new_node, old_node)		Replaces the child node old_node with the new child node object new_node, and returns the old child node.
selectNodes(pattern)	Ext	Applies a specified pattern to this node's context and returns a node list object containing matching nodes. The string pattern specifies the XSL pattern-matching operation to be used.
selectSingleNode (pattern)	Ext	Applies a specified pattern to this node's context and returns just the first node object that matches. The string pattern specifies the XSL pattern-matching operation to be used.
transformNode (stylesheet)	Ext	Processes this node and its children using an XSL style sheet specified in the stylesheet argument, and returns the resulting transformation. The style sheet must be either a Document node object, in which case the document is assumed to be an XSL style sheet, or a Node object in the xsl namespace, in which case this node is treated as a standalone style sheet fragment.

Implementation — the IXMLDOMImplementation Object

This object provides access to methods that are application-specific and independent of any particular instance of the document object model. It is a child of the `Document` object.

Implementation Method

Name	Description
hasFeature(feature, version)	Returns `true` if the specified version of the implementation supports the specified feature.

IE5-Specific XML Parser Objects

While the document object is quite tightly standardized as far as the structure of the document is concerned, there are other peripheral activities that any XML application must handle. This includes managing and reporting errors, originating and handling HTTP requests, and interfacing with style sheets. These are all application-specific tasks, and in IE5 are managed by three subsidiary objects:

- ❑ ParseError (the `IDOMParseError` object)
- ❑ HttpRequest (the `IXMLHttpRequest` Object)
- ❑ Runtime (the `IXTLRuntime` object)

ParseError — the IDOMParseError Object

The properties of this object return detailed information about the last error that occurred while loading and parsing a document. This includes the line number, character position, and a text description. In the following table, all are marked 'Ext' to indicate that the W3C recommendations do not cover this area of the DOM.

ParseError Properties

Name		Description
errorCode	Ext	Returns the error number or error code as a decimal integer.
filepos	Ext	Returns the absolute character position in the file where the error occurred.
line	Ext	Returns the number of the line in the document that contains the error.
linepos	Ext	Returns the character position of the error within the line in which it occurred.

Table Continued on Following Page

Name		Description
reason	Ext	Returns a text description of the source and reason for the error, and can also include the URL of the DTD or schema and the node within it that corresponds to the error.
srcText	Ext	Returns the full text of the line that contains the error or an empty string if the error cannot be assigned to a specific line.
url	Ext	Returns the URL of the most recent XML document that contained an error.

HttpRequest — the IXMLHttpRequest Object

This object provides client-side protocol support for communication with HTTP servers. A client can use the HttpRequest object to send an arbitrary HTTP request, receive the response, and have the IE5 DOM parse that response. In the following table, all are marked 'Ext' to indicate that the W3C recommendations do not cover this area of the DOM.

HttpRequest Properties

Name		Description
readyState	Ext	Indicates the current state of the XML document being loaded:
		0 ("uninitialized") - the object has been created but the load() has not yet been executed.
		1 ("loading") - the load() method is executing.
		2 ("loaded") - loading is complete and parsing is taking place.
		3 ("interactive") - some data has been read and parsed and the object model is now available. The data set is only partially retrieved and is read-only.
		4 ("completed") - document has been completely loaded. If successful the data is available read/write, if not the error information is available.
responseBody	Ext	Returns the response as an array of unsigned bytes.
responseStream	Ext	Returns the response as an IStream object.

Name		Description
responseText	Ext	Returns the response as an ordinary text string.
responseXML	Ext	Returns the response as an XML document. For security reasons, validation is turned off during this process to prevent the parser from attempting to download a linked DTD or other definition file.
status	Ext	Returns the status code sent back from the server as a long integer.
statusText	Ext	Returns the status text sent back from the server as a string.

HttpRequest Methods

Name		Description
abort()	Ext	Cancels a current HTTP request.
getAllResponseHeaders()	Ext	Returns all the HTTP headers as name/value pairs delimited by the carriage return-linefeed combination.
getResponseHeader (header_name)	Ext	Returns the value of an individual HTTP header from the response body as specified by the header name.
open(method, url, async, userid, password)	Ext	Initializes a request, specifying the HTTP method, the URL, whether the response is to be asynchronous, and authentication information for the request.
send()	Ext	Sends an HTTP request to the server and waits to receive a response.
setRequestHeader (header_name, value)	Ext	Specifies an HTTP header to send to the server.

Runtime — the IXTLRuntime Object

This object implements a series of properties and methods that are available within XSL style sheets. In the following table, all are marked 'Ext' to indicate that the W3C recommendations do not cover this area of the DOM.

Runtime Properties

Name		Description
attributes	Ext	Returns a collection of the Attribute (or Attr) objects for this node as a NamedNodeMap object.
baseName	Ext	Returns the node name with any namespace removed. For example, in a node declared as `<nspace:elemname>` it returns the "elemname" part.
childNodes	Ext	Returns a NodeList containing all the child nodes of this node, for nodes that can have child nodes.
dataType	Ext	Sets or returns the data type for this node.
definition	Ext	For EntityReference nodes, returns the entry in the DTD or schema containing the definition for the entity, i.e. "`<!ENTITY entityname 'entity value'>`". For other nodes, returns null.
firstChild	Ext	Returns a reference to the first child node of this node.
lastChild	Ext	Returns a reference to the last child node of this node.
namespaceURI	Ext	Returns the URI for the namespace as a string. For example, in the namespace declaration `xmlns:name="uri"` it returns the "uri" part.
nextSibling	Ext	Returns a reference to the next sibling node of this node, i.e. the next node in the source data file at the same level of the hierarchy.
nodeName	Ext	Returns the name of the node, which will depend on the node type. See the list of Node Types at the end of this appendix for more details.
nodeTypeString	Ext	Returns the node type as a string. See the list of Node Types at the end of this appendix for more details.
nodeType	Ext	Returns the node type as a number. See the list of Node Types at the end of this appendix for more details.

Name		Description
nodeTypedValue	Ext	Sets or returns the strongly typed value of the node, expressed in its defined data type. If no data type has been defined for the node, its nodeValue is returned.
nodeValue	Ext	Sets or returns the value of the node as plain text.
ownerDocument	Ext	Returns the root node of the document that contains the node.
parentNode	Ext	Returns the parent node of this node, for nodes that can have parents.
parsed	Ext	Returns true if this node and all its descendants have been parsed and instantiated.
prefix	Ext	Returns the element namespace prefix as a string. For example, in a node declared as <nspace:elemname> it returns the "nspace" part.
previousSibling	Ext	Returns a reference to the previous sibling node of this node, i.e. the previous node in the source file at the same level of the hierarchy.
specified	Ext	Indicates whether the node value is explicitly specified or derived from a default value in the DTD or schema. Normally only used with attribute nodes.
text	Ext	Sets or returns the entire text content of this node and all its descendant nodes.
xml	Ext	Returns the entire XML of this node and all descendant nodes of this node.

Runtime Methods

Name		Description
absoluteChildNumber (this_node)	Ext	Returns the index of a specified node within its parent's childNodes list. Values start from "1".

Table Continued on Following Page

345

Name		Description
ancestorChild Number(node_ name, this_node)	Ext	Finds the first ancestor node of a specified node that has the specified name, and returns the index of that node within its parent's childNodes list. Values start from "1". Returns null if there is no ancestor.
appendChild(new_ node)	Ext	Appends the node object new_node to the end of the list of child nodes for this node.
childNumber (this_node)	Ext	Finds the first node with the same name as the specified node within the specified node's parent's childNodes list (i.e. its siblings). Returns the index of that node or null if not found. Values start from "1".
cloneNode (recurse_ children)	Ext	Creates a new node object that is an exact clone of this node, including all descendant nodes of this node if recurse_children is set to true.
depth(start_node)	Ext	Returns the depth or level within the document tree at which the specified node appears. The documentElement or root node is at level 0.
elementIndex_ List(this_ node, node_name)	Ext	Returns an array of node index numbers for the specified node and all its ancestors up to and including the document root node, indicating each node's position within their parent's childNodes list. The ordering of the array starts from the root document node.
		When the node_name parameter is not supplied, the method returns an array of integers that indicates the index of the specified node with respect to all of its siblings, the index of that node's parent with respect to all of its siblings, and so on until the document root is reached.
		When the node_name parameter is specified, the returned array contains entries only for nodes of the specified name, and the indices are evaluated relative to siblings with the specified name. Zero is supplied for levels in the tree that do not have children with the supplied name.
		Although this method is included in the Microsoft documentation, it was not supported by IE5 at the time of writing.

Name		Description
formatDate (date, format, locale)	Ext	Formats the value in the date parameter using the specified formatting options. The following format codes are supported:
		m - Month (1-12)
		mm - Month (01-12)
		mmm - Month (Jan-Dec)
		mmmm - Month (January-December)
		mmmmm - Month as the first letter of the month
		d - Day (1-31)
		dd - Day (01-31)
		ddd - Day (Sun-Sat)
		dddd - Day (Sunday-Saturday)
		yy -Year (00-99)
		yyyy - Year (1900-9999)
		The locale to use in determining the correct sequence of values in the date. If omitted the sequence month-day-year is used.
formatIndex (number, format)	Ext	Formats the integer number using the specified numerical system.
		1 - Standard numbering system
		01 - Standard numbering with leading zeroes
		A - Uppercase letter sequence "A" to "Z" then "AA" to"ZZ".
		a - Lowercase letter sequence "a" to "z" then "aa" to "zz".
		I - Uppercase Roman numerals: "I", "II", "III", "IV", etc.
		i - Lowercase Roman numerals: "i", "ii", "iii", "iv", etc.

Table Continued on Following Page

347

Name		Description
`formatNumber` `(number,` `format)`	Ext	Formats the value number using the specified format. Zero or more of the following values can be present in the format string:
		# (pound) – Display only significant digits and omit insignificant zeros.
		0 (zero) – Display insignificant zeros in these positions.
		? (question) – Adds spaces for insignificant zeros on either side of the decimal point, so that decimal points align with a fixed-point font. You can also use this symbol for fractions that have varying numbers of digits.
		. (period) – Indicates the position of the decimal point.
		, (comma) – Display a thousands separator or scale a number by a multiple of one thousand.
		% (percent) – Display number as a percentage.
		E or e - Display number in scientific (exponential) format. If format contains a zero or # (hash) to the right of an exponent code, display the number in scientific format and inserts an "E" or "e". The number of 0 or # characters to the right determines the number of digits in the exponent.
		E- or e- Place a minus sign by negative exponents.
		E+ or e+ Place a minus sign by negative exponents and a plus sign by positive exponents.

Name		Description
formatTime (time, format, locale)	Ext	Formats the value in the time parameter using the specified formatting options. The following format codes are supported:
		h - Hours (0-23)
		hh - Hours (00-23)
		m - Minutes (0-59)
		mm - Minutes (00-59)
		s - Seconds (0-59)
		ss - Seconds (00-59)
		AM/PM - Add "AM" or "PM" and display in 12 hour format
		am/pm - Add "am" or "pm" and display in 12 hour format
		A/P - Add "A" or "P" and display in 12 hour format
		a/p - Add "a" or "p" and display in 12 hour format
		[h]:mm – Display elapsed time in hours, i.e. "25.02"
		[mm]:ss - Display elapsed time in minutes, i.e. "63:46"
		[ss] - Display elapsed time in seconds
		ss.00 - Display fractions of a second
		The locale is used to determine the correct separator characters.
hasChildNodes ()	Ext	Returns true if this node has any child nodes.
insertBefore (new_node, this_node)	Ext	Inserts a new node object new_node into the list of child nodes for this node, to the left of the node object this_node or at the end of the list if this_node is omitted.
removeChild (this_node)	Ext	Removes the child node this_node from the list of child nodes for this node, and returns it.
replaceChild (new_node, old_node)	Ext	Replaces the child node old_node with the new child node object new_node, and returns the old child node.

Name		Description
selectNodes (pattern)	Ext	Applies a specified pattern to this node's context and returns a node list object containing matching nodes. The string pattern specifies the XSL pattern-matching operation to be used.
selectSingleNode (pattern)	Ext	Applies a specified pattern to this node's context and returns just the first node object that matches. The string pattern specifies the XSL pattern-matching operation to be used.
transformNode (stylesheet)	Ext	Processes this node and its children using an XSL style sheet specified in the stylesheet argument, and returns the resulting transformation. The style sheet must be either a Document node object, in which case the document is assumed to be an XSL style sheet, or a Node object in the xsl namespace, in which case this node is treated as a standalone style sheet fragment.
uniqueID (this_node)	Ext	Returns the unique identifier for the specified node.

The DOM NodeTypes

Each node exposes its type through the nodeType property. In IE5, there is also a nodeTypeString property, which exposes the node type as a named string rather than an integer. This saves having to explicitly convert it each time. Each node type also has a named constant. These make up the IDOMNodeType enumeration.

IDOMNodeType Enumeration

The IDOMNodeType enumeration specifies the valid settings for particular DOM node types. This includes the range and type of values that the node can contain, whether the node can have child nodes, etc. Note that default string and numeric entities (such as &) are exposed as text nodes, rather than as entity nodes.

Named Constant	nodeType	nodeName	nodeValue	nodeTypeString(IE5)
NODE_ELEMENT	1	tagName property	null	"element"

Can be the child of a `Document, DocumentFragment, EntityReference, Element` node.
Can have child nodes of type `Element, Text, Comment, ProcessingInstruction, CDATASection, EntityReference`.

NODE_ATTRIBUTE	2	name property	value property	"attribute"

Cannot be the child of any other node type. Only appears in other nodes' `attributes` node lists.
Can have child nodes of type `Text, EntityReference`.

NODE_TEXT	3	"#text"	content of node	"text"

Can be the child of an `Attribute, DocumentFragment, Element, EntityReference` node.
Cannot have any child nodes.

NODE_CDATA_ SECTION	4	"#cdata-section"	content of node	"cdata section"

Can be the child of a `DocumentFragment, EntityReference, Element` node.
Cannot have any child nodes.

NODE_ENTITY_ REFERENCE	5	entity reference name	null	"entity reference"

Can be the child of an `Attribute, DocumentFragment, Element, EntityReference` node.
Can have child nodes of type `Element, ProcessingInstruction, Comment, Text, CDATASection, EntityReference`.

NODE_ENTITY	6	entity name	null	"entity"

Can be the child of a `DocumentType` node.
Can have child nodes that represent the expanded entity, that is `Text, EntityReference`.

NODE_PROCESSING_ INSTRUCTION	7	target property	content of node excluding target	"processing instruction"

Can be the child of a Document, DocumentFragment, Element, EntityReference node.
Cannot have any child nodes.

NODE_COMMENT	8	"#comment"	comment text	"comment"

Can be the child of a Document, DocumentFragment, Element, EntityReference node.
Cannot have any child nodes.

NODE_DOCUMENT	9	"#document"	null	"document"

Represents the root of the document so cannot be a child node.
Can have a maximum of one Element child node, and other child nodes of type Comment, DocumentType, ProcessingInstruction.

NODE_DOCUMENT_TYPE	10	doctype name	null	"document type"

Can be the child of the Document node only.
Can have child nodes of type Notation, Entity.

NODE_DOCUMENT_FRAGMENT	11	"#document-fragment"	null	"document fragment"

Represents an unconnected document fragment, so cannot be the child of any node type.
Can have child nodes of type Element, ProcessingInstruction, Comment, Text, CDATASection, EntityReference.

NODE_NOTATION	1 2	notation name	null	"notation"

Can be the child of a DocumentType node only.
Cannot have any child nodes.

ADO Recordsets Reference

The ADO 2.0 Recordset Object

Methods

Name	Returns	Description
AddNew		Creates a new record in an updateable Recordset object.
Cancel		Cancels execution of a pending asynchronous Open operation.
CancelBatch		Cancels a pending batch update.
CancelUpdate		Cancels any changes made to the current record, or to a new record prior to calling the Update method.
Clone	Recordset object	Creates a duplicate Recordset object from an existing Recordset object.
Close		Closes the Recordset object.
CompareBookmarks	CompareEnum	Compares two bookmarks and returns an indication of their relative values.
Delete		Deletes the current record or group of records.

Table Continued on Following Page

Name	Returns	Description
Find		Searches the Recordset for a record that matches the specified criteria.
GetRows	Variant	Retrieves multiple records of a Recordset object into an array.
GetString	String	Returns a Recordset as a string.
Move		Moves the position of the current record in a Recordset.
MoveFirst		Moves the position of the current record to the first record in the Recordset.
MoveLast		Moves the position of the current record to the last record in the Recordset.
MoveNext		Moves the position of the current record to the next record in the Recordset.
MovePrevious		Moves the position of the current record to the previous record in the Recordset.
NextRecordset	Recordset object	Clears the current Recordset object and returns the next Recordset by advancing through a series of commands.
Open		Opens a Recordset.
Requery		Updates the data in a Recordset object by re-executing the query on which the object is based.
Resync		Refreshes the data in the current Recordset object from the underlying database.
Save		Saves the Recordset to a file.
Supports	Boolean	Determines whether a specified Recordset object supports a particular functionality.
Update		Saves any changes made to the current record of a Recordset object.
UpdateBatch		Writes all pending batch updates to disk.

Properties

Name	Data Type	Description
AbsolutePage	PositionEnum	Specifies in which page the current record resides.
AbsolutePosition	PositionEnum	Specifies the ordinal position of a Recordset object's current record.
ActiveCommand	Object	Indicates the Command object that created the associated Recordset object. Read only.
ActiveConnection	Variant	Indicates to which Connection object the specified Recordset object currently belongs.
BOF	Boolean	Indicates whether the current record is before the first record in a Recordset object. Read only.
Bookmark	Variant	Returns a bookmark that uniquely identifies the current record in a Recordset object, or sets the current record to the record identified by a valid bookmark.
CacheSize	Long	Indicates the number of records from a Recordset object that are cached locally in memory.
CursorLocation	CursorLocation Enum	Sets or returns the location of the cursor engine.
CursorType	CursorTypeEnum	Indicates the type of cursor used in a Recordset object.

Table Continued on Following Page

Name	Data Type	Description
DataMember	String	Specifies the name of the data member to retrieve from the object referenced by the DataSource property. Write only.
DataSource	Object	Specifies an object containing data to be represented as a Recordset object. Write only.
EditMode	EditModeEnum	Indicates the editing status of the current record. Read only.
EOF	Boolean	Indicates whether the current record is after the last record in a Recordset object. Read only.
Fields	Fields collection	Contains all of the Field objects for the current Recordset object.
Filter	Variant	Indicates a filter for data in the Recordset.
LockType	LockTypeEnum	Indicates the type of locking placed on records during editing.
MarshalOptions	MarshalOptionsEnum	Indicates which records are to be marshaled back to the server.
MaxRecords	Long	Indicates the maximum number of records to return to a Recordset object from a query. Default is zero (no limit).
PageCount	Long	Indicates how many pages of data the Recordset object contains. Read only.
PageSize	Long	Indicates how many records constitute one page in the Recordset.

Name	Data Type	Description
Properties	Properties collection	Contains all of the `Property` objects for the current `Recordset` object.
RecordCount	Long	Indicates the current number of records in the `Recordset` object. Read only.
Sort	String	Specifies one or more field names the `Recordset` is sorted on, and the direction of the sort (ascending or descending).
Source	String	Indicates the source for the data in a `Recordset` object.
State	Long	Indicates whether the recordset is open, closed, or whether it is executing an asynchronous operation. Read only.
Status	Integer	Indicates the status of the current record with respect to match updates or other bulk operations. Read only.
StayInSync	Boolean	Indicates, in a hierarchical `Recordset` object, whether the parent row should change when the set of underlying child records changes. Read only.

All properties are read/write unless otherwise stated.

Events

Name	Description
EndOfRecordset	Fired when there is an attempt to move to a row past the end of the `Recordset`.
FetchComplete	Fired after all the records in an asynchronous operation have been retrieved into the `Recordset`.
FetchProgress	Fired periodically during an asynchronous operation, to report how many rows have currently been retrieved.

Table Continued on Following Page

Name	Description
FieldChangeComplete	Fired after the value of one or more `Field` objects has been changed.
MoveComplete	Fired after the current position in the `Recordset` changes.
RecordChangeComplete	Fired after one or more records change.
RecordsetChangeComplete	Fired after the `Recordset` has changed.
WillChangeField	Fired before a pending operation changes the value of one or more `Field` objects.
WillChangeRecord	Fired before one or more rows in the `Recordset` change.
WillChangeRecordset	Fired before a pending operation changes the `Recordset`.
WillMove	Fired before a pending operation changes the current position in the `Recordset`.

Method Calls Quick Reference

```
Recordset.AddNew([FieldList As Variant], [Values As Variant])
Recordset.Cancel
Recordset.CancelBatch([AffectRecords As AffectEnum])
Recordset.CancelUpdate
Recordset = Recordset.Clone([LockType As LockTypeEnum])
Recordset.Close
CompareEnum = Recordset.CompareBookmarks(Bookmark1 As Variant,
Bookmark2 As Variant)
Recordset.Delete([AffectRecords As AffectEnum])
Recordset.Find(Criteria As String, [SkipRecords As Integer],
[SearchDirection As SearchDirectionEnum], [Start As Variant])
Variant = Recordset.GetRows([Rows As Integer], [Start As Variant], [Fields
As Variant])
String = Recordset.GetString(StringFormat As StringFormatEnum,
[NumRows As Integer], ColumnDelimeter As String, RowDelimeter As String,
NullExpr As String)
Recordset.Move(NumRecords As Integer, [Start As Variant])
Recordset.MoveFirst
Recordset.MoveLast
Recordset.MoveNext
Recordset.MovePrevious
Recordset = Recordset.NextRecordset([RecordsAffected As Variant])
Recordset.Open([Source As Variant], [ActiveConnection As Variant],
[CursorType As CursorTypeEnum], [LockType As LockTypeEnum], [Options
As Integer])
```

```
Recordset.Requery([Options As Integer])
Recordset.Resync([AffectRecords As AffectEnum], [ResyncValues As
ResyncEnum])
Recordset.Save([FileName As String], [PersistFormat As
PersistFormatEnum])
Boolean = Recordset.Supports(CursorOptions As CursorOptionEnum)
Recordset.Update([Fields As Variant], [Values As Variant])
Recordset.UpdateBatch([AffectRecords As AffectEnum])
```

ADO Standard Constants

The following constants are predefined by ADO. For scripting languages these are
included in `adovbs.inc` or `adojava.inc`, which can be found in the `Program
Files\Common Files\System\ado` directory. For Visual Basic these are
automatically included when you reference the ADO library.

AffectEnum

Name	Description
adAffectAll	Operation affects all records in the recordset.
adAffectAllChapters	Operation affects all child (chapter) records.
adAffectCurrent	Operation affects only the current record.
adAffectGroup	Operation affects records that satisfy the current `Filter` property.

BookmarkEnum

Name	Description
adBookmarkCurrent	Default. Start at the current record.
adBookmarkFirst	Start at the first record.
adBookmarkLast	Start at the last record.

CommandTypeEnum

Name	Description
adCmdFile	Indicates that the provider should evaluate `CommandText` as a previously persisted file.
adCmdStoredProc	Indicates that the provider should evaluate `CommandText` as a stored procedure.

Table Continued on Following Page

Name	Description
adCmdTable	Indicates that the provider should generate a SQL query to return all rows from the table named in CommandText.
adCmdTableDirect	Indicates that the provider should return all rows from the table named in CommandText.
adCmdText	Indicates that the provider should evaluate CommandText as textual definition of a command, such as a SQL statement.
adCmdUnknown	Indicates that the type of command in CommandText unknown.

CompareEnum

Name	Description
adCompareEqual	The bookmarks are equal.
adCompareGreaterThan	The first bookmark is after the second.
adCompareLessThan	The first bookmark is before the second.
adCompareNotComparable	The bookmarks cannot be compared.
adCompareNotEqual	The bookmarks are not equal and not ordered.

ConnectModeEnum

Name	Description
adModeRead	Indicates read-only permissions.
adModeReadWrite	Indicates read/write permissions.
adModeShareDenyNone	Prevents others from opening connection with any permissions.
adModeShareDenyRead	Prevents others from opening connection with read permissions.
adModeShareDenyWrite	Prevents others from opening connection with write permissions.
adModeShareExclusive	Prevents others from opening connection.

Name	Description
adModeUnknown	Default. Indicates that the permissions have not yet been set or cannot be determined.
adModeWrite	Indicates write-only permissions.

ConnectOptionEnum

Name	Description
adAsyncConnect	Open the connection asynchronously.
adConnectUnspecified	The connection mode is unspecified.

CursorLocationEnum

Name	Description
adUseClient	Use client-side cursors supplied by the local cursor library.
adUseClientBatch	Use client-side cursors supplied by the local cursor library.
adUseNone	No cursor services are used.
adUseServer	Default. Uses data provider driver supplied cursors.

CursorTypeEnum

Name	Description
adOpenDynamic	Opens a dynamic type cursor.
adOpenForwardOnly	Default. Opens a forward-only type cursor
adOpenKeyset	Opens a keyset type cursor.
adOpenStatic	Opens a static type cursor.
adOpenUnspecified	Indicates as unspecified value for cursor type.

DataTypeEnum

Name	Description
adBigInt	An 8-byte signed integer.
adBinary	A binary value.
adBoolean	A Boolean value.
adBSTR	A null-terminated character string.
adChapter	A chapter type, indicating a child recordset.
adChar	A String value.
adCurrency	A currency value. An 8-byte signed integer scaled by 10,000, with 4 digits to the right of the decimal point.
adDate	A Date value. A Double where the whole part is the number of days since December 30 1899, and the fractional part is a fraction of the day.
adDBDate	A date value (yyyymmdd).
adDBFileTime	A database file time.
adDBTime	A time value (hhmmss).
adDBTimeStamp	A date-time stamp (yyyymmddhhmmss plus a fraction in billionths).
adDecimal	An exact numeric value with fixed precision and scale.
adDouble	A double-precision floating point value.
adEmpty	No value was specified.
adError	A 32-bit error code.
adFileTime	A DOS/Win32 file time. The number of 100 nanosecond intervals since Jan 1 1601.
adGUID	A globally unique identifier.
adIDispatch	A pointer to an IDispatch interface on an OLE object.
adInteger	A 4-byte signed integer.
adIUnknown	A pointer to an IUnknown interface on an OLE object.
adLongVarBinary	A long binary value.

Name	Description
adLongVarChar	A long String value.
adLongVarWChar	A long null-terminated string value.
adNumeric	An exact numeric value with a fixed precision and scale.
adPropVariant	A variant that is not equivalent to an Automation variant.
adSingle	A single-precision floating point value.
adSmallInt	A 2-byte signed integer.
adTinyInt	A 1-byte signed integer.
adUnsignedBigInt	An 8-byte unsigned integer.
adUnsignedInt	An 4-byte unsigned integer.
adUnsignedSmallInt	An 2-byte unsigned integer.
adUnsignedTinyInt	An 1-byte unsigned integer.
adUserDefined	A user-defined variable.
adVarBinary	A binary value.
adVarChar	A String value.
adVariant	An Automation Variant.
adVarNumeric	A variable width exact numeric, with a signed scale value.
adVarWChar	A null-terminated Unicode character string.
adWChar	A null-terminated Unicode character string.

EditModeEnum

Name	Description
adEditAdd	Indicates that the AddNew method has been invoked and the current record in the buffer is a new record that hasn't been saved to the database.
adEditDelete	Indicates that the Delete method has been invoked.
adEditInProgress	Indicates that data in the current record has been modified but not saved.
adEditNone	Indicates that no editing is in progress.

365

ErrorValueEnum

Name	Description
adErrBoundToCommand	The application cannot change the ActiveConnection property of a Recordset object with a Command object as its source.
adErrDataConversion	The application is using a value of the wrong type for the current application.
adErrFeatureNot Available	The operation requested by the application is not supported by the provider.
adErrIllegalOperation	The operation requested by the application is not allowed in this context.
adErrInTransaction	The application cannot explicitly close a Connection object while in the middle of a transaction.
adErrInvalidArgument	The application is using arguments that are the wrong type, are out of the acceptable range, or are in conflict with one another.
adErrInvalidConnection	The application requested an operation on an object with a reference to a closed or invalid Connection object.
adErrInvalidParamInfo	The application has improperly defined a Parameter object.
adErrItemNotFound	ADO could not find the object in the collection.
adErrNoCurrentRecord	Either BOF or EOF is True, or the current record has been deleted. The operation requested by the application requires a current record.
adErrNotExecuting	The operation is not executing.
adErrNotReentrant	The operation is not reentrant.
adErrObjectClosed	The operation requested by the application is not allowed if the object is closed.
adErrObjectInCollection	Can't append. Object already in collection.
adErrObjectNotSet	The object referenced by the application no longer points to a valid object.
adErrObjectOpen	The operation requested by the application is not allowed if the object is open.

Name	Description
adErrOperationCancelled	The operation was cancelled.
adErrProviderNotFound	ADO could not find the specified provider.
adErrStillConnecting	The operation is still connecting.
adErrStillExecuting	The operation is still executing.
adErrUnsafeOperation	The operation is unsafe under these circumstances.

EventReasonEnum

Name	Description
adRsnAddNew	A new record is to be added.
adRsnClose	The object is being closed.
adRsnDelete	The record is being deleted.
adRsnFirstChange	The record has been changed for the first time.
adRsnMove	A Move has been invoked and the current record pointer is being moved.
adRsnMoveFirst	A MoveFirst has been invoked and the current record pointer is being moved.
adRsnMoveLast	A MoveLast has been invoked and the current record pointer is being moved.
adRsnMoveNext	A MoveNext has been invoked and the current record pointer is being moved.
adRsnMovePrevious	A MovePrevious has been invoked and the current record pointer is being moved.
adRsnRequery	The recordset was requeried.
adRsnResynch	The recordset was resynchronized.
adRsnUndoAddNew	The addition of a new record has been cancelled.
adRsnUndoDelete	The deletion of a record has been cancelled.
adRsnUndoUpdate	The update of a record has been cancelled.
adRsnUpdate	The record is being updated.

EventStatusEnum

Name	Description
adStatusCancel	Request cancellation of the operation that is about to occur.
adStatusCantDeny	A Will event cannot request cancellation of the operation about to occur.
adStatusErrorsOccurred	The operation completed unsuccessfully, or a Will event cancelled the operation.
adStatusOK	The operation completed successfully.
adStatusUnwantedEvent	Events for this operation are no longer required.

ExecuteOptionEnum

Name	Description
adAsyncExecute	The operation is executed asynchronously.
adAsyncFetch	The records are fetched asynchronously.
adAsyncFetchNonBlocking	The records are fetched asynchronously without blocking subsequent operations.
adExecuteNoRecords	Indicates CommandText is a command or stored procedure that does not return rows. Always combined with adCmdText or adCmdStoreProc.

FieldAttributeEnum

Name	Description
adFldCacheDeferred	Indicates that the provider caches field values and that subsequent reads are done from the cache.
adFldFixed	Indicates that the field contains fixed-length data.
adFldIsNullable	Indicates that the field accepts Null values.
adFldKeyColumn	The field is part of a key column.
adFldLong	Indicates that the field is a long binary field, and that the AppendChunk and GetChunk methods can be used.
adFldMayBeNull	Indicates that you can read Null values from the field.

Name	Description
adFldMayDefer	Indicates that the field is deferred, that is, the field values are not retrieved from the data source with the whole record, but only when you access them.
adFldNegativeScale	The field has a negative scale.
adFldRowID	Indicates that the field has some kind of record ID.
adFldRowVersion	Indicates that the field time or date stamp used to track updates.
adFldUnknownUpdatable	Indicates that the provider cannot determine if you can write to the field.
adFldUpdatable	Indicates that you can write to the field.

FilterGroupEnum

Name	Description
adFilterAffectedRecords	Allows you to view only records affected by the last Delete, Resync, UpdateBatch, or CancelBatch method.
adFilterConflictingRecords	Allows you to view the records that failed the last batch update attempt.
adFilterFetchedRecords	Allows you to view records in the current cache.
adFilterNone	Removes the current filter and restores all records to view.
adFilterPendingRecords	Allows you to view only the records that have changed but have not been sent to the server. Only applicable for batch update mode.
adFilterPredicate	Allows you to view records that failed the last batch update attempt.

GetRowsOptionEnum

Name	Description
adGetRowsRest	Retrieves the remainder of the rows in the recordset.

LockTypeEnum

Name	Description
adLockBatchOptimistic	Optimistic batch updates.
adLockOptimistic	Optimistic locking, record by record. The provider locks records when Update is called.
adLockPessimistic	Pessimistic locking, record by record. The provider locks the record immediately upon editing.
adLockReadOnly	Default. Read only, data cannot be modified.
adLockUnspecified	The clone is created with the same lock type as the original.

MarshalOptionsEnum

Name	Description
adMarshalAll	Default. Indicates that all rows are returned to the server.
adMarshalModifiedOnly	Indicates that only modified rows are returned to the server.

ObjectStateEnum

Name	Description
adStateClosed	Default. Indicates that the object is closed.
adStateConnecting	Indicates that the object is connecting.
adStateExecuting	Indicates that the object is executing a command.
adStateFetching	Indicates that the rows of the recordset are being fetched.
adStateOpen	Indicates that the object is open.

PersistFormatEnum

Name	Description
adPersistADTG	Default. Persist data in Advanced Data TableGram format.
adPersistXML	Persist data in XML format. This format was not supported in ADO 2.0 but is supported in ADO 2.1, which ships with Internet Explorer 5.

PositionEnum

Name	Description
adPosBOF	The current record pointer is at BOF.
adPosEOF	The current record pointer is at EOF.
adPosUnknown	The Recordset is empty, the current position is unknown, or the provider does not support the AbsolutePage property.

RecordStatusEnum

Name	Description
adRecCanceled	The record was not saved because the operation was cancelled.
adRecCantRelease	The new record was not saved because of existing record locks.
adRecConcurrencyViolation	The record was not saved because optimistic concurrency was in use.
adRecDBDeleted	The record has already been deleted from the data source.
adRecDeleted	The record was deleted.
adRecIntegrityViolation	The record was not saved because the user violated integrity constraints.
adRecInvalid	The record was not saved because its bookmark is invalid.
adRecMaxChangesExceeded	The record was not saved because there were too many pending changes.
adRecModified	The record was modified.

Table Continued on Following Page

Name	Description
adRecMultipleChanges	The record was not saved because it would have affected multiple records.
adRecNew	The record is new.
adRecObjectOpen	The record was not saved because of a conflict with an open storage object.
adRecOK	The record was successfully updated.
adRecOutOfMemory	The record was not saved because the computer has run out of memory.
adRecPendingChanges	The record was not saved because it refers to a pending insert.
adRecPermissionDenied	The record was not saved because the user has insufficient permissions.
adRecSchemaViolation	The record was not saved because it violates the structure of the underlying database.
adRecUnmodified	The record was not modified.

ResyncEnum

Name	Description
adResyncAllValues	Default. Data is overwritten and pending updates are cancelled.
adResyncUnderlyingValues	Data is not overwritten and pending updates are not cancelled.

SearchDirectionEnum

Name	Description
adSearchBackward	Search backward from the current record.
adSearchForward	Search forward from the current record.

XML Schemas and Data Types

While XML documents can be successfully defined using a **Document Type Definition** (DTD), there is felt to be a requirement for a more flexible way of defining the structure of XML documents. It is also accepted that there needs to be a way for the data type to be indicated within the design of the XML document to make it easier for the handling of XML documents to be mechanized.

To this end, the W3C are — at the time of writing — working on a group of proposals that come under the general heading of **XML Schemas and Data Types**. This includes the proposed **Document Content Definition** (DCD) language. Internet Explorer 5 supports a reasonably standard implementation of XML Schemas and Data Types, as described in this reference section. This technology is still developing in IE5 and not all of the attributes listed here may work as described at the present time.

XML Schemas

An **XML Schema** is a description or definition of the structure of an XML document. The schema is itself written in XML. This makes it easier for newcomers to understand, when compared to the need to learn the SGML-like syntax of the Document Type Definition (DTD).

Internet Explorer 5 includes an implementation of XML Schemas that provides eight predefined elements for use in defining XML documents:

Name	Description
Schema	The overall enclosing element of the schema, which defines the schema name.
ElementType	Defines a type of element that will be used within the schema.
element	Defines an instance of an element declared for use within an <ElementType> element.
AttributeType	Defines a type of attribute that will be used within the schema.

Table Continued on Following Page

Name	Description
attribute	Defines an instance of an attribute declared for use within an `<ElementType>` element.
datatype	Defines the type of data that an attribute or element can contain.
description	Used to provide information about an attribute or element.
group	Used to collect elements together to define specific sequences of elements.

IE5 XML Schema Elements

This section describes each of the XML Schema elements in alphabetical order, complete with their attributes.

The attribute Element

The `<attribute>` element is used to define specific instances of an attribute that is used within an `<AttributeType>` or `<ElementType>` element.

Element Name	Attribute	Description
attribute	default	The default value for the attribute, used when `required` is `"no"`. If `required` is `"yes"` then the value provided in the document must be the same as the default value.
	required	Specifies if a value for this attribute is required. Can be either `"yes"` or `"no"`.
	type	Specifies the `<AttributeType>` of which the attribute is an instance.

The AttributeType Element

The `<AttributeType>` element is used to define a type of attribute that is used within elements in the schema. Specific instances of the attribute can be further specified using the `<attribute>` element.

Element Name	Attribute	Description
AttributeType	default	The default value for the attribute. If the attribute is an enumerated type, the value must appear in the list.

Element Name	Attribute	Description
AttributeType	dt:type	The data type that the attribute will accept.
	dt:values	A set of values that form an enumerated type, for example "roses carnations daisies"
	name	A unique string that identifies the <AttributeType> element within the schema and provides the attribute name.
	model	Defines whether the attribute can accept content that is not defined in the schema. The value "open" allows undefined content to appear, while the value "closed" allows only content defined in the schema to appear.
	required	Specifies if a value for this attribute is required. Can be either "yes" or "no". This and default are mutually exclusive when required is "yes".

The dt:type and dt:values are used in the same way as in the <datatype> element:

```
<AttributeType name="flowername"
               default="rose"
               dt:type="enumeration"
               dt:values="rose carnation daisy lilac" />
```

Note that, although dt is the usual namespace prefix for data types, we can replace it with a different prefix.

The datatype Element

The <datatype> element is used to define the type of data that an attribute or element can contain. At the time of writing, support for this element was particularly limited.

Element Name	Attribute	Description
datatype	dt:max	The maximum (inclusive) value that the element or attribute can accept.

Table Continued on Following Page

Element Name	Attribute	Description
datatype	dt:maxExclusive	The maximum exclusive value that the element or attribute can accept, that is, the value must be less than this value.
	dt:maxlength	The maximum length of the element or attribute value. For strings this is the number of characters. For number and binary values this is the number of bytes required to store the value.
	dt:min	The minimum (inclusive) value that the element or attribute can accept.
	dt:minExclusive	The minimum exclusive value that the element or attribute can accept, that is, the value must be more than this value.
	dt:type	One of the specific or primitive data types listed at the end of this appendix.
	dt:values	For an enumeration, the list of values in the enumeration.

The description Element

The <description> element is used to provide information about an attribute or element.

Element Name	Attribute	Description
description	*none*	The descriptive text for the element or attribute.

The element Element

The <element> element is used to define specific instances of an element that is used within an <ElementType> element.

Element Name	Attribute	Description
element	type	The name of an element type defined in this or another schema, and of which this element is an instance.

Element Name	Attribute	Description
element	minOccurs	Defines whether the element is optional in documents based on the schema. "0" denotes that it is optional and does not need to appear, while "1" denotes that the element must appear at least once. The default if omitted is "1".
	maxOccurs	Defines the maximum number of times that the element can appear at this point within documents based on the schema. "1" means only once, while "*" means any number of times. The default if omitted is "1".

The ElementType Element

The <ElementType> element is used to define a type of element that is used within the schema. Specific instances of the element can be further specified using the <element> element.

Element Name	Attribute	Description
ElementType	content	Defines the type of content that the element can contain. "empty" means no content, "textOnly" means it can contain only text (unless the model is "open"), "eltOnly" means it can contain only other elements and no free text, and "mixed" means it can contain any mixture of content.
	dt:type	One of the specific or primitive data types listed at the end of this appendix.
	model	Defines whether the element can accept content that is not defined in the schema. The value "open" allows undefined content to appear, while the value "closed" allows only content defined in the schema to appear.
	name	A unique string that identifies the <ElementType> element within the schema and provides the element name.

Table Continued on Following Page

Element Name	Attribute	Description
ElementType	order	Defines how sequences of the element can appear. The value "one" means that only one of the set of enclosed element elements can appear, "seq" means that all the enclosed elements must appear in the order that they are specified, and "many" means that none, any or all of the enclosed elements can appear in any order.

For examples of the content and order attributes, see the section on the <group> element next.

The group Element

The <group> element is used to collect series of <element> and/or <attribute> elements together so that they can be assigned a specific sequence in the schema. This can precisely control the order that they can appear in documents that are based on this schema.

Element Name	Attribute	Description
group	minOccurs	Defines whether the group is optional in documents based on the schema. "0" denotes that it is optional and does not need to appear, while "1" denotes that the group must appear at least once. The default if omitted is "1".
	maxOccurs	Defines the maximum number of times that the group can appear at this point within documents based on the schema. "1" means only once, while "*" means any number of times. The default if omitted is "1".
	order	Defines how sequences of the groups and element types contained in this group can appear. "one" means that only one of the set of enclosed groups or element types can appear, "seq" means that all the enclosed groups or element types must appear in the order that they are specified, and "many" means that none, any or all of the enclosed groups or element types can appear in any order.

380

The next example shows some of the ways that groups and element types can be used to define the ordering and appearance of elements in a document:

```
<ElementType name="first" content="empty" />
<ElementType name="second" content="textOnly" dt:type="string" />
<ElementType name="thirdEqual" content="empty" />

<ElementType name="third" content="eltOnly" order="many">
    <element type="thirdEqual" />
</ElementType>

<ElementType name="fallen" content="empty" />
<ElementType name="unplaced" content="empty" />
<ElementType name="last" content="empty" />

<ElementType name="raceorder" order="seq">

    <element type="first" />
    <element type="second" />
    <element type="third" />

    <group minOccurs="1" maxOccurs="1" order="one">
        <element type="fallen" />
        <element type="unplaced" />
        <element type="last" />
    </group>

</ElementType>
```

Because the main element `raceorder` has the attribute `order="seq"`, the `<first>`, `<second>` and `<third>` elements must appear at least once in the order shown. This also applies to the `group` element; however, of the three elements that are defined within the group, only one can occur in the document. So, the following combinations are some of the legal and valid possibilities:

```
<first />
<second>too slow again</second>
<third />
<fallen />
```

```
<first />
<second />
<third>
    <thirdEqual />
</third>
<unplaced />
```

```
<first />
<second>still too slow</second>
<third>
    <thirdEqual />
    <thirdEqual />
    <thirdEqual />
</third>
<last />
```

The Schema Element

The `<Schema>` element is the enclosing element of the schema. It defines the schema name and the namespaces that the schema uses.

Element Name	Attribute	Description
Schema	name	Defines a name by which the schema will be referred to.
	xmlns	Specifies the default namespace URI for the elements and attributes in the schema.
	xmlns:dt	Specifies the namespace URI for the datatype attributes in the schema.

```
<Schema name="myschema"
       xmlns="urn:schemas-microsoft-com:xml-data"
       xmlns:dt="urn:schemas-microsoft-com:datatypes">
```

As we noted above, the datatype namespace prefix does not have to be dt, but this is the usual value, and clearly indicates to a (human) reader that the attributes prefixed by it belong to the datatype namespace. However, the namespace definitions (the URN parts) *must* be as they appear here.

The IE5 XML Schema Structure

The following code shows the overall structure of an IE5 XML Schema, with the type of value expected for each attribute. Where elements can appear in more than one place, the subsequent occurrences have the attribute list removed to avoid excessive duplication.

```
<Schema name="schema_name"
       xmlns="namespace_URI"
       xmlns:dt="namespace_URI" >

    <AttributeType default="default_value"
                   dt:type="xml_data_type"
                   dt:values="enumerated_value_list"
                   name="name_or_id"
                   model="open"|"closed"
                   required="yes"|"no">

        <datatype dt:max="maximum_value"
                  dt:maxExclusive="maximum_value_exclusive"
                  dt:maxlength="maximum_length"
                  dt:min="minimum_value"
                  dt:minExclusive="minimum_value_exclusive"
                  dt:type="xml_data_type" />
                  dt:values="enumerated_value_list" />

        <description>description_text</description>

    </AttributeType>

    <AttributeType>
        ... etc ...
    </AttributeType>

    <ElementType content="empty"|"textOnly"|"eltOnly"|"mixed"
                 dt:type="xml_data_type"
                 model="open"|"closed"
                 name="name_or_id"
                 order="one"|"seq"|"many" >
```

```
    <description>description_text</description>

    <datatype ... etc ... />

    <element type="element_type"
             minOccurs="0"|"1"
             maxOccurs="1"|"*" />

    <attribute default="default_value"
               required="yes"|"no" />

    <attribute ... etc ... />

    <group minOccurs="0"|"1"
           maxOccurs="1"|"*"
           order="one"|"seq"|"many" >

      <attribute ... etc ... />

      <element ... etc ... />

    </group>

  </ElementType>

</Schema>
```

XML Datatypes

Data types are referenced from the data type namespace, which is declared within the XML <Schema> element of the schema using the xmlns : *datatypename* attribute.

The data types that are proposed by W3C, and supported in Internet Explorer 5, are shown in the next table, which includes all highly popular types and all the built-in types of popular database and programming languages and systems such as SQL, Visual Basic, C, C++ and Java. This table is taken from the W3C note at http://www.w3.org/TR/1998/NOTE-XML-data/

Name	Parse type	Storage type	Example
string	pcdata	string (Unicode)	Ομωνυμα λεγαται ων ονομα μονον κο ινον, ο δε κατα του νομα λογος της ουσ ιας ετερος, οιον ζυο ν ο τε ανθροπος και το γεγραμμενον.

Table Continued on Following Page

Name	Parse type	Storage type	Example
number	A number, with no limit on digits, may potentially have a leading sign, fractional digits, and optionally an exponent. Punctuation as in US English.	string	15, 3.14, -123.456E+10
int	A number, with optional sign, no fractions, no exponent.	32-bit signed binary	1, 58502, -13
float	Same as for number	64-bit IEEE 488	.314159265358979 E+1
fixed. 14.4	Same as number but no more than 14 digits to the left of the decimal point, and no more than 4 to the right.	64-bit signed binary	12.0044
boolean	"1" or "0"	bit	0, 1 (1=="true")
dateTime .iso8601	A date in ISO 8601 format, with optional time and no optional zone. Fractional seconds may be as precise as nanoseconds.	Structure or object containing year, month, hour, minute, second, nanosecond.	19941105T 08:15:00301
dateTime .iso8601 .tz	A date in ISO 8601 format, with optional time and optional zone. Fractional seconds may be as precise as nanoseconds.	Structure or object containing year, month, hour, minute, second, nanosecond, zone.	19941105T 08:15:5+03

Name	Parse type	Storage type	Example
date. iso8601	A date in ISO 8601 format. (no time)	Structure or object containing year, month, day.	19541022
time. iso8601	A time in ISO 8601 format, with no date and no time zone.	Structure or object exposing day, hour, minute	
time. iso8601. tz	A time in ISO 8601 format, with no date but optional time zone.	Structure or object containing day, hour, minute, zone-hours, zoneminutes.	08:15-05:00
i1	A number, with optional sign, no fractions, no exponent.	8-bit binary	1, 255
i2	as above	16-bit binary	1, 703, -32768
i4	as above	32-bit binary	
i8	as above	64-bit binary	
ui1	A number, unsigned, no fractions, no exponent.	8-bit unsigned binary	1, 255
ui2	as above	16-bit unsigned binary	1, 703, -32768
ui4	as above	32-bit unsigned binary	
ui8	as above	64-bit unsigned binary	
r4	Same as number	IEEE 488 4-byte float	
r8	as above	IEEE 488 8-byte float	
float. IEEE.754. 32	as above	IEEE 754 4-byte float	

Table Continued on Following Page

Name	Parse type	Storage type	Example
float. IEEE.754. 64	as above	IEEE 754 8-byte float	
uuid	Hexadecimal digits representing octets. Optional embedded hyphens should be ignored.	128-bytes Unix UUID structure	F04DA480-65B9-11d1-A29F-00AA00C14882
uri	Universal Resource Identifier	Per W3C spec	http://www.ics.uci.edu/pub/ietf/uri/draft-fielding-uri-syntax-00.txt http://www.ics.uci.edu/pub/ietf/uri/ http://www.ietf.org/html.charters/urn-charter.html
bin.hex	Hexadecimal digits representing octets	no specified size	
char	String	1 Unicode character (16 bits)	
string. ansi	String containing only ASCII characters <= 0xFF.	Unicode or single-byte string.	This does not look Greek to me.

The dates and times above reading iso8601xxx actually use a restricted subset of the formats defined by ISO 8601. Years, if specified, must have four digits. Ordinal dates are not used. Of formats employing week numbers, only those that truncate year and month are allowed.

Primitive XML Data Types

The W3C also recommends tokenized data types for use in XML 1.0. These are sometimes referred to as **primitive types**. The primitive types supported in Internet Explorer 5 are:

Name	Description
entity	The XML ENTITY type.
entities	The XML ENTITIES type.
enumeration	An enumerated type, i.e. a list of permissible values.
id	The XML ID type.
idref	The XML IDREF type.
idrefs	The XML IDREFS type.
nmtoken	The XML NMTOKEN type.
nmtokens	The XML NMTOKENS type.
notation	A NOTATION type.
string	Represents a generic String data type.

CSS Properties

This appendix lists the properties of CSS Level 2 (which includes all the properties of CSS1). However, not all these properties are implemented by IE5, although the level of support is likely to be increased with successive releases. As ever, to see if a property works, just try it!

I shall cover the properties under the same headings you'll find in the specification:

- ❑ Box Model
- ❑ Visual Formatting Model
- ❑ Visual Formatting Model Details
- ❑ Visual Effects
- ❑ Generated Content, Automatic Numbering and Lists
- ❑ Paged Media
- ❑ Colors and Backgrounds
- ❑ Font Properties
- ❑ Text Properties
- ❑ Tables
- ❑ User Interface
- ❑ Aural Style Sheets

The tables on the following pages list all the properties that can be applied to HTML and XML elements through a CSS style sheet. For more information about each of the properties, you should refer to the specification that may be found at http://www.w3.org/TR/1998/REC-CSS2/. You could also take a look at the Wrox Press title *Professional Style Sheets for HTML and XML* (1-861001-65-7).

Box Model

These properties are covered in section 8 of the CSS2 specification.

Property Name	Possible Values	Initial Value	Applies to	Inherited
margin-top	`<length>` | `<percentage>` | `auto` `<percentage>` refers to the parent element's width. Negative values are permitted.	0	All	No
margin-right	*as above*	0	All	No
margin-bottom	*as above*	0	All	No
margin-left	*as above*	0	All	No
margin	`[<length>` | `<percentage>` | `auto]{1,4}` If 4 values are given they apply to top, right, bottom, left, in that order. 1 value applies to all 4. If 2 or 3 values are given, the missing value is taken from the opposite side. `<percentage>` refers to the parent element's width. Negative values are permitted.	Undefined	All	No

Property Name	Possible Values	Initial Value	Applies to	Inherited
padding-top	`<length> | <percentage>` `<percentage>` refers to the parent element's width. Negative values are *not* permitted.	0	All	No
padding-right	*as above*	0	All	No
padding-bottom	*as above*	0	All	No
padding-left	*as above*	0	All	No
padding	`[<length> | <percentage>]{1,4}` If 4 values are given they apply to top, right, bottom, left, in that order. 1 value applies to all 4. If 2 or 3 values are given, the missing value is taken from the opposite side. `<percentage>` refers to the parent element's width. Negative values are *not* permitted.	0	All	No
border-top-width	`thin | medium | thick | <length>`	medium	All	No
border-right-width	`thin | medium | thick | <length>`	medium	All	No
border-bottom-width	`thin | medium | thick | <length>`	medium	All	No

Table Continued on Following Page

Property Name	Possible Values	Initial Value	Applies to	Inherited
border-left-width	thin | medium | thick | \<length\>	medium	All	No
border-width	[thin | medium | thick | \<length\>] {1,4}	Undefined	All	No
	If 4 values are given they apply to top, right, bottom, left, in that order.			
	1 value applies to all 4.			
	If 2 or 3 values are given, the missing value is taken from the opposite side.			
border-top-color	\<color\>	The element's color property	All	No
border-right-color	\<color\>	The element's color property	All	No
border-bottom-color	\<color\>	The element's color property	All	No
border-left-color	\<color\>	The element's color property	All	No

Property Name	Possible Values	Initial Value	Applies to	Inherited
border-color	<color>{1,4} | transparent If 4 values are given they apply to top, right, bottom, left, in that order. 1 value applies to all 4. If 2 or 3 values are given, the missing value is taken from the opposite side.	The element's color property	All	No
border-top-style	none | hidden | dotted | dashed | solid | double | groove | ridge | inset | outset	none	All	No
border-right-style	none | hidden | dotted | dashed | solid | double | groove | ridge | inset | outset	none	All	No
border-bottom-style	none | hidden | dotted | dashed | solid | double | groove | ridge | inset | outset	none	All	No
border-left-style	none | hidden | dotted | dashed | solid | double | groove | ridge | inset | outset	none	All	No
border-style	[none | hidden | dotted | dashed | solid | double | groove | ridge | inset | outset]{1,4}	none	All	No

Table Continued on Following Page

Property Name	Possible Values	Initial Value	Applies to	Inherited
border-top	<border-top-width> || <border-top-style> || <color>	Undefined	All	No
border-right	<border-right-width> || <border-right-style> || <color>	Undefined	All	No
border-bottom	<border-bottom-width> || <border-bottom-style> || <color>	Undefined	All	No
border-left	<border-left-width> || <border-left-style> || <color>	Undefined	All	No
border	<border-width> || <border-style> || <color>	Undefined	All	No

Visual Formatting Model

This is a new category of property in CSS2, and is covered in section 9 of the specification.

Property Name	Possible Values	Initial Value	Applies to	Inherited
`display`	`block` | `inline` | `list-item` | `none` | `run-in` | `compact` | `marker` | `table` | `inline-table` | `table-row-group` | `table-column-group` | `table-header-group` | `table-footer-group` | `table-row` | `table-cell` | `table-caption` | `table-column`	`inline`	All	No
`position`	`static` | `relative` | `absolute` | `fixed`	`static`	All (but not generated content)	No
`top` (box offsets)	`<length>` | `<percentage>` | `auto` `<length>`: the box offset is a fixed distance from the reference edge. `<percentage>`: the box offset is a percentage of the containing block's width (for `left` or `right`) or height (for `top` and `bottom`). `auto`: the value depends on which of the other box offset properties are `auto` as well.	`auto`	Positioned elements	No

Table Continued on Following Page

Property Name	Possible Values	Initial Value	Applies to	Inherited
left (box offsets)	*as above*	auto	Positioned elements	No
bottom (box offsets)	*as above*	auto	Positioned elements	No
right (box offsets)	*as above*	auto	Positioned elements	No
float	left | right | none Note: float removes inline elements from the line.	none	All but positioned elements and generated content	No
clear	block | inline | list-item | none	none	Block elements	No
z-index	auto | \<integer\>	auto	Positioned elements	No
direction	ltr | rtl ltr: left-to-right rtl: right-to-left	ltr	All	Yes
unicode-bidi	normal | embed | bidi-override	normal	All	No

Visual Formatting Model Details

This is another new section in CSS2, and is covered in section 10 of the CSS2 specification.

Property Name	Possible Values	Initial Value	Applies to	Inherited
`width`	`<length>` | `<percentage>` | `auto` `<percentage>` refers to parent element's width.	`auto`	All but non-replaced inline elements, table columns and column groups	No
`min-width`	`<length>` | `<percentage>`	Depends on user agent	All but non-replaced inline elements and table elements	No
`max-width`	`<length>` | `<percentage>` | `none`	`none`	All but non-replaced inline elements and table elements	No
`height`	`<length>` | `<percentage>` | `auto`	`auto`	All but non-replaced inline elements, table rows and row groups	No

Table Continued on Following Page

Property Name	Possible Values	Initial Value	Applies to	Inherited
min-height	`<length>` | `<percentage>`	0	All but non-replaced inline elements and table elements	No
max-height	`<length>` | `<percentage>` | none	none	All but non-replaced inline elements and table elements	No
line-height	normal | `<number>` | `<length>` | `<percentage>` `<number>`:- line-height = font-size x num. `<percentage>` is relative to font-size.	normal	All	Yes
vertical-align	baseline | sub | super | top | text-top | middle | bottom | text-bottom | `<percentage>` | `<length>` `<percentage>` is relative to element's line-height property	baseline	Inline and table-cell elements	No

Visual Effects

This is a new category of property in CSS2. It is covered in section 11 of the specification.

Property Name	Possible Values	Initial Value	Applies to	Inherited
overflow	visible | hidden | scroll | auto	visible	Block-level and replaced elements	No
clip	<shape> | auto	auto	Block-level and replaced elements	No
visibility	visible | hidden | collapse | inherit	inherit	All	No

Generated Content, Automatic Numbering and Lists

Again, this is a new category of property in CSS2, covered in section 12 of the specification. In CSS2 it is possible to generate content in several ways:

Using the content property in conjunction with the :before and :after pseudo-elements.

In conjunction with the cue-before and cue-after aural properties

Elements with a value of list-item for the display property

The style and location of generated content is specified with the :before and :after pseudo-elements. These are used in conjunction with the content property, which specifies what is inserted. Unsurprisingly, :before and :after pseudo-elements specify content before and after an element's document tree content. See the specification (section 12) for further details.

Property Name	Possible Values	Initial Value	Applies to	Inherited
content	[<string> | <uri> | <counter> | attr(X) | open-quote | close-quote | no-open-quote | no-close-quote]+	empty string	:before and :after pseudo-elements	No
quotes	[<string> <string>]+ | none	Depends on user agent	All	Yes
counter-reset	[<identifier> <integer>?]+ | none	none	All	No
counter-increment	[<identifier> <integer>?]+ | none	none	All	No
marker-offset	<length> | auto	auto	Elements with the display property set to marker	No
list-style-type	disc | circle | square | decimal | decimal-leading-zero | lower-roman | upper-roman | lower-greek | lower-alpha | upper-alpha | none | lower-latin | upper-latin | hebrew | armenian | georgian | cjk-ideographic | hiragana | katakana | hiragana-iroha | katakana-iroha	disc	Elements with the display property set to list-item	Yes
list-style-image	<uri> | none	none	List-items	Yes
list-style-position	inside | outside	outside	List-items	Yes

Paged Media

All the following paged media properties are new to CSS2 and are covered in section 13 of the specification.

Property Name	Possible Values	Initial Value	Applies to	Inherited
list-style	<list-style-type> || <list-style-position> || <list-style-image>	Undefined	List-items	Yes
size	<length>{1, 2} | auto | portrait | landscape	auto	Page context	N/A
marks (crop marks)	[crop || cross] | none	none	Page context	N/A
page-break-before	auto | always | avoid | left | right	auto	Block-level elements	No
page-break-after	auto | always | avoid | left | right	auto	Block-level elements	No
page-break-inside	avoid | auto	auto	Block-level elements	Yes
page (for using named pages)	<identifier> | auto	auto	Block level elements	Yes
orphans	<integer>	2	Block-level elements	Yes
widows	<integer>	2	Block-level elements	Yes

Colors and Backgrounds

These properties (which are unchanged from CSS1) are in Section 12 of the CSS2 specification.

Property Name	Possible Values	Initial Value	Applies to	Inherited
color	keyword | numerical RGB specification	Depends on user agent	All	Yes
background-color	<color> | transparent	transparent	All	No
background-image	<uri> | none	none	All	No
background-repeat	repeat | repeat-x | repeat-y | no-repeat	repeat	All	No
background-attachment	scroll | fixed	scroll	All	No
background-position	[[<length> | <percentage>]{1,2} | [top | center | bottom] || [left | center | right]]	0%, 0%	Block and replaced elements	No
background	[<background-color> || <background-image> || <background-repeat> || <background-attachment> || <background-position>]	Undefined	All	No

Font Properties

These properties are unchanged in CSS2 from CSS1, and are covered in section 15 of the specification.

Property Name	Possible Values	Initial Value	Applies to	Inherited

`font-family`	`[ [<family-name> |`
	`<generic-family>] , ]*`
	`[<family-name> | <generic-family>]`
	
	Use any font family name.
	
	`<generic-family>` values are:
	
	serif
	sans-serif
	cursive
	fantasy
	`monospace`
		Depends on user agent	All	Yes

`font-style`	`normal | italic | oblique`	`normal`	All	Yes
`font-variant`	`normal | smallcaps`	`normal`	All	Yes

`font-weight`	`normal | bold | bolder | lighter |`
	`100 | 200 | 300 | 400 | 500 | 600 |`
	`700 | 800 | 900`
		`normal`	All	Yes

Table Continued on Following Page

Property Name	Possible Values	Initial Value	Applies to	Inherited
font-stretch	normal | wider | narrower | ultra-condensed | extra-condensed | condensed | semi-condensed | semi-expanded | expanded | extra-expanded | ultra-expanded	normal	All	Yes
font-size	\<absolute-size> | \<relative-size> | \<length> | \<percentage> \<absolute-size>: xx-small | x-small | small | medium | large | x-large | xx-large \<relative-size>: larger | smaller \<percentage>: In relation to parent element	medium	All	Yes
font-size-adjust	\<number> | none	none	All	Yes
font	[[\<font-style> || \<font-variant> || \<font-weight>]? \<font-size> [/\<line-height>]? \<font-family>] | caption | icon | menu | message-box | small-caption | status-bar	Undefined	All	Yes

Text Properties

The text properties are covered in section 16 of the CSS2 specification.

Property Name	Possible Values	Initial Value	Applies to	Inherited
text-indent	`<length>` | `<percentage>`	0	Block elements	Yes
text-align	`left` | `right` | `center` | `justify` | `<string>`	Depends on user agent and writing direction	Block elements	Yes
text-decoration	`none` | [`underline` || `overline` || `line-through` || `blink`]	none	All	No
text-shadow	`none` | [`<color>` || `<length>` `<length>` `<length>?` ,]* [`<color>` || `<length>` `<length>` `<length>?`]	none	All	No
letter-spacing	`normal` | `<length>`	normal	All	Yes
word-spacing	`normal` | `<length>`	normal	All	Yes
text-transform	`none` | `capitalize` | `uppercase` | `lowercase`	none	All	Yes
white-space	`normal` | `pre` | `nowrap`	normal	Block elements	Yes

Tables

All the `table` properties are new to CSS2 and can be found in section 17 of the specification.

Property Name	Possible Values	Initial Value	Applies to	Inherited
caption-side	top | bottom | left | right	top	Table-caption elements	Yes
border-collapse	collapse | separate	collapse	Table and in-line-table elements	Yes
border-spacing	<length>	0	Table and in-line-table elements	yes
table-layout	fixed | auto	auto	Table and in-line-table elements	No
empty-cells	show | hide	show	Table-cell elements	Yes
speak-header	once | always	once	Elements that have header information	Yes

User Interface

The user interface properties are new to CSS2 and can be found in section 18 of the specification.

Property Name	Possible Values	Initial Value	Applies to	Inherited
cursor	[[<uri>,]* [auto | crosshair | default | pointer | move | e-resize | ne-resize | nw-resize | n-resize | se-resize | sw-resize | s-resize | w-resize| text | wait | help]]	auto	All	Yes
outline	<outline-color> || <outline-style> || <outline-width>	See individual properties	All	No
outline-width	border-width	medium	All	No
outline-style	border-style	none	All	No
outline-color	border-color | invert	invert	All	No

Aural Style Sheets

These are a new addition in CSS2 and can be seen in further detail in section 19 of the specification.

Property Name	Possible Values	Initial Value	Applies to	Inherited
volume	`<number>` | `<percentage>` | `silent` | `x-soft` | `soft` | `medium` | `loud` | `x-loud`	medium	All	Yes
speak	`normal` | `none` | `spell-out`	normal	All	Yes
pause-before	`<time>` | `<percentage>`	Depends on user agent	All	No
pause-after	`<time>` | `<percentage>`	Depends on user agent	All	No
pause	[[`<time>` | `<percentage>`]{1, 2}]	Depends on user agent	All	No
cue-before	`<uri>` | `none`	none	All	No
cue-after	`<uri>` | `none`	none	All	No
cue	[`<cue-before>` || `<cue-after>`]	Undefined	All	No
play-during	`<uri>` `mix`? `repeat`? | `auto` | `none`	auto	All	No

Property Name	Possible Values	Initial Value	Applies to	Inherited
azimuth	<angle> | [[left-side | far-left | left | center-left | center | center-right | right | far-right | right-side] || behind] | leftwards | rightwards	center	All	Yes
elevation	<angle> | below | level | above | higher | lower	level	All	Yes
speech-rate	<number> | x-slow | slow | medium | fast | x-fast | faster | slower	medium	All	Yes
voice-family	[[<specific-voice> | <generic-voice>],]* [<specific-voice> | <generic-voice>]	Depends on user agent	All	Yes
pitch	<frequency> | x-low | low | medium | high | x-high	medium	All	Yes
pitch-range	<number>	50	All	Yes
stress	<number>	50	All	Yes
richness	<number>	50	All	Yes
speak-punctuation	code | none	none	All	Yes
speak-numeral	digits | continuous	continuous	All	Yes

IE5 XSL Reference

IE5 broadly supports the **Transformations** section of the working draft of XSL released by W3C on 16th December 1998, though there are some minor differences. It does *not* support the proposals for **Formatting Objects** or **Flow Objects**. This reference section details the XSL support available in IE5 final release.

XSL defines a set of XML elements that have special meaning within the `xsl` namespace (that is, each is prefixed with the `xsl` namespace identifier). These elements perform the transformation of the document into a new format. From here, under the W3C proposals, Formatting Objects would be used to define the actual output format for each element transformation. In IE5, we will generally use HTML within the transformations to define the new document format.

Bear in mind that XSL can also be used to transform *any* XML document into another (different) XML document, or into a document in almost any other format. This means, for example, that it can be used to transform an XSL stylesheet document into another XSL stylesheet document, or into some custom format that defines the styling in a way suited to some other application.

The IE5 XSL Elements

XSL in IE5 provides twenty elements that are used to create XSL stylesheets, or style sections within an XML document. The elements are:

Name	Description

`xsl:apply-`
`templates`
	Used inside a template to indicate that XSL should look for and apply another specific template to this node. The attributes are:
	
	`order-by="[+|-] xsl-pattern"`
	
	`select="xsl-pattern"`

Table Continued on Following Page

Name	Description
`xsl:attribute`	Used to create a new `Attribute` node and attach it to the current element. The single attribute is: `name="attribute-name"`
`xsl:cdata`	Used to create a new `CDATASection` at this point in the output. Has no attributes.
`xsl:choose`	Used with the `xsl:when` and `xsl:otherwise` to provide a selection mechanism based on individual conditions for the same or different nodes. Similar to an `If...ElseIf...Else` construct. Has no attributes.
`xsl:comment`	Used to create a new `Comment` node at this point in the output. Has no attributes.
`xsl:copy`	Used to copy the current node in its entirety to the output. Has no attributes.
`xsl:define-template-set`	Used to define a set of templates that have a specific scope in the stylesheet. Has no attributes.
`xsl:element`	Used to create a new `Element` node at this point in the output. The single attribute is: `name="element-name"`
`xsl:entity-ref`	Used to create a new `EntityReference` node at this point in the output. The single attribute is: `name="entity-reference-name"`
`xsl:eval`	Used to evaluate a string expression and insert the result into the output. The string can be a mathematical or logical expression, an XSL function or a custom script function. The single attribute is: `language="language-name"`

`xsl:for-each`	Used to create a loop construct similar to a `For...Next` loop, allowing the same template to be applied to multiple more than one node. The attributes are:
	
	`order-by="[+|-] xsl-pattern"`
	`select="xsl-pattern"`

`xsl:if`	Used to create conditional branches within a template, in the same way as an `If...Then` construct, to allow a template to provide different output based on a condition. The single attribute is: `match="condition-pattern"`

Name	Description
xsl:node-name	Used to insert the name of the current node into the output as a text string. Has no attributes.
xsl:otherwise	*see* xsl:choose (above). Has no attributes.
xsl:pi	Used to create a new ProcessingInstruction node at this point in the output. The single attribute is: name="*processing-instruction-name*"
xsl:script	Used to define an area of the template that contains global variable declarations and script code functions. The single attribute is: language="*language-name*"
xsl:stylesheet	Used to define the 'root' element of an XSL stylesheet, the scripting language used, whether to preserve any white space in the input document when creating the output document, and a namespace declaration for the xsl prefix. The attributes are: xmlns:xml="http://www.w3.org/TR/WD-xsl" language="*language-name*" indent-result="[yes|no]" (default is "no") **NOTE:** The namespace **must** be as shown here for XSL to work in IE5.
xsl:template	Used to define a template which containing contains the instructions for transforming the XML input into the output for nodes that match a specific pattern. The attributes are: language="*language-name*" match="*xsl-pattern*"
xsl:value-of	Used to evaluate an XSL pattern in the select attribute, and insert into the template as text the value of the matching node and its descendants. The single attribute is: select="*xsl-pattern*"
xsl:when	*see* xsl:choose (above). The single attribute is: match="*xsl-pattern*"

XSL Stylesheet Structure

The following shows the more common ways in which the XSL elements are used to construct an XSL style sheet, showing the kinds of structures that can be created. This isn't by any means the only combination, as most of the elements can be nested within most of the other elements. However, in general, each stylesheet will consist of one template that matches the root element in the document, followed by others that apply specific style and formatting to specific elements within the document.

```
<xsl:stylesheet xmlns:xsl="http://www.w3.org/TR/WD-xsl">

    <xsl:template match="...">
        <xsl:value-of select="..." />
        <xsl:eval> ... </xsl:eval>
        <xsl:if match="..."> ... </xsl:if>
        <xsl:copy />

        <xsl:choose>
            <xsl:when match="..."> ... </xsl:when>
            <xsl:otherwise> ... </xsl:otherwise>
        </xsl:choose>

        <xsl:for-each select="...">
            <xsl:value-of select="..." />
            <xsl:eval> ... </xsl:eval>
            <xsl:if match="..."> ... </xsl:if>
            <xsl:copy />
            <xsl:apply-templates />
        </xsl:for-each>

        <xsl:apply-templates select="..." />
    </xsl:template>

    <xsl:define-template-set>
        <xsl:template match="..."> ... </xsl:template>
        <xsl:template match="..."> ... </xsl:template>
    </xsl:define-template-set>

    <xsl:script> ... </xsl:script>

</xsl:stylesheet>
```

Creating New Nodes in XSL

The XSL elements that create new nodes in the output document are xsl:attribute, xsl:cdata, xsl:comment, xsl:element, xsl:entity-ref and xsl:pi.

To create the XML node <![CDATA[This is a CDATA section]]> we could use:

```
<xsl:cdata>This is a CDATA section</xsl:cdata>
```

To create the XML node <!ENTITY copy "©"> we could use:

```
<xsl:entity-ref name="copy">©</xsl:entity-ref>
```

To create the XML node <!--This is the comment text--> we could use:

```
<xsl:comment>This is the comment text</xsl:comment>
```

To create the XML node `<?WroxFormat="StartParagraph"?>` we could use:

```
<xsl:pi name="WroxFormat">StartParagraph</xsl:pi>
```

To create the XML element `<title>Instant JavaScript</title>` we could use:

```
<xsl:element name="title">Instant JavaScript</xsl:element>
```

and to add a `print-date` attribute to it we could use:

```
<xsl:attribute name="print_date">1998-02-07</xsl:attribute>
```

This gives us the XML result:

```
<title print_date="1998-02-07">Instant JavaScript</title>
```

XSL Stylesheet Runtime Methods

The `xsl:eval` element can be used to execute a number of built-in methods available in XSL in IE5. The `IXTLRuntime` object provides these methods:

Name	Description
`absoluteChildNumber (this_node)`	Returns the index of a specified node within its parent's `childNodes` list. Values start from `"1"`.
`ancestorChildNumber (node_name, this_node)`	Finds the first ancestor node of a specified node that has the specified name, and returns the index of that node within its parent's `childNodes` list. Values start from 1. Returns 0 if there is no ancestor.
`childNumber (this_node)`	Returns the index of the specified node within its parent's `childNodes` list of children with the same name (that is, its index within the list of the node's identically named siblings) or 0 if not found. Values start from 1.
`depth(start_node)`	Returns the depth or level within the document tree at which the specified node appears. The `XMLDocument` or root node is at level 0.

Table Continued on Following Page

Name	Description
`elementIndexList (this_node, node_name)`	Returns an array of node index numbers for the specified node and all its ancestors up to and including the document root node, indicating each node's position within their parent's `childNodes` list. The ordering of the array starts from the root document node.

When the node_name parameter is not supplied, the method returns an array of integers that indicates the index of the specified node with respect to all of its siblings, the index of that node's parent with respect to all of its siblings, and so on until the document root is reached.

When the node_name parameter is specified, the returned array contains entries only for nodes of the specified name, and the indices are evaluated relative to siblings with the specified name. Zero is supplied for levels in the tree that do not have children with the supplied name.

Although this method is included in the Microsoft documentation, it was not supported by IE5 at the time of writing. |
| `formatDate(date, format, locale)` | Formats the value in the date parameter using the specified formatting options. The following format codes are supported:

m - Month (1-12)

mm - Month (01-12)

mmm - Month (Jan-Dec)

mmmm - Month (January-December)

mmmmm - Month as the first letter of the month

d - Day (1-31)

dd - Day (01-31)

ddd - Day (Sun-Sat)

dddd - Day (Sunday-Saturday)

yy -Year (00-99)

yyyy - Year (1900-9999)

The locale to use in determining the correct sequence of values in the date. If omitted the sequence month-day-year is used. |

Name	Description
formatIndex (number, format)	Formats the integer number using the specified numerical system. 1 - Standard numbering system 01 - Standard numbering with leading zeros A - Uppercase letter sequence "A" to "Z" then "AA" to"ZZ". a - Lowercase letter sequence "a" to "z" then "aa" to "zz". I - Uppercase Roman numerals: "I", "II", "III", "IV", etc. i - Lowercase Roman numerals: "i", "ii", "iii", "iv", etc.
formatNumber (number, format)	Formats the value number using the specified format. Zero or more of the following values can be present in the format string: # (pound) – Display only significant digits and omit insignificant zeros. 0 (zero) – Display insignificant zeros in these positions. ? (question) – Adds spaces for insignificant zeros on either side of the decimal point, so that decimal points align with a fixed-point font. You can also use this symbol for fractions that have varying numbers of digits. . (period) – Indicates the position of the decimal point. , (comma) – Display a thousands separator or scale a number by a multiple of one thousand. % (percent) – Display number as a percentage. E or e - Display number in scientific (exponential) format. If format contains a zero or # to the right of an exponent code, display the number in scientific format and inserts an "E" or "e". The number of 0 or # characters to the right determines the number of digits in the exponent. E- or e- Place a minus sign by negative exponents. E+ or e+ Place a minus sign by negative exponents and a plus sign by positive exponents.

Table Continued on Following Page

Name	Description
formatTime(time, format, locale)	Formats the value in the time parameter using the specified formatting options. The following format codes are supported: h - Hours (0-23) hh - Hours (00-23) m - Minutes (0-59) mm - Minutes (00-59) s - Seconds (0-59) ss - Seconds (00-59) AM/PM - Add "AM" or "PM" and display in 12 hour format am/pm - Add "am" or "pm" and display in 12 hour format A/P - Add "A" or "P" and display in 12 hour format a/p - Add "a" or "p" and display in 12 hour format [h]:mm – Display elapsed time in hours, as in "25.02" [mm]:ss - Display elapsed time in minutes, as in "63:46" [ss] - Display elapsed time in seconds ss.00 - Display fractions of a second The locale is used to determine the correct separator characters.
uniqueID(this_node)	Returns the unique identifier for the specified node.

As an example, this code transforms a number which is the content of the current element into Roman numerals using the built-in formatIndex() method:

```
<xsl:eval>
   intNumber=parseInt(this.text);
   formatIndex(intNumber, "i");
</xsl:eval>
```

Note that the content of the element must first be transformed from string format (which is the default for all XML content, unless we specify otherwise in the XML document's schema using data types).

The IE5 XSL Pattern-Matching Syntax

Using the elements described earlier, XSL can create a stylesheet document that contains one or more XSL `template` elements. These templates are applied to individual elements or sets of elements in the source document to create a particular section of the output document. To define which template applies to which of the source elements or nodes, a **pattern** is used. This pattern has one of two generic forms, and can define the node or nodes that match through:

❏   The **position** and **hierarchy** of the node or nodes within the source document

❏   The application of a **filter** that selectively targets one or more nodes

Node Position and Hierarchy

To select or match nodes (i.e. elements) through their position and hierarchy within the source document, we use a series of **path operators** to build up a pattern string. The path operators are:

Operator	Description
/	A forward slash is the **child** path operator. It selects elements that are direct children of the specified node, in much the same way as we use it to specify paths in a URL. For example, we use `book/category` to select all `<category>` elements that are children of `<book>` elements. To indicate the root node, we place this operator at the start of the pattern, for example: `/booklist/book`.
//	Two forward slashes indicate the **recursive descent** path operator. It selects all matching nodes at any depth below the current node (all descendants), for example: `booklist//title` to select all `<title>` elements that are descendants at any level of the `<booklist>` element. When it appears at the start of the pattern, it indicates recursive descent from the root node, that is, all elements in the document.
.	The period or 'full stop' is the **current context** path operator. It is used to indicate specifically the current node or 'context', for example: `.//title` to select all `<title>` elements at any level below the current element. The combination `./` always indicates the current context and is usually superfluous — for example `./book/category` is the same as `book/category`.
@	The 'at' operator is the **attribute** path operator. It indicates that this part of the pattern refers to attributes of the current element. For example, `book/@print_date` selects the `print_date` attributes of all `<book>` elements.

Table Continued on Following Page

Operator	Description
*	The asterisk is a **wildcard** path operator, and is used when we want to select all elements or attributes regardless of their name, for example book/* to select all child elements of all book elements, or book/@* to select all the attributes of all <book> elements.

Node Index Position

The path operators always return all elements or nodes that match the pattern. The node **index** can be used to specify a particular node within the set (or collection) of matching nodes, and the special XSL end() function can be used to specify the last node:

```
/booklist/book[0]      'first <book> element in root <booklist> element
/booklist/book[2]      'third <book> element in root <booklist> element
/booklist/book[end()]  'last <book> element in root <booklist> element
```

Note that the following three examples select different nodes within the same document:

```
book/category[2]       'second <category> element from all <book> elements
book[2]/category[2]    'second <category> element in second <book> element
(book/category)[2]     'second <category> element within the set of all ...
                       '... <category> elements from all <book> elements
```

In the last example, think of the pattern within the parentheses being applied first to create the set of all category elements from all book elements, followed by the index operator selecting just the second one.

XSL Filters and Filter Patterns

An **XSL filter** has the generic form [operator pattern] where operator is an optional **filter operator** that defines how the pattern is applied, and pattern is the required XSL **filter pattern** that selects one or more elements based on a range of criteria. One or more whitespace characters separate the filter operator and the filter pattern. The optional operator part can also consist of more than one filter operator expression if required. If omitted, any or all nodes that match the criteria in the filter pattern will be selected.

Filter Patterns

XSL filter patterns are very powerful, and offer an almost infinite number of pattern combinations. The following is a broad guide to the different kinds of ways that they can be used. The examples cover:

❑ Selecting by **child node name**

❑ Selecting by **node value**

❑ Selecting by **attribute existence**

❑ Selecting by **attribute value**

❑ Selecting by a **combination** of these

Selecting by Child Node Name

The position and hierarchy syntax we looked at earlier works by selecting elements based on their name as well as their position within the document. For example, `book/category` selects all `<category>` elements that are child elements of `<book>` elements. This is equivalent to the filter:

```
book[category]/category
```

because the filter `book/category` is actually a shorthand way of saying we want to select all `<book>` elements that have a `<category>` element (equivalent to `book[category]`), and then select the `<category>` element. A more useful way of using the longhand technique is when you want to specify a *different* child element to return. For example,

```
book[title]/category
```

means select only the `<category>` elements of books that have a `<title>` child element. To find all books that have both a `<category>` and a `<title>` child element, we use two filters:

```
book[title][category]
```

Selecting by Node Value

Extending the filter pattern that selects a node by its name, we can also select by value:

```
book[category = 'Scripting']
```

will select all `<book>` elements that have a `<category>` element with the value 'Scripting'. If we want to get the titles of books in this category, we would use:

```
book[category = 'Scripting']/title
```

To specify a value for the current element, we can include the period path operator. For example:

```
book/title[. = 'Instant JavaScript']
```

selects the title of the book 'Instant JavaScript'.

Selecting by Attribute Existence

The '@' attribute operator can also be used in a filter pattern to specify that the element must have a matching attribute:

```
book[@print_date]
```

selects only `book` elements that have a `print_date` attribute.

421

Selecting by Attribute Value

We can also specify the value that the attribute must have in order to match the pattern:

```
book[@print_date = '1998-05-02']
```

Selecting by a Combination of Methods

And, of course, we can combine all these methods to select exactly the element or node we require. For example:

```
book[@print_date = '1998-05-02']/title[. = 'Instant JavaScript']
```

to find the book titled 'Instant JavaScript' that was printed on 2nd May 1998, or:

```
/booklist//cover_design[issue = "final"]/*[@url = 'images']
```

to select all elements that:

- ❑ Have *any* name, but also have an attribute named `url` that has the value 'images' (from the `*[@url = 'images']` part);

- ❑ Are child elements of `cover_design` elements that themselves also have a child element named `issue` with the value 'final' (from the `cover_design[issue = "final"]` part);

- ❑ Are descendants of the root `booklist` element (from the `/booklist//` part).

Note that the values of elements and attributes can be enclosed in single or double quotes.

Comparison Operators

The above examples all use the normal equality operator '=' to test if two values are equal. This works for numbers as well as strings. All XML values are strings by default, but IE5 casts them to appropriate data types before carrying out the comparison if possible. The data type chosen is based either on the content of the node value string, or on a **schema** (if one is present) that specifies the data type. This means that a comparison such as `[price = 29.95]` (without quotes around the numeric value) is perfectly valid.

> *If a schema is present and the content of the node cannot be cast into the type specified in the schema, for example if it contains characters that are illegal for that data type, such as letters in a numeric value, it is omitted from the set of matching nodes.*

As well as the equality operator, there is a full set of other comparison operators:

Shortcut	Operator	Description
=	eq	Case-sensitive equality, for example [price = 29.95]
!=	ne	Case-sensitive inequality, for example [category != 'Script']
< *	lt	Case-sensitive less than, for example [radius lt 14.73]
<= *	le	Case-sensitive less than or equal, for example [age le 18]
>	gt	Case-sensitive greater than, for example [name > 'H']
>=	ge	Case-sensitive greater than or equal, for example [speed >= 55]
	ieq	Case-insensitive equality
	ine	Case-insensitive inequality
	ilt	Case-insensitive less than
	ile	Case-insensitive less than or equal
	igt	Case-insensitive greater than
	ige	Case-insensitive greater than or equal

** Note that the '<' and '<=' operators cannot be used 'un-escaped' in XSL attributes, because these have to follow XML standards of well formed-ness. Instead, it is better to use the equivalent lt and le. Also note that all filter operator **names** (such as eq) are case sensitive, that is, they must be all lower-case.*

The shortcut operators perform exactly the same operation as the longer version, so the following are equivalent:

```
[category = 'Scripting']
[category $eq$ 'Scripting']
```

as are:

```
[category != 'Scripting']
[category $ne$ 'Scripting']
```

The case-insensitive operators have no shortcut operator syntax. They are useful, however, when you need to match irrespective of case. There is no UCase or LCase function included in XSL (unless you provide your own script function), so it saves having to do multiple tests, i.e.:

```
[category = 'html' $or$ category = 'HTML']
```

423

Instead, we just use:

```
[category $ieq$ 'html']
```

Logical Filter Operators

As well as single comparison tests, we can use logical operators to combine patterns to build up more complex ones (as seen in the final example in the previous section). The logical operators are:

Shortcut	Operator	Description
&&	and	Logical AND
||	or	Logical OR
	not	Negation, logical NOT

So, using these we can do things like selecting books that have a `<category>` element that is either 'Scripting' or 'HTML':

```
book/[category = 'Scripting' $or$ category = 'HTML']
```

or which have the title 'Instant JavaScript' (case-insensitive match), but are not in the category 'Scripting':

```
book/[category $ne$ 'Scripting' $and$ title $ieq$ 'Instant JavaScript']
```

The not operator simply changes the 'truth' of the match, so the following are equivalent, and match `<book>` elements which have a child `<category>` element with the value 'Scripting' but no child `<category>` element with the value 'HTML' (thus excluding `<book>` elements which have child `<category>` elements with both values):

```
book/[category = 'Scripting' $and$ category $ne$ 'HTML']
book/[category = 'Scripting' $and$ $not$ category = 'HTML']
```

Filter Set Operators

Remember that all the above examples of filter patterns that use comparison operators rely on the fact that the default filter action, if no operator is specified in the filter, is to return any or all nodes that match the pattern. However, there are ways that we can specify more exactly which of the matching elements we want, in a similar way to using an index to specify the first element. We use the **set** operators, any and all:

Operator	Description
all	Returns True only if the specified pattern matches all of the items in the collection.
any	Returns True if the specified pattern matches any of the items in the collection.

The easiest way to appreciate the difference is to think about the way that elements are selected. For an element named <book>, we can specify that we want it to be included in the results if it has a <category> child element with the value 'HTML' by using the pattern:

```
book[category = 'HTML']
```

However, this will only match the <book> element if the *first* <category> element has the value 'HTML'. If it doesn't have this value, even if other (later) child elements do, the <book> element will not be selected. However, if we use the pattern:

```
book[$any$ category = 'HTML']
```

we will get a match for this <book> element, because we specified that we want the <book> elements where *any* of the child elements has the value 'HTML'. If we use the alternative set operator, all, we are specifying that we only want to select <book> elements where *all* of their category child elements have the value 'HTML', not just the first one or any one or more of them. For the book to be included in the results, they must all have the value 'HTML':

```
book[$all$ category = 'HTML']
```

Of course, if the book only has one <category> child element, with the value 'HTML', all three of these filters will return this book element. The differences only appear when the pattern specifies elements with more than one matching child (or other) element.

XSL Built-In Methods

We saw one of the built-in methods of XSL earlier on when looking at selecting elements by their index. The last node in a collection of matching nodes is returned by the end() method:

```
booklist/category[end()]
```

The Information Methods

Other **information** methods are available to help isolate a specific node in a collection:

Name	Description
end()	Selects and returns the last node in a collection.
index()	Selects and returns the index (number) of the current node within its collection.
nodeName()	Selects and returns the tag name of the current node, including any namespace prefix.
nodeType()	Selects and returns as a number the type of the node (as used in the DOM).

Table Continued on Following Page

425

Name	Description
date()	Returns a value in date format.
text()	Selects and returns the text content of the current node.
value()	Returns a type cast version of the value of the current node.

The value() method is the default, so the following are equivalent:

```
book[category!value() = "Script"]
book[category = "Script"]
```

*The exclamation mark operator (sometimes called the **'bang'** operator) denotes that* value() *is a method of the* <category> *element. The normal use of a period here is not legal. It would be confused with the **current path** operator.*

The index() method is also optional when we want a specific element:

```
book[index() = 5]
book[5]
```

However, it is useful for selecting several elements, for example the fourth and fifth <book> elements only:

```
book[index() > 3 $and$ index() < 6]
```

The Collection Methods

It's also possible to select elements or other nodes using the **collection** methods supported by XSL in IE5:

Name	Description
ancestor()	Selects the ancestor node nearest to the current node that matches the pattern, starting at the parent node and working back up the document hierarchy. Returns a single element or null if none matches.
attribute()	Selects all attribute nodes of the current node, returning them as a collection. The optional parameter can specify the attribute name to match.
comment()	Selects and returns as a collection all child comment nodes.
element()	Selects all child element nodes of the current node, returning them as a collection. The optional parameter can specify the element name to match.

Name	Description
node()	Selects and returns as a collection all child nodes that are not attributes.
pi()	Selects and returns as a collection all child processing instruction nodes.
textnode()	Selects and returns as a collection all child text nodes.

As an example, we can select all of the comment elements within our <book> elements using:

```
book/comment()
```

The attribute() and element() methods accept a text parameter that can be used to limit the matching nodes:

```
book/attribute('print_date')
```

Of course, this is equivalent to the '@' operator we saw earlier, so these provide the same result:

```
book/attribute('print_date')
book/@print_date
```

And the element() method is equivalent to the earlier syntax as well — these two provide the same result:

```
book/element('category')
book/category
```

The ancestor() method also accepts a text parameter containing the pattern to be matched. For example:

```
ancestor(book/category)
```

will match the nearest <category> ancestor node which is a child of a <book> element. Note that this method cannot occur to the right of a '/' or '//' in the pattern, and that, unlike the attribute() and element() methods, the name of the node to be matched should not be placed in quotes.

Important Note

Remember that, of all of the XML-related technologies, XSL is probably the most volatile at the moment, in terms of changes that will come about in the language and syntax. There are subtle differences between the W3C working draft and Microsoft's implementation of XSL in IE5. You may wish to confine your development effort to experimental and induction projects until the future standards are more firmly established.

XML Behaviors Reference

Internet Explorer 5 provides features that allow programmers to create custom **behaviors** that can be attached to elements in a document. These behaviors are built as HTML Components (HTCs), using XML syntax elements and scripting code. As well as creating **custom behaviors**, authors can take advantage of a range of **default behaviors** that are part of Internet Explorer 5. This appendix describes these default behaviors, then goes on to describe the syntax and elements that are used when creating custom behaviors.

Default Behaviors Reference

Internet Explorer provides the following default behaviors:

- ❏ anchor (anchorClick) - used to open a folder in Web Folder view.
- ❏ clientCaps - provides information about the capabilities of the client browser.
- ❏ download - can be used to download HTML pages and other files to the client.
- ❏ homePage - allows you to query and change the user's Home Page setting
- ❏ httpFolder - used to open a folder in Web Folder, DAV or WEC view.
- ❏ saveFavorite - allows the state of the page to be saved as a Favorites entry.
- ❏ saveHistory - allows the state of the page to be saved as a History entry.
- ❏ saveSnapshot - allows the state of the page and script variables to be saved.
- ❏ userData - can be used to save values from controls between sessions.

The anchor (anchorClick) Default Behavior

Used to open a folder in Web Folder view.

Instantiated within an HTML element:

```
<element_name
    HREF="url_default"
    FOLDER="url_folder"
    TARGET="window_name"
    ID="unique_id"
    STYLE="behavior:url(#default#anchorClick)">
```

where:

`element_name` is the name of a visible HTML element to be used to start the process

`url_default` is the address of the page to open if the browser doesn't support the `anchor` behavior

`url_folder` is the address of the folder to open in Web Folder view

`window_name` (optional) is the name of a browser window or frame to open the view within, or "`_self`" to open in the current window (the default if omitted) or "`_blank`" to open in a new window

`unique_id` (optional) is the ID to apply to the element if required

The style can also be defined as a class, and applied to elements using the CLASS attribute:

```
<STYLE TYPE="text/css">
    .myanchors {behavior:url(#default#anchorClick);}
</STYLE>
...
<A CLASS="myanchors"... etc ... >
```

Instantiated as a custom XML element:

```
<namespace:element_name
    ID="unique_id"
    STYLE="behavior:url(#default#anchorClick)" />
```

where:

`namespace` is the optional namespace definition in the page's <HTML> element
`element_name` is the name to be used to declare the element
`unique_id` (optional) is the ID to apply to the element if required

For example:

```
<HTML XMLNS:myNS="http://www.mysite.com/ns">
...
<myNS:MYANCHOR ID="xmlAnchor" STYLE="behavior:url(#default#anchorClick)" />
```

Note that the anchor *behavior requires special software to be installed on the server. It was not working reliably in the version we used when writing this book.*

The clientCaps Default Behavior

Provides information about the capabilities of the client browser.

Instantiated as a custom XML element:

```
<namespace:element_name
    ID="unique_id"
    STYLE="behavior:url(#default#clientCaps)" />
```

where:

namespace is the optional namespace definition in the page's <HTML> element
element_name is the name to be used to declare the element
unique_id (optional) is the ID to apply to the element if required

For example:

```
<HTML XMLNS:myNS="http://www.mysite.com/ns">
...
<myNS:MYCAPS ID="xmlCCaps" STYLE="behavior:url(#default#clientCaps)" />
```

clientCaps Properties

The clientCaps object provides the following properties for the client browser or
user agent:

Name	Description
availHeight	Returns the available height of the screen in pixels, excluding toolbars etc.
availWidth	Returns the available width of the screen in pixels, excluding toolbars etc.
bufferDepth	Returns the number of bits per pixel for the screen buffer on the client.
colorDepth	Returns the number of bits per pixel that can be displayed on the client screen.
connectionType	Returns the type of network connection that the client is using.
cookieEnabled	Returns true if the client browser is set to accept cookies.
cpuClass	Returns the type of processor in use, for example 'x86'
height	Returns the overall height of the screen in pixels, including toolbars etc.

Table Continued on Following Page

Name	Description
javaEnabled	Returns true if the client browser has Java code execution enabled.
platform	Returns the type of operating system in use, e.g. 'Win32'
systemLanguage	Returns the language code set in the client's operating system.
userLanguage	Returns the language code set in the client's browser.
width	Returns the overall width of the screen in pixels, including toolbars etc.

clientCaps Methods

The clientCaps object provides the following methods for use in scripting:

Name	Description
addComponentRequest ("componentID", "IDType", "minimum_version")	Adds a request to the browser's component install queue for a component that must be downloaded before the page completes loading and starts to execute. A minimum version number can optionally be specified.
clearComponentRequest ("componentID", "IDType")	Removes a component download request from the download queue.
result=compareVersions ("version1", "version2")	Compares two component versions based on their version numbers. Returns –1 if version1 is older than version2, 0 if they are the same, and 1 if version1 is more recent than version2.
success=doComponentRequest()	Starts the download of all the queued component requests, and returns true if it succeeds.
version=getComponentVersion ("componentID", "IDType")	Returns the current version of a specified component if it is installed on the client, or null otherwise.
isComponentInstalled ("componentID", "IDType", "minimum_version")	Returns true if the specified component is already installed on the client and the version is equal to or higher than the optional minimum_version.

The list of components that `clientCaps` can identify, together with their identifiers, is available from Microsoft at http://www.microsoft.com/workshop/author/behaviors/reference/methods/installable.asp.

The possible (case-insensitive) values for the `"IDType"` parameter are:

Value	Description
`"clsid"`	The CLSID of the component.
`"componentid"`	The Active Setup ID of the component.
`"mimetype"`	The MIME-type of the component.
`"progid"`	The ProgID of the component.

The download Default Behavior

Can be used to download HTML pages and other files to the client.

Instantiated as a custom XML element:

```
<namespace:element_name
    ID="unique_id"
    STYLE="behavior:url(#default#download)" />
```

where:

`namespace` is the optional namespace definition in the page's <HTML> element
`element_name` is the name to be used to declare the element
`unique_id` (optional) is the ID to apply to the element if required

For example:

```
<HTML XMLNS:myNS="http://www.mysite.com/ns">
...
<myNS:MYDLOAD ID="xmlDLoad" STYLE="behavior:url(#default#download)" />
```

download Method

The `download` object provides the following method for use in scripting:

Name	Description
`startDownload("file_url", callback_function)`	Starts downloading the file specified. When complete, the function named in the second parameter is executed automatically.

The homePage Default Behavior

Allows you to query and change the user's Home Page setting.

Instantiated as a custom XML element:

```
<namespace:element_name
    ID="unique_id"
    STYLE="behavior:url(#default#homePage)" />
```

where:

namespace is the optional namespace definition in the page's <HTML> element
element_name is the name to be used to declare the element
unique_id (optional) is the ID to apply to the element if required

For example:

```
<HTML XMLNS:myNS="http://www.mysite.com/ns">
...
<myNS:MYHOME ID="xmlHOME" STYLE="behavior:url(#default#homePage)" />
```

homePage Methods

The homePage object provides the following methods for use in scripting:

Name	Description
isHomePage("page_url")	Returns true only if the specified page is the user's current Home Page and it is on the same domain as the currently executing page, or false if it is on a different domain or is not the user's current Home Page.
navigateHomePage()	Loads the user's current Home Page.
setHomePage("page_url")	Sets the user's current Home Page to the specified page (providing the user grants permission, which is requested in a dialog box).

The httpFolder Default Behavior

Used to open a folder in Web Folder, DAV or WEC view.

Instantiated within an HTML element:

```
<element_name
    ONCLICK="function_name()"
    ID="unique_id"
    STYLE="behavior:url(#default#httpFolder)">
```

where:

element_name is the name of a visible HTML element to be used to start the process
function_name is the name of a script function that will execute the object's methods
unique_id (optional) is the ID to apply to the element if required

The style can also be defined as a class, and applied to elements using the CLASS attribute:

```
<STYLE TYPE="text/css">
    .myfolders {behavior:url(#default#httpFolder);}
</STYLE>
...
<SPAN CLASS="myfolders"... etc ... >
```

Instantiated as a custom XML element:

```
<namespace:element_name
    ID="unique_id"
    STYLE="behavior:url(#default#httpFolder)" />
```

where:

namespace is the optional namespace definition in the page's <HTML> element
element_name is the name to be used to declare the element
unique_id (optional) is the ID to apply to the element if required

For example:

```
<HTML XMLNS:myNS="http://www.mysite.com/ns">
...
<myNS:MYHTTP ID="xmlHttp" STYLE="behavior:url(#default#httpFolder)" />
```

httpFolder Methods

The httpFolder object provides the following methods for use in scripting:

Name	Description
navigate("page_url", "protocol")	Opens the page specified in the current window or frame using the protocol specified. This can be "Folder" for Web Folder view, "DAV" for Distributed Authoring and Versioning view or "WEC" for Web Extender Client (i.e. MS FrontPage) view.
navigateFrame("page_url", "window_name", "protocol")	Opens the page specified in the window or frame specified using the protocol specified. The window name can be the usual "_self", "_blank", "_parent", "_top", the name of an existing or the name for a new window.

Note that the `httpFolder` *behavior requires special software to be installed on the server. It was not working reliably in the version we used when writing this book.*

The saveFavorite Default Behavior

Allows the state of the page to be saved as a Favorites entry. It is saved in an `.ini` file, and retrieved when the page is next loaded from the Favorites list.

Instantiated within an HTML element:

```
<element_name
    ID="unique_id"
    ONSAVE="function_name()"
    ONLOAD="function_name()"
    STYLE="behavior:url(#default#saveFavorite)">
```

where:

`element_name` is the name of an HTML element to which the behavior will be applied
`function_name` is the name of a function to execute in response to that event
`unique_id` (optional) is the ID to apply to the element if required

The style can also be defined as a class, and applied to elements using the CLASS attribute:

```
<STYLE TYPE="text/css">
    .myfavorites {behavior:url(#default#saveFavorite);}
</STYLE>
...
<INPUT CLASS="myfavorites"... etc ... >
```

A `<META>` element is also required in the `<HEAD>` section of the page to indicate that the page is persistent. For example:

```
<META NAME="save" CONTENT="favorite">
...
<SCRIPT LANGUAGE="JScript">
function saveData() {
    // set the control's persistent attribute value
    txtSaved.setAttribute("myvalue", txtSaved.value);
}

function loadData() {
    // retrieve the persistent attribute value
    txtSaved.value = txtSaved.getAttribute("myvalue");
}
</SCRIPT>
...
<INPUT TYPE="TEXT" ID="txtSaved" CLASS="myfavorites"
        ONSAVE="saveData()" ONLOAD="loadData()">
```

The `saveFavorites` behavior does not automatically persist values. The page author must use the `setAttribute()` method to persist the values and the `getAttribute()` method to retrieve them. This is usually done in response to the `onsave` and `onload` events.

saveFavorite Methods

The `saveFavorite` object provides the following methods for use in scripting:

Name	Description
getAttribute ("attribute_name")	Returns the value attached to the element by the `setAttribute()` method under the specified attribute name.
setAttribute ("attribute_name", value)	Attaches the specified value to the element as a persistent attribute using the specified name.

saveFavorite Events

The `saveFavorite` object provides the following events for use in scripting:

Name	Description
onload	Occurs when the page is opened from the user's Favorites list.
onsave	Occurs when the page is added to the user's Favorites list.

The saveHistory Default Behavior

Allows the state of the page to be saved as a History entry. The information is saved in memory, and is lost when the browser is closed.

Instantiated within an HTML element:

```
<element_name
    ID="unique_id"
    ONSAVE="function_name()"
    ONLOAD="function_name()"
    STYLE="behavior:url(#default#saveHistory)">
```

where `element_name` is the name of an HTML element to which the behavior will be applied, `function_name` (optional) is the name of a script function that will execute the object's methods, and `unique_id` (optional) is the ID to apply to the element if required.

The style can also be defined as a class, and applied to elements using the CLASS attribute:

```
<STYLE TYPE="text/css">
    .myhistory {behavior:url(#default#saveHistory);}
</STYLE>
...
<INPUT CLASS="myhistory"... etc ... >
```

437

A <META> element is also required in the <HEAD> section of the page to indicate that the page is persistent. For example:

```
<META NAME="save" CONTENT="history">
...
<INPUT TYPE="TEXT" ID="txtSaved" CLASS="myhistory">
```

The saveHistory behavior automatically persists values for form elements that have this behavior style. However, the setAttribute() and getAttribute() methods and the onsave and onload events are still available and can be used to persist other values if required.

saveHistory Methods

The saveHistory object provides the following methods for use in scripting:

Name	Description
getAttribute ("attribute_name")	Returns the value attached to the element by the setAttribute() method under the specified attribute name.
setAttribute ("attribute_name", value)	Attaches the specified value to the element as a persistent attribute using the specified name.

saveHistory Events

The saveHistory object provides the following events for use in scripting:

Name	Description
onload	Occurs when the page is loaded from the user's History list.
onsave	Occurs when the page is saved in the user's History list.

The saveSnapshot Default Behavior

Allows the state of the page and script variables to be saved. The values are inserted into the HTML of the page as it is saved, making it permanent in the saved copy. Note that array variables are not persisted.

Instantiated within an HTML element:

```
<element_name
    ID="unique_id"
    STYLE="behavior:url(#default#saveSnapshot)">
```

where:

element_name is the name of an HTML element to which the behavior will be applied

unique_id (optional) is the ID to apply to the element if required

The style can also be defined as a class, and applied to elements using the CLASS attribute:

```
<STYLE TYPE="text/css">
   .mysnapshot {behavior:url(#default#saveSnapshot);}
</STYLE>
...
<SCRIPT CLASS="mysnapshot"... etc ... >
```

A <META> element is also required in the <HEAD> section of the page to indicate that the page is persistent. For example:

```
<META NAME="save" CONTENT="snapshot">
...
<SCRIPT LANGUAGE="JScript" ID="myscript" CLASS="mysnapshot)">
... persisted variables ...
</SCRIPT>
...
<INPUT TYPE="TEXT" ID="txtSaved" CLASS="mysnapshot)">
```

The saveSnapshot behavior automatically persists values for form elements and variables (with the exception of array variables) in <SCRIPT> sections that have this behavior style.

The userData Default Behavior

Can be used to save values from controls between sessions. Values are saved in a local XML store that can be accessed using normal DOM scripting methods.

Instantiated within an HTML element:

```
<element_name
   ID="unique_id"
   STYLE="behavior:url(#default#userData)">
```

where:

element_name is the name of an HTML element to which the behavior will be applied
unique_id (optional) is the ID to apply to the element if required

The style can also be defined as a class, and applied to elements using the CLASS attribute:

```
<STYLE TYPE="text/css">
   .myuserdata {behavior:url(#default#userData);}
</STYLE>
...
<INPUT CLASS="myuserdata"... etc ... >
```

The userData methods provide access to the user's local XML store for persisting values:

```
<SCRIPT LANGUAGE="JScript">
function saveUserData() {
   // set the control's persistent attribute value
   txtSaved.setAttribute("myvalue", txtSaved.value);
   // then save it in the XML store
   txtSaved.save("myXmlBranch");
}
```

```
function loadUserData() {
   // retrieve the attribute from the XML store
   txtSaved.load("myXmlBranch");
   // then get the attribute value
   txtSaved.value = txtSaved.getAttribute("myvalue");
}
</SCRIPT>

<INPUT TYPE="TEXT" ID="txtSaved" CLASS="myuserdata">

<INPUT TYPE="BUTTON" VALUE="Save Data" ONCLICK="saveUserData()">
<INPUT TYPE="BUTTON" VALUE="Load Data" ONCLICK="loadUserData()">
```

The userData behavior does not automatically persist values. The page author must use the setAttribute() and save() methods to persist the values and the getAttribute() and load() methods to retrieve them as required. Of course, you can do this in the onload event of the page if you wish:

```
<BODY BGCOLOR="#FFFFFF" ID="myBody" ONLOAD="loadUserData()">
```

userData Methods

The userData object provides the following methods for use in scripting:

Name	Description
getAttribute ("attribute_name")	Returns the value attached to the element by the setAttribute() method under the specified attribute name.
setAttribute ("attribute_name", value)	Attaches the specified value to the element as a persistent attribute using the specified name.
load("xmlstore_name")	Retrieves stored attributes from the local persistent XML store and attaches them to the element.
save("xmlstore_name")	Stores the attributes attached to the element in the local persistent XML store.

Accessing the XML Store

When data is saved into an XML store, it can be accessed using the same techniques that are used for accessing the XML DOM in script. The persisted element provides an XMLDocument property which returns a reference to the persisted XML data store, for example:

```
var XMLStoreDoc = myPersistedObject.XMLDocument;
```

The XML store is in Windows/Application data/Microsoft/UserData, and consists of a series of XML files that are based on an element named <ROOTSTUB>, for example:

```
<ROOTSTUB PersistedValue="value" />
```

The Experimental time Behavior

The experimental behavior named `time` extends HTML elements, such as the `<IMG>` element, to allow more control over the way the content is loaded and displayed. It is designed to be used to display or insert a range of different media types into a document. The behavior can be referenced through any of the internal names: `animation`, `audio`, `img`, `media`, `par`, `seq`, `time` and `video`. It provides a single implementation for all these, so the same properties and methods are available.

Instantiated within an HTML element:

```
<element_name
   ID="unique_id"
   STYLE="behavior:url(#default#time)"
   ACCELERATE="percentage"
   AUTOREVERSE="true" | "false"
   BEGIN="hh:mm:ss.fff" | "number[ h | min | s | ms]"
   BEGINAFTER="elementID"
   BEGINEVENT="elementID.eventname"
   BEGINWITH="elementID"
   DECELERATE="percentage"
   DUR="hh:mm:ss.fff" | "number[ h | min | s | ms]"
   END="hh:mm:ss.fff" | "number[ h | min | s | ms]"
   ENDEVENT="elementID.eventname"
   ENDHOLD="true" | "false"
   ENDSYNC="first" | "last" | "none"
   EVENTRESTART="true" | "false"
   REPEAT="number" | "indefinite"
   REPEATDUR="hh:mm:ss.fff" | "number[ h | min | s | ms]"
   SYNCBEHAVIOR="canslip" | "locked"
   TIMEACTION="display" | "none" | "onOff" | "style" | "visibility"
   TIMELINE="none" | "par" | "seq"
   TIMESTARTRULE="onDocLoad" | ""
>
```

"`hh:mm:ss.fff`" is the **absolute** time, for example `10:25:40.000`, where `fff` indicates the number of hundredths of a second.

"`number[ h | min | s | ms]`" is the **relative** time, for example `6h` for 6 hours, `500ms` for 500 milliseconds, etc.

The style can also be defined as a class, and applied to elements using the CLASS attribute:

```
<STYLE TYPE="text/css">
   .mytime {behavior:url(#default#time);}
</STYLE>
...
<IMG CLASS="mytime"... etc ... >
```

The attributes of the element are equivalent to the properties that can be read and set using script code at runtime.

time Behavior Properties

Name	Description
accelerate	The rate at which the local timeline will accelerate smoothly from a stop.

Table Continued on Following Page

Name	Description
autoReverse	Specifies if the timeline on the element will immediately reverse after completing in the forward direction.
begin	The absolute or relative time when the timeline will begin playing.
beginAfter	The element that must end its timeline before the timeline of this element starts.
beginEvent	An event in the page that will start the timeline of the element.
beginWith	The element that the timeline of this element will start at the same time as.
currTime	Returns the current time on the local timeline (read only).
decelerate	The rate at which the local timeline will decelerate smoothly to a stop.
dur	The absolute or relative time during which the element will remain active or displayed.
end	The absolute or relative end time for the element.
endEvent	An event in the page that will end the timeline of the element.
endHold	Specifies if the element will remain active if its timeline ends before the timeline of its parent element ends.
endSync	Specifies that the timeline of the element ends when the timeline on one of its child elements ends.
eventRestart	Specifies whether the element can restart if a beginEvent property or beginElement() method call occurs while the local timeline is already running.
repeat	Specifies the number of times that the element's timeline will repeat.
repeatDur	The absolute or relative time during which the element's timeline will loop.
syncBehavior	The synchronization rules for the element's timeline.
timeAction	The action that will be taken on the element while the timeline is active.
timeline	The type of timeline to associate with the element.
timeStartRule	Specifies if the element's timeline will start with the document's onload event. At the time of writing, the only permissible value was "onDocLoad".

time Behavior Methods

Name	Description
beginElement()	Starts the element running on the timeline.
endElement()	Stops the element running.
pause()	Pauses the timeline on the element (applies only to the <BODY> element).
resume()	Resumes a paused timeline on the element (applies only to the <BODY> element).

time Behavior Events

Name	Description
onbegin	Fires when the timeline on an element starts.
onend	Fires when the timeline on an element ends.
onpause	Fires when the behavior is paused.
onrepeat	Fires when the timeline on an element repeats, after the first iteration.
onresume	Fires when the behavior is resumed after pausing.
onreverse	Fires when the timeline on an element begins to play backward.

For more details of the time behavior and its current implementation, check out:
http://www.microsoft.com/workshop/author/behaviors/reference/behaviors/time.htm

The Microsoft Behaviors Library

Microsoft makes available a range of custom behaviors as script files that you can download and use or modify yourself. At the time of writing the list consisted of:

Name	Description
calendar	Implements a calendar control in the document.
moveable	Implements a control that can be dragged and moved.
coolbar	Implements a flat 'coolbutton' for use in a 'coolbar'.
coolbutton	Implements a flat 'coolbar', as in the latest applications.
menu	Implements a collapsible menu in the document.

Table Continued on Following Page

Name	Description
mask	Adds the 'masked edit' behavior to certain HTML controls.
imageRollover	Adds a 'rollover' effect to images.
rowover	Provides alternate row shading and highlighting in HTML tables.
tooltip	Implements rich 'tooltip' objects in the document with HTML.
soundRollover	Adds an audio rollover effect to objects in the document.
slider	Implements a slider control in the document.

For the current list of behaviors that are available, go to
http://www.microsoft.com/workshop/author/behaviors/library/behaviorslibrary.asp.

Custom Behaviors Reference

Custom Behaviors can be constructed in a range of ways: as HTCs (HTML components) as scriptlets, or as compiled components using languages such as C++, Visual Basic, Delphi, Java, or J++. This reference section is concerned with custom behaviors created as HTCs. The technique of creating scriptlet-based behaviors is now obsolete.

> To see more about the way that Microsoft see the whole topic of scriptlets and behaviors going, check out
> http://www.microsoft.com/workshop/languages/clinic/xmlscript.asp and
> http://www.microsoft.com/sitebuilder/magazine/ie5behave.asp.

HTC Structure

HTCs are constructed using XML elements and script code. The basic structure is:

```
<PUBLIC:COMPONENT URN="component_identifier">

    <PUBLIC:ATTACH EVENT="name_of_external_event"
                   FOR="document" | "element" | "window"
                   HANDLER="function_name"
                   URN="source_event_urn" />

    <PUBLIC:PROPERTY NAME="property_name"
                     ID="unique_id"
                     INTERNALNAME="function_name"
                     PERSIST="True" | "False"
                     GET="function_name"
                     PUT="function_name"
                     VALUE="default_value" />

    <PUBLIC:METHOD NAME="method_name"
                   INTERNALNAME="function_name" />
```

```
<PUBLIC:EVENT NAME="custom_event_name"
              ID="unique_id" />

<SCRIPT LANGUAGE="language_name">
  ...
  // functions that implement the behavior
  ...
</SCRIPT>

</PUBLIC:COMPONENT>
```

Alternatively, properties can be defined using separate XML GET and PUT elements:

```
...
<PUBLIC:PROPERTY NAME="property_name"
                 ID="unique_id"
                 INTERNALNAME="function_name"
                 PERSIST="True" | "False">

  <PUBLIC:GET INTERNALNAME="function_name" />
  <PUBLIC:PUT INTERNALNAME="function_name" />

</PROPERTY>
...
```

The HTC Element Attributes

Element	Description and attributes
COMPONENT	Defines the file as being an HTC. The equivalent element `<HTC>` can also be used. URN - a unique URN identifier for the component.
ATTACH	Attaches an event in the source document to a function in the component. EVENT - the name of the event occurring in the source document that the component will react to. FOR - the source of the event that the component will react to, either `"document"`, `"element"` or `"window"` (optional). HANDLER - the name of the function that will be called when the external event occurs. URN - a unique URN identifier for the event (optional).
METHOD	Defines a method that can be called from the source document. NAME - the name of the method as seen from outside the component. INTERNALNAME - specifies the name of the function within the component that implements the method (optional if same as method name).

Table Continued on Following Page

445

Element	Description and attributes
EVENT	Defines an event that will be raised by the component. NAME - the name of the event as seen from outside the component. ID - a unique identifier for the event (optional).
PROPERTY	Defines a method that can be accessed from the source document. NAME - the name of the property as seen from outside the component. ID - a unique identifier for the property (optional). INTERNALNAME - specifies the name of the property as used within the component (optional if same as property name). PERSIST - specifies if the property value will be persisted as part of the page if the page is persisted using one of the default behaviors (optional). GET - name of the function that will be called to retrieve the value. PUT - name of the function that will be called to set the value. VALUE - the default value to use, if the user does not provide a value.
GET	Defines the function that will be called when retrieving the value of a property. INTERNALNAME - name of the function that will be called.
PUT	Defines the function that will be called when setting the value of a property. INTERNALNAME - name of the function that will be called.

It is also possible to use the attachEvent() method to attach an external event to a function in the behavior component, instead of using an <ATTACH> element:

```
attachEvent("event_name", function_name);
```

for example:

```
attachEvent("onmouseover", hiliteElement);
```

HTC Objects, Methods and Events

HTC behavior components can take advantage of several objects, methods and events that are pre-defined:

HTC Object

Name	Description
element	This object can be referenced within a behavior component, and returns the element that the behavior is attached to as an object. Equivalent to the JavaScript this keyword.

HTC Method

Name	Description
createEventObject()	Creates and returns a standard Dynamic HTML event object. The properties can then be set and the event object passed to the original script when the event fires.

HTC Events

Name	Description
oncontentchange	Occurs when the element that the behavior is attached to has been parsed on loading, and each time the content of the element changes afterwards.
ondocumentready	Occurs after the complete document that contains the element to which this behavior is attached has been loaded and parsed. Useful for running initialization scripts that need to access the document.

Behavior-Related Properties and Methods

In order to integrate behaviors into the existing Dynamic HTML document object model (DOM), several new properties and methods have been added to the DOM. These can be accessed through DHTML script code. They are:

Behavior-Related Properties

Name	Description
srcUrn	Property of the event object only. Returns the URN property of the behavior that caused the event.
uniqueID	Generates and returns a unique ID for an element or the document, for the current session only. Can be different each time the page is loaded. Applies to all HTML elements.

Behavior-Related Methods

Name	Description
`behaviorID=addBehavior ("source_url")`	Attaches the specified behavior to an element. Returns a unique numeric ID that can be used to remove the behavior later. Applies to all HTML elements.
`success=attachEvent ("event_name", function_name)`	Attaches the specified event to an element, so that the specified function is executed when the event occurs. Returns `true` on success. Applies to all HTML elements. Can also be used in HTCs instead of the `<ATTACH>` element.
`collection=behaviorUrns()`	Returns a collection of the URNs of all the behaviors currently attached to an element. Applies to all HTML elements.
`detachEvent("event_name", function_name)`	Disconnects the specified event from an element, so that the specified function is no longer executed when the event occurs. Returns `true` on success. Applies to all HTML elements.
`success=removeBehavior (behaviorID)`	Disconnects a behavior previously added by the `addBehavior()` method, using the unique numeric ID. Returns `true` on success. Applies to all HTML elements.
`collection=urns(urn)`	Returns a collection of the HTML element objects to which a behavior with the specified `urn` is currently attached. Applies to the `all`, `areas`, `elements` and `forms` collections and the `<SELECT>` element.

Support and Errata

One of the most irritating things about any programming book can be when you find that bit of code you've just spent an hour typing simply doesn't work. You check it a hundred times to see if you've set it up correctly and then you notice the spelling mistake in the variable name on the book page. Grrr! Of course, you can blame the authors for not taking enough care and testing the code, the editors for not doing their job properly, or the proofreaders for not being eagle-eyed enough, but this doesn't get around the fact that mistakes do happen.

We try hard to ensure no mistakes sneak out into the real world, but we can't promise that this book is 100% error free. What we can do is offer the next best thing by providing you with immediate support and feedback from experts who have worked on the book and try to ensure that future editions eliminate these gremlins. The following section will take you step by step through the process of posting errata to our web site to get that help. The sections that follow, therefore, are:

- ❏ Wrox Developers Membership
- ❏ Finding a list of existing errata on the web site
- ❏ Adding your own errata to the existing list
- ❏ What happens to your errata once you've posted it (why doesn't it appear immediately?)

There is also a section covering how to e-mail a question for technical support. This comprises:

- ❏ What your e-mail should include
- ❏ What happens to your e-mail once it has been received by us

So that you only need view information relevant to yourself, we ask that you register as a Wrox Developer Member. This is a quick and easy process, that will save you time in the long-run. If you are already a member, just update membership to include this book.

Wrox Developer's Membership

To get your FREE Wrox Developer's Membership click on Membership in the navigation bar of our home site

www.wrox.com.

This is shown in the following screen shot:

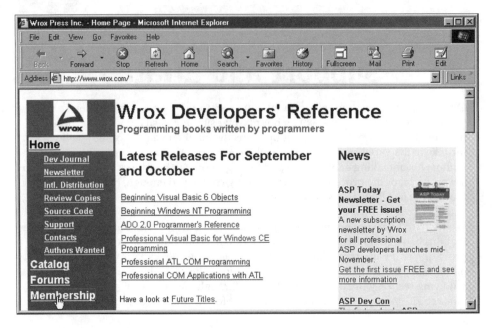

Then, on the next screen (not shown), click on New User. This will display a form. Fill in the details on the form and submit the details using the submit button at the bottom. Before you can say 'The best read books come in Wrox Red' you will get the following screen:

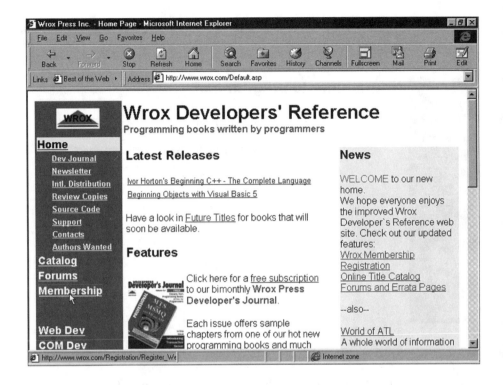

Finding Errata on the Web Site.

Before you send in a query, you might be able to save time by finding the answer to your problem on our web site: http:\\www.wrox.com.

Each book we publish has its own page and its own errata sheet. You can get to any book's page by clicking on support from the left-hand side navigation bar.

From this page you can locate any book's errata page on our site. Select your book from the pop-up menu and click on it.

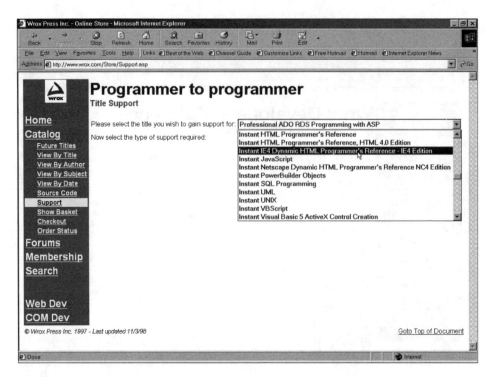

Then click on Enter Book Errata. This will take you to the errata page for the book. Select the criteria by which you want to view the errata, and click the apply criteria button. This will provide you with links to specific errata. For an initial search, you are advised to view the errata by page numbers. If you have looked for an error previously, then you may wish to limit your search using dates. We update these pages daily to ensure that you have the latest information on bugs and errors.

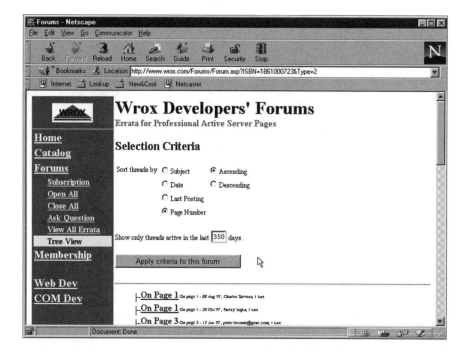

Adding Errata to the Sheet Yourself.

It's always possible that you may find your error is not listed, in which case you can enter details of the fault yourself. It might be anything from a spelling mistake to a faulty piece of code in the book. Sometimes you'll find useful hints that aren't really errors on the listing. By entering errata you may save another reader hours of frustration, and of course, you will be helping us provide even higher quality information. We're very grateful for this sort of advice and feedback. You can enter errata using the 'ask a question' of our editors link at the bottom of the errata page. Click on this link and you will get a form on which to post your message.

Fill in the subject box, and then type your message in the space provided on the form. Once you have done this, click on the Post Now button at the bottom of the page. The message will be forwarded to our editors. They'll then test your submission and check that the error exists, and that the suggestions you make are valid. Then your submission, together with a solution, is posted on the site for public consumption. Obviously this stage of the process can take a day or two, but we will endeavor to get a fix up sooner than that.

E-mail Support

If you wish to directly query a problem in the book with an expert who knows the book in detail then e-mail support@wrox.com, with the title of the book and the last four numbers of the ISBN in the subject field of the e-mail. Your e-mail MUST include the title of the book the problem relates to, otherwise we won't be able to help you. The diagram below shows what else your e-mail should include:

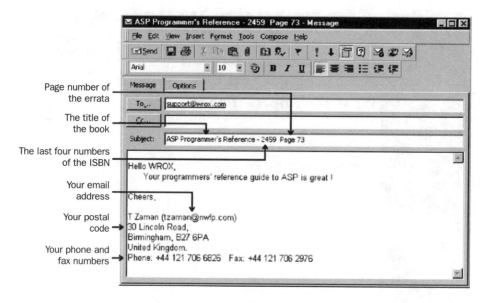

We won't send you junk mail. We need the details to save your time and ours. If we need to replace a disk or CD we'll be able to get it to you straight away. When you send an e-mail it will go through the following chain of support:

Customer Support

Your message is delivered to one of our customer support staff who are the first people to read it. They have files on most frequently asked questions and will answer anything general immediately. They answer general questions about the book and the web site.

Editorial

Deeper queries are forwarded to the technical editor responsible for that book. They have experience with the programming language or particular product and are able to answer detailed technical questions on the subject. Once an issue has been resolved, the editor can post the errata to the web site.

The Authors

Finally, in the unlikely event that the editor can't answer your problem, s/he will forward the request to the author. We try to protect the author from any distractions from writing. However, we are quite happy to forward specific requests to them. All Wrox authors help with the support on their books. They'll mail the customer and the editor with their response, and again all readers should benefit.

What we can't answer

Obviously with an ever growing range of books and an ever-changing technology base, there is an increasing volume of data requiring support. While we endeavor to answer all questions about the book, we can't answer bugs in your own programs that you've adapted from our code. So, while you might have loved the help desk systems in our Active Server Pages book, don't expect too much sympathy if you cripple your company with a live adaptation you customized from Chapter 12. But do tell us if you're especially pleased with the routine you developed with our help.

How to tell us exactly what you think.

We understand that errors can destroy the enjoyment of a book and can cause many wasted and frustrated hours, so we seek to minimize the distress that they can cause.

You might just wish to tell us how much you liked or loathed the book in question. Or you might have ideas about how this whole process could be improved. In which case you should e-mail feedback@wrox.com. You'll always find a sympathetic ear, no matter what the problem is. Above all you should remember that we do care about what you have to say and we will do our utmost to act upon it.

Index

Symbols

 # (pound mark)
XML and, 100
* (asterisk)
wildcard path operator (XSL), 226
. (period)
current context path operator (XSL), 226
/ (forward slash)
child path operator (XSL), 226
// (double forward slash)
recursive descent path operator (XSL), 226
@ (at)
attribute path operator (XSL), 226
| (vertical bar)
XML and, 100

A

<A> element (HTML), 92, 94, 101, 102, 122
abort() method
Document object (XML DOM), 167
HttpRequest object (XML DOM), 179
actions (XSL), 223
Active Server Pages
see ASP
ActiveX Data Objects
see ADO
ActiveX Objects
RDS, 114
TDC (Tabular Data Control), 114
actuate attribute (XLink), 96
addBehavior() method, 254, 256, 264, 271
addNew() method, 130
ADO (ActiveX Data Objects), 121
XML data and, 121
XML recordsets and, 137

Advanced Data Connector
see RDS
#all candidate element type, 107
ancestor relative term (XPointer), 103, 106
anchorClick behavior, 269
anchors, 92
ANY keyword (XML), 53
appendChild() method
Node object (XML DOM), 157
appendData() method
CharacterData object (XML DOM), 174
<APPLET> element (HTML), 117, 122
applets (Java), 117
applications
XML and, 26-30
  universal data formats, 27
ASP (Active Server Pages), 114, 208
objects
  see under objects
ASP2XML specialist component, 29
async property
Document object (XML DOM), 164, 169
<ATTACH> element (XML), 258, 259
attachEvent() method, 253, 255, 258
<ATTLIST> element (XML), 51, 54, 59
Attr object
see Attribute object
attribute declarations (XML), 51, 54
<attribute> element (XML Schemas), 84
default attribute, 84
required attribute, 84
attribute location terms, 110
attribute namespaces, 47
Attribute object (XML DOM), 149, 173, 176, 202, 208, 237
name property, 173
tagName property, 173
value property, 173
attribute path operator (@) (XSL), 226
attribute values, 12

links, 90, 98
extended, 92, 94, 97
inline, 94
locators, 100
out-of-line, 94
simple, 94
traversing of, 93
XLink and, 93
links (HTML), 37
literals (DTDs), 56
load() method
Document object (XML DOM), 167, 169
loadXML() method
Document object (XML DOM), 167
location terms
attribute, 110
spanning, 108
string, 109
locators, 100
XPointer, 101

M

markup (DTDs), 56
<MARQUEE> element (HTML), 123
mask behavior, 270
master/detail HTML tables, 127
master/detail recordsets, 125
XML files and, 126
maxOccurs attribute (XML Schemas)
<element> element, 83
menu behavior, 270
<METHOD> element (XML), 259
methods
abort()
Document object (XML DOM), 167
HttpRequest object (XML DOM), 179
addBehavior(), 254, 256, 264, 271
addNew(), 130
appendChild()
Node object (XML DOM), 157
appendData()
CharacterData object (XML DOM), 174
attachEvent(), 253, 255, 258
behaviorUrns(), 254
cancelUpdate(), 130
cloneNode()
Node object (XML DOM), 157
createAttribute()
Document object (XML DOM), 165
createCDATASection()
Document object (XML DOM), 165

createComment()
Document object (XML DOM), 165
createDocumentFragment()
Document object (XML DOM), 165
createElement()
Document object (XML DOM), 165
createEntityReference()
Document object (XML DOM), 165
createEventObject(), 263
createNode()
Document object (XML DOM), 167
createProcessingInstruction()
Document object (XML DOM), 165
createTextNode()
Document object (XML DOM), 165
delete(), 130
deleteData()
CharacterData object (XML DOM), 174
detachEvent(), 255
end(), 227
eval(), 210
fire(), 263
formatNumber()
IXTLRuntime interface (XML DOM), 245
getAllResponseHeaders()
HttpRequest object (XML DOM), 179
getAttribute(), 277, 279
Element object (XML DOM), 172, 186
getAttributeNode()
Element object (XML DOM), 172
getClientCaps()
clientCaps behavior, 280
getElementsByTagName()
Document object (XML DOM), 166, 185, 209
Element object (XML DOM), 172
getNamedItem()
NamedNodeMap object (XML DOM), 161, 186
getQualifiedItem()
NamedNodeMap object (XML DOM), 162
getResponseHeader()
HttpRequest object (XML DOM), 179
hasChildNodes()
Node object (XML DOM), 157
hasFeature()
Implementation object (XML DOM), 176
htmlEncode()
Server object (ASP), 199

ASP Today

www.asptoday.com

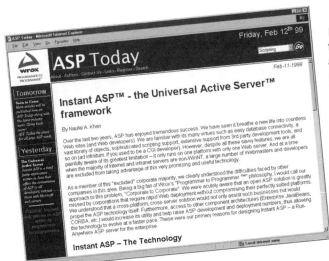

It's not easy keeping up to date with what's hot and what's not in the ever-changing world of internet development. Even if you stick to one narrow topic like ASP, trawling through the mailing lists each day and finding new and better code is still a twenty-four-seven job. Which is where we come in.

You already know Wrox Press from its series of titles on ASP and its associated technologies. We realise that we can't bring out a book everyday to keep you all up to date, so from March 1, we're starting a brand new website at www.asptoday.com which will do all the hard work for you. Every week you'll find new tips, tricks and techniques for you to try out and test in your development, covering ASP components, ADO, RDS, ADSI, CDO, Security, Site Design, BackOffice, XML and more. Look out also for bug alerts when they're found and fixes when they're available.

We hope that you won't be shy in telling us what you think of the site and the content we put on it either. If you like what you'll see, we'll carry on as we are, but if you think we're missing something, then we'll address it accordingly. If you've got something to write, then do so and we'll include it. We're hoping our site will become a global effort by and for the entire ASP community.

In anticipation,
Dan Maharry, ASPToday.com

WROX PRESS INC.

Wrox writes books for you. Any suggestions, or ideas
about how you want information given in your
ideal book will be studied by our team.
Your comments are always valued at Wrox.

Free phone in USA 800-USE-WROX
Fax (312) 397 8990

UK Tel. (0121) 687 4100   Fax   (0121) 687 4101

NB. If you post the bounce back card below in the UK, please send it to:
Wrox Press Ltd., Arden House, 1102 Warwick Road, Acocks Green, Birmingham. B27 6BH. UK.

XML IE5 Programmer's Reference

Name

Address

City   State/Region

Country   Postcode/Zip

E-mail

Occupation

How did you hear about this book?

☐ Book review (name)

☐ Advertisement (name)

☐ Recommendation

☐ Catalog

☐ Other

Where did you buy this book?

☐ Bookstore (name)   City

☐ Computer Store (name)

☐ Mail Order

☐ Other

What influenced you in the
purchase of this book?

☐ Cover Design

☐ Contents

☐ Other (please specify)

How did you rate the overall
contents of this book?

☐ Excellent   ☐ Good

☐ Average   ☐ Poor

What did you find most useful about this book?

What did you find least useful about this book?

Please add any additional comments.

What other subjects will you buy a computer
book on soon?

What is the best computer book you have used this year?

Note: This information will only be used to keep you updated
about new Wrox Press titles and will not be used for any other
purpose or passed to any other third party.

Check here if you DO NOT want to receive further support for this book

1576

wrox
PROGRAMMER TO PROGRAMMER™